PRESUMED LOST

Other Books by Stephen L. Moore

War of the Wolf. Texas' Honored Lost Boat: World War II's Famous Submarine Seawolf. Dallas, TX: Atriad Press, 2008.

Savage Frontier: Rangers, Riflemen, and Indian Wars in Texas. Volume III: 1840–1841. Denton, TX: University of North Texas Press, 2007.

Savage Frontier: Rangers, Riflemen, and Indian Wars in Texas. Volume II: 1838–1839. Denton, TX: University of North Texas Press, 2006.

Spadefish: On Patrol With a Top-Scoring World War II Submarine. Dallas, TX: Atriad Press, 2006.

Eighteen Minutes: The Battle of San Jacinto and the Texas Independence Campaign. Plano, TX: Republic of Texas Press, 2004.

Savage Frontier: Rangers, Riflemen, and Indian Wars in Texas. Volume I: 1835–1837. Plano, TX: Republic of Texas Press, 2002.

Taming Texas. Captain William T. Sadler's Lone Star Service. Austin, TX: State House Press, 2000.

With William J. Shinneman and Robert W. Gruebel. *The Buzzard Brigade: Torpedo Squadron Ten at War.* Missoula, MT: Pictorial Histories Publishing Co., 1996.

For more information, visit www.stephenlmoore.com

PRESUMED
LOST

The Incredible Ordeal of America's
Submarine POWs during the Pacific War

STEPHEN L. MOORE

NAVAL INSTITUTE PRESS
Annapolis, Maryland

Naval Institute Press
291 Wood Road
Annapolis, MD 21402

Library of Congress Cataloging-in-Publication Data

Moore, Stephen L.
    Presumed lost : the incredible ordeal of America's submarine veteran POWs of World War II / Stephen L. Moore.
        p. cm.
    Includes bibliographical references and index.
    ISBN 978-1-59114-530-1 (alk. paper)
    1. World War, 1939–1945—Naval operations—Submarine. 2. World War, 1939–1945—Naval operations, American. 3. World War, 1939–1945—Prisoners and prisons, Japanese. 4. Prisoners of war—Japan. 5. Prisoners of war—United States. 6. World War, 1939–1945—Pacific Area. I. Title.
    D783.M667 2009
    940.54'7252—dc22
                        2009015644

Printed in the United States of America on acid-free paper

15 14 13 12 11 10 09   9 8 7 6 5 4 3 2
First printing

Photo retouching courtesy of Brian McKenzie. Cover photo of USS *Perch* crew aboard Japanese destroyer courtesy of Robert Lents.

Contents

Preface

Much tribute has been paid to the veterans of the United States Submarine Force of World War II. These gallant submariners accounted for some 55 percent of all Japanese vessels sunk in the war, although their service only accounted for 1.5 percent of the U.S. Navy. More than 3,500 U.S. submariners, remain on "eternal patrol," lost aboard 52 boats during the war. Of some 16,000 men who fought in the "Silent Service" during World War II, more than 20 percent did not come home. This casualty rate was the highest of all American armed forces and was six times greater than that in the surface navy.

Of the 52 U.S. submarines lost in World War II, prisoners of war were taken by Japan from only seven of the boats. From Attu in the Aleutians, Port Darwin and Fremantle in Australia, and Pearl Harbor, 525 officers and men departed with their submarines on what would be their final war patrols. Only 158 of them would ever see the United States again after the war.

When each of these seven boats failed to return to port from patrol, they were officially listed by the Navy as "overdue and presumed lost." Loved ones were notified by the War Department that their siblings, spouses, and sons were missing in action and presumed lost.

The stories of how members of these brave crews survived the sinking of their ships and endured months and often years of captivity are remarkable. In the case of *Perch* and *Grenadier*, these subs were so badly damaged by enemy attacks that their crews were forced to scuttle their ships and take to the ocean. Two other U.S. subs—*Sculpin* and *S-44*—went down fighting to the end on the surface with heavy losses of lives. *Tang* and *Tullibee* fell victim to their own faulty, circling torpedoes during surface torpedo attacks against Japanese forces. Only one sailor survived *Tullibee*'s violent destruction. Nine officers and men from *Tang* were picked up by the Japanese, five of whom had escaped their sunken, burning submarine from 180 feet below the ocean surface. The seventh lost boat, *Robalo* had a small group of men survive after the ship struck a mine, but none of them would survive the war.

Those submariners who were fortunate enough to be taken as prisoners by the Japanese military quickly found that their fight to survive was just beginning. They were slapped, kicked, punched, beaten, tortured, and humiliated. Some endured bamboo splints driven under their fingernails and cruel water tortures. Most went days on end without any food or water. When food was supplied, it was often only starvation rations or merely rice laden with worms and maggots. During winter months, the men worked under slave-like conditions in factories, shipyards, mines, and caves without proper clothing to keep warm.

Subjected to endless interrogation sessions, the former submariners refused to crack. Instead, they often refused to answer the questions or made up grandiose lies concerning American military secrets. Malnutrition, abuse, and disease took heavy tolls on their weary bodies. Pneumonia, beriberi, dysentery, malaria, and other ailments claimed Allied POWs throughout the war.

Dozens of these submarine force prisoners were never officially listed as POWs by Japan. Many crewmen from *Perch*, lost in 1942, endured 1,298 days of captivity without their families ever being told that they were alive. Only those men who made it to official POW camps on the Japanese mainland were registered with the International Red Cross during the war.

In exchange for holding America's military secrets sacred—including the U.S. submarine service's Ultra shipping-intercept transmissions—and sacrificing their lives for the good of their country, a small percent of these sub force veterans were honored with commendations shortly after the war. All of the survivors still living as of 1985 became eligible to receive the newly approved POW Medal—issued more than 40 years after their capture.

Two of the submariners from these seven lost boats were awarded the nation's highest honor, the Congressional Medal of Honor. Captain John Cromwell, patrolling with *Sculpin* as a wolfpack commander, chose to go down with the ship to avoid giving up military secrets under torture. Commander Dick O'Kane, the skipper of *Tang*, narrowly survived his time in various Japanese POW camps and received his Medal of Honor from President Harry Truman in 1946.

For the *Tang* tragedy, I have reviewed the primary statements of the survivors as well as recollections some of them gave many years later. As a longtime scuba diver who once made a free emergency ascent (breathing out as you ascend) from 60 feet during dive training, I have long been fascinated with the fact that *Tang*'s men made their ascents from three times that depth—one without a Momsen lung for most of his ascent. On the day of *Tang*'s loss, Dick O'Kane and his eight surviving ship-mates agree that 13 men total swam out from *Tang*'s forward torpedo room escape hatch. To this day, Bill Leibold believes the number 13 to be accurate—although the names and sequence of escape attempts is conflicting. My presentation of the *Tang* escape pulls the pieces together to best reach this agreed upon number.

This is the story of tragic loss and inspiring courage. It is the story of men who bravely fought through bitter circumstances to defend the liberties offered by their home country. Many of these veterans found that the only way to get beyond their memories of abuse was to live for the present. "If you walk around with hate in your heart, the only person that really ever hurts is you," former *Grenadier* prisoner of war Charles "Tim" McCoy stated recently.

As of this writing, only about two dozen of the 158 submarine service POWs are still living. Through their stories and contributions, this history of their ordeal is possible. Those former POWs of the submarine force who directly shared their stories were: Norman Albertson, Elbert Arnette, Joseph Baker, Floyd Caverly, Bill Cooper, Gordon Cox, Kevin Harty, Riley Keysor, Cliff Kuykendall, Bill Leibold, Robert Lents, Charles "Tim" McCoy, Dempsey McGowan, Thomas Moore, Virgil Ouillette, Ernest Plantz, Joseph Price, George Rocek, Herbert Thomas, Alfred Toulon Jr., Marion "Turk" Turner, Charles Ver Valin, and Bernard Witzke. Personal details were also contributed by: David A. Hurt Jr.; Theodore Reh via his nephew Ken Lohmann; John McBeath via his daughter Veronica Mayo; and Lee K. Ryder, daughter of John Ryder. Notes, letters, photos and general recollections from Charles "Johnny" Johnson and Lee "Pappy" Shaw were provided by Kim Reed, Pat Havel, Peggy Pepper, and Sandra Fahnert Wofford Stacy.

For each submarine, there were those who went out of their way to make sure ample materials were available for this manuscript. Robert Whitemore, son of *S-44* survivor Bill Whitemore, provided photos, telegrams, newspaper clippings, and family records. Jack Cleverdon and Jamie Hulsey provided a photo and information on *S-44*'s pharmacist's mate, Tom Cleverdon. Janet M. David provided details of her uncle Phil Jaworski's escape from *S-44*, his subsequent death, and assisted in photo identification. For *Tullibee*, lone survivor Cliff Kuykendall was a constant source of material, eagerly fielding my calls and letters. For *Tang*, Bill Leibold provided detailed responses to my queries and generously supplied photos from his collection. Submarine veteran Gene Kellar made available a three-hour videotape of Clay Decker's experiences. *Back From the Deep* author Carl LaVO shared much of his research and photos pertaining to *Sculpin*, including survivor statements, war crimes testimony and letters from ex-POWs. For *Grenadier*, Gordon Cox, Chuck Ver Valin, Al Albertson, Tim McCoy, and Kevin Harty all contributed photos, newsletters, memoirs, and other papers relating to their ship. Turk Turner, Bob Lents, Ernie Plantz, and author Greg Michno provided documents, newsletters, and photos pertaining to *Perch*'s loss. Service papers and POW experiences of

Paul Richter were supplied by his sisters, Frances Richter Swinny and Marguerite Richter Nemky.

Personal accounts from dozens of other submarine POWs came in the form of diaries, memoirs, and the 1945 statements taken from these men by intelligence officers after their liberation from Japanese prisoner camps.

Charles Waggoner of the University of Wyoming provided important papers from Kenneth Schacht and John Fitzgerald from the Clay Blair archives. Wendy Culley of the Submarine Force Museum in Groton, Connecticut, kindly provided POW statements, newspaper clippings, and photos. Charles Hinman of the *Bowfin* Museum at Pearl Harbor provided many photographs, POW statements, and general support for this project. Roger Mansell, Director of the Center for Research, Allied POWs Under the Japanese, offered assistance with contacts, photos, and information from his detailed website. W. G. "Doc" Sweany put me in contact with John Crouse at the St. Mary's Submarine Museum in Georgia to find Bill Whitemore's *S-44* POW statement. Matt Staden, Navy Records Manager in Washington, offered his expertise in culling through the various reports housed by the Navy and the National Archives.

For proofing various chapters, suggesting improvements, correcting errors and adding other interesting details along the way, I must especially thank Chuck Ver Valin, Gordon Cox, Kevin Harty, Tim McCoy, Cliff Kuykendall, Turk Turner, Bob Lents, Ernie Plantz, Elbert Arnette, and Bill Leibold. One could not ask for more qualified expert readers: they lived this story.

1
Perch in Peril

"Forward room, open the outer doors."

The call from battle stations talker Tom Moore was welcomed. The word sent down from the conning tower indicated all was ready. Fire control solutions had been worked out. The course to the enemy ships had been meticulously tracked on the plotting table. Now it was time for the submariners to earn their keep. Their Mark 14 torpedoes were armed and ready.

Torpedoman first class Samuel Ford Simpson, a 26-year-old from Richmond, Virginia, was the senior man in the forward torpedo room of the submarine USS *Perch* (SS-176). Simpson joined the Navy in 1936 and did time on surface ships before completing Submarine School at New London, Connecticut, in April 1938. Two months later he reported on board *Perch* as a seaman who stood regular watches and served as second loader on the ship's 3-inch .50-caliber deck gun. Sam Simpson had started as a torpedoman striker in the forward torpedo room, serving under CTM Charlie Cross. Nearly four years later, he was in charge of the forward room and Cross was chief of the boat, *Perch*'s senior enlisted man aboard.[1]

His team—TM2c Warren Atkeison, TM3c Richard Evans, and TM3c Bob Lents—was ready for action. Atkeison, 21, had joined the Navy in April 1937 from his hometown of Mobile, Alabama and later volunteered for submarine service. He and his buddy Robert Wayne Lents were both making their second war patrols on *Perch*. A skilled torpedoman, Lents served as the angle setter in the forward room, insuring that the torpedoes were properly adjusted to the required firing angles. Born in rural Union County, Iowa, Lents was raised on a farm. He wanted to join the U.S. Navy right out of high school. "They wouldn't take me at first," he recalled. "I had a bad ear."

After the war started in England, however, things changed. "I got a letter that they wanted me to come. "I went down there in November 1939 and they said my ear was good enough then."

Bob Lents volunteered for either air duty or submarines. "I got submarines and did my boot camp training at Great Lakes," he later stated. "Then, I went to the Submarine Base, Pearl Harbor, and worked in the mine school." Lents also worked in the base torpedo shop, where he picked up some valuable schooling. When the submarine *Seawolf* (SS-197) came through en route to the Philippines for duty on the China Station, Lents was transferred on board as a torpedoman striker, a non-rated seaman studying to earn his TM3c rating.

After six months on Captain Freddie Warder's *Seawolf*, he was transferred to a submarine tender for more torpedo schooling. "When I was finished, the *Seawolf* was gone," he recalled. "But, the *Perch* needed another torpedoman and that's where I ended up." On *Perch*'s first patrol, Lents and his fellow torpedo gang drew first blood when their war fish connected with a Japanese freighter on 27 December. This ship was later claimed to be the 7,190-ton *Nojima Maru*, which was never heard from again.

With one successful war patrol under his belt, Lents was wearing the battle phones in the forward room on 1 March 1942, as his ship set up to fire on another Japanese merchantman. "They would call down the angles in my headphones that they wanted set on the torpedoes," he said.

As fate had it, *Perch* did not have time to fire her Mark 14 warfish this day.

On the bridge, Lt. Cdr. Dave Hurt was conning his submarine into a favorable attack position. As *Perch* prepared to attack, a lookout suddenly shouted, "Captain, there's something on the other side of that ship!"

The previously unnoticed vessel was an escort ship which had spotted the American submarine. The Japanese ship opened fire, missing with its first shot. The second shell was right on the money. Within an instant of the sight of the gun flash in the distance, there was a jarring explosion and flash as the shell made contact with *Perch*'s bridge.

Being hit by shell fire while surfaced was one of the greatest dangers a submarine could face. If her pressure hull was pierced, she would not be able to dive again. Lt. Cdr. Hurt and his men on the bridge regained their footing and quickly scanned the damage to see if their boat could dive.

For the 59-man crew of the USS *Perch*, fate had just dealt them an unlucky card. They could little expect, however, that a most unfortunate series of circumstances was only beginning.

———

David Albert Hurt Sr. was a father figure to many young sailors he commanded on his submarine. Born 4 August 1903, in Pounding Mills, Virginia, he had completed one year of local college before Senator Carter Glass of Virginia appointed him to the U.S. Naval Academy in Annapolis in 1921. Hurt was a member of the Junior Varsity crew and of the class track team prior to his graduation on 4 June 1925. His first assignments after graduation were aboard the cruiser *Raleigh*, submarine tender *Bushnell*, and the old *S-7*.

Dave Hurt attended submarine school at New London in 1929 before spending his next three years as a junior officer on the submarine *R-14*. During the following two years, he attended postgraduate school at Annapolis, before joining *S-34* in June 1934. Hurt then commanded *S-35* for more than two years before returning to the Academy in June 1937 to serve another two years as an instructor in the department of electrical engineering.

His first wife Kathryn Vurdidge Hurt died of pneumonia shortly after giving birth to their first son, David Jr., in 1926. Remarried to Constance Wickham, Hurt became the proud father of two more sons during his early naval career. On 3 June 1939, he took command of USS *Perch*. Like other submarines of the U.S. Navy, she was named for a fish. The Electric Boat Company in Groton, Connecticut, had laid down the boat's keel on 25 February 1935. A *Porpoise*-class submarine, *Perch* was launched on 9 May 1936, sponsored by Mrs. Thomas Withers.

Perch was caught at the Cavite Navy Yard in the Philippines preparing for an overhaul on 8 December 1941—which was one day earlier in Hawaii—when World War II commenced for America. She departed Manila Bay on 10 December, narrowly escaping destruction by Japanese bombers. Lieutenant Commander Hurt's first torpedo attack on Christmas Day 1941 was very nearly his last. Firing four torpedoes from the surface at a darkened steamer, he watched three Mark 14 torpedoes run straight at the target ship. The Mark 14s were later found to run much deeper than their settings, and these passed harmlessly under the Japanese vessel.

The fourth broached at launching, took its depth and then began circling around back toward *Perch*. *Perch*'s second-in-command, or executive officer, was Lt. Beverly Robinson Van Buskirk from the Academy class of 1934. Bev Van Buskirk recalled how close his sub had come to causing her own demise.[2]

> *Tullibee* and *Tang* were sunk by their own torpedoes. *Perch* was almost the first. It was Christmas night 1941, when four torpedoes were fired. The first surfaced and commenced to circle. It ended up heading directly for the conning tower. Just before it hit, it exploded, with parts of it raining all over topside. The crew below decks were cheering, thinking that one of our first torpedoes had made a direct hit. It almost did.

The following day, 26 December, *Perch* fired two torpedoes at a merchant ship and again suffered deep runners. *Perch* drew her first blood on 27 December when she fired two fish at what Hurt perceived to be a large tanker. One hit and exploded, causing the target ship to take on a heavy list. A Japanese aircraft and escort ships kept *Perch* from making a final attack on this cripple.

Perch was directed to pass through Makassar Strait and to refuel at Balikpapan on Borneo's eastern coast. She did so and proceeded toward Darwin, Australia, per orders. Hurt made a submerged attack against Japanese destroyers on 12 January, firing two torpedoes at one of the slower moving tin cans. One of the torpedoes exploded prematurely en route to target. *Perch* dived to avoid counterattack and never learned what happened to the second torpedo.[3]

Dave Hurt called on his torpedo and gunnery officer, 28-year-old Lt. Kenneth George Schacht, to resolve the issue. "We set up a fool-proof procedure for obtaining target course and speed solutions," Schacht related. The plan would allow the officers to rule out their firing data as a potential issue but could do nothing to offset the real culprit—faulty Mark 14 torpedoes.[4]

Known simply as "K.G." to the wardroom officers, *Perch*'s fourth officer was a 1935 graduate of the Naval Academy. Schacht had played football with such star Navy submarine officers as Robert Edson "Dusty" Dornin and Slade Deville Cutter. After graduation, Ensign Schacht had spent his first two years aboard the battleship *New Mexico* as a junior officer. He entered submarine school in December 1937 and upon completion in June 1938 was assigned to join *Perch* at Manila on China Station. During that time, he had worked his way up to full lieutenant and was *Perch*'s torpedo and gunnery officer. His new firing principles would be put to the test on *Perch*'s next patrol.

In addition to K. G. Schacht, Dave Hurt had three other solid officers to help him command his 54 enlisted men. Lt. Bev Van Buskirk was the exec and third officer Lt. John French Ryder—a 1936 Naval Academy graduate who hailed from Portland, Oregon—served as *Perch*'s engineering and diving officer. The fifth officer, Lt. (jg) Jacob Jay "Jake" Vandergrift Jr., was another Academy man who came from an affluent Pennsylvania family. He had reported on board in May 1941 as the communications and commissary officer.

Perch entered Darwin Harbor on 17 January and moored alongside the sub tender *Otus* (AS-20). Lt. Cdr. Hurt was awarded the Navy Letter of Commendation and his ship was given wartime credit for sinking one 5,000-ton Japanese freighter although this credit was later stripped postwar. Many years later, the research of retired Navy commander John D. Alden found Japanese records showing that they had lost the 7,190-ton armed ammunition ship *Nojima Maru* to *Perch* off Hong Kong.[5]

The crew had a short time ashore in Australia before departing on the second patrol, but they found little to do. "There was nothing there," said Bob Lents. "It had all been abandoned. All there was was empty houses. All I found to do was walk around the jungles."

Seaman first class Thomas Moore made the most of his time ashore. On board, he was striking for his torpedoman third class rating in Sam Simpson's forward room, but was still "a low man on the totem pole. I wasn't assigned there full time, so my big job was mess cooking when the war started."

For 19-year-old Tom Moore, Navy life was a chance to make something of himself. "I was one of these guys who had a tough life in the United States," he later said. "I was a hobo and an orphan and abandoned so I had my treatment before I even got in the Navy." Born in New Jersey, he had lived in an orphanage in Port German, New York, from age two for the next eight years. He and his brother worked farms in upstate New York as they grew older. Tom literally lived the life of a hobo until he turned 18 and enlisted in the Navy "to get something to eat and some shoes."

By the end of the first patrol, Hurt was impressed enough with Moore's ability on the battle phones that he made him his battle stations talker. "During any actions or torpedo attacks, I was down in the control room as his talker while the skipper conned from the bridge or conning tower," Moore said.

Dave Hurt may have had second thoughts about his choice when Tom Moore reported back on board *Perch* from Port Darwin. "There wasn't much to do there and we were not allowed to talk to the natives," he said. Moore acquired some booze from one of the natives and proceeded to get drunk. "It's all red clay down there and it was monsoon season," he recalled. "Of course, in my whites I got caught in a rainstorm drunk out there and I looked like a red man. When I woke up and had to go back to the ship, the appearance of my uniform revealed all of what I'd done."

The captain was not pleased with his new battle talker and confined Moore until they sailed. "I was always in trouble," he admitted. "I was confined to the ship, but with what was to happen to us, what the hell was the difference?"

Perch took on additional Mark 14 torpedoes and departed Australia on 3 February 1942 at the time the Japanese campaign to secure the Netherlands East Indies was at its height. An invasion of Borneo or Java seemed imminent and *Perch* was ordered to go into the Java Sea to scout Makassar Strait on her second patrol. Between 3 February and 23 February, Dave Hurt was sent several reports concerning enemy concentrations in the area. On 25 February, he was directed to go through the Sallier Strait and patrol along the curve northeast of the Kangean Islands as part of the force fighting to defend Java.

Perch was patrolling off the southern exits of Kendari on the night of 25 February 1942 when the Japanese supply ship fired on her. The fire control method looked good on paper. The only thing Lt. K. G. Schacht and his skipper had not prepared for was an enemy gun crew firing on them first.

"All worked perfectly, except that the night was not as black as assumed," Schacht recalled. "We had been visually observed for some time."[6]

"Right full rudder," Hurt called down to his helmsman.

Perch heeled over to starboard as she lined up her prey. "Stand by to fire," the skipper called.

At that instant, the enemy supply ship suddenly opened up with its forward deck gun. "The first round was short," Schacht remembered, "the second a direct hit (2-ft. hole) in the conning tower fairwater." The shell's explosion ruptured *Perch*'s antenna trunk, severing electrical leads, flooding the standard compass, rupturing an air line, and causing other minor damage.[7]

TM3c Bob Lents in the forward torpedo room, "knew we were hit somewhere from the jar and the explosion. The shell luckily hit the guard rail around the conning tower first and then started exploding before it hit our pressure hull." In the maneuvering room, EM3c Marion McDaniel "Turk" Turner felt the jar. "It shocked us because we didn't know what was going on up above. We hadn't heard the part about another ship being spotted."

For a submarine, getting hit by a shell was potentially fatal. One rupture to her pressure hull and diving would be out of the question. In *Perch*'s case, the damage was not substantial.

Turk Turner had volunteered for the Navy once he heard of the great war breaking out overseas. At the time, he was serving in the Civilian Conservation Corps because steady work had been hard to find in the late 1930s. "I had always wanted to go to college so once I got into the Navy, I was determined I would make the most of my learning," Turner recalled. He studied his books hard and in only 13 months he was advanced from fireman to third class petty officer (EM3c).

Three months into the war, Turner was already leading something of a charmed life. In late 1940, he had passed on the chance to join the submarine *Shark* (SS-174), opting to let an electrician's mate who was three days his junior in seniority take the slot. In early February 1942, this man and 57 others were killed when *Shark* fell victim to a Japanese depth charge attack and became the first U.S. submarine of World War II to be lost with all hands. Turner had instead been assigned to the newer boat *Sealion* (SS-195) in November 1940. *Sealion* joined the U.S. Asiatic Fleet in the Philippines but Turner was transferred in January 1941 to the submarine tender *Canopus* with a bad case of dengue fever.

On 1 March, Turk Turner was transferred to *Perch*. He would soon find that assignment was again fortunate for his survival. When the Japanese bombed the Cavite Naval Yard in Manila on 10 December, *Sealion*'s hull was ripped apart by a bomb which exploded deep in her engineering space. The electrician who had replaced Turner when he became ill—EM3c Vallentyne Lester Paul—was one of four men killed by the bomb. He had already cheated death twice when *Perch* was shelled on 25 February.

Lieutenant Commander Hurt's radio gang repaired the radio trunk quickly and a message was sent to ComSubsAsiatic telling him that radio reception was possible but transmission was uncertain. Hurt headed his boat south and continued on his patrol as planned.

————

Winged by the enemy, *Perch* was back on the attack just days later on 1 March. Dave Hurt had received a message directing all submarines to attack the invading convoy at the landing point. By the evening of 28 February, a large convoy of Japanese troopships was reported to be heading for Surabaya, on the coast of the island of Java.

Perch ran surfaced at top speed during the night, heading for the Japanese landing point. At 1755, two enemy destroyers were sighted while approximately 20 miles northeast of Surabaya. Much later in the war, Cdr. Sam Dealey of Texas would become the famed "destroyer killer" skipper for attacking and sinking Japanese men-of-war. Dave Hurt was equally brazen as he weighed his chances of taking out such prime warships so early into the Pacific War. He had already fired on a Japanese destroyer unsuccessfully on his first patrol.

Unknown to Lieutenant Commander Hurt and his crew, Japanese naval forces had engaged Allied warships on 27 February in what became known as the Battle of the Java Sea. The Allied forces consisted of the U.S. heavy cruiser *Houston* (CA-30), British heavy cruiser *Exeter*, Australian light cruiser *Perth*, Dutch light cruisers *DeRuyter* and *Java*, plus ten American, British, and Dutch destroyers. In this battle, *DeRuyter* and *Java* were sunk, along with two destroyers. Following this battle, the destroyer *Pope* (DD-225) was caught by dive bombers from the Japanese light carrier *Ryujo* on 1 March and was mortally damaged. Her crew was forced to abandon ship. The Japanese heavy cruisers *Ashigara* and *Myoko* closed in that afternoon and pounded the remains of the 1,190-ton destroyer under the waves. After three days adrift, 149 survivors from *Pope* were picked up by a Japanese destroyer and taken to Makassar City on Celebes Island, where they would join other American, Dutch, and British POWs.[8]

The seas around Surabaya were alive with Japanese warships when *Perch* approached that area on 1 March. Sweeping the horizon atop *Perch*'s periscope shears was S1c Tom Moore. "The captain was on the bridge with us," he said. "Lieutenant Schacht, the gunnery officer, was the officer of the watch. We were in shallow water when these two destroyers spotted us."

The two destroyers Hurt's submarine had spotted were *Amatsukaze* and *Hatsukaze*, which were just returning to the area from refueling. Steaming at 20 knots, *Hatsukaze*'s lookouts spotted *Perch* and the destroyer charged on the diving U.S. submarine. Tameichi Hara, skipper of *Amatsukaze*, had his lookouts intently scanning the ocean for American submarines this night.[9]

Captain Hara's *Amatsukaze* was unable to make proper sonar contact due to the destroyer's high speed. *Hatsukaze*'s sonar, however, made a solid lock and she charged toward the spot where *Perch* had dived.

At 2000, *Perch* made a quick dive. "We were absolutely flabbergasted at having been sighted," said torpedo officer K. G. Schacht. "It was at night and the moon favored us." *Amatsukaze* and *Hatsukaze* raced bow-on toward the American submarine at 25 knots.

With the attack opportunity lost, Hurt kept *Perch* at periscope depth. He happily watched as the DDs passed well clear astern of his boat. After going on ahead on course for about five miles, one of the destroyers suddenly turned and came back toward *Perch*.

"The course of one of the enemy ships would bring it across our stern and I prepared to fire the aft tubes," Hurt recorded in his report. "There was a full moon and I was able to take periodic periscope observations. After taking my last look, the destroyer was only a thousand yards away. He had changed course sharply to the right and was speeding directly our way."

Tom Moore, having scrambled down from the periscope shears, was now wearing the battle talker's headset in the control room, relaying his skipper's orders to the after room. Chief of the Boat Charlie Cross stood sentry at the Christmas tree, the red and green light hull opening indicator panel. Diving officer Jack Ryder supervised the planesmen.

In the after torpedo room, TM1c Glenn Taylor and his crew—TM3c Francis Alboney, TM3c Gilbert Shaefer, TM3c John Greco, and their strikers—were ready. When the range had closed to about 800 yards and the firing point was almost reached, *Hatsukaze* suddenly changed course. He turned sharply in *Perch*'s direction and increased speed. "Whether he spotted our periscope or picked us up by sonar, we'll never know," Ken Schacht wrote.[10]

Thinking that he had 200 feet of water under his boat, Lieutenant Commander Hurt called out, "Take her to one hundred eighty feet! Prepare for depth charge attack!"

In the control room, Lieutenant Ryder ordered his planesmen to nose the boat down for the bottom. The charts showed 200 feet of depth in this area, although the fathometer had not been used to avoid detection by the destroyers. *Perch* had just reached 100 feet when *Hatsukaze* raced overhead and dropped six depth charges. Before each resonating blast, the men could hear the deadly click of the firing pin on the detonators.

Click–BOOM! Click–BOOM!

Each blast shook the boat as she continued diving for the ocean floor. *Perch* found the bottom long before the anticipated 180 feet she was clawing for. At 147 feet, the submarine hit bottom in the mud of the Java Sea's floor. The motors were still turning over as men suddenly were knocked from their feet. In Sam Simpson's forward torpedo room, Bob Lents felt there was "nothing much you can do but hang on when the depth charges came rattling down. They were right on us. It knocked out the lights and knocked gauges off the bulkhead. It broke glass from the gauges and heaved in some of the hull."

EM2c Turk Turner was on duty in the maneuvering room. He and his buddy, EM1c Edward "Doggie" Van Horn, were answering calls from the annunciator. "If they wanted us to back down, they would show us astern with the annunciator," Turner recalled. "We thought we had more water under us than we actually did."

The first depth charges did no serious harm and the accidental bottoming of the ship had not seriously damaged her. The second string of ashcans was another story.

Hatsukaze's screws were heard clearly by the soundmen as he raced in for another run. This time, the splashes of four trash-can-sized depth explosives were heard. *Hatsukaze*'s skipper was right on the money. There was not even the delayed click before the explosions. *Perch* was punished by four crippling explosions that bent and twisted her hull. Men were knocked down as the water outside her hull exploded violently. The lights went out and cork insulation pelted the sailors like hail.

"This one hurt," Lieutenant Schacht recalled. "Broken glass [was] all over the place." He noted differing reactions on the faces of nearby men, "mostly numb." The blasts were so close that Schacht felt no concussion. He felt "like an animal trapped in a drum when someone beats on it with a hammer."[11]

Maximum damage and shock was absorbed in the motor room and engine room. Power was lost on one shaft. Ninety percent of the engine-room gauges were broken. The high-pressure air bank in the after battery started a bad leak. Number Five main-ballast vents were frozen closed. In the after battery, the hull was compressed for about six feet by one foot, to a depth of 2.5 inches. The crew's porcelain toilet was shattered.

"There were many indentations in the hull but none were broken through," recalled EM3c Daniel Crist. Born on Valentine's Day in 1920, Crist had joined the Navy in 1939. At the moment, his recently celebrated 22nd birthday was beginning to look like his last. "All the lights were put out by the first direct hits," he recalled.

"I thought I was a goner," battle talker Tom Moore said. "I was 19 years old and I figured, well, that's the end of me." Jack Ryder's planesmen were helpless as their boat lay stuck in the muddy bottom, her engines dead. Their fate lay solely in the skill or lack thereof possessed by the Japanese sailors rolling the depth charges off their stern racks some 147 feet above them.

In *Perch*'s engine room, F1c Elbert Hugh Arnette found that "the damage was heavy" from this depth charge attack. A 20-year-old from Perdido, Alabama,

Arnette's Southern accent had quickly earned him the nickname "Alabama." He had first served on the battleship *New Mexico* before volunteering for submarine duty. "They paid $25 more a month for submarine duty, and I wanted to get that to send back home," Arnette recalled. "So, I went from Hawaii to Manila Bay and joined the *Perch* before her first patrol."

Ironically, Alabama Arnette had the option to skip *Perch*'s last patrol. Prior to his ship's second war patrol, he had been on night duty helping to service the diesels while *Perch* was moored alongside the tender *Otus* in Port Darwin. "I was the youngest one on duty that night," he recalled, "so they sent me over to the tender to get some cold water." Arnette went topside with a water jug to cross the catwalk between the ships. Although it was pitch black, he called back to the deck watchman, "You can turn off your flashlight. I can see all right."

With his next step, Arnette missed the plank and plunged down into Darwin's harbor between the sub tender and *Perch*. He received a nasty slash on his left wrist that cut a major vein to his little finger. "I had blood all over the place so they rushed me over to the tender," Arnette said. *Otus'* medical staff and *Perch* pharmacist Philip Dewes tended to the sailor, who was offered the chance to stay behind. "No, I want to be with my buddies," Arnett protested. "If they all die, I want to die with 'em." Soon after *Perch* departed Darwin, Dewes removed the bandages and allowed the machinist to continue his duties.

Arnette had spent some time on the stern diving planes during battle stations before being permanently assigned to CMM Henry Yates' engine room. "We had four main engines and two auxiliaries," he later said. "I was assigned to one of the engines with a man named Joe Foley, who was my instructor." Foley, Chief Yates, and CMM Albert Newsome had trained the Alabama youth well, but little could prepare him for the pounding his ship was taking this day.

"The air in the boat was bad and it was hot," Arnette stated. "Guys were walking around the ship stark naked—it was that hot. Sweat was pouring right down into my shoes."

The destroyer came swishing back over for a third run, passing directly overhead like a steam train. He laid down another five ashcans, these exploding once again with maximum damage to *Perch*'s midships area. In the control room, the hull exhaust-duct section flooded, soaking the fire-control panel. "All depth gauges except the bow planes and the gauges in the Commanding Officer's room were broken," Lieutenant Van Buskirk later detailed. The conning tower was compressed two inches above the chart desk. The Number Two periscope was frozen. The Number One periscope would raise, but it took four men to turn it. The engine-room hatch, conning tower hatch, and conning tower door gaskets were crimped so that they leaked steadily. The air-conditioning water-supply flange cracked at the weld and leaked heavily.[12]

"They really had us precisely located," K. G. Schacht later wrote. "Being unable to free the boat was a frustrating experience."[13]

Perch was the figurative sitting duck, motionless and fully located. One more good string of explosives might cave in her battered hull completely. The temperature soared in the boat as the men sat silently, looking up at the hull and listening for the sounds of the approaching screws again. Thankfully, they became more distant for the time.

Dave Hurt joined Lieutenant Ryder in the control room and ordered his diving officer to get the boat up out of the mud. Their only chance lay in putting some ocean between their attackers and their current predicament. Ryder and his men soon managed to break their submarine from the mud. "After two hours of cat-and-mouse, we were able to elude the enemy vessels," Hurt wrote.

It was discovered later that loss of air and oil had convinced the enemy that the submarine had been demolished, and the Japanese had discontinued their attack accordingly. Their depth charges had been set shallow and detonated above *Perch*. Japanese depth charges were designed for a limited number of depth settings and would not detonate if they bottomed before making their set depth. So they could not be set for 200 feet. "I think the only thing that saved us was the muddy bottom," said EM3c Ernest Virgil Plantz, making his second run on *Perch*. "It was soft and we sank right down into it. If we'd been on rock, it would have ripped us apart."[14]

Born in 1922 in Spring Hill, West Virginia, as the first of four children, Ernie Plantz graduated from South Charleston (West Virginia) High School in 1939. The effects of the Great Depression made jobs scarce. Although he was a member of the CCC, Plantz elected to join the U.S. Navy, enlisting for six years in 1940. After boot camp at Norfolk, he reported on board the battleship *New Mexico* at Long Beach, California. Determined to become an electrician's mate, Plantz soon found that the Navy had plans for him to become a boatswain's mate striker against his will.[15]

To escape this fate, Ernie Plantz volunteered for submarine duty. He was accepted and was sent straight to Manila in 1941—without the benefit of submarine school—to report on board *Perch*. "I wanted to be an electrician, but I literally qualified for my dolphins in July of 1941 while I was mess cooking and I made third class electrician just as the war started."

Plantz was greatly relieved to find how sturdy his submarine, "pretty badly beat up," was proving to be. At 0300 on 2 March, *Perch* surfaced—seven hours after first diving to avoid the destroyers. Fortunately, the Japanese destroyers *Hatsukaze* and *Amatsukaze* had orders to rejoin a large Japanese warship force and they had moved on.

After surfacing, *Perch*'s crew surveyed their boat. They found the fresh air to be rejuvenating, but the damage was appalling. Turk Turner recalled, "We were pulling huge pieces of depth charges off the deck that had exploded during the attack." K. G. Schacht was impressed that his ship survived. "The deck was covered with crinkled strips of what had to be depth charge casings."[16]

Lieutenant Schacht had reported on board in 1939 as *Perch*'s commissary officer and worked his way up the wardroom ladder. During pre-war torpedo exercises in Subic Bay, he and fire controlman John Ellison had once spent 36 hours straight dismantling and reassembling the TDC, only to have their repair work give way again the following day. On another occasion, he had gone into the water in Manila Bay with torpedoman Sam Simpson to inspect a jammed outer door on one of *Perch*'s forward torpedo tubes. "Sam and I were in swim trunk in the water inspecting," Schacht recalled. "We were amazed to spot a large green snake with blue and yellow spots, lying there at No. 4 tube, looking us in the eye. We retreated and postponed our inspections."[17]

The damage control work faced by Schacht's crew on 2 March 1942 was beyond any expectations. Both periscope windows were broken and both scopes were flooded. As Ryder's engineers fired up the diesels, the No. 1 engine ran away on starting and the No. 4 main-engine camshaft was broken. The No. 2 main engine was put on battery charge and the No. 3 engine was put on propulsion.

Auxiliarymen and electricians removed sections of duct between the after battery blower and flappers, discharging the battery exhaust into the dinette. The forward battery ventilation was reconfigured to discharge directly into the officers' quarters through the ship's ventilation exhaust duct. The gyro follow-up system was out, so steering was accomplished from the control room using the master gyro.

Hurt headed *Perch* for the position of the Japanese landing to carry out an attack in spite of his boat's severe damage. At 0347, less than an hour after surfacing, two destroyers were sighted with dawn still two hours away. Fate worked in the favor of Captain Hara during the early hours of 2 March. Although his lookouts had not spotted *Perch* in time to attack the previous day, Hara's starboard lookout, Bunichi Ikeda, was first to spot *Perch* this day.[18]

Hara ran his *Amatsukaze* up to 26 knots and ordered his gun crews to their stations. As his ship raced in toward firing range, Hara noted that the U.S. submarine appeared to be adrift. As the distance dropped to 2,700 meters, *Amatsukaze* snapped on a searchlight, lit up the target and came around to port. "Open fire!" Captain Hara barked. *Amatsukaze* fired six shells in three salvos and *Hatsukaze* fired two salvos, although all missed.[19]

Perch dived at 0350 and headed for the ocean floor. "This time, we made no attempt to evade," wrote Lt. Schacht. "Too short on battery and air. We'd just sit there and sweat it out." To run submerged in the condition his boat was in, Dave Hurt needed the noisy trim pumps to stay in operation but on the bottom all machinery could be stopped and the boat could lie quietly at 200 feet. Hurt had used this tactic of lying on the bottom during a depth charge attack on his first patrol off Formosa. Unfortunately, *Perch* had been sighted and the Japanese destroyers homed in on her with a vengeance this time.[20]

"The Japanese had either sighted us on the surface or else located our boat with sound gear," Hurt wrote. "They ran straight for the *Perch*." One destroyer passed directly overhead and dropped six depth charges. The first string dealt her no additional damage. The second string of five charges was terrible. The air-conditioning circulating-water-supply flange leaked quarts as the flange studs elongated under successive shocks.

The same casualty caused bad leaks on the lines of the high-pressure air-compressor circulating water system. No. 1 main-ballast vent was damaged and it proved impossible to blow the tank. Air could be heard passing up alongside the hull when blowing, but the tanks would not hold air. There were leaks in the engine circulating water line and in various high-pressure air lines, including the after torpedo room. The transmitter was now inoperable due to leakage of the antenna trunk.

The porcelain toilet bowls in the maneuvering room and after battery were shattered. "There was such sharp jolts that it just shaved the toilet bowls right off even with the deck," recalled engineman Alabama Arnette. "It was just like someone had cut them off with a knife."

Perch was badly damaged, suffering internally when a third string of five charges landed directly overhead from stern to bow. The bow planes, on a 20-degree rise, were rigged in by the force of the explosions, a violence that burned up the bow-plane rigging panel. The JK soundhead and receiver were knocked out of commission. Torpedoes No. 1 and No. 2 made hot runs in their forward tubes. These fish were jarred into starting and safety cut-offs eventually stopped them.

Bob Lents knew the Mark 14s were not able to arm themselves, but the whine of their propellers did little to soothe his nerves. "We just sat there and hoped they didn't get hot enough to go off," he said. "They gave off a lot of smoke and heat, making it even harder to breathe." Lents knew that the whining propellers presented more problems than the fear they were currently facing. "The sound of those torpedoes gave us away to the depth chargers. I saw a lot of praying, a lot of praying! I was not really religious at that time, although I got religion!"

In the maneuvering room, EM3 Ernie Plantz was on duty with Turk Turner and EM2 Jesse Robison. "I was their third man," he recalled. "I was their coffee runner and just about anything else they could think of for me to do." During the worst of this round of depth charging, there was little for the electricians to do but sweat it out. "We really took a beating," said Plantz.

"The destroyer is turning," sound operator Ted Reh reported, as he switched on the speaker. The pinging was initially slow and deliberate as the DD sonar operators pinged for the stricken sub. As the range shortened, the tempo increased. The destroyer's screws became louder as he began his next approach run.

"The screws are heard clearly through the submarine's hull, sounding like the old N.Y. City elevated railway!" Schacht later narrated. "The pinging stops. He is overhead. The range is opening. You await the first charge; while bad, it is never the worst. The next is closer. The string's middle charges shake the ship. The lights go off; more air hissing and glass shattering are heard."[21]

Above, the destroyer made his fourth run paralleling *Perch* and dropped four more tooth-shakers. The bow planes had to be operated by hand from then on. The officers' toilet bowl was shattered and thrust out into the passageway. Leading petty officers quietly moved about, effecting what damage control they could during the attack. All joking and casual bantering had ceased. "Air pressure, CO_2, sweat, stink, fatigue, and frustration were bad enough," said K. G. Schacht, "but our inability to fight back was the worst aspect."[22]

The final blast of three depth charges proved the most severe. This came at about 0830 on the morning of 2 March. At one explosion, the depth gauge suddenly changed from 178 feet to an additional 30 feet of depth as the ship was compressed deep into the muddy ocean floor.

A cell cracked in the after battery; 19 cells had previously cracked in the forward battery. All the electric alarm system and telephone circuits went dead. On the engine-room deck the supporting stanchions between the overhead and the deck were broken at the hull weld. "The bolts that held down the engines just sheared off," said Alabama Arnette.

Working to control *Perch*'s damage this day was 31-year-old MM1c Stephen Michael Orlyk, a New Yorker who had already served 15 years in the Navy. Since most of his service had been on submarines, Orlyk needed little instruction on how to pitch in. He and his shipmates had quite a job on their hands if *Perch* was to be saved. "The boat was really a total wreck," Orlyk stated.[23]

At least 30 depth charges had been dropped on *Perch* during a two and a half hour period. Seeing large air bubbles break the surface and a widening oil slick, the Japanese destroyer skipper felt certain that the American sub had been crushed. Returning to the same area, Captain Hara on *Amatsukaze* also witnessed a great oil slick rising to the surface.[24]

After this savage attack, the Japanese destroyers steamed away, confident of a kill. They were nearly correct.

2
"A Miracle Was Needed"

With the Japanese destroyers departing, the mission of saving *Perch* took over. Fortunately, no chlorine gas leaks had been started. Lieutenant Commander Hurt decided that they should conserve oxygen and not risk further depth chargings during the day. He kept his boat down on the bottom while men set to work. "The pressure within the boat was high," said Lt. K. G. Schacht. "No gauges to tell us how high, but the squeaky sound of voices was an indicator."[1]

Two air tanks were completely empty from leaks. Two others had no more than 2,500 pounds of pressure each. This last reserve of air would have to be conserved for when *Perch* could safely make an attempt to dig herself out of the mud. Leaks throughout the ship required continuous operation of trim and drain pumps to keep the motor room, engine room and pump room bilges below the precious electrical gear that could ground out.

"We were getting very low on oxygen," recalled torpedoman Bob Lents. "You could hear water running into the boat like waterfalls from all the leaks. The air got so bad in the boat that if someone wanted to smoke, they couldn't even light a match." In the forward torpedo room, they spread the CO_2 absorbent powder around on the deck to help when the oxygen supply became low. Lents removed his shoes during the depth charge attack to help maintain silence. He now walked through the powder, pools of sweat, and water that seeped into his ship.

The crew was steady throughout their ordeal. *Perch* was fortunate to have a good percentage of very experienced men aboard. Helping to listen for the Japanese destroyers on the sonar gear was 26-year-old RM2c Ray Normand from

Massachusetts, who had joined the Navy in 1939. Having served as a radioman on board the heavy cruiser *San Francisco* prewar, Normand had volunteered for sub duty when he heard about the extra pay and extended shore leaves between patrols that was involved.[2]

During the afternoon, the engineers isolated the damaged motors of the starboard side, leaving two motors on the starboard shaft for propulsion. With the depth gauge in the control room showing *Perch* to be below 200 feet, it appeared that the explosions had forced the ship to slide down an embankment in the mud. Dave Hurt waited until after sunset on 2 March to try and free his ship.

They found her main vents would not hold air and the emergency vents had to be closed. By going ahead and astern at maximum power on both shafts, *Perch* took an hour to free herself. "We pulled forward and back, forward and back," recalled Turk Turner. "At the same time, the diving officer would blow air out of the ballast tanks to try and break us free from the mud."

Tom Moore recalled that Lt. Schacht used human ballast to help free *Perch*. "All hands to the control room," he called over the 1MC. When Moore and dozens others packed into the control room, they were ordered to walk forward through the ship and then turn and walk back while Schacht blew the ballast. "They decided to blow the port forward ballast tank and see if we could get to the surface," recalled Alabama Arnette. "As they blew the tank, the boat jarred and shook a while."

The rocking motion of the extra weight helped to free the ship from the muddy bottom. "Pretty soon we could hear this sucking noise," Moore said. "It was like a miracle. The stern started going up all by itself."[3]

Perch took a natural, high up-angle during her rise to the surface. "All of a sudden, she went up head first," said Arnette. "I'll tell you, that was the most wonderful feeling." *Perch*'s second surfacing of the day came at 2100. Lieutenant Van Buskirk reported that it "required two men to hold quartermaster opening [the] conning tower hatch. Air pressure in boat so high that both men though well braced were just able to prevent the quartermaster from being carried up with the escaping blast."[4]

Alabama Arnette remembered that the fresh air rushing into the stale, hot boat "was like heaven on earth." Lookouts made quick sweeps of the horizon. "Our periscope was knocked out and we just had to go by sight," Arnette explained. Fortunately, the lookouts quickly reported to Dave Hurt, "No ships in sight, sir."

After successively trying all engines, the black gang was finally able to get one on the line. Chief Victor "Pete" Pederson's electricians began charging the badly depleted batteries on the No. 1 and No. 2 auxiliary engines. *Perch* got under way, making 5 knots. Fifty percent of the holding-down studs on No. 3 main engine had snapped, and this engine vibrated so badly that the head covers raised one inch. There were numerous short circuits caused by spray from salt water leaks under pressure, many gaskets were badly crimped, and lube oil was lost constantly.

Perch senior electrician Pete Pederson sent junior electrician's mate Ernie Plantz into the battery wells to inspect their condition. "At least half the cells were cracked and were leaking," Plantz said. "The battery well was lined with vulcanized rubber. All of the cells were sitting on the rubber. You could look down between the cells with a flashlight and see the electrolyte down there."

The steering gear was badly damaged. On left rudder, the rudder could be moved only with difficulty; upon reaching the amidships position it would suddenly snap over against the stops to starboard. Hull leaks proved so bad on the surface that both trim and drain pumps were required at full capacity to keep bilges from flooding. *Perch* limped forward at 5 knots on one engine. She headed north, her crew dreaming that they could still somehow nurse their battered ship back to a friendly port and a long Navy yard overhaul. Hurt hoped to get away from the Japanese invasion forces and Surabaya by running east through the Flores and Banda seas toward Australia, some 1700 miles distant.[5]

Ken Schacht, the torpedo and gunnery officer, also held the role of the ship's first lieutenant. His men slaved through the night repairing leaks in the conning tower and after battery compartment. Commissary officer Jake Vandergrift had his cooks prepare a hearty breakfast during the early morning to feed the damage controlmen. Dave Hurt decided to make a trim dive before sunrise to see what progress had been made. About 0500 on 3 March, he ordered a running dive.

With the ship going ahead at one-third speed on one engine, he opened the vents to take in water to dive the boat. In spite of every effort to make the ship light and catch a trim by flooding in, she was found heavy on the dive. Before the descent could be checked, the injured *Perch* went down to 60 feet. "I intended to make a running dive, but the ship took a big up-angle and began to drop stern first," Lieutenant Commander Hurt wrote. "I thought, as we went deep, that air pressure would seal the leaks—but this was not the case."

Jack Ryder started blowing the safety tank, the No. 3, and No. 6 main-ballast tanks at 75 feet. Water began pouring into the engine room at the exhaust blowers. The conning tower and engine-room hatches had failed to seat and were leaking heavily. In the engine room, Chief Yates reported water entering the engine room at the ship's ventilation exhaust blowers. By the time *Perch* regained the surface, water in the engine-room bilges was up to the generators. After surfacing it was possible to expose only the forward half of the deck. Her stern underwater, *Perch* chugged ahead like a wounded whale.

Her conning tower hatch was badly twisted and could not be closed properly. Handicapped by their darkened ship, the crew tried to adjust the dogs on the hatch. "The dive was a dismal failure," wrote Ken Schacht. "We knew then that a miracle was needed."[6]

Dave Hurt called his four other officers and Chief of the Boat Charlie Cross to the wardroom. In a short meeting, they reviewed the combat status of their ship.

Hurt said that he did not believe they could get the ship back to the surface if they dived again. The crew was to continue making repairs, but unless they could reach shallow water, the men should be prepared to scuttle the boat on short notice to avoid it being captured by the Japanese.

Reality had set in for most of the crew by this point. "We knew we was really finished," said engineman Alabama Arnette. "We were having to do everything by hand, turning hand wheels to let water in and pump water out."

Jake Vandergrift scurried about, stuffing mail bags with classified material and weights. "We were worried about water depth, fearful that the enemy could reach her with divers and perhaps salvage useful material," recalled Lt. Schacht. He went to the safe in his room and stuffed his wallet into his pocket. "I dreamed of getting to the nearest land, 75 miles away," Schacht wrote. "No doubts. However, I did write a note and sealed it in a jar just in case."[7]

In the galley, SC1c Vernon Bolton shoved a couple of turkeys into the oven, thinking that the men should at least enjoy the best food aboard while they could. The gunner's mates found that they were unable to train or elevate the deck gun and that its sights were shattered.

At this inopportune moment, the OOD suddenly reported ships on the horizon. Unable to dive, *Perch* was defenseless. This group of approaching ships turned out to be two cruisers and four destroyers. Cruisers *Nachi* and *Haguro* were in company with the destroyers *Sazanami*, *Amatsukaze*, *Hatsukaze*, and *Ushio*. Japanese ships had been active over the past days, picking up numerous survivors of the Battle of the Java Sea. These included British men from the heavy cruiser *Exeter* and destroyer *Encounter* plus Americans from the destroyer *Pope*.

Lookouts on Lt. Cdr. Uesugi Yoshitake's *Ushio* and sister destroyer *Sazanami* both sighted a surfaced submarine at 0652 (Japanese time). *Ushio*'s skipper thought it might be a Japanese submarine and tried unsuccessfully to contact *Perch* with his ship's blinker gun. With no reply after another seven minutes, Yoshitake had *Ushio* open fire with her 5-inch guns from 5,250 yards.[8]

Aboard *Perch*, lookouts watched as the first shell fell 300 yards short and 50 yards forward. The second and third shells were on in deflection but fell short. Daylight was coming, however, and the Japanese gunners would not be long in finding their mark. *Perch*'s situation was hopeless. Unable to fire the deck gun or any of the torpedo tubes, "the general feeling was more one of frustration than desperation," wrote Lt. Schacht.[9]

Hurt decided to abandon ship and ordered his boat scuttled. Torpedomen Sam Simpson and Warren Atkeison departed their forward room immediately. As they passed through the control room, Chief of the Boat Charlie Cross on the air manifold warned them, "You had better hurry. She is settling in the water and could go at any time." Simpson scrambled out the conning tower hatch, ran aft and sat down to take off his shoes to avoid any added drag on his feet as he swam.

"She slipped from under me and I floated off the deck into the sea. I recall several persons diving from the A-frames into the sea just before she went down."[10]

Jake Vandergrift dropped all the classified material he had gathered over the sides in their weighted bags. He then took to the water with a life jacket and a Momsen lung. Vandergrift chose to pin his lung to his trousers, enabling him to float with his feet up without difficulty.

In the engine room, Chief Henry Yates' black gang got the word over the emergency speaker to abandon ship. Alabama Arnette and Joe Foley wasted no time in getting "topside to the deck." Bob Lents was the last man out of the forward torpedo room. When the call came to abandon ship, his buddies scurried for the conning tower. "I turned around and everybody was gone," he said. "I think I was about the last one out of the forward end of the submarine. They were all up on deck when I got there." Lents surveyed the situation topside for a moment and saw the Japanese warships approaching. "Their shells were whistling over and cutting the antenna wires above us." Needing no further prompting, Lents simply stepped over the side and began swimming.

Electricians Doggie Van Horn and Turk Turner were on duty in the maneuvering room when the call to abandon ship came.

"Hey, let's go," said Van Horn.

The pair started for the conning tower. Just as they reached the control room, the order came to stop all engines. Turner raced back to the maneuvering room and stopped the engines. He grabbed a flashlight and came up through the conning tower onto the main deck. By the time he made it topside, there were only two men left aboard who were scuttling the ship. "Our stern was already underwater, so I just walked right off into the water," he said.

Hurt and Exec Bev Van Buskirk were topside. Their men wore life belts and carried off whatever personal effects they could. Pharmacist Philip Dewes, a warrant officer, passed out watertight contraceptives that the men partially inflated to house their pictures and personal effects. Battle talker Tom Moore never found time to collect any of his personal effects. With his life jacket on, he waited until the water was literally underneath his armpits and he floated away from his submarine carrying only his flashlight.

Two men were left below to scuttle the boat, GM3c Earl "Bud" Harper and Lt. K. G. Schacht. Schacht went aft to the engine room, opened some vents, then dashed for the conning tower. When he arrived, he had to fight his way up the hatch through a wall of water. For his work in depriving the Japanese of *Perch's* secret gear, he was later awarded the Navy Cross.[11]

Electrician Ernie Plantz was down in the pump room working on the IC motor generator, trying to restore AC power to the ship. He somehow missed hearing the word to get topside. Another sailor finally stuck his head through the hatch and yelled, "Hey, we're abandoning ship! You'd better get up here!"

Plantz thus had no time to grab any personal effects and left with only the clothes on his back. As he came up out of the pump room, he saw Lt. Schacht and Bud Harper heading aft. En route to the after engine room, Schacht spotted the young electrician and said, "What the hell are you doing here?"

"I came back to help you guys," Plantz offered.

"Get the heck out of here," he was told. "The boat is going to sink." Plantz made it topside before Schacht and Harper. "We each had our life jacket on and we just floated away from the ship as she went down," Plantz said.

Among the last to leave *Perch* with them was fireman Alabama Arnette. He stood for a moment near Bud Harper watching as sea water poured down through the open hatch into his crippled submarine. "I'll never forget the color of that water," Arnette recalled. "It was a beautiful aqua color."

Momentarily engrossed in the surreal view, he was slapped back into reality by the warning shout of a shipmate, "Get away from that hatch! It could suck you under!"

With that, Arnette decided it was time to go overboard. "I was just a kid and I thought I'd just dive right into the water like I used to do in the old days in Perdido Creek," he later stated. "I climbed up onto one of the rails that go around the ship to dive in. By the time I got ready to dive, the ship just sunk out from under me."

K. G. Schacht, clinging to a Momsen lung, watched his ship slide below the surface of the Java Sea. He later reflected:[12]

> One highly intelligent officer, when the word was passed to "abandon and scuttle ship," quickly went to his locker and put on his oldest pair of shoes. He didn't want to ruin those he was wearing in salt water.
>
> The amount of personal gear most of the men managed to take with them, and keep dry, was amazing. Pictures, razors, soap, combs, socks, wallets, watches, etc. How? The pharmacist mate apparently maintained (unbeknownst to the wardroom) a large supply of contraceptives. These, stuffed and secured, provided efficient, water-tight containers.

All the men got into the warm water safely. From a distance, they watched *Perch* start for the bottom. The ocean poured in through her open conning tower hatch and she was gone a moment later. She slid beneath the surface silently, producing but a few big bubbles to mark her passing as she made her last dive toward the ocean floor. Most of her crew were a mere 100 yards away as she went down.

Alabama Arnette, as he drifted away from his plunging submarine, saw that her "colors were flying to the last." Sam Simpson said *Perch* went "down by the stern, raising her prow to an angle of about 35° and silently slipped backwards into the sea."[13]

Seaman first class Gordon Bennett "Ben" Clevinger felt that his ship would have survived had she been in deeper water during the depth charge attacks. "It took two days and 71 depth charges to get us," he recalled. A native of poor Kentucky coal-mining country, Clevinger had joined the Navy at age 18, one of only 26 applicants accepted when he applied. He had been in his bunk on board *Perch* at Manila when the war started. "The Japs just bombed Pearl Harbor," was suddenly announced. "Pearl Harbor's not here," another sailor muttered as he rolled back over to sleep. For Ben Clevinger, the war had become real at that moment and now his fate seemed in jeopardy.[14]

As they watched their ship go down, men realized everything they owned was gone. Bob Lents lost $37 in his locker that was now heading for Davy Jones' locker. Ernie Plantz longed for his prized bolo knife with its decorative scabbard—which he had purchased from a merchant in Mindanao—also tucked away in his locker. "Seeing the sub go down was like seeing my home go down," Plantz thought.[15]

Many men were carrying flashlights they had used on their power-stricken submarine. It was dark as they entered the water.

"I wonder if they are going to pick us up?" someone asked.[16]

"Let's turn our lights on them," another sailor suggested.

Lieutenant Van Buskirk recalled, "That seemed like a good idea, so we started shining our lights toward the Japs. They thought they had sunk a submarine, when the entire city of Scottsdale illuminated the horizon."

Japanese gunners opened up on the shining lights. As the shells began whistling overhead and splashing into the ocean, the men hurriedly attempted to turn off their flashlights. "If you soaked them in salt water, then turned them on, they were grounded and would continue to burn," Van Buskirk wrote.

The men tried frantically to turn them off. CMM Henry Yates finally yelled, "Why don't you drop the damn things?"

Van Buskirk joked that only one person out of a 59-man crew was thinking clearly. "I guess that is about par for the course."

The weary submariners watched the Japanese ships close in. "They fired at us while we were in the water," recalled EM3c Dan Crist. "Destroyers came over where the ship went down and dropped more depth charges."

Sam Simpson was wearing both a life jacket and Momsen lung, which caused him to float "shoulder high in the water. It was dark. I could not recognize anyone." Due to leaving *Perch* at varying times during her final dive, some of the men had become scattered about in the Java Sea. "Our men were spreading," recalled Simpson, who called out to a shipmate to encourage everyone to stay together.[17]

After the *Perch* men had been in the water about an hour, the Japanese began picking them up. One of the destroyers, Cdr. Uesugi Yoshitake's *Ushio*, lowered two wooden whaleboats and began collecting the survivors. Captain Hara's *Amatsukaze* dropped six depth charges "to clinch the job" and then departed the area with *Hatsukaze*. Ernie Plantz and others felt that *Amatsukaze* had dropped the depth charges to make sure that *Perch* was indeed destroyed. "They had evidently surmised that part of the crew had abandoned ship as a decoy while the submarine made an escape," Plantz said.[18]

As the whaleboat crews paddled amongst the dozens of American sailors, the Japanese at first tried to pick up only the *Perch* officers. "Nobody would go," said Turk Turner. "We told them to take everybody or nobody, so they took all of us." Commissioned in November 1931, *Ushio* was 378 feet in length, weighed 2,050 tons, carried 197 crewmen and had a top speed of 37 knots. Although damaged several times in combat, *Ushio* would be the only destroyer out of 20 ships in her class to survive World War II and would be the only survivor of 22 combat ships in the 1941 Pearl Harbor assault force.[19]

The whaleboats brought the submariners alongside *Ushio*, where the Americans climbed up a Jacob's ladder to the main deck. Turner found that his skipper, who had been sick before the last fight of the *Perch*, was worn out. "Go ahead, Turner," he said.

"No, come on, Captain, you go," Turner said. Swimming up behind his skipper, he gave him a boost. "I got him on my shoulder and pushed him up to where he could get his knee on the ladder." Turner then followed Hurt up the ladder.

Tom Moore looked up at the Japanese destroyer and saw the rails lined with Japanese faces. "Every one of them was leering at us. They all had guns." He was certain that they would begin shooting the submariners in the water. MM1c Joe Foley, floating beside Moore, called to his buddy, "Tom, turn your head. Then they'll hit you in the back of the head with their bullets."[20]

When a whaleboat approached Foley and Moore, they were pulled on board and thrown in the bilge. Japanese sailors put their feet on the Americans to keep them from moving. "We were so exhausted it didn't matter," Moore recalled. As Lt. (jg) Vandergrift scrambled up the rope ladder to the Japanese deck—wearing his life jacket and Momsen lung pinned to his trousers—he noted the sun was just rising.

Torpedoman Bob Lents was one of the last to be picked up. He and a group of five others swam as far away from the enemy ships as possible, hoping to escape their shell fire. Lents was suffering from an unknown pain in the back of his neck. "I found out later that I had chipped a piece of bone in the fifth vertebra in my neck," he said. "Something had apparently flown off the bulkhead during the depth charge explosions and hit me in the neck." When the destroyer's whaleboat approached, "I didn't know what was gonna happen," Lents thought. "I think we were scared of them and they were a little scared of us."

Alabama Arnette found it difficult to make it onto *Ushio*'s deck. "Every time I'd try to step onto the destroyer's deck, they'd knock me down," he said. "All I could think was, 'Why are they knocking me down for?'"

One of his shipmates finally called out, "You're supposed to salute when you come aboard their ship!" Arnette was knocked to the deck three times by angry Japanese sailors before he finally gave a salute to their flag. "I really hated to support that Japanese flag," he recalled. After giving in, he was finally allowed to take a seat on the destroyer's deck with the rest of his crew. "That's where it all started for us," Arnette related.

Ushio was the only warship to retrieve *Perch*'s survivors. She would pick up the entire 59-man crew: five officers and 54 enlisted men. "After stripping men of life jackets and lungs and most all articles that were personal, they put us on the starboard side, aft," related Arnette. "Aboard this vessel, we were kept aft on the main deck during an eighteen-hour trip to a small bay," stated Lieutenant (jg) Vandergrift. Once on board the destroyer, Turk Turner still had some cigarettes and he shared one with his skipper as they nervously awaited what the Japanese would do with them.

Dave Hurt and Exec Bev Van Buskirk were transferred to the heavy cruiser *Ashigara*, flagship for the 3rd Japanese Fleet, for questioning two hours after being picked up. The first amusing fact that Van Buskirk heard was that his submarine was the 66th American sub that had been sunk by the Japanese in the first three months of war. "I refused to answer questions and I was threatened by the Chief of Staff that he would have me decapitated," he recalled. "Happily for me, he did not execute these threats, but it was an example of their conduct when endeavoring to obtain information."[21]

The other three officers and the *Perch* enlisted men remained on board *Ushio* throughout the afternoon. They were left seated topside and were not interrogated. "They gave us tea, hard tack, and cigarettes," related Dan Crist. Ernie Plantz found that the Japanese sea biscuits "were about ten times more tasty than ours were. They told us we'd better eat and drink because they wouldn't be so good to us where we were going." Lt. K. G. Schacht found the *Ushio* crew to be decent to the American survivors. "The DD skipper offered his condolences to our skipper on the loss of his ship. Our morale took a dip when they showed us Nipponese magazine pictures of the Pearl Harbor bombing damage."[22]

Ushio brought her catch of *Perch* men directly to southeastern Borneo, as did *Inazuma* with her *Pope* survivors, the latter reaching the port on 5 March. *Ushio* entered the harbor during the late hours of 3 March. The men topside saw a hospital ship already docked in the harbor. "We were on the destroyer until they moved us during the night," said Tom Moore. "They used pulling whaleboats, rowboats to transfer us." At 0220 on 4 March, the *Perch* prisoners were moved from the Japanese warship to the larger captured Dutch vessel. The Dutch ship was the *Op ten Noort*, built in 1927 as a 6,076-ton passenger ship and later converted to a hospital ship. They found nearly 1,000 prisoners aboard her from *Exeter*, *Encounter*, and the Dutch destroyer *DeRuyter*. *Perch*'s skipper and exec were reunited with them and the crew was kept contained like cattle on the large ship for several days.[23]

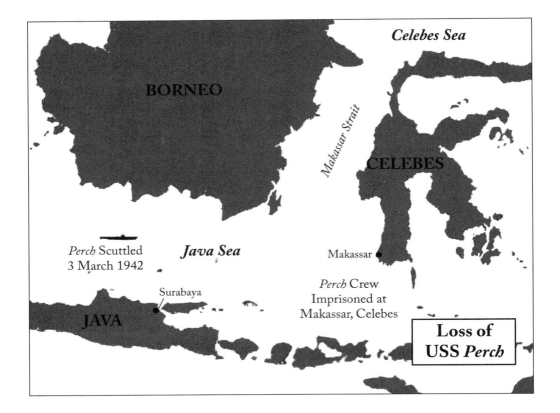

"We were not restrained while we were topside on the hospital ship," recalled Turk Turner. "I could have swam to the coast easily and I was contemplating that until I looked into the water under the ship and saw them big sharks down there. I decided not to try that."

Taken below into the holds of the hospital ship, the *Perch* crew was not provided for at all. They were kept locked in an old coal hold that had only one ladder leading up to the main deck. "We had no water, no food, no nothing for three days," recalled Ernie Plantz. Crowded among British and Dutch survivors, Plantz debated with his fellow crewmen on what nourishment they might receive.[24]

> Some guys were wondering what they would feed us. Robbie Robison told me when we had been swimming in the ocean before they picked us up that it would be rice, because that's what the Japanese ate. I said I hoped they would give us sugar and cream with it, because I couldn't eat rice without sugar and cream. Well, three days later when they finally fed us for the first time, I ate that rice without sugar and cream.

The *Perch* crew was in better physical condition aboard *Op ten Noort* than some of their Allied counterparts from *Exeter, Encounter,* and *DeRuyter.* "It was pretty crowded down in that old hull with no ventilation," said Plantz. "Some of those poor British and Dutch sailors had second and third degree burns from the sun. They had been in the water a couple of days."

After a week on board the hospital ship, the *Perch* crew was taken off onto a pier, where they were formed in ranks four abreast. They were marched into Makassar City on 10 March. "It was in the afternoon and it was hot, being a half degree off the equator," said Plantz. "Some of the guys who didn't have shoes on blistered the soles of their feet on the blacktop. Their soles just peeled off later. They marched us through the city, showing off the submarine crew they had captured."

Outside Makassar City, the *Perch* crew was marched to an Army camp on the outskirts of town. They walked along an unpaved road of stones, passing various houses and Indonesian shops along the way. "I thank God that I had kept my shoes on my feet," said Arnette. "It was hot and some of those shoeless guys were hopping around."

From within one of the buildings, Turk Turner heard an English voice calling out, "Hey Yanks! Hey, Yanks!" Turner and his fellow crewmen would soon find out that these men were Allied POWs the Japanese had captured from *Exeter* and various Dutch military personnel.

They at last arrived at a former Dutch army post which was surrounded by a barbed wire fence. Inside the complex were two large buildings of similar size on either side of the road. The officers and crew were all kept together, allowing them the opportunity to compare notes on their ship's loss.

"My skipper, Dave Hurt, expressed the desire that I try and get some paper and write a report pointing out the structural weaknesses of the *Perch* as a result of the depth charging," Bev Van Buskirk related. "It was his hope that I would be able to smuggle it through the war so that the Navy could correct those weaknesses."[25]

A Dutch officer in camp helped to smuggle a writing tablet and pencils through the fence to the *Perch* officers. "I began interviewing the officers and leading petty officers, and in a short time I had a very detailed 20-page report on the subject, which I turned over to the officers to memorize," Van Buskirk wrote.

Feeding the newly arrived American POWs was not a priority for the Japanese. Lt. Jack Ryder recalled, "The camp was not prepared to take care of the large number of prisoners at first, either in food or housing conditions." Jake Vandergrift agreed, "there was no apparent organization for the care of the POWs and as a result of the unpreparedness, we missed several meals at first."

Bob Lents remembered that the Americans were all kept in the same barracks, separated from the British prisoners. "They shut the doors on us and we stayed there all night," he said. "The next morning, they opened up the doors and said we could go down and get a drink of water. They had running water in the camp down in the toilets. Finally, they gave us a little sea biscuit. Food was mighty scarce," said Lents. "We would eat grass or leaves or anything we could eat."

Two weeks later, the *Pope* crew was brought into the Makassar prison camp, after two weeks in a prison near the harbor after their original arrival on 5 March. Lt. (jg) John Joseph Aloysius Michel, one of the destroyer's junior officers, was pleased to see men he knew. Jake Vandergrift was a Naval Academy classmate of his and Lt. Cdr. Hurt had been one of their instructors. Michel found Vandergrift hard to recognize at first due to his full beard. He also noted the other *Perch* officers—Van Buskirk, Schacht, and Ryder—"all looked bedraggled and unshaven."[26]

The Makassar camp contained about 3,000 prisoners of all nationalities. Of this, 186 were American, mostly from *Perch* and *Pope*. This became known as the Makassar-Celebes POW camp, although the Japanese would never report the existence of such a camp nor its occupants. The *Pope* and *Perch* men would remain listed as missing and their families in most cases believed them to be dead.

The lack of food was most trying. During the first few weeks, the *Perch* crew received only a daily piece of bread about the size of a hamburger bun. "I tried eating grass and those grub worms you find in rotten wood," recalled Ernie Plantz. He learned to lie on his back with a heavy log on his stomach to try and control his hunger pangs. A man of 180 pounds, Plantz found that his weight began dropping quickly during the first weeks.[27]

The days at Makassar passed slowly for Turk Turner. "It was mighty boring," he said. "We were on pins and needles, not knowing what was going to happen." Turner was kept in a little cubicle in the barracks with four Americans—Ernie Plantz and Jesse Robison from *Perch* and two men from *Pope*, including a mess attendant. In their cell one day, the mess attendant was standing, looking out the window, when a Japanese guard entered. The guard proceeded to beat this man for no apparent reason. Turner was furious. "I came up off the deck and said to myself, 'I'm gonna get me a Jap!'"

Fortunately, one of Turner's shipmates subdued him. "He jumped on top of me and held me down," Turner said. "The guard beat that guy from the *Pope* all around with his fist for no reason at all. He didn't do nothing."

Alabama Arnette was locked into a cell with four members of the *Perch* black gang: Chief Henry Yates, Chief Albert Newsome, Joe Foley, and F2c Tom Kerich, who was striking to be a machinist. Confined in such close quarters, they learned to look out for one another. Foley, who had been young Arnette's instructor aboard ship for qualification in submarines, became close friends with his former understudy.

Toward the end of March, the Japanese guards moved the American and British officers into cottages situated along the southern side of camp. In the little cottages, the officers found some meager furniture, a welcome relief from weeks of sitting on the floor. Lt. William Wilson from *Pope* received permission from the Japanese to use two Filipino officers' stewards—CK1c Macario Sarmiento from

Perch and StM1c Fermin Beriontes from *Pope*—to work for the American officers in their cottages.[28]

Morale for the officers was boosted with these new living quarters at Makassar. Food rations at this time also improved for the enlisted men, as the Japanese guards were able to sort out the dilemma of properly feeding them. On 1 April, the food finally reached a level that Jake Vandergrift deemed "sufficient." Mess cooks Sarmiento and Beriontes were able to barter with natives who lived behind the camp, and occasionally added duck eggs or fish to the officers' meager food rations.[29]

The enlisted men had not been confined at Makassar long before they began taking chances to improve their odds of survival. "We could see other buildings out there near our barracks and we decided to see what was in them," Turk Turner recalled. He and cubicle mate Ernie Plantz slipped out one night under the barbed wire behind the prisoners' latrine. They broke into an unused building which proved to be some type of old auditorium. They acquired some old mattresses to bring back to their barracks to soften the boards they had been sleeping on. "The best thing we found were wormy raisins," related Turner. "Worms were all over them but those worms had to look out for themselves because we ate those raisins fast, I guarantee you that!"

The two *Perch* prisoners had to hide in the auditorium's attic when Japanese guards entered the building. Turner and Plantz were fearful when they saw the Makassar prisoners lined up the next morning for a muster call. Fortunately, Robbie Robinson and their other cellmates were able to slip in and out of the line, yelling out the names and hometowns of the two missing prisoners. That night, they waited for the all-clear signal and slipped back into their barracks. "That night and for the rest of the time we were in that camp," said Turner, "we were able to sleep on those mattresses."

After only a week of staying in improved quarters, all good things came to an end for the *Perch* officers. Notice was received that some of the American and British officers were to be transferred to Japan. A total of 32 men were rounded up, including nine officers from *Exeter* and all five *Perch* officers—Hurt, Van Buskirk, Schacht, Ryder, and Vandergrift. Four *Pope* officers were also called out: Lt. Cdr. Welford Charles Blinn, the destroyer's skipper; Lt. William Ritchie Wilson Jr.; Lt. Robert Van Rensselaer Bassett Jr.; and Lt. (jg) William Oscar Spears Jr. Five *Pope* officers remained at Makassar: Lieutenant (jg) Michel, Lt. (jg) William Rawlins Lowndes, Lt. (jg) Allen Jack Fisher, Ens. Donald Ellsworth Austin, and the exec, Lt. Richard Nott Antrim.[30]

The Japanese apparently thought these men were most likely to have knowledge of war plans and codes. With them would go all three *Perch* radiomen: RM1c Ted Reh, RM2c Ray Normand, and RM3c Robert Berridge. *Perch* torpedoman Sam Simpson recalled that skipper Dave Hurt kindly divided all his remaining money among his crew; each man received 60 cents.[31]

Perch was officially listed as "overdue and presumed lost." The next of kin of her crew were notified of the status of their loved ones. Prior to *Perch*'s loss, *Sealion* had been destroyed at Cavite, *S-26* sank after a collision off Panama, and *Shark* was reported overdue in the Pacific. *Perch* was the fourth submarine reported lost by the Navy in the first months of World War II. When the news was issued from Washington, the *New London Day* carried a headline on 11 April 1942, "Submarine *Perch* Lost in Pacific."

The 59 *Perch* prisoners were just beginning the fight of their lives. Back home in the United States, their loved ones could only maintain silent hope while they grieved for those now officially "presumed lost."

3
The First Months of Hell

The eight *Perch* officers and radiomen who were marched out of the Makassar prison camp on 2 April 1942 were just beginning a new and terrible chapter in their ordeal. Loaded aboard the 10,380-ton armed transport ship *Hakusan Maru*, they would spend more than three weeks en route to mainland Japan.

Perch's third officer, Jack Ryder, later stated, "On 2 April, [we] left Makassar on the *Hakusan Maru* for Japan. The trip took 23 days with stopovers at Takao, Taiwap and Sasebo Naval Base, Kyushu. The ship sailed to the eastward of the Philippines, through Formosa Straits to Sasebo and then south of Kyushu and Shikoku to Yokohama. Our quarters were the third class dining saloon on army cots."

Lt. (jg) Jake Vandergrift, *Perch*'s most junior officer, felt "treatment aboard ship was fair. We had a mess of our own." The food they received aboard ship was far better than what they would find after their arrival in Japan. Although the trip to Japan was delayed due to the Doolittle raid, *Hakusan Maru* made port at Yokosuka Naval Base in Yokohama on 25 April and the POWs were marched ashore.

"We arrived in Yokohama on Easter Sunday, 1942," recalled Lt. Bev Van Buskirk. He had carefully folded up the handwritten loss report on *Perch* that his officers and leading petty officers had helped to write. He stuffed it into his shoe before the men were led to a train station the following morning.

They were then put aboard a train on 26 April and taken on a ride about 20 minutes into the hills southwest of Yokohama to the camp known as Ofuna for questioning. This secret Japanese Navy interrogation camp was opened 7 April 1942 to temporarily house captured Allied prisoners. The Ofuna compound consisted of flimsy wooden building structures called *Ikku*, *Nikku*, and *Sanku*—One, Two and Three in Japanese. The three barrack wings were connected to a main building that housed latrines, an officer's headquarters, and the kitchen—where all meals were prepared for prisoners and guards.[1]

After departing the train, the *Perch* survivors were marched approximately five miles to camp and were introduced to the camp commandant, Warrant Gunnery Officer Ouchi. The *Perch* prisoners were the first American submariners to be moved into the new Ofuna compound. The officers and radiomen were shocked to find that they were not considered POWs, and would not be entitled to any privileges of prisoners of war until after they were transferred from Ofuna. Ouchi then ordered them to remove their clothing.

"You mean shoes, too?" Lieutenant Van Buskirk asked the interpreter, as he feared them finding his *Perch* report.[2]

"No, leave your shoes on," he said.

Van Buskirk watched the guards go through the Americans' clothing "as if they were looking for a needle in a haystack. It turned out that they were looking for pencil and paper so that we could not exchange notes with each other on questions that we might be asked during the long sessions of interrogation."

Following this inspection, the men were allowed to redress. "There was to be no talking among prisoners. Any talking would be to Japanese guards in Japanese," stated Jack Ryder. "Discipline would be hard." They were placed into a horse-shoe-shaped building with about 16 two-man cells per wing. Upon arrival, each man was placed in solitary confinement. "We lived in small wooden cells without books or any form of entertainment," recalled Jake Vandergrift. "Food was very scarce—truly a starvation ration."

In his cell, Bev Van Buskirk removed the report from his shoe and tried to find a better place to hide it. He had obtained needle and thread at Makassar, and he now carefully sewed the report into his hip pocket to avoid its detection.[3]

Since they had each been thoroughly searched upon arrival, he felt like that would be the last search. "How wrong can one be?" he recalled. The next morning, 27 April, the Japanese guards came running through the barracks, yelling at the men to get out on the parade ground for inspection.

Van Buskirk was the last to line up. He nervously noted the guards frantically frisking each man. Recalling that the last page of his handwritten report was blank, he quickly stepped forward out of line. "The guards were all over me," he recalled. "They called me things that morning that I never did find out what they meant. Even the interpreter was yelling at me, and I kept yelling at him."

The *Perch* Exec snapped at the interpreter, "What are you looking for?"

He finally understood that the guards were looking for paper. "I think I have some," Van Buskirk offered.

"Where is it?"

He stated that he had some in his cell. "Well, go get it!" the interpreter yelled.

With that, Van Buskirk took off running so fast that the guards did not even think to follow him. While racing down the passageway toward his cell, he tore at the hip pocket in which he had sewed the *Perch* loss report. "When I got to my cell, with my pants down, I practically tore the pocket off," he wrote. "I grabbed the report, took off the last page, threw the rest under my blanket, and as nonchalantly as possible, walked back to that mad milling mob of mugs waving this piece of paper in their faces."

The guards were enraged that he had smuggled in the paper, but Van Buskirk achieved what he had desired. He left the interpreter and his guards pleased for the moment that they had found some paper. When the POWs were dismissed back to their cells, his concern became what to do with the other 19 handwritten pages stashed under his bedding. Seated in the corner of his four-foot by eight-foot cell with his back to the wall, he was in a position where a guard peeping in could only see the lower portion of his legs and not the upper portion of his body.

Van Buskirk decided to destroy the secret report the only certain way he could—by eating it! "If you think cheese is binding, you should try 20 sheets of pencil paper without any water," he wrote.

Lieutenant Ryder later offered some detail on the daily routine the *Perch* prisoners learned during their first weeks at Ofuna.

> Except when doing menial tasks about the camp or doing mass exercising, we were confined to our rooms, either one or two occupants. Infractions of rules (real or imaginary) brought beatings either with clubs or fists. The clubs varied in size. Physical exercise was often carried out to the point of exhaustion. The diet was just enough in calories to keep us from starving but not to prevent deficiency diseases.

The starvation was soon learned to be a means of breaking down the prisoners into talking. "Our diet consisted of one teacup of rice three times daily; two teacups of soybean paste once a day, a few cooked vegetables once daily and occasionally a small portion of sardines or pork," Lieutenant Commander Hurt recalled. "The average weight loss was 20 to 25 pounds in 3–5 months."

Ofuna was a naval questioning camp and the prisoners were routinely taken in for interrogation. Dave Hurt was grilled on all types of questions pertaining to his ship, its operational bases, and the men he commanded. Jake Vandergrift, *Perch*'s communications officer, maintained a strict routine of playing stupid. "Their main questions concerned communications and sound apparatus," he stated. "They were looking for someone who had seen our Electric Coding Machine, someone who could work our Call Sign Cipher, and someone who would describe our sound gear."

Vandergrift was beaten frequently for saying that he knew nothing. When pressed, he admitted that sonar was used for detection of ships, something the Japanese already knew. When asked how it worked, Vandergrift again pleaded ignorance. They asked what he did when it needed repair; he answered that it was sent to the sub tender to be fixed. They asked him why, if he was in charge of this equipment, he didn't even want to know how it worked. Vandergrift replied that he never liked his job and that he was always relaxing in Manila. At this, the interrogator stood up and shouted, "Get out. You are a disgrace to the American Navy."[4]

Lt. (jg) Vandergrift's ploy worked. "I was never questioned again," he recalled.

Dave Hurt and Lt. Cdr. Welford Blinn of *Pope* were not as fortunate. They were roughed up and interrogated frequently during their long stay at Ofuna. Engineering officer Jack Ryder believed that he was questioned by Japanese civilian engineers. He found that as long as he gave them at least some answer, no punishment was given to him. "It was only necessary to avoid being caught in a lie."

Lt. K. G. Schacht's first serious grilling came on 6 May. "Refusal to talk brought on an immediate beating and ration reduction, whereas the questioners usually seemed satisfied with a lie or an 'I don't know' for an answer." Schacht and the *Perch* officers followed a policy of releasing facts which could be found in *Jane's Fighting Ships*. Concerning modern fire-control methods, they played dumb. They lied about *Perch* having a TDC and said that her torpedoes were similar to the old World War I vintage Mark 10.3s. "It was considered mandatory that each officer quickly pass on the questions asked and answers given immediately after each interview in order to avoid conflicting answers," Schacht said.

On *Perch* issues, Schacht gave the total crew number as 49 and stated that his ship was lost due to depth charges causing excessive leaking. He did not mention that he had personally helped scuttle the submarine. The Japanese wanted to know where *Perch* refueled after leaving Manila, what her patrol course was, and where she met up with any submarine tender. Schacht offered Balikpapan as his ship's refueling port, swore that *Perch* never was serviced by a tender, and lied about the route his ship had taken on patrol.

Somewhat content with his answers during this first session, the Japanese worked on other officers for a week before calling K. G. Schacht back in on 12 May. This time, the questions were more personal. The interrogators started with his submarine schooling and whether he had volunteered. When asked about the school boats, Schacht said there were only six small R-class submarines at New London when he went through. The Japanese turned to more specific questions on *Perch*'s torpedoes. Schacht's lies were enough to keep them thoroughly confused.

He told them that the U.S. torpedoes could make 35 knots, travel 8,000 yards and had only one speed, with no ability to change their angles other than 90-degree right or left. Schacht continued to lie about the number of men kept on watch and that his submarine never ran on the surface in the daylight.

Having given up on Jake Vandergrift, the Japanese grilled Schacht, Van Buskirk, Ryder, and Dave Hurt during the next weeks. On 22 May, Lieutenant Schacht was quizzed on the duties of the officers during torpedo attacks and the methods in which they determined the range to Japanese ships. He told them U.S. subs must close to within 1,000 yards to fire and that their sound equipment was only for listening, not ranging. At the end of this interrogation, Schacht was warned: "This interview has been very unsatisfactory. We warn you that we have means of checking your answers and refreshing your memory."

The next week, a guard who was helpful to the U.S. prisoners warned Schacht that the camp authorities considered him "half bad." They were not happy with his answers and felt that he was disrespectful to the officers interrogating him. "Unless my conduct improved," he stated, "I would be severely punished."

Finally, on 15 June, the interrogators had their fill of lies. Two lieutenants, Van Buskirk and Schacht, received the worst of it, both being placed in solitary confinement. They were given starvation diets for ten days "because our answers to the same question did not agree," said Van Buskirk.

When Schacht was quizzed that day, they wanted to know how a Japanese destroyer had mysteriously blown up while making depth charge runs above a U.S. submarine. Schacht could only guess that a torpedo with a damaged rudder had made a circular run, but he told the Japanese that the destroyer must have been blown up by her own depth charges exploding prematurely.

He was led back to a solitary cell and given no food. He was brought out again the next day and asked the same questions. He gave only the same answers. Schacht was returned to another cell and given very little food, allowed only to leave his cell to use the toilet. "My ration was cut to about a quarter of the regular ration, which had already reduced the weights of all the prisoners," he recalled. "Two or three times, prisoner friends managed to slip me some of their food."

On 17 June, he again refused to give different answers. Five days later, the Japanese asked him, "Are you ready to talk?"

"No," Lieutenant Schacht answered.

Finally, on 25 June, he was suffering from ten days of near starvation diet when he was brought in once again for questioning. "How do you feel?" he was asked.

"Damn weak!" Schacht honestly answered.

"Are you ready to talk?"

"I can't add a thing to what I've already told you," he said. "You can starve me as long as you like. My story is the same."

During the questioning, the sunken "destroyer" was this time called a "torpedo boat" by the Japanese. Schacht protested that a torpedo fired at the attacking ship could only have been done by a "rough guess of the range."

"How accurate are these bearings obtained over your listening instruments?" he was asked.

Schacht explained that currents, water temperatures, and target speed could affect bearings so that the torpedo officer must expect "a ten degree error" ratio.

"That seems rather high," the officer replied.

"It is," lied Schacht, "but there isn't much we can do about it."

After this reply, he heard "much jabbering in Nipponese." The interpreter finally asked if the American smoked. Schacht nodded and the Japanese passed over a pack of Philip Morris cigarettes. Amazingly, the guards laughed and told him that they believed his story for now. "We warn you that if a later check-up shows you've been lying, the consequences will be most serious."

"I understand," he replied weakly.

Ken Schacht was returned to his regular cell, much worn down from the starvation that he had endured. That night, Schacht was given all the guards' mess leftover rice, potatoes, and cucumbers that he could eat. He kept good record of his interrogation sessions, writing down the Japanese questions on scraps of clothing that he wore for future reference. During this same period, Jake Vandergrift contracted a bad case of dysentery. He was placed in the naval hospital at Yokosuka Naval Base from 3 July through 17 July. "Treatment was good during this period," he said. "After recovery, I was returned to the camp at Ofuna."

Jack Ryder also contracted dysentery, and he was similarly transferred to the Yokosuka Naval Hospital on 19 July after Vandergrift's return. During his time there, eleven patients had to use seven beds. Three guards stood sentry over the sick prisoners with one, S1c Saito, administering frequent beatings. Ryder later offered details on his treatment at the naval hospital at Yokosuka.

> The sick prisoners only wore kimonos of the thinnest material so there was no protection against beatings. For such infractions as looking out windows at Japanese planes, eating food in the wrong sitting position (not cross-legged), etc., patients were given from 5 to 20 strokes of a club on the buttocks or hit in the face with closed fist. I personally was beaten across the buttocks 20 times with a heavy club for looking out the window while a plane was passing overhead. The plane could not be seen. The skin was broken and bleeding resulted and diarrhea increased.
>
> Another time for not sitting cross-legged (nearly impossible to do in the required position), I was struck in the face 10 times by the guard's fist.

After 12 days at the hospital, Lieutenant Ryder was returned to Ofuna on 30 July. Still very weak, he was immediately forced to rejoin the daily physical training drills and to run races. "The latter caused me to black out," he stated.

Lt. Ken Schacht was twice sent to the Yokosuka Naval Hospital for treatment for the dysentery epidemic that had swept the Ofuna camp. On 27 July, Schacht was given 20 blows from a guard's club in the kidneys and buttocks for speaking to a nurse. "This resulted in my acquiring a high temperature, increasing diarrhea and stool blood content," he testified.

The following day, Schacht was asleep in his bed when a Japanese plane flew over the hospital. For "observing" this plane while sleeping, he was aroused by "five to ten hard blows to the jaw." Another prisoner at the hospital, RT1c R. N. Shilton, was so sick from beriberi that he could not handle his dishes properly. When he spilled some of his rice on 31 July, Saito beat him across the buttocks with a club until his skin ruptured and bled.

Lieutenant (jg) Vandergrift was the first *Perch* officer transferred from Ofuna on 2 August 1942, along with a few officers. The first prisoners to be sent out were the ones that the Japanese had deemed unworthy of offering any more relevant testimony. Vandergrift's group was sent to Zentsuji Camp on Shikoku Island.

During early fall 1942, more prisoners arrived at Ofuna. They soon became two to a cell. The guards carried clubs the size of softball bats and used them frequently on those caught talking. "They used them on the least provocation," recalled Bev Van Buskirk. "In fact, they didn't need any provocation. The standard punishment for being accused of talking was 18 swats across the small of your back. With six guards present, each guard gave three swats. He put his all into it, just in case he did not have another chance at you. One or two swats across the small of your back would cause you to pass blood in your urine for two or three days."[5]

Jack Ryder recalled the Japanese enlisted man responsible for formal punishment was usually seaman first class Shimada. Another seaman guard, Endo, invariably followed his direct orders by bashing prisoners in the head with a club. "Severe and often brutal punishment was given for such things as refusing to answer a questioner, being what was considered disrespectful to a questioner, lying or being suspected of lying, talking to other prisoners (roommate not excepted), sitting on or leaning against blankets." Ryder found that in addition to beatings, punishment sometimes included solitary confinement on almost no rations for as long as two weeks. "Minor infractions were punished by slapping the face or hitting the face with fist one or two times, or by a few blows to the head or body with a club," Ryder stated. "Sometimes beatings were so brutal that the victim fell unconscious."

Skipper Dave Hurt felt, "The beatings were designed to break the morale of the POWs to secure information. I know of no beatings which drew blood or caused broken bones. But the beaten areas—from the mid-back down to the knees—would turn purple for two months."

Every Saturday night during the summer months of 1942, about ten Ofuna prisoners would be lined up for swats from the bats by the Japanese guards. The other prisoners would be lined up to watch the torture. "A Lieutenant Commander from the HMS *Exeter* received 35 or 40 blows when he was caught smiling when the commandant read from the newspaper a second claim by the Japanese of sinking the USS *Saratoga* within a 30-day period," related Lieutenant Van Buskirk.

Jack Ryder was the second *Perch* officer transferred from Ofuna. On 8 September, he and 13 other prisoners were sent to Zentsuji on Shikoku Island, where he reunited with Jake Vandergrift.

During October, another British officer, Lt. Cdr. Geoffrey Percival Packard, arrived at Ofuna and refused to answer questions. Packard was taken behind the Ofuna barracks and worked over with bats by the guards. "I counted between 65 and 70 blows," recalled Van Buskirk. "He later said that about four canes were broken across his back." British reserve officer Lt. William G. Warner was also beaten severely in early November until he could no longer stand. Van Buskirk testified, "The beating and kicking then continued until he was unconscious."

As the winter approached, conditions worsened for the prisoners. "Any time someone complained about the cold, he was forced to run double time around the prison," recalled Ken Schacht. "There was no lying down from reveille to taps."

In September 1942, command of Ofuna passed from warrant officer Ouchi to warrant officer Kakuzo Iida. When the Japanese considered them of no further value, the two lieutenants Schacht and Van Buskirk were transferred on 4 December to Yokohoma POW Camp Despatch No. 1. During his seven months at Ofuna, Van Buskirk had dropped from 155 to 96 pounds.[6]

Dave Hurt remained at Ofuna throughout the fall and into 1943, the only U.S. submarine officer left there. His three radiomen were the only enlisted submariners to be kept at Ofuna with him. The winter months were brutal in the drafty barracks sleeping on a straw mat. "Our clothing was tropical weight and inadequate for [a] climate which I would compare to that of Maryland," he stated.

Among the men who spent time with Hurt at Ofuna were four naval aviators from the carrier *Enterprise* who had been shot down during the 26 October 1942 carrier battle of Santa Cruz: Ens. Raleigh Edward "Dusty" Rhodes, Ens. Albert Edward Mead, AMM3c Murray Glasser, and ARM1c Thomas Churchill Nelson Jr. Al Mead and Dusty Rhodes had given conflicting written statements to their captors while at Truk concerning the composition of the U.S. Navy's task force at Santa Cruz. Rhodes "had stretched the numbers, but Al had decided to make them smaller than they actually were."[7]

After reaching Ofuna on 24 November 1942, Rhodes and Mead were beaten unconscious for lying about their fleet. Welford Blinn instructed Rhodes the following day to at least give the Ofuna interrogators some information by entertaining them "with stories about all kinds of useless shit." *Perch* skipper Dave Hurt similarly passed instructions to the new *Enterprise* aviators while frequently talking to one of the Japanese guards in English. "But Hurt wasn't really talking to them," Rhodes recalled. "He was saying things for the benefit of the other prisoners."[8]

The three older American officers—Hurt, Blinn, and Al Maher—were given the worst treatment while trying to protect the younger enlisted men. Dusty Rhodes recalled that during long periods outside in the cold, Lieutenant Commander Hurt took turns sharing an olive drab jacket with him for warmth. When the guards were rotated the following month, the head guard became a short, stocky CPO named Hirabaya who carried a riding crop. When Hirabaya forced the Ofuna inmates to do calistentics, Hurt and Blinn struggled with the deep knee bends and seemed to be holding each other up. Al Maher, also struggling, was cracked by the new officer's riding whip. Maher fell over and the guard proceeded to beat him severely in the head, face and hands with the stick. Ensign John Lawrence "Larry" Coulter, former co-pilot of Lt. Carlton Clark's PBY, soon nicknamed this abusive guard "Shithead." As Rhodes recalled, "like all appropriate nicknames, it stuck."[9]

The next week, Hirabaya had the prisoners run laps around the compound until their malnourished bodies faltered. When Dave Hurt began slowing down and limping on his right foot, Rhodes saw that "Shithead was on him in a minute, cracking him across the thighs with the riding crop." Blinn and Leonard J. Birchall, a Royal Canadian Air Force PBY pilot, soon fell and were beaten on their rears and chests until bloodstains appeared on Blinn's khaki shirt.[10]

At the end of April 1943, Dusty Rhodes, Birchall, Larry Coulter, and three others were transferred from Ofuna to make room for a group of incoming POWs from another lost U.S. sub. Rhodes said goodbye to his three fellow *Enterprise* aviators, Dave Hurt, Welford Blinn, and to Al Maher as he left.

Perch's skipper and his three radiomen were the only U.S. submariners left at Ofuna after a full year, and they were still not officially listed as POWs.

Makassar: 1942

When the *Perch* officers were transferred to Japan at the beginning of April, the only American officers remaining at the Makassar compound were five from *Pope*, with Lt. Richard Antrim being the senior. Of the 51 remaining *Perch* enlisted men, chief of the boat Charlie Cross was now their senior man.

The Allied officers lived in their little cottages and the enlisted men remained in the barracks. The *Perch* men were divided into small groups, separated from the next group by partitions. "You got together with the people you clicked with," recalled GM3c Bud Harper. "It was a real family thing."[11]

A short time after the *Perch* officers were transferred on to Japan, Makassar's compound received a new group of prisoners. They were Dutch troops who had been holding out in the hills of Celebes until they were forced to surrender. Their senior officer was a Lieutenant Colonel Gortmans, who began holding a conference every morning which the senior American and British officers also attended. The *Pope* officers had some money which had not been taken from them and they generously proposed that this be used for the needs of both their own crewmen and those of the *Perch*, who now had no officers present to represent them.[12]

Lieutenant Antrim and Lt. Cdr. Thomas Alton Donovan, an American prisoner who had served on the carrier *Langley*, persuaded the Japanese guards to allow the Allied prisoners to barter with a native merchant for necessary items. The Japanese would allow this merchant in camp on rest day, Sunday, each week to sell items such as soap, fruit, and tobacco to the prisoners.[13]

After three weeks in camp, the *Perch* crew was only receiving one cup of rice per day. In early April, the Japanese began calling up work parties to labor in or near the camp. Some were taken to work at the local Makassar hospital, while others cleaned rubbish, cut down grass, cleaned latrines, worked on roads, or unloaded supplies. Torpedoman Sam Simpson found the best part of working was the extra meal they earned. "Then we got two cups of rice, one in the morning and one at night." Simpson considered this to be "third grade rice, full of weevil worms and husks." The *Perch* and *Pope* prisoners learned to steal by necessity—pinching medicine, food, and supplies from the hospital, the Japanese, or buildings in which they worked. Because of being frisked upon return from work details, the Americans created "loot sacks," bags with strings at each end which were tied to a man's legs inside his trousers.[14]

"We smuggled food into prison camp for two or three years before they ever caught us," said TM3c Bob Lents. "We had the loot sacks tied below our knees. They'd search us all the way down to our knees but never searched us below our knees." Knowing that the Dutch had money, the Americans learned that by stealing, they could bargain with the Dutch to acquire money. "We'd take this money and then buy stuff from the natives and got things going. We acquired a pretty good amount of loot," said Lents. "That was the only thing that kept you alive, was what you could steal or buy from the natives."

Electrician Ernie Plantz later described how the *Perch* crew resorted to black market trading with goods acquired from Celebes natives to stay alive.

> Typically, the working party was 50 men and there would be one or two Jap guards. It was hard with all of us working there to try and make contact with the natives. We went in there without money. The Dutchmen went in there with trunkloads of money that they had stashed outside of camp. We were all starving, so we figured how to smuggle food in. We'd eat part of it and sell part of it to the Dutchmen for big money. The natives made a candy exactly like our peanut brittle. You could buy that for almost a penny a square or a dime for a bundle. We smuggled it in and we'd sell part of it to the Dutchmen for a dime apiece.

Each little group of men took care of each other. "You stole for each other, shared food," said Plantz. "If a man couldn't do that, if he couldn't get along, he didn't stay with the group."[15]

Plantz was kept in his cell with Bill Seward from *Pope* and EM2c Turk Turner and EM2c Jesse Robison from *Perch*. "We stayed together and helped each other out," said Turner. "We stole vitamins out of the hospital where they had us work. You could hide them on your person and put them in your shoes. We had to supplement our so-called food."

Alabama Arnette was among the first from *Perch* to be publicly abused for his trading efforts. His cell mate Joe Foley had managed to acquire some smoking tobacco from the natives. In order to smoke it, the prisoners needed papers, which happened to be stored in quantity in eight- by eight-inch sheets in some of the old Dutch warehouses at Makassar. During one of his working details at the hospital, Arnette decided to steal some of the tobacco paper sheets, which the Japanese were using for toilet paper. "I rolled up about eight of those sheets real tight and pinned them in my pants as we got ready to leave," he said. The plan faltered when the Japanese guards did a pat-down search of the prisoner work detail and one felt the lump stuffed into his shorts.

"I had to take my pants off and they beat me around," said Arnette. He was ordered to fall back into line and the prisoners were marched to camp. "There, they called me out of the ranks," Arnette related. As the other prisoners were stood at attention to watch, one of the guards stepped forward with a club. "I had to hold my hands up over my head and put my feet out stretched," said Arnette. "He started beating me with that baseball bat right across the cheeks of my buttocks."

From the prisoner ranks, a shipmate hollered, "Don't yell out, Arnette! That's what they want you to do!"

"I just gritted my teeth and took it," Arnette related. "After about 21 licks, he just quit, threw the bat down, and walked off. That was their way of punishing people. My butt swelled up so big that it almost busted."

Tom Moore felt that every day "was hell," filled with beatings for anyone who stepped out of line. "We got up at 5 a.m. and ate a cup of watery rice and drank a cup of weak coffee," Moore related. "For lunch, we had a dipper of rice and some horrible-tasting cooked greens. At night, they'd run a piece of caribou meat through water and called it soup. It was served with a double handful of cooked rice. That was it. We worked eight to 15 hours a day, depending on the job."[16]

One work detail rebuilt a dam at a water buffalo wallow, a three-quarter-acre hole in the middle of a stream, near the camp. "I think they were just looking to keep us working," recalled Bud Harper. On one Sunday, a Japanese guard took a group of Americans to the little pond to bail over the dam with buckets and to catch fish. Turk Turner stayed out of the water after "getting leeches in my leg." The men sunk into mud up to their shoulders as they bailed the water. "When you came out of the water and mud there were black leeches stuck all over your body," Sam Simpson said. "Some natives on the bank would spit tobacco juice on them and they would drop off." As the water was drained, the men were able to scoop up fish and put them in garbage cans. The guards ate all the large fish that were caught, leaving only small, mud-encrusted fish for the prisoners. Ernie Plantz chose to pass on the small fish because of their filthy condition. He was pleased that when the Japanese guards "filleted them, breaded them and fried them, they all got sick." Simpson heard that "the Japs got the shits when they ate the fish. I hope so."[17]

In the American barracks, a rag-tag musical group was put together, which consisted of several men with musical abilities using leftover Dutch musical instruments. One of the Japanese guards became angry at this little swing band and confronted Lt. (jg) Allen Fisher from *Pope*.[18]

The guards sentenced Lieutenant (jg) Fisher to 40 lashes across the buttocks from a four-foot length of manila hawser. Fisher was lashed severely while other American prisoners watched. By the fifteenth lash, Fisher went down. The guard kicked at his head and connected with his shoulder. As the Japanese continued to beat Fisher, *Pope*'s exec, Dick Antrim, stepped in and shouted, "Enough! I'll take the rest!"[19]

The Japanese were greatly disturbed by the former Naval Academy football player's selfless offer to take the beating. Guard Yoshida refused to accept Antrim as a substitute. The senior Japanese guard finally arrived and listened to Antrim's protests and to Yoshida's stories. The senior guard decided that the bloodied officer had been punished enough and ordered Fisher back to his cottage.[20]

"During our first year at Makassar, we were beaten often and usually did not know why," Turk Turner stated. "We would stand around with our arms crossed. Due to the language barrier, it took us some time to figure out that the Japanese saw this as a sign of disrespect."

On one occasion, the cruel guard Yoshida conducted a mass beating of the prisoners for a minor event. A short time later, another group of prisoners was accused of stealing firewood from the galley. They had actually bought it from Dutchmen who had brought it to town, but one of the sentries beat them for their "crime." When Lieutenant Commander Donovan tried to stop the beatings, the guard ordered him to assume the position and proceeded to beat him severely.

The officers' living arrangements and food supply was better than that of the enlisted men confined in the barracks. The Filipino mess attendants, Sarmiento from *Perch* and Beriontes from *Pope*, cleaned their cottages and prepared decent meals from the food they could acquire. "Sarmiento was the comedian of the pair and always had a wisecrack," recalled *Pope*'s John Michel. The officers rewarded the Filipinos with extra food and tobacco.[21]

Perch's other enlisted men were not as fortunate during the early months at Makassar. Dan Crist later related, "The food was very bad. We ate only two times a day for several weeks. Many men were beaten for not understanding. After a few days, we were made to work cleaning up in the city."

When men contracted serious diseases, the Japanese sent the most critically ill to the local hospital for treatment or back to the hospital ship *Op ten Noort* in the harbor until they were deemed healthy enough to go back to work. One of the few forms of recreation the Japanese allowed the prisoners to enjoy was baseball. "After several tries, we were able to get bats and leather with which to make a baseball," wrote John Michel. "Because no gloves were to be had, it was decided that a softball should be made." The *Pope* crew organized a team and another from the *Perch* took to the field with Lieutenant (jg) Fisher pitching for the *Pope* team and 2nd Lt. Walter D. Haines of the U.S. Army Air Corps pitching for the *Perch* team. "We were allowed to play baseball and football on the recreational fields during our first year of captivity," recalled Turk Turner. "We could even play cards, but this also was taken away after the first year." [22]

During the summer, three British and Dutch men escaped from the Makassar camp. They were captured by the natives within 24 hours and turned over to the Japanese. "Three men tried to escape but were captured," said Dan Crist. "The Japs read the sentence to all hands. The three men would be shot. They were taken out of the camp and never returned."

Ernie Plantz learned that the escapees were set up by the native chief they had paid to help them escape. "They brought them back, put them in the brig, and beat them every day for about a week. Then they just disappeared. We learned from the natives that they had been taken and made to dig their own graves. The Japanese made them kneel, then cut off their heads and kicked them into the grave."

The Makassar guards then pulled 30 men—ten for each escapee—and confined them to the brig. "Every day when the Japanese changed guards, every three hours, they would curse them out, slap these men around, punch them out, and tell them how bad they were," Plantz related. "These 30 guys were either friends of those who escaped or men who slept near them. They threatened to put them to death for not telling them that these other guys were planning to escape."

Seaman Tom Moore had been one of the boldest in terms of slipping out to steal at night. "Whenever I could, I'd sneak out of the camp," he said. "I got together with a couple of Limies off the *Exeter*. They would include me on any of their escapades." During the day, Moore and the *Exeter* sailors would make contact with the natives to meet them at night for exchanges. "We'd pick up extra chow and smokes. That didn't last long." Whatever was acquired was shared with his cell mates. "That's all you could do to help each other. If you couldn't, you just had to sustain yourself the best way you could." When word was passed about the execution of the Dutch escapees, however, Moore halted his excursions for some time. "We cooled that right there," he said. "That was a good lesson."

Torpedoman Warren Atkeison was alarmed that even cell mates of an escapee would now be executed. "We were placed in groups by the Japs," Atkeison later stated. "If a man of the group escaped, the others were taken out and executed."

Surprise inspections became more frequent after this botched escape attempt. In late August, the Japanese designated that a number of the Makassar prisoners would soon be shipped out. The Navy prisoners were ordered to supply 24 enlisted men and one officer, along with 2nd Lt. Walt Haines. Senior *Pope* officer Dick Antrim selected Lt. (jg) John Michel to take the spot of the American officer. The British would be sending ten officers and 215 enlisted men, while the Dutch would ship out 12 officers and 738 enlisted men. This movement would effectively cut the camp size almost in half.[23]

The 24 enlisted men were pulled from the destroyer *Pope* and submarine *Perch* crews. The ship's engineers, all rated machinist's mates, were the men of most interest to the Japanese from the *Perch* crew. In fairness, the Americans opted for a two-thirds/one-third split of *Pope/Perch* prisoners, since *Pope* had twice as many men to choose from. The eight *Perch* men selected for transfer were: MM2c Larry Dague, MM2c Bernie Deleman, MM1c Joe Foley, MM1c Calvin Goodwine, MM2c Rudy Klecky, CMM Jim McCray, MM1 Frank McCreary, and MM2c Felix Walton. Five others rated as machinist's mates, including chiefs Albert Newsome and Henry Yates, were to be left at Makassar. Electrician Turk Turner said, "They didn't want the electricians. They took the machinists to Japan to question them."

The large contingent of Allied prisoners did not ship out right away. They were ordered to be available in camp at all times and were not detailed for working parties. Each morning, this large group was marched to the athletic field and given calisthenics to improve their physical conditions. They were also drilled on various commands in the Japanese language and on the proper courtesies that were to be shown to Japanese officials. Clearly, they were heading for Japan.[24]

Although the men expected to depart within days, a month passed. On 1 October, they were finally lined up to draw rations for their trip to Japan. Each man received two blankets, several pairs of socks, two undershirts and underpants, cotton sailor uniforms, and tennis shoes for those who had no shoes at all.[25]

The prisoners were marched back through town down the road on which they had first marched in. In port, they could see the familiar *Op ten Noort* moored in her berth in Makassar's harbor. Admiral Mori addressed the men and told them they were heading for Japan. They were placed aboard the former luxury liner *Asama Maru*, which had once boasted berths for 680 passengers. Converted to an armed transport ship, *Asama Maru* was 16,975 tons, had a 17-knot cruising speed, and would be used often during the war for the transportation of Allied POWs.[26]

The officers were given third-class staterooms, while the *Perch* and *Pope* enlisted men were ordered into a hold at the foot of a ladder that led to the upper decks. *Asama Maru* got under way for Japan on 4 October.

For eight months, Makassar's prison camp had been the only life the eight *Perch* machinists had known. As they sailed from Celebes in the dark confines of *Asama Maru*, they wondered what new hell awaited them in Japan.

4
"Hard Labor, Poor Conditions"

The Allied prisoners of war aboard *Asama Maru* in October 1942 received decent treatment. This ship would, however, ferry other POWs during the course of the war, and most would come to despise her as just another of the so-called "hell ships." The *Perch* and *Pope* prisoners were allowed to bathe in salt water and were given ample drinking water. As *Asama Maru* steamed closer to Japan, the air grew cooler. The ship came within sight of the island chain on 23 October and anchored near Nagasaki. The prisoners were told that their camp was not ready and that they would have to wait another day before debarking.[1]

On the morning of 24 October, the prisoners were mustered on *Asama Maru*'s forecastle deck. The men were herded into two ferryboats and landed at a pier just inside a shipyard. They were led along a muddy road through the cold air into an open square before several buildings. There, a group of Japanese addressed the men and informed them of their new status.[2]

They were told that they would have to work hard and that any attempt to escape would be met with severe punishment. Soon thereafter, the Allied POWs were marched from the square up a small rise and then down a steep path toward their new camp. They would soon learn that this was designated Camp Fukuoka No. 2—located on the water's edge a quarter mile from the square and about half a mile from the Nagasaki shipyard.[3]

In camp, the men were assigned barracks by their ranks, with the officers quartered separately. Group photographs were taken the next day for the Japanese to help identify their prisoners. "The unfinished state of the camp became increasingly apparent," *Pope* officer John Michel recalled. "The only water supply within the camp was a shallow well; the water was not fit to drink without boiling."[4]

MM2c Rudy Klecky, one of the machinists from *Perch*, later stated, "The treatment here was just as bad and the men had very little clothing to keep them warm in the winter months. The food was scarce and what we did get was very poor food. The medical care was poor and a lot of our men needed attention, but they were neglected." Klecky found that with no bathing facilities "we were lucky if we got three baths during the winter months. We received quite a lot of beatings here, for which they termed 'petty'."

After the first few days, work parties were organized and men were sent to various jobs, which involved drilling, welding, camp work, and various other details about the Japanese shipyard. Reveille was at 0500 each day and work parties were assembled by 0640. Normal work days were from 0730 to 1700 with only a 30-minute break at lunchtime. The first death in this camp, an Indonesian man with malaria, occurred less than a week after the arrival of *Perch* and *Pope*'s prisoners. For Christmas 1942, the Fukuoka inmates were allowed to attend a mass religious ceremony in honor of the Christian holiday. Work at the docks was suspended to observe the New Year, but the hiatus was all too brief.[5]

Winter, malnutrition, and illness claimed the first *Perch* prisoner at Fukuoka on 4 January 1943. MM1c Frank McCreary, born in St. Louis and respected by his shipmates, died from pneumonia this day. Known to all as "Big Mac," McCreary had only been sick for three days prior to his death. "The doctor had not considered him sick enough to send to sick bay, which was crowded with pneumonia cases, mostly Dutch and British," recalled John Michel. "Mac had received only aspirin, because the most serious cases were given medicine from the minute supply available."[6]

Rudy Klecky stated that McCreary "would have lived but they did not give him any medical attention. Later in the winter there were fifty deaths. Most of these men were Dutch." The following day, a small group of pallbearers took the bodies of McCreary and a Dutchman, who had died hours later, in wooden caskets on a small boat to Nagasaki for cremation. MM1c Calvin Goodwine from *Perch* and another man gathered the ashes of their fallen comrades into urns and took them to a small Japanese church to be kept until they could be taken home.[7]

Two weeks later, WT2c William Albert Kirk from *Pope* died of pneumonia on 18 January. Water was hard to come by and when it was available, it was agonizing for the men to wash their clothes in the cold weather. On 4 May 1943, Rudy Klecky and his fellow *Perch* machinist mates—Rudy Klecky, Joe Foley, Larry Dague, Calvin Goodwine, Bernie Deleman, Jim McCray, and Felix Walton—were sent from Fukuoka to a mining camp by the name of Orio, where they stayed through 1945. "The treatment here was the same," Klecky related. "Sometimes we were exposed to civilians and were beaten and humiliated."

Orio was located on the northern side of Kyushu at the town of Mitzumaki in the Fukuoka district. This POW camp was established in 1943 as Fukuoka No. 15-B, was later redesignated as Fukuoka 9-D, and was officially Fukuoka 6-B at war's end. More than 1,000 American, Dutch, British, and Australian prisoners were housed in barracks at this camp during the war, forced to work in the trying conditions of the Orio coal mines.

MM2c Bernie Deleman, a 22-year-old Pennsylvania native, had enlisted in the Navy in October 1939. After two years as a machinist on surface ships, he volunteered for submarine service for the extra pay and new experiences. Assigned to *Perch* prior to her first war patrol, Deleman worked the Orio mines with his fellow *Perch* machinists until the Japanese discovered his aptitude for all things mechanical. Deleman was then assigned to special duty in the Japanese shipyards—where the strenuous work and the abuse was debilitating enough that his body would never fully recover.

The *Perch* officers were scattered throughout 1943. Lieutenant Commander Hurt remained at Ofuna, while Lt. Bev Van Buskirk had been transferred to a camp in Yokohama on 4 December. There, the men were forced to work in the Mitsubishi shipyard, helping to build Japanese ships. "I was senior American officer and kept track of the work records," wrote Van Buskirk. "The Japs furnished me an old Underwood typewriter to keep those records."[8]

After a short time of casing out his new camp, Van Buskirk busied himself with rewriting the *Perch*'s loss report once he had figured out the routine of the guards. Back at Makassar, he had been forced to eat the original 19-page report to avoid its discovery. This time, he was determined to create a report that the Japanese guards could not find. Using the front and back side of a single sheet of paper, he rewrote the report from memory, using very few spaces and only one or two letters to represent a word. Fellow prisoners soldered sheet metal into a small capsule into which he placed the single page report before it was soldered tight.

"I could now hide it from the Japs by inserting it into my rectum," Van Buskirk wrote. "I didn't look forward to that with any anticipation. Surely, there must be a better way. The inspiration came when I realized that the Jap guards, for some reason, had a terrific fear of venereal disease."

With this idea in mind, Van Buskirk acquired an opaque jar of cold cream, into which he inserted the little capsule to the bottom. Smoothing over the cream's surface, he replaced the cap and simply kept the clear jar of cream in plain sight at the head of his bunk. When a new Japanese guard came in to inspect, he often pointed at the jar of cream and demanded to know what it was. "I was able to convince him that I had a terrible case of venereal disease," wrote Van Buskirk.

"This was medicine for it—would he like to have some? He would back away from it like it was an atomic bomb." In this manner, the *Perch* exec was able to keep his secret report safely hidden in a jar of cold cream throughout the war.

Lt. K. G. Schacht was transferred to Tokyo POW Camp No. 2 in Yokohama on 4 December. He found that Captain Nishizawa, the camp commandant, "was extremely negligent in the matter of providing medical supplies. Prisoners died who, according to the British medical officer A. C. Price, could have been saved had drugs been brought into camp." Schacht found pneumonia took the greatest toll on the Yokohama camp prisoners in their dirty, crowded warehouse barracks. "Rainy days meant the POWs marched off to work in wet clothing the following morning. Nipponese overcoats were provided in January." If the Mitsubishi ship-yard sent men back to camp for being too sick, they were slapped, tripped, and beaten with bamboo. "Those too sick to work were placed on one-half to one-third rations," related Lieutenant Schacht. "The officers were forced to work by stand-ing them, sick and well, outside on a cold winter day until they signed a statement volunteering to work."

Lt. (jg) Jake Vandergrift and Lt. Jack Ryder had been sent to Zentsuji on Japan's Shikoku Island. Ryder found Zentsuji "was uneventful as far as punishment was concerned. Food was good at first, later became very small in amount and so poor in quality as to be inedible, even by a very hungry person."

Zentsuji Camp did offer some perks. "Here, we were made official POWs and given fair treatment," stated Vandergrift, "being allowed to send messages via radio and mail. All hands engaged in light gardening or similar labor. While the food ration here was definitely inadequate and living conditions poor, the treatment was not bad and the Red Cross was able to get supplies to us periodically, saving many lives."

During March 1943, Jack Ryder was allowed to send a radio message out. He stated that all officers and men of *Perch* were alive and requested that the wives of Bev Van Buskirk and Dave Hurt be notified that their husbands were alive. Ryder's mother received two letters from him during early 1943 that had been written in September and October of 1942. The letters came via Germany—delayed due to censors four times—but they included pictures of him. Ryder's letter stated:

> I am quite well, uninjured and treated well. The food is alright, so don't worry. I've been in Japan for five months now and expect to be here until the end of the war. This is my third camp. We all hated to see the *Perch* go down for she meant a great deal to us. There was no choice and we are thankful to be alive. All hands were rescued. We did our duty as long as possible.

Just as Bev Van Buskirk was able to successfully hide the *Perch* report during the war, Ryder was able to sew his Academy class ring into the waist of his pants and carry it throughout his internment. Enough reports from Zentsuji and other camps filtered out to America for the families to learn that Ryder, Van Buskirk, Vandergrift, and Schacht were alive and registered as POWs. It was not until 4 August 1943 that a message from another former Ofuna prisoner mentioned that Commander Al Maher from the cruiser *Houston* and Lt. Cdr. Dave Hurt of *Perch* were both alive and well.[9]

––––––––––

The enlisted men of *Perch* remaining on Celebes kept order based on their seniority. The most senior enlisted men remaining were chief of the boat Charlie Cross and five CPOs: CMM Albert Newsome, CEM Houston Edwards, CQM Sidney Boersma, CEM Pete Pederson, and CMM Henry Yates. "Our chiefs took over just like the officers and did a darn fine job," Ernie Plantz later stated. "They got beat just like the officer did if we did something we weren't supposed to do."

Torpedoman Sam Simpson had already lost two shipmates from his former Dutch Army barracks cubicle to transfers. Radioman Ted Reh had been sent to Japan with the officers and machinist Larry Dague had been shipped out in October, leaving Simpson with only John Greco and Bud Harper. Some shuffling of prisoners occurred and F3c Orville "Red" Peters soon joined their cubicle for the duration of their stay in the barracks.[10]

When the Americans were sent out in working parties, they were generally managed by at least two Japanese guards. "We didn't know any Jap and they didn't know any English," explained Simpson. "They usually made what they wanted clear enough. Our customs and ways of doing things was the biggest problem. You had to act immediately: no smiling, no questioning, no hesitating or misunderstanding. They all carried a stick and used it."[11]

Each *Perch* chief petty officer was put in charge of a group of men but some of the senior petty officers were also given similar responsibilities. Simpson and MM1c Tommy Brynes were also detailed to oversee work parties. Their duties included keeping accurate counts of their men and learning enough of the basic Japanese language to relay orders to their group. Any failure to promptly follow a command was met with swift consequences. On one occasion, Simpson witnessed a large Japanese guard drop Chief Pete Pederson "with a right to the jaw."[12]

The *Perch* crew often worked on building bomb shelters and in tearing down the old fort section of the Makassar camp where the Japanese had bombed it. "That's where we lost our first man on one of these working parties," recalled electrician Turk Turner. "They would have us push these walls down. If the wind came up, the walls would start weaving and then break and fall down."

The prisoners had left some tools at the base of one of the old bomb-damaged walls when a heavy wind came up. The guards wanted the men to retrieve the tools before knocking off from work. One of the *Pope* survivors, TM3c Robert James Gilbert, volunteered to run back and fetch the tools. "To heck with them," said Turner. "We can get them later." Gilbert instead ran back to the wall and began collecting the tools as the old wall creaked in the wind. As others watched in horror, the high brick wall collapsed and crushed him. A large chunk of the wall crushed Gilbert's thorax and broke bones. He lay comatose before passing away. Sam Simpson, who had become friends with Gilbert, was selected as one of six to attend a funeral that the Japanese allowed for the fallen *Pope* sailor, the first American casualty at Makassar. "I don't know why, but I don't recall any funerals being held for others," Simpson related.[13]

Turk Turner recalled unloading a Dutch merchant ship in Makassar's harbor around Christmastime. "They had us hauling freight out onto the docks," he said. "As we were unloading one of the holds, we found hundreds of cases of Heineken beer among the cargo. So, as we unloaded them, we were careful to let just a few drop here and there. We would kick the bottles off around the corner as we were walking with our loads. When the guards weren't looking, we took some swigs. It may not have been a white Christmas, but it was the next best thing."

According to Ernie Plantz, "We were still looking for the Americans to land any night by the first Christmas of 1942. For more than a year, we slept with a little packet of everything we wanted to take with us, just ready to grab it and run." With time, this optimism began to fade. "The Americans didn't bomb anything, they didn't show, and we didn't get any news," recalled Plantz. "The Japs acted like they had won the damn war, were in total control, and would stay that way. It began to look like the Japs were right and we were all wrong. There was nothing for us but hunger and disappointment."

The chance of acquiring food compelled the POWs to take chances. Plantz decided in camp one day that he would try to climb a coconut tree that stood on the other side of the fence of their Makassar campground. That night, he slipped under the fence with Robbie Robison and Turk Turner to go after coconuts. Plantz shimmied halfway up the steep coconut tree before he lost his grip. "He slid down the tree, scraping his bare belly up on the rough bark," recalled Turner. "All we could do was laugh. We never did get any of those coconuts." According to Sam Simpson, TM2c Andrew Eaton from *Pope* acquired a set of leg spurs and was able to occasionally scale the coconut trees successfully when the guards were not nearby.[14]

Bob Lents was among the many who learned to survive by bartering with the locals. "We'd steal out of the Jap warehouses when we were working there. We'd steal cigarette paper and sell it to the natives," he said.

As 1942 rolled into 1943, "hard labor and poor conditions" were the Makassar routine for the *Perch* men, according to Alabama Arnette. "American prisoners of war in Celebes were allowed no mail and no Red Cross from the time captured.

In the months of January, February, March and April, many men died," he said. "Many died from lack of proper food and medical attention."

Arnette credited his spirituality for pulling him through the tougher times. "I always believed in God because I was brought up in a Christian home," he recalled. "I prayed silently to myself and I believe He got me through every day." Arnette's faith was sorely tested by frequent abuse, including one beating he endured with a shovel by a Japanese guard. In spite of this, he clung to the happier moments. During one cool, clear night, Arnette and a buddy laid on the ground and looked up at the stars. "I thought, well here I am," he related. "A lot of people are dying right now, I thought. But I was still alive and I was happy for that."

Tom Moore, a stocky member of the crew, was singled out for extra physical labor. Moving heavy loads was often accomplished with a lever system the POWs called a "yo-yo pole," a wooden pole with ropes to which heavy loads of dirt, rock, or other items could be attached—all of which was balanced across the prisoner's shoulders. "They used to make me lift things, just to see what I could lift," Moore remembered.

On one occasion, the guard called over two other Japanese to see if they could lift the amount of weight that Moore was hauling with the yo-yo pole. "He told one of them to get on the other side from me on the end of the pole, and he told us to lift it. This guy crunched right to the ground and he couldn't lift it. The Japanese just shook his head and he didn't even ask the other guy to try and lift it. He was embarrassed."

Many of the Americans were put to work constructing a crushed coral road through the jungle. "For weeks, we would wade into the sea and locate large lumps of coral," recalled Sam Simpson. "We dug them out and carried them ashore to be loaded into carts and hauled to a road area two miles away." The coral was moved in carts along a narrow gauge railroad, unloaded by other POWs, and then crushed into small pieces to "pave" the jungle road. The crushed coral "was later pressed down by an old steam roller that was pulled by more or less 30 POWs on a rope with no shoes on," Simpson related.[15]

Other prisoners were taken to the harbor to unload coal ships using bushel baskets on the end of bamboo yo-yo poles. The cargo holds were sweltering and anyone who stumbled was swatted on the rear with sticks or thumped in the forehead by the guards. "The men referred to it as a hell hole and the guards as the bulls of the coal pile," said Simpson.[16]

The work parties offered the prisoners a chance to trade with the local natives for sugar, salt, tobacco, candy, and other supplies. Sam Simpson's cubicle mates John Greco, Red Peters, and Bud Harper managed to acquire "a grass sack apiece and we stuffed grass in them to lay on at night." Peters took chances by slipping out at night, dodging camp guards en route to the pig pen, and stealing corn from the supply. "Everything was divided and we would put a little in our rice,"

Simpson related. When he took his turn slipping out to steal more corn, Simpson was caught. Fortunately for him, a more lenient guard was present and he was not severely punished. Bartering and stealing were simply ways of life at Makassar. "We had nothing and were given nothing," Simpson wrote.[17]

Still presumed lost by their loved ones, these *Perch* enlisted men clung to their faith, and survived by stealing and whatever means they could find as the months passed.

5
The Fight to Save *Grenadier*

Lt. Kevin Denis Harty was so focused on the enemy convoy ahead that he was startled by the call.

"Plane on the port quarter!" the after lookout cried from the periscope shears.

Harty was on the bridge, manning the after TBT of USS *Grenadier* (SS-210). The ship's communications officer, his job this day was to help plot the course of these ships. A native of River Edge, New Jersey, Kevin Harty had joined the Navy in 1940 and completed the torpedo course at the Naval Torpedo Station in Keyport, Washington, by the summer of 1941. He was then ordered to join the sub tender *Otus* in the Asiatic Fleet stationed at Manila. Lieutenant Harty reported on board *Grenadier*, his first submarine, from *Otus* in Albany, Western Australia, following the sub's third war patrol. *Grenadier* was in pursuit of two Japanese tankers and Harty, making his third war patrol, was intently cutting in the convoy's smoke through his binoculars on the target bearing transmitter.

The date was 21 April 1943 and the time was 0835. Lieutenant Harty and *Grenadier*'s skipper, Lt. Cdr. John Fitzgerald, quickly swung their glasses in the direction of the reported aircraft. "Not wishing to be deceived by having it turn out to be some bird or false alarm, I turned around and identified the object as a plane myself," Fitzgerald later wrote. It appeared to be a twin-engined bomber.[1]

"Clear the bridge!" shouted Fitzgerald. "Dive! Dive!"

As the officers and lookouts scrambled down the ladder into the conning tower, their submarine was already plowing under the waves. *Grenadier* had been spotted by many an enemy aircraft in her previous patrols and had thus far been successful in evading the best of their efforts. Fate would, however, deal the *Grenadier* crew a different hand this time.

———

Grenadier, a *Tambor*-class fleet submarine built by the Portsmouth Navy Yard, was commissioned 1 May 1941, seven months before Pearl Harbor. Weighing 1,475 tons and named for a relative of the cod, *Grenadier* was just over 307 feet in length and capable of 20 knots surfaced.

Grenadier's war had not started with great success. She had three different skippers during her first four war patrols but was only credited officially postwar with one confirmed sinking. Prior to her fifth patrol, *Grenadier* was assigned her fourth skipper. Lt. Cdr. John Allison Fitzgerald took command on 24 December 1942.

Born in Craig, Missouri, Fitzgerald attended high school in Oxnard, California, and was appointed to the Naval Academy in 1927. In addition to his academic studies, he was a member of the Academy boxing team for years. Following his 1931 graduation, Ensign Fitzgerald served as a junior officer on board the battleship *Texas* until entering Submarine School at New London, Connecticut, in July 1934. After his graduation, he was the assistant boxing coach at the Naval Academy from December 1934 until March 1935. During the next few years, he worked his way up the ranks as a submarine officer on board the old *S-32* and *R-11* before returning to Annapolis in 1938 for postgraduate school in Operating Engineering. He returned to surface duty, serving briefly as the destroyer *Yarnell*'s engineering officer in 1939 and then as executive officer of the destroyer *Dupont* through 1940.[2]

When the war broke out, John Fitzgerald was executive officer of *Gar* (SS-206) and made four war patrols on her, earning the Silver Star Medal. During her first three patrols, *Gar* managed to sink only one 1,500-ton ship that postwar analysis would confirm to her credit. An aggressive submariner, Fitzgerald urged his captain, Donald McGregor, to take greater risks by going closer to the beach and staying nearer the surface. After another lackluster patrol on *Gar*, Fitzgerald requested to be transferred to a more aggressive boat.[3]

Admiral Lockwood gave John Fitzgerald a chance to command his own boat, *Grenadier*. Fitzgerald quickly proved his intention to aggressively seek out and destroy enemy shipping. Patrolling the Java Sea, he made six attacks, damaging two freighters with torpedoes and sinking three smaller vessels with his deck gun. Fitzgerald would later be awarded the Letter of Commendation for "meritorious conduct in action" during *Grenadier*'s fifth patrol.[4]

"The new skipper was very aggressive," wrote one of *Grenadier*'s young crewmen, S1c Gordon Charles Cox. As fourth loader on *Grenadier*'s 3-inch deck gun, Cox noted that Lieutenant Commander Fitzgerald kept his submarine engaged with a tanker even when it fired back. "We could hear the projectiles pass by our heads," recalled Cox. Fitzgerald closed on the tanker, sinking both it and the barge it was towing with gun fire.[5]

Gordon Cox was born in Crossfield, Alberta, Canada, in 1923, on his grandfather's farm. His farming family moved to Yakima, Washington, in 1937, where he attended high school through much of the eleventh grade. Hearing that the U.S. Navy was taking enlistments, Cox enlisted against his mother's wishes. "I had to wait for papers from Canada before they would take me, which happened on January 28, 1941," he wrote.[6]

Cox finished in the top 20 percent of his San Diego boot camp class. He attended communication school, and ended up as a "volunteer" for submarine duty in August 1941. When the call came for men to volunteer for submarine duty, several of his buddies stepped forward right away. "When they were giving last call, I got a big push from behind and ended up a couple steps out of line," Cox recalled.[7]

Cox rode the battleship *Tennessee* from California to Pearl, a second-class seaman making $36.00 per month. In October 1941, he was assigned to the submarine *Sculpin*, which had located the sunken *Squalus* in 1939. Due to a shortage of submarine sailors, some men were taken aboard for on-the-job training versus being sent to New London's submarine school. Such was the case with three good friends joining *Sculpin* who had attended communications school together: seamen second class Cox, Odis S. Taylor, and James Q. Harper. In statistics typical of the World War II submarine service, two of these three buddies would be aboard submarines that were lost in combat. Cox would ultimately survive his ordeal but Harper went down with *Sculpin* in 1944.[8]

Seaman Cox made two war patrols on *Sculpin* and then was transferred in Fremantle, Australia, to the tender *Holland*. Months passed and he was later transferred to another tender, *Pelias*. At the end of December 1942, he found himself still aboard the sub tender in the relief crew, chipping paint. "It was a dirty job in very confined spaces, so I got to feeling sorry for myself," Cox wrote. "I had been in the Navy almost two years by then, had been in the Asiatic Fleet, and made a couple of war patrols."[9]

Cox glanced over at the next pair of brown shoes in coveralls and "proceeded to tell him what I thought." As it turned out, the "sailor" in coveralls was Lt. Alfred Joseph Toulon Jr., an officer in the relief crew. Toulon proceeded to chew out the 19-year-old sailor, who then asked to see the commanding officer. Lt. Toulon gladly brought Cox before the relief crew commander, where the young sailor voiced his complaints about spending the war chipping paint. "You'll be at sea tomorrow!" his skipper snapped.[10]

Gordon Cox reported on board *Grenadier* on 1 January 1943, prior to her fifth patrol with a large number of new hands who were not yet submarine qualified. As fate would have it for young Cox, Al Toulon also joined *Grenadier* from the *Pelias* relief crew at the same time. Toulon, 25, was well qualified in submarines. He had served in 1942 on skipper James "Red" Coe's *Skipjack*, which was given wartime credit for four sinkings in one patrol. Toulon, the son of a Navy surgeon, became *Grenadier*'s torpedo officer.

Following *Grenadier*'s successful fifth patrol, Lt. Cdr. Fitzgerald received three new officers in Fremantle, including two lieutenants, Arthur Greenville McIntyre and Harmon Bradford Sherry, the latter the new diving officer. Sherry had completed four patrols aboard the successful *Gudgeon*. The other officers whom Fitzgerald had experience with were fourth officer Lieutenant Toulon—making his second patrol on *Grenadier*—Lt. Kevin Harty, and Lt. George Harris Whiting, the ship's exec.

Whiting, a 28-year-old born in South Carolina, was a 1936 Academy graduate who had already made seven prior war patrols. He started the war aboard *Triton*, aboard which he earned a Bronze Star for his work as her TDC operator during three patrols. Whiting joined *Grenadier* as her torpedo and gunnery officer but had advanced to second in command by his fourth run with John Fitzgerald, who considered Whiting to possess "excellent leadership and coolness under fire."

The night before *Grenadier* departed on patrol, MoMM1c Chuck Ver Valin accepted five dollars from his engine-room buddy Raymond Leslie to take his place. Ver Valin stood his watches while Leslie went ashore for one last night of partying. "I wouldn't have traded with him had I known I would never get to spend that five dollars!" Ver Valin recalled.

Grenadier left Fremantle on 20 March 1943 to conduct her sixth war patrol in the Malacca Strait, west of Malaysia. Targets were scarce, but she managed to torpedo a small freighter on 6 April near Pilgrim Island. She fired two stern torpedoes from 1,605 yards at the Japanese maru. Gunfire erupted from the Japanese ships and *Grenadier* dodged the escorts by going around Pilgrim Island to escape.[11]

Satisfied that his *Grenadier* had sunk one ship, Fitzgerald patrolled in Malacca Strait, and he decided to investigate the approaches to the Malaysian seaport of Penang. During the night of 21 April 1943, the ship was ten miles to the west of Lem Valon Strait. The watch soon picked up smoke and *Grenadier* ran surfaced through the night to get into position ahead of two Japanese merchant ships.[12]

Gordon Cox found that skipper John Fitzgerald was as aggressive of a captain as he could hope for. After a lengthy time as seaman first class, he was finally about to be rated as a quartermaster third class. "I'm putting you in for third class when we get into port," the skipper told him after coming off watch in the conning tower on the sixth patrol. "It would be a long time before I saw that third class," Gordon Cox later wrote.[13]

The Japanese aircraft which forced *Grenadier* down on the morning of 21 April 1943 was typical of all previous aircraft contacts the ship had endured, with one exception: this pilot had better aim.

Lieutenant Commander Fitzgerald had been heading west of Lem Valon Strait with *Grenadier* surfaced, making a run to get into attack position when the Japanese aircraft appeared. When the plane was spotted approaching, Fitzgerald, Harty, and their lookouts cleared the bridge as the ship made a crash dive. The new diving officer, Lt. Harmon Sherry, was supervising the men on the bow and stern planes in the control room as the boat clawed for depth. Kevin Harty felt that the ship "lost diving control at 85 to 90 feet," as Fitzgerald ordered an evasive maneuver of right 15 degrees rudder. Lieutenant Sherry was able to have his men quickly regain control and continue the ship's descent to the starboard side of the path of the incoming aircraft. As *Grenadier* was passing 120 feet at 0837, Exec George Whiting remarked to Captain Fitzgerald, "We ought to be safe enough now."[14]

Whiting's statement was immediately followed by a powerful explosion that his skipper felt was as strong as if "two express trains collided." The Japanese pilot had dropped a depth bomb right on the mark. It exploded directly above *Grenadier* near the bulkhead between the maneuvering room and the after torpedo room. "The force of the explosion healed the boat over 10- or 15-degrees," wrote Fitzgerald. "All lights and power were lost."[15]

In the crew's mess, MoMM1c Charles Henry Ver Valin was finishing up breakfast with F1c John Schwartzly following his 0400 to 0800 watch. "It was one hell of a big thud," Ver Valin said of the explosion. "The lights went out. It opened the valves from the sinks and water came rushing out all over the deck." The force of the bomb pushed the ship's stern down. As others raced to stop the water flow in the galley, Ver Valin instinctively struggled to his feet against the ship's up-angle and headed through the after battery for his station in the engine room.

Ver Valin reported to his boss, CMoMM Charlie Erishman, who was head of the engine gang on *Grenadier*. Ver Valin had enlisted in the Navy while only a junior in high school. "After serving on the battleship *Maryland* in Hawaii, I put in for submarine duty and was shipped back to New London in the spring of 1941," he related. When war broke out, Chuck Ver Valin was serving on board the submarine *Gudgeon*, which became the first U.S. submarine to sink a Japanese submarine, the *I-173*. Following four productive runs on this boat, Ver Valin was making his second run on *Grenadier*. All of his previous experience would be put to the test this day.

The force of the explosion heeled *Grenadier* over sharply and she coasted helplessly downward for the ocean bottom. The ship's yeoman, Robert Wiley Palmer, was in the control room, manning the battle phones for the skipper. "We were going down fast at an 18-degree up-angle," he recalled. Palmer had always been able to think fast under pressure. His mother had died when Bob was age nine, leaving him and his older brother to take care of themselves. After joining the Navy, he took advantage of offers when they came. "I was on the old USS *Wright*, painting the officers' head when the yeoman came in and asked me if I could type," Palmer related. "I had failed that twice in one year in high school, but what would you say?"[16]

Bob Palmer rated yeoman and made runs on *Tuna* before being assigned to *Grenadier* on 8 October 1942. His calm voice and coolness under pressure had helped him earn the duty of battle stations talker for Lieutenant Commander Fitzgerald. As he felt his submarine plunging for the bottom now, things were not so in control. At 180 feet, he heard his skipper shout to diving officer Harmon Sherry, "Blow everything at 300!"

"I phoned the after torpedo room, but there was no answer," Palmer recalled. "I kept waiting for all stations to report, 'All battle stations manned.'"

Under the circumstances, most departments found little time to report their status. Men were more concerned with keeping their footing as *Grenadier*'s stern plunged following the bomb blast. *Grenadier* sank until she came to rest on the ocean floor around 270–276 feet, according to Lieutenant Harty. As she hit bottom, men were pitched off their feet once again.

Long before she hit bottom, *Grenadier*'s crew was in action. Gunner's mate first class Fred Zufelt later said, "I was in my bunk when the excitement started." In the after torpedo room, TM1c Norman Arthur "Al" Albertson was the senior petty officer in charge. Born in Muskegon, Michigan, he joined the Navy right after the Great Depression "to start a career and get a paying job." He put *Grenadier* into commission and had been a senior torpedoman in her forward room for the previous five runs before wanting a change and taking charge of the after torpedo room for the ship's sixth patrol.

On duty with Al Albertson at the time of the explosion was S1c Charles H. McCoy, a Texas boy striking for his torpedoman rating. Aboard ship, McCoy was known simply as "Skeeter" to his buddies. Raised in Lubbock and Dallas before joining the Navy at age 17, McCoy had been awarded the Silver Star in 1942 for his efforts on board the submarine *Trout* when she had hauled gold out of the Philippines for the treasury department to prevent the Japanese from capturing it. He had felt enough depth charges already to know that this blast was serious. "The bomb hit between the maneuvering room and our after torpedo room and blew us to Kingdom Come," McCoy said. Men around him were thrown about like rag dolls.

QM3c Joe Minton—a 19-year-old from Florida who had come on board *Grenadier* in October 1942 at Albany from the tender *Pelias*—was napping above the torpedoes in his port side aft bunk. Across from him in the starboard side aft bunk was MoMM1c John Pianka, the ship's senior auxiliaryman. When the bombs hit close outside this compartment, both Minton and Pianka were instantly airborne.

Pianka's mattress hit the deck and he ended up between the torpedo tubes. Minton came flying down and landed right on Pianka's mattress. Suddenly awakened and sore, Joe "Baby Duck" Minton was making his third patrol on *Grenadier* and he knew to report in.[17]

In his excitement, Minton was shouting into the speaker for the control room, "Control! Control! Control!" When the control room failed to answer, he soon realized he had forgotten to hold the talk button down. Minton's shipmates would tease him later over his errant attempt to report the damage. When he was able to finally call the control room to report on the after torpedo room, Minton's voice was the first that battle talker Palmer would hear from.[18]

The force of the blast also knocked S2c Albert John Rupp from his bunk in the after battery compartment. "Parts of the upper bunks, mattresses, and even the cork from the overhead began to engulf me," he later wrote. Al Rupp had been sworn into the Navy on 13 December 1941 at age 15, after altering his birth certificate and pleading with his mother to sign as his guardian. He had made his first patrol on board *Gudgeon*, the boat shipmate Chuck Ver Valin had also served on. The skipper made him "captain of the head." In his zeal to make the toilet area sparkle, he used a creosote solution to scour the toilet bowls. Days later, *Gudgeon* was found to be bleeding a milky substance into the water that was traced to the creosote solution Rupp poured in the toilet bowls.[19]

After a second run-in with *Gudgeon*'s skipper while in Albany for refit from the tender *Holland*, Rupp was transferred to the sub division command. After spending some time mess-cooking, he was assigned to *Grenadier* when she came into Fremantle. Following the bomb blast on *Grenadier*, 16-year-old Rupp picked himself up off the deck as the red glow of the emergency lights began to fill the berthing department. He later wrote, "We were going down fast."[20]

Seaman Gordon Cox was also thrown from his bunk when the bomb exploded. "As I awoke, a large T-handle wrench came flying off the overhead and just missed my head," Cox recalled. Throughout the boat, talkers called Bob Palmer to report their damage to the skipper. The yeoman, knocked to the deck by the explosion, was now wrapped around the No. 2 periscope with his headphones still on.[21]

Communications with the after compartments went out. Then the word was passed, "Fire in the maneuvering room!" Smoke surged from the compartment, men groped about blindly, coughing, and as the fire got out of hand, Fitzgerald ordered the compartment sealed. Over the torpedo room, where the bulkhead adjoined the maneuvering room, the bomb had wreaked havoc on the electrical workings of the ship.[22]

In the maneuvering room, flames licked into the hull-insulation cork, cables, stores, and cleaning rags. The main motor cables had been gashed, and arcing and sparks from the resulting short circuit had started the blaze. F1c Virgil Ouillette found himself in a tight spot. Raised in Michigan, he had made three previous patrols on *Grenadier* and had worked on overhauling *Triton* and *Gudgeon* before joining *Grenadier* for three of her previous patrols.

Ouillette donned a Momsen lung and went in to fight the fire in the maneuvering room. Chuck Ver Valin soon offered to help, although he was inexperienced with the Momsen lung. "I couldn't get my damn one on properly and Ouillette showed me how," said Ver Valin. "I followed him in there and helped put the fire out. We had CO_2 and sprayed it all over. There were sparks flying out of this cable."

Virgil Ouillette was caught by the ship's lathe on the starboard side by the electrical cage. He soon found himself unable to escape the room again, as thousands of volts were arcing between the cage and the bulkhead. He noted that the volts were in a series which came at regular intervals. He steeled his nerves and prepared to act just as a child jumping rope. Ouillette leaped through during the next "off-arc" and managed to turn the juice off at its source to help prevent further fires.[23]

Even after Ver Valin and Ouillette were able to douse the fire with CO_2, the area was dangerous. "There was still a lot of spitting and sputtering when you put out an electrical fire," Ver Valin recalled. "There were still little pops. We had all the smoke in there, plus the mixture of the damn CO_2."

Lieutenant Sherry was on hand to direct the efforts in the maneuvering room. Ouillette and EM2c Lester Barker spent the better part of the afternoon cleaning up the mess in this area. "We had to wash the whole area off with fresh water to get rid of the salt water," he said. Barker and Ouillette then spent hours trying to bring the shorted out batteries back on line.

In the fire-fighting process, two men were overcome by the smoke. One of them was Ouillette, who finally had to leave Barker behind. "I got sick and went and crashed for most of the day," he said. When the fire was finally smothered, the maneuvering room was a wreck. The induction valve had been knocked off its seat, and a two-inch stream of water was pouring in. The hard patch above the main motor-controller had ruptured, admitting a spray that soaked the maze of electrical apparatus. Short circuits and grounds started a pyrotechnic sputter. No sooner was one blaze extinguished than another started.

Yeoman Bob Palmer found his skipper to be an encouraging force. Fitzgerald spoke quietly over the intercom to his people, "Steady men. We're OK. Everything is all right." A bucket brigade hustled between the maneuvering room and the forward torpedo room, trying to keep the water level below the main motors. Gordon Cox joined this effort. "When we started, you would just take a bucket of water and pass it to the next man," he wrote. In a short time, men began passing out from the heat, exertion, and foul air. "We would move them aside and continue," Cox related. "Before long, I was running buckets the length of a compartment. It was tough in the heat and foul air."[24]

Another young sailor who joined the bucket brigade was 18-year-old F1c Dempsey Ernest McGowan, a native of Charlotte, North Carolina. His mother had allowed him to join the Navy in June 1941, and he had been at diesel school in New London when Pearl Harbor was attacked. McGowan had finished his duty, visited the mess hall, and just crawled into his bunk when *Grenadier* was rocked by the explosion. As he and his shipmates quickly surveyed the damage, the engineman realized that war in the boats may have been more than he bargained for. He had spent the first year of war stuck aboard the sub tender *Pelias* because of his own advanced engine schooling.

"They wanted to keep me there permanently but I finally convinced them to let me go to sea," McGowan recalled. He was scheduled to join two different submarines but his *Pelias* superiors had kept him aboard both times. "I think the Good Lord was with me there, because both of the submarines that I was scheduled to go out on were sunk," he said. With his *Grenadier* now in a harrowing condition, McGowan raced aft and began helping to pass the buckets of water forward. "Water was leaking into the after torpedo room and the motor room," he related. "We were flooding bad and we had to get the water forward. We didn't have any pumps so we just had to do everything manually."

Chuck Ver Valin joined those battling the rising water. Water spurted from the stuffing glands around the shafts into the motor room. "Several enginemen and me tightened them up as much as we dared to because you couldn't bust the damn studs off," he said. "The water was up to your knees where it was seeping in."

Eventually a jury rig was installed between the main battery and a drain pump, so that the pump could be put on the motor room bilge. "They soon secured the bucket brigade, and we were ordered to lie down so not to use up any more oxygen than was necessary," wrote Gordon Cox.[25]

Grenadier had suffered serious internal injuries. In the forward end of the after torpedo room, the hull on the starboard side had been dished in from four to six inches. The after tubes had been forced to port, bending the main shafts. All the hull frames in the maneuvering room and the after torpedo room were bent inward. The door between the maneuvering room and the after torpedo room was sprung and would not close properly. Water sprayed in through the damaged after torpedo room loading hatch. Later the crew discovered that about two-fifths of the gasket in this hatch was chopped up. "The hatch itself was elliptical in shape to the extent that I could put my hand in between the knife edge and hatch cover itself," Lieutenant Commander Fitzgerald later wrote.[26]

The ship's auxiliary gang was heavily taxed with repair work. MoMM1c John Pianka, the senior auxiliaryman, had two assistants, MoMM2c Lee Shaw and F1c Joseph Thomas Price. Having joined the Navy in 1941 before Pearl Harbor, Joe

Price was making his second run on *Grenadier*. When the bomb exploded, he had just come off midnight watch and gone to sleep in his bunk. "The damage was so extensive that everyone had to participate in the work," Price said. "We had a bucket brigade until the pumps got back on line. I stood watch in the control room after that, going wherever I was needed at the time."

The ship's "Fuel King" was motor machinist's mate first class Ver Valin. He was also busy throughout the afternoon, checking his tanks and pumping ballast as directed by Al Toulon and Harmon Sherry. During one of his rounds of checking the tank levels, he popped into the captain's cabin to read the fuel gauge there. He found John Fitzgerald sitting there with his head in his hands. Ver Valin noted that the CO was staring at a picture of his wife and family. He directed Ver Valin to make the grounded boat lighter by pumping out as much excess fuel as possible.

The radio transmitter in the conning tower had been jarred from its foundation. Minor damage extended all the way to the forward battery room where dishes and phonograph records had been shattered. "Sunrise Serenade" was a favorite on *Grenadier* and it had been playing when the bomb went off. Lt. Harty recalled that another result of the bomb damage "was that 'Der Fuhrer's Face' record was broken."[27]

MoMM1c Raymond Leslie, a veteran submariner who served on S-boats in prewar China Station duty, recalled that a strong current moved the ship along a little and that *Grenadier* "sorta bounced" along the bottom for some time.[28]

Chuck Ver Valin recalled that the situation was tense:

> A lot of guys tried to sleep, but not really anybody I know did. They were in groups, talking about what we would do next. As a whole, everybody took it really good. There was only a couple of guys that kinda spooked out a little bit. But, with other guys hollering at them to shut up, they did.

Grenadier's crew labored throughout the day to regain propulsion. Electricians did everything they could to shield vulnerable equipment from the salt bath showering from the maneuvering room overhead, but intermittent electrical fires and persistent leaks frustrated their best efforts. The radio, however, was put back in commission, and the motors were at last revived. At 2130, the submarine struggled to the surface. Somehow, Lieutenant Sherry, the diving officer, managed to keep her on an even keel.

Grenadier began moving slowly, as compressed air blown into her tanks drove out the heavy seawater and began making her more buoyant. On the battle phones, Bob Palmer "called depth up to 200 feet; then we surfaced very fast."

As she rose to periscope depth, the skipper swept the horizon with his periscope and found it clear of Japanese shipping. With the lifting of the hatch, a rush of fresh air swept down through the conning tower and into the control room. The vacuum force sucked out the smells of smoke, burnt wiring, and sweat that had accumulated over 15-plus hours below. The skipper also ordered the forward torpedo room hatch opened.

While the engineers and electricians struggled to regain propulsion, others of the crew found that they had little to do. Gordon Cox recalled that chief commissary steward Charlie Westerfield and his cooks "had laid out sandwiches and coffee for the crew that very few touched. The stress and strain of the last 24 hours had left most of them in somewhat of a daze. Some of the crew had broken out their personal stock of hidden booze and were secretly having a snort."[29]

TM3c Riley Keysor recalled that shipmate Dean Shoemaker "went down in the pit in the forward torpedo room with me and helped drink a pint of whiskey when things were not looking so good for us." A new member of Al Albertson's forward torpedo gang for this patrol, Keysor had survived six war patrols on *Grayling* before being assigned to *Grenadier*. His pint of whiskey was a small relief to the stress of this day and it would be many years before he confessed to others of his crew about this little forbidden episode.[30]

John Fitzgerald had hoped that on the surface they could stem the leakage and restore the electrical equipment. The submarine was cleared of smoke, and the engineers and electricians got to work on the damaged power plant. By means of jury rigs, they finally managed to turn over one shaft at slow speed. But the shaft was badly bent and it was impossible to get the contact levers into the second stage of resistance.[31]

Skeeter McCoy felt that it was over. "One screw turned over about ten times and then froze in its bearings and the other screw wouldn't even turn," he said. "The whole ship was just really, truly devastated."

After a heartbreaking attempt, the engineering officer, Lt. Al Toulon, and the electricians reported to Fitzgerald on the bridge that their efforts were stymied. This was sometime after 0400 when Fitzgerald received the news that they had exhausted all efforts to regain propulsion.[32]

About dawn, the Skipper ordered CEM Charles Whitlock to secure the power. With her deck gun out of commission, *Grenadier* could neither fight nor run away. He ordered the bridge guns, the 20mm and 30-calibers, manned. He soon had his crew working on a sail that might take his boat closer to the beach where the men could disembark and blow up *Grenadier*. Fireman Dempsey McGowan recalled Lt. Cdr. Fitzgerald talking to the crew to explain their chances of survival. He concluded by telling them that after sunrise, "We'll just wait and see what happens."

Pharmacist John McBeath and others toiled on sewing sheets together. At age 17, McBeath had signed up for the Navy before he finished high school, because he "wanted to travel." At age 18, he began his basic training in 1938 at Newport, Rhode Island, right out of high school. His superiors enrolled him in medical training and by the time of the attack on Pearl Harbor, McBeath was a PhM2c stationed aboard the sub tender *Pelias*. He was getting ready to go ashore at 0800, when the battle stations alarm suddenly sounded.[33]

He ran to his battle station as the ships of Pearl Harbor were blasted by bombs and torpedoes. After the second wave, he went topside on *Pelias* and saw that "the whole harbor was aflame. There was black smoke everywhere." Once the Japanese planes departed, the young pharmacist joined others to go aboard other ships to help save the wounded. "There were mostly corpses, pieces of corpses, things like that," McBeath stated. "It was a bad deal." Aboard small launches, he and others carried the bodies to the grounds of the naval hospital and laid them out on the lawn. In the aftermath of the surprise attack, McBeath helped with the grim duty of transporting the bodies to the Punchbowl for burial.[34]

McBeath's world abruptly changed on 7 December 1941. "I knew we were at war," he said. "I wasn't going to war—I was at war." The young pharmacist volunteered for submarine service and was assigned to the submarine *Perch*. Little could McBeath imagine that his handiwork with a needle would be called upon to help sew sheets to try and power a modern naval warship. "We were vulnerable," recalled Doc McBeath. "We couldn't get under way and we could never get back down again." His makeshift sail was tied to the No. 1 periscope on 22 April 1943 and the other end down to the radio antenna staff. But the sail proved useless in the breathless doldrums of a tropic sunrise.

EM3c Charles "Johnny" Johnson, who was topside near the stern assisting the efforts, recalled that MoMM2c Lee Shaw volunteered to go over the side and check for damages to *Grenadier*'s hull. Shaw, a rugged Texan who was approaching his 30th birthday, was known as "Pappy" by his shipmates. He had been stationed for some time in Australia and had only come aboard *Grenadier* as a replacement for an ill crewman. Pappy Shaw wrote a letter to his sister Peggy (Shaw) Pepper back in San Antonio on 16 March 1943, just four days before *Grenadier*'s last patrol. "I guess this will be the last letter you will get from me for awhile, so don't worry. Seems like I always manage to come back." It would be years, in fact, before Peggy's brother would "come back."[35]

At about 0600, John Fitzgerald was on the bridge of his mortally wounded submarine when things went from bad to worse. "I noticed, coming from the northwest out of Lem Valon Strait, a ship which at that time appeared to me to be a large destroyer or light cruiser. Shortly thereafter I noticed smoke from a patrol or escort vessel to the southeast."[36]

The skipper took stock of his situation and found that neither fighting nor fleeing was a viable option. "I ordered preparations to be made for abandoning ship, thinking it imprudent to engage the approaching ships with machine guns."

Lieutenant Harty, "sent [a] message at five or six [a.m. on] 22 April 1943, in British number code giving condition of ship and intentions to abandon *Grenadier*." Radiomen Joe Knutson and Lou Poss dispatched their skipper's message.

The men who began gathering topside brought up all kinds of personal effects. A rubber raft was broken out and inflated and filled with large quantities of cigarettes. "The men that had them broke out their personal pistols," recalled Gordon Cox. He also noted MM2c George Stauber toting two German pistols. Stauber had "one in a holster like the old westerns, and the other he stuck in his belt." The gunner's mates carried the ship's issue rifles, including one rifle that skipper John Fitzgerald had once used off the west coast of Sumatra to shoot a pesky bird from his periscope shears.[37]

As the Japanese escort ship and a merchant ship were seen to be approaching, everything considered confidential was weighted and thrown overboard. Kevin Harty made sure that all the publications he had gathered were sunk. "We smashed SD and SJ, XYZ, radio equipment, TDC and CT sound gear," Harty related. "We stuffed the secret documents and materials into weighted bags and sank them over the side."

As the efforts continued to destroy all confidential gear, lookouts suddenly spotted a single-engine Japanese plane approaching. Seaman first class William Michael Cunningham was among those topside manning one of the .30-caliber machine guns. TM1c Al Albertson reached the deck just as "everything was going on. I was just standing there as this plane came in to attack."[38]

Dempsey McGowan had joined the ammunition handling line to assist the gunners who now faced an incoming enemy aircraft. "We didn't pass up but two shells to the 3-inch gun because they found out it was bent and jammed," he said. "So, I helped pass up the .50-caliber and 20mm ammunition." The aircraft made a beeline for the stricken submarine. *Grenadier* was not completed paralyzed, however. Cunningham watched the Japanese plane coming in on the starboard side on the sub's beam. Withholding fire until the position angle was about 65°, Fitzgerald ordered the gunners to open up with two 20mm and two .30-caliber machine guns. The enemy plane was so close that Cunningham could see the pilot in the cockpit before he opened up with his .30-caliber.[39]

The attacking plane was hit and the pilot was unable to complete his first run. "The plane, to the best of my knowledge, was hit three times," wrote Fitzgerald.[40]

The aircraft pulled its nose up sharply and the pilot changed course to the left to try a run up *Grenadier*'s port side. The submariners blazed away as the plane roared in. GM1c Fred Zufelt, manning one of the 20mm bridge guns, made his shots count. Chuck Ver Valin popped away at the incoming plane with one of *Grenadier*'s Browning automatic rifles. "Those were the only shots I took at an enemy during the war," he later stated. The pilot released his two bombs while almost directly overhead. Fortunately, they sailed past and exploded in the water about 200 yards from *Grenadier*. The submarine crew later found that this miss cost this airman his life. He was badly wounded and he struggled to keep his plane aloft as he flew off toward the distant shoreline. He died that night as a result of bullet wounds and a crash landing when he returned to Penang.[41]

In addition to shooting up an enemy aircraft, one of *Grenadier*'s crew had to shoot another menace. After the personnel records and confidential files had been collected, they were brought topside to be given the deep six in a weighted gunny sack. When it was tossed overboard, it refused to completely sink.

Lieutenant Commander Fitzgerald called out to one of his men on deck, "Skeeter, swim out there and get that sack so we can weight it down better."

Skeeter McCoy dived in and swam out to the bag of documents. "As I was swimming back toward the *Grenadier* towing this sack, a giant sea snake came up and started following me," he recalled. Shipmates noticed the long serpent and began hollering at McCoy. As fate would have it, MM2c George Stauber—a long-time gun collector—was on deck, preparing to toss his two prized German Mauser pistols into the ocean.

Loader Gordon Cox, topside with the gunners, estimated that the sea snake was about six feet in length. Cox watched as Stauber "pulled the one from the holster and shot, hitting the snake in the head. Was that just a lucky shot or was he that good? He never said anything, just put the gun back into the holster and walked away."[42]

Greatly relieved, McCoy then "swam over to the bow planes, which were rigged out." Shipmate Bob Palmer helped him back aboard, where the records bag was properly weighted down.

By this time, the Japanese ships were approaching and it was likely that the attacking aircraft had sent out further warnings. Fitzgerald came over the intercom and ordered all hands to assemble on deck forward of the conning tower. He told the crew of his intentions to abandon ship. Young seaman Al Rupp looked at his skipper and noticed that "the gleam had disappeared from his eyes. He had not slept since this nightmare began and the strain was apparent on his face. He made a decision which all commanding officers pray they will never have to make."[43]

"The skipper said nobody was going to get his submarine," recalled TM3c Riley Keysor.

Lieutenant Commander Fitzgerald ordered his men to get rid of anything that would show they had come from Australia, including money. Lt. Al Toulon lost more than most men: he had a considerable sum of money he had won from his shipmates in cribbage games.

Seaman John Gunderson watched as Chief Charles Whitlock also sadly "had to throw a couple hundred pounds" of Australian money over the side. There could be no connection to the secret advanced submarine bases in Australia. Gordon Cox recalled that Whitlock kept his rolled wad of money hidden in a flashlight. On the previous patrol, Chuck Ver Valin noted that Whitlock "had lost big playing poker. On our last run, he drew all the money he had coming to him," intent on winning back his poker losses at the first opportunity. He would not get the chance. "He threw the roll out on the ocean, with the roll unrolling as it spread the bills all the way," wrote Cox.[44]

With the prospect of being picked up by the Japanese, some men disposed of other impractical items. George Stauber—who had just joined *Grenadier* before her sixth run—gave up his prized snake-killing pistols into the ocean.[45]

Among the last to make it topside from the demolition work were S1c John Gunderson and GM2c Bill Wise. Wise scrambled up toward the bridge with his buddy right behind. "He hit the control room without touching anything but the guy under him, me," recalled Gunderson. They took time to scuttle some of the ship's Momsen lungs, which were stenciled with SS-210. As Wise reached the deck, he was momentarily blinded by the spotlight from the Japanese corvette.[46]

John Fitzgerald had every member of his crew topside except for Chief of the Boat Buck Withrow, who had been ordered below to open the vents to finish flooding the submarine. Withrow opened the vents and scrambled topside as *Grenadier* began settling in the water. Al Rupp recalled his skipper's final words on deck to be, "Abandon ship, and God bless you."[47]

It was a bitter moment for all, particularly for the man who had fought the system to gain his own command. Seaman Cox was struck by his skipper's resolve. "When the skipper ordered us over the side, there were tears running down his cheeks, and his voice was shaky. It was very sad to see this tough little fighter lose his ship and the home we had all known for a time."[48]

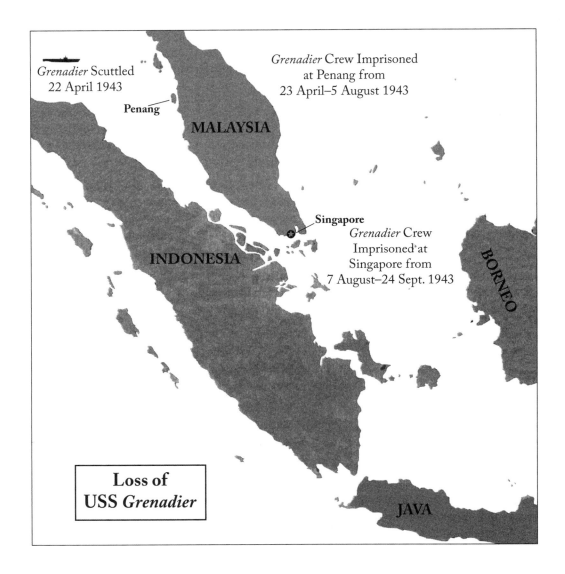

Grenadier Scuttled
22 April 1943

Penang

MALAYSIA

Grenadier Crew Imprisoned
at Penang from
23 April–5 August 1943

Singapore

INDONESIA

Grenadier Crew
Imprisoned at
Singapore from
7 August–24 Sept. 1943

BORNEO

**Loss of
USS *Grenadier***

JAVA

6
"Where Hell Started"

In the control room, Chief Withrow opened the dive vents to start *Grenadier* on her final dive. The Japanese merchant ship and the corvette were approaching the battered American submarine on the surface. While he waited for his chief of the boat to return from below, John Fitzgerald moved among the SS-210 sailors gathered on the ship's forecastle. As they began going over the side with the rising water, he reassured them, "Take it easy. We'll come through."

Those who were sick or unable to swim were assigned to cling to the rubber lifeboat. As the submarine began settling by her stern, John Simpson recalled that mess attendant Thomas "T. J." Trigg was among the non-swimmers who begged to be allowed into the raft. A husky man and the ship's only African American, Trigg had made it into submarines without ever learning to swim.[1]

Tom Courtney jumped in without his shoes, while EM1c Ralph Adkins thought to bring along an extra pair for some reason. Joe Price was not about to leave without his. "I had bought a new pair of shoes before I left on this run, so I put them on thinking they'd probably have to last a long time."

Chuck Ver Valin was more than a little apprehensive about entering the water. He had always been a poor swimmer and had once had a close brush with drowning. His sister had actually drowned while he was a young boy, adding to his fears. "Before I went over the side," Ver Valin said, "I made damn sure that my life belt was fully inflated."

F1c Bernie Witzke had no time to gather any extra belongings before going overboard. "I was up on the periscope shears as battle lookout with two other guys while those Japanese ships were approaching," he said. "The word was passed that the ship was going to be scuttled." The exec, George Whiting, told the other lookouts to come down and grab shoes, clothing, or whatever personal items they desired before entering the water.

A member of the engine-room gang who was striking for his motor machinist's mate rating, Witzke had been happy to join *Grenadier*. After finishing high school in St. Paul, Minnesota, he had his parents sign the papers in March 1941 for him to enlist in the Navy for six years. He volunteered for sub duty and was attending sub school at the time Pearl Harbor was attacked. Following this, he was assigned to a relief crew and eventually ended up in Australia, where he put in eleven months as a relief crewman before finally securing an assignment to *Grenadier*.

As the Japanese closed in on his doomed submarine, Bernie Witzke was left to maintain a lonely vigil atop the shears after word was passed to abandon ship. "The captain waited to abandon until the Japanese merchant ship was close, so we would not be in the water long. After the other lookouts were allowed to get their shoes, I had to remain up there all alone," he said. "They never got around to relieving me on the periscope." He felt some relief in that he was already wearing a life belt around his waist.

Witzke stayed on the shears until Chief Withrow reappeared from below after opening the vents. He then scrambled down and was among the very last to leave the ship. "When I went over the side, I had on only what I was wearing for lookout duty—a T-shirt, my trousers and a pair of sandals," he said.

The last of the crew went over the side as *Grenadier* went down by the stern. Fitzgerald waited for Buck Withrow to come up from below, and then the pair went over the side as the Japanese circled *Grenadier*, taking pictures.

George Whiting called to the men to stay together in the water. Some grabbed onto a buddy's life jacket to keep from drifting away. Bill Cunningham, one of the .30-caliber gunners who had scored hits on the Japanese plane, jumped off *Grenadier* with an inflated life jacket. In the ocean, however, he soon found his air escaping. Another shipmate had both a life jacket and a Momsen lung, so he gave Cunningham the lung to swim with.[2]

As he bobbed in the Indian Ocean of Malacca Strait, seaman Gordon Cox felt a "feeling of peacefulness and relaxation as we rose and fell with the swell, after the stress of the last 24 hours. A person could have fallen asleep under different circumstances."[3]

One of the Japanese ships fired a gun as it circled around the site of where *Grenadier* had dipped below the waves. Fireman Dempsey McGowan, who had jumped into the ocean wearing his dungarees and shoes, was alarmed by this shell. "A couple of us figured right then and there, that was it," he said. The Japanese dropped a dye marker while the smaller corvette stood off at a distance. The larger ship made a circle around the area and Japanese sailors unleashed a few machine-gun blasts, apparently as a warning. Some feared the worst. "I couldn't describe how scared I was," John McBeath later stated. "We expected to be machine-gunned."

The ship then stopped her engines and drifted into the survivors. She lowered Jacob's ladders and cargo nets. "I was the first one they picked up," said torpedo-man Al Albertson. "Just luck of the draw, I guess. They threw over a Jacob's ladder and I climbed up it and stepped over the gunnel." As soon as Albertson reached the deck, he was greeted by one of the Japanese who smashed him in the head with his rifle butt.

Lieutenant Commander Fitzgerald was picked up and he took his place on the deck among his crew. Seaman Skeeter McCoy noticed that the skipper instinctively reached for a cigarette, pulling a waterproof tin of sea store cigarettes from his top pocket. "They had guards all around us, but people that smoke just automatically reach for their cigarette and don't always know what they're doing," recalled McCoy. Fitzgerald put a cigarette in his mouth and started to light it with the metal lighter he carried in the tin. "One of the guards hit him with a rifle butt and knocked him across the deck," said McCoy. "That's when I realized that this was war and it wasn't any fun!"

Lt. Kevin Harty came on board the ship wearing a pith hat he had purchased in Ceylon in January. "On reaching the Jacob's ladder of the Japanese vessel after treading water for a long while, I had a trying time mounting the ladder," Harty recalled. "On reaching the deck, a Japanese sailor rapped me over the head with his rifle and bashed in the top of my pith 'topee.' Luckily, the top absorbed any shock, but it messed up my hat."

As Gordon Cox reached the deck, he was hit by a Japanese sailor and knocked down. On deck, the submariners faced men shouting and waving at them in a language they could not understand. "Regaining my feet, I was punched forward toward a Jap with a rifle pointed at me with the bayonet mounted," Cox recalled.[4]

The Japanese sailor inspecting auxiliaryman John Pianka as he came on board found a piece of paper in one of his pockets. "Pianka grabbed that paper back from the Japs and threw it overboard," Chuck Ver Valin recalled. The excited Japanese had one of their sailors spear the paper and bring it back on board for inspection. "Pianka nearly lost his life over that paper," said Ver Valin. "It turns out all it was was some handwritten instructions he had made for Joe Price on running compressors."

One of the Japanese moved among the men, signaling to them to remove their clothing. Whatever possessions they had escaped with were now taken. The corvette moved to the largest group of *Grenadier* survivors, hauled them aboard and stripped them. The rubber raft with non-swimmer T. J. Trigg was pulled alongside the ship. After all the men had climbed on board, a Japanese sailor went over the side with a bayonet and punctured the life raft, letting it sink with its stash of cigarettes.

Virgil Ouillette was another of those who watched the Japanese destroyer moving around, picking up the sailors. "Minton was with me in the water when we got picked up," he said. "We were the last ones who went aboard."

In short order, all 76 men—8 officers and 68 enlisted men—from *Grenadier* were picked up by this ship. The *Grenadier* men were forced to sit upon a large canvas-covered hatch that was very hot from exposure to the sun. "It must have been some sight, all these naked snow-white men that hadn't seen daylight for many days, sitting on this hot hatch cover," Gordon Cox wrote.[5]

After more than an hour and a half of sitting on the hot deck, the men noticed some of the Japanese sailors returning with their clothes. The hot tropical sun had already started burning much of their white flesh. The Japanese guards on the forecastle each had rifles with bayonets affixed. With much screaming and gesturing, they lined up the American sailors and then allowed them to grab their clothing.

Most men grabbed whatever they could, often putting on someone else's shirt or pants. Little could they guess at how long they would each wear that set of clothing. Seaman Tom Courtney, who left *Grenadier* barefooted, was happy to find that Ralph Adkins had jumped overboard with an extra pair of shoes.[6]

In the early afternoon, the Japanese came by with a gallon jug of loose cigarettes that had been confiscated from the *Grenadier* crew. "We were each given one cigarette," wrote Al Rupp. "Only one was lighted. Each of us were allowed to get a light from the closest shipmate. I soon realized the cigarette was lunch."[7]

During the afternoon, the guards removed the *Grenadier* skipper and led him before the ship's captain. The Japanese wanted to know what other submarines were operating in the area. Although the captain had Fitzgerald beaten for not answering, "he received nothing of importance which he could transmit to Tokyo. Threats of being bayoneted and shot still gave him no information," he related.[8]

When skipper Fitzgerald was led back to his crew in the late afternoon, they could see the effects of his questioning. As the sun set that evening, the guards ordered the *Grenadier* crew to lie down. Many fell asleep from their exhaustion from the past two days of damage control, swimming, and sun exposure. Anyone needing to relieve himself did so in the large bucket provided by the guards.[9]

The Japanese ship arrived in Penang around 0700 on 23 April 1943. A short while after the ship had docked, the *Grenadier* crewmen were individually led to the ship's starboard side and were forcibly herded into a large bus waiting on the dock. The vehicle transported the *Grenadier* men to a Catholic school in Penang along a twisting and turning road from the harbor. According to Bill Cunningham, the men were not blindfolded, but taken on a bus that had its windows boarded up. When they exited the bus, they passed through a high, solid wooden gate. There were buildings on either side and in front as they moved through a small alley to the porch of a building. The enlisted men were split into two large groups and led into two large classrooms of about 20 x 30 feet. The floors were concrete and the walls appeared to be the same.[10]

The men lined up in the rooms as if at muster, shoulder to shoulder in two rows with just enough room for the guards to move through. Four guards wearing the uniforms of the Japanese Army remained in the room. "I thought they would probably feed us soon, take a head count, and report our capture to the International Red Cross, declaring all of us prisoners of war," thought naive 16-year-old Al Rupp. "Boy, was I ever wrong!"[11]

In the words of Seaman Tom Courtney, the school at Penang "began a living hell for the members of that crew." Chief of the Boat Buck Withrow would later agree of Penang: "That's where hell started." Torpedoman Riley Keysor concurred. "When they took us to Penang, they turned us over to the Army and all hell broke loose."[12]

Fitzgerald was told that his men would be fed soon after their arrival at the school. "Sandwiches had been put out on board the *Grenadier*, but because of the nervous tension and excitement, hardly anyone had eaten," he wrote. In the Catholic school, the officers were taken to rooms on the second floor where they sat on the wooden decks. "There were about four of us officers together and the others were in a different part of the girls' school," stated Kevin Harty. "I was with the captain and Exec."[13]

Some of the enlisted men had not slept in more than a day. The guards moved among them, punishing anyone who did not stand at strict attention. "If you moved or shifted on your feet a guard would hit you with his rifle butt," recalled Gordon Cox. Bernie Witzke occupied his mind by staring out the classroom's window. He saw "white flowers on a tree outside the window. They looked like Easter lilies." The flowers made Witzke realize that his family was likely enjoying Easter weekend back home.[14]

By dusk, some of the men were slumping. As it became dark, the lights were turned on in the classroom and the men were forced to remain at attention. Anyone who slumped was poked with a bayonet and forced to regain his feet. If someone passed out during the night, shipmates on either side supported him in an upright position. "We were clubbed for the slightest movement of body or eyelash until late evening," related Bob Palmer. "Then positions changed to hands over head, knees bent."

Dawn came and went on 24 April without food or water. The tropical heat began to fill the room and little strength was left in the men. The guards selected a crewman at random and punched him in the face while the others laughed. Trips to the head were allowed with three men at a time going. Al Rupp, badly dehydrated, scooped water from the toilet to drink while another man urinated.

Toward evening on the second day, Rupp's leg muscles gave out, forcing his friend Bill Cunningham and a gunner's mate to support him.[15]

The crew remained at attention through another night without food or water. During their third night, the three little shutters on the three windows in the room were opened. The light in their room was turned off. For the first time, they could see what looked like a greenhouse in a triangular grassy area beyond the porch outside. The crew saw two guards dragging a stumbling, khaki-clad officer across the grass toward the greenhouse. Two more guards were waiting in the greenhouse. As the officer entered the lit room, they could see that it was their own skipper, John Fitzgerald, who was thrown outstretched on a table. The guards doused him with water and began beating his wet body with leather straps.[16]

After witnessing this first public torture of their CO, the men found that their individual beatings or punches to the face were not as bad. They refused to show reaction to their guards. "It was a spirit of extreme disgust and just as strong was that spirit of survival which they had created," Rupp wrote.[17]

————

Lt. Cdr. John Fitzgerald endured his own private hell, secluded from his enlisted men. His first day at Penang was spent without food. By dawn of the 24th, Captain Fitzgerald felt "that old gnawing pain in the midriff." He was the first to be called down for questioning by the Japanese. In the interrogation room, he saw food spread out before him. "It was maddening to go to that questioning room and see the Japs eating bananas and sandwiches in front of us; let alone their drinking cool limeade and milk. No doubt it was one of their aims to get us to break down. It was very apparent to all of us that if they were going to kill us, they would have already done so."[18]

When Fitzgerald did not give answers that they wanted, no food was given to his crew. "Persuasive measures such as clubs, about the size of indoor ball bats, pencils between the fingers, and pushing the blade of a pen knife under the fingers" were used to try and make him talk. The sight of the coconuts lying on the ground outside his window teased Fitzgerald over the next days. One day, he encountered a guard who spoke Spanish and they began conversing. "He had lived in Brazil a number of years, but returned to Japan just prior to the war in the Pacific," Fitzgerald related. "All I could get from him was one cigarette. As to the coconuts lying in the yard, 'No peude, señor.'"

The Japanese worked on the other *Grenadier* officers as well. "We kept our stories straight because the captain and exec passed information back in Penang," related Lieutenant Harty. "We had a few points that we made sure that we would stick to and it seemed to work out pretty well." While Fitzgerald was given "special treatment" by the Penang interrogators, the methods used on the other *Grenadier* officers were plenty brutal. "They used bats, fists, any types of intimidation," Harty said.

Lt. Al Toulon recalled that there were generally two people in charge of guarding the officers. Toulon summarized the treatment the *Grenadier* officers endured.

> We were threatened with death in the questioning room and beaten until we passed out. Beatings varied from using fists on your face to sticks everywhere; rifle butts, down to using little twigs swishing across your cheeks until they were all bloody. In the questioning rooms, they went a little further. The usual treatment was just being beaten with clubs.
>
> A little variation from this at times—sticking pencils between your fingers and squeezing and putting twigs under your finger nails. Japanese kneeling position and step on your instep, and kicking in general. When you got up and were asked if you would talk now and you said, "No," they would beat you some more until you passed out.

———

The *Grenadier* crewmen were still standing on 26 April, their fourth day in the Penang classroom. After three full days and nights on their feet without food or water, they often slept while leaning against another man. Gordon Cox recalled:[19]

> While we were standing there, the Japs decided to amuse themselves. They made one line about face and punch the man across from you. Naturally, you didn't want to punch your shipmate, so they'd hit you with a club. Then, when you did hit him, they would indicate hit harder. Then they would hit you again. It became clear that they were trying to break us down physically and mentally.

For other amusement, the guards had the crew drop into pushup position on their toes and hands. The men were made to hold this position as the Japanese walked among them. When someone collapsed from exhaustion and could not return to the push-up position, he was kicked, beaten, and dragged away from the others.[20]

Bill Cunningham noticed that Gordon Cox wired himself to a slatted door with "what looked like an old coat hanger so he could drop off to sleep without moving." Cox had moved to the back of the room and found a piece of wire hooked to a stud in the concrete wall. "I made a loop in the wire, putting it under my arms and over my chest," he wrote. "That way I could hang there and get a nap until the wire started cutting in and woke me up. Then I would trade off with another short fellow standing by me. You had to be short for it to work."[21]

During the first few days at Penang, "they didn't work on any of us," said Skeeter McCoy. The Japanese were intently working over Skipper Fitzgerald. "Day and night we heard those bloodcurdling calls of pain and torture," McCoy later sadly related.

The routine changed for the *Grenadier* crewmen on 26 April, the day after witnessing skipper Fitzgerald's greenhouse torture session. Around 0900, a short, heavyset guard appeared. The enlisted men were assembled and told that they would be fed and then questioned. After more than 72 hours of standing at attention, the men were returned to their classrooms and ordered to sit. "When we were finally allowed to sit, we all crowded around the room with our backs against the walls," recalled Bernie Witzke. "I ended up sitting right by the door to the classroom with my back pressed against the wall, thinking that this would be a good spot."

The crewmen were issued straw mats to stretch out on, although they offered little comfort from the hard floor. Nothing in the way of food was offered to the crew during their first four days at the Penang school. Finally, on 27 April, food was delivered at 1700, but it was barely edible. TM2c Warren Roberts testified that the *Grenadier* crew had been "made to stand for five days with no food at all."

The interpreter who had quickly become known to the enlisted men as the "Dragon" appeared in their classroom in the late afternoon. "You will all eat now," he said. Soldiers entered the room with primitive gourd-like bowls. Each man was given a ladle-full of warm broth that smelled like some kind of fish soup. "Not a gourmet's delight, but the first thing to resemble food since leaving *Grenadier*," Al Rupp wrote.[22]

Bob Palmer found it less than satisfying. "Evening of fifth night, we got maggoty, wormy rice broth." Many men collapsed into exhaustive sleep now, broken only by occasional jabs from the guards. They were left to sleep or whisper until after nightfall that day. Rupp decided to keep track of the number of days he was a prisoner by scratching a mark on his left leg near the knee. He figured if he went deep enough to draw blood, it would leave a small scar that he could count. He was on day five.[23]

The guards also allowed the men to smoke one cigarette that night. Bill Cunningham found that smoking it made the men "a little high" due to their starved condition. Many held their cigarette until it was burning the ends of their fingers before finally relinquishing it to the butt can.[24]

Dawn of the sixth day started with guards in the classrooms, hollering and slapping people's feet with their sticks to wake them up. The Dragon informed them that they were going to learn to count in Japanese. The interpreter walked them through the lesson twice, making them repeat after him. Each man then had to give the proper number for his place in the line. Anyone getting the number wrong was slapped in the face until he pronounced it correctly. Radioman Lou Poss recalled that the guards gave them 30 seconds to count off in Japanese. They were then dispersed and told to fall back into line again. Anyone who did not fall back into line in the same numeric order was beaten. They were also instructed on how to bow at the waist, not at the neck. Incorrect bowing brought raps over the head from the sticks.[25]

Around 1000 on 28 April, an Army corporal entered one of the classrooms and stared intently at the *Grenadier* men. Suddenly, he turned and pointed to the man seated closest to the door, Bernie Witzke, and ordered him to stand and follow. Witzke found that his selected position of sitting closest to the classroom door had only insured his being the first to be singled out for interrogation. The men were prepared to offer false information to their captors. "When we were sitting on the destroyer's deck by the foscle, the skipper had passed the word that we were not to reveal the *Grenadier*'s operating base," Witzke recalled. "He said to say we were operating out of Frisco. So, I told the interpreter that we had departed from Frisco."

This name seemed to confuse the Japanese, who produced a map and told Witzke to show them where in the world "Frisco" was. "After the first four guys got through the interrogation process, the Japanese figured out that we were lying about things," he said.

About 90 minutes after selecting his first crewman, the corporal returned and selected F1c Virgil Ouillette. Witzke was not returned to the room. Unknown to those left behind, the ones interrogated were placed into a third classroom once finished.

Ouillette sat through the endless questions of where he was from and how long he had been in the service. "I answered the questions I could," he related. "They worked on me and beat the shit out of me." During the course of his interrogations, one of the guards grabbed Ouillette's arm and yanked his shoulder out of joint. "It was painful. They turned it around in front of me." After they had worked over Ouillette, he was dumped in the other empty classroom with Witzke. The corporal then returned to the larger classroom and selected another victim.

At mid-afternoon, the crew was fed a milky, watery soup that contained a few grains of rice in each bowl. In all, about half a dozen men from each of the two classrooms were taken away for interrogations that day. GM1c Fred Zufelt recalled, "I was mistreated considerably. When I asked an officer to repeat a question, I was threatened to be killed. They slapped me around quite a bit. It made them very angry when I did not reveal the information they desired."[26]

When EM1c James Dennis "Denny" Landrum would not reveal the location of other American ships, they shoved bamboo splinters under his fingernails and lit them on fire, but Landrum refused to cooperate. MoMM2c Pappy Shaw later related that when the Japanese could not get information from him, "They put my head in a window, slammed it down on my neck, and stuck bamboo straws up my nose and my fingernails." In the classroom, the men there could hear the interrogations' effects. "The screams of pain were very recognizable and worked on our nerves," recalled Gordon Cox.[27]

Yeoman Bob Palmer said that he was a cook. He recalled that the men were "taken one at a time to a room, the door of which was marked 'Art Room' and tortured by clubbing with flat of sword and round club. Matches were struck under fingernails." F1c Dempsey McGowan found that everyone "was treated just about the same except for the captain, who was treated worse." RM1c Lou Poss' interrogation was "so rough that I passed out for a time. They asked us what submarine we were on. I told them the *Goldfish*. I had been given instructions to tell them a fictitious name."

That night, the crew was once again forced to stand and look out their windows toward the little greenhouse. Skipper Fitzgerald was led into the building and placed prone on a table which was tilted and his arms and legs were bound. One guard held his mouth while another poured water from a gallon jug into his nostrils, allowing him only quick breaths through his mouth to get enough air to keep swallowing. "If he tried to get some air by turning his head, they would beat him," wrote Gordon Cox. When the jug was emptied, the guard in charge stood on the table beside Fitzgerald. He leaped up and landed with both feet squarely in the middle of Fitzgerald's stomach. "The gush of fluid that came forth from the Skipper's mouth and nose in immediate response was horrifying," thought Al Rupp.[28]

Grenadier crewmen who refused to watch were struck by the guards. Fitzgerald was forced to consume another large jug of water while his mouth was held shut, after which the guard jumped forcefully on his stomach. "They'd jump on his stomach and pound him in his belly," remembered Chuck Ver Valin. After the second round, the skipper was unconscious and was carried from the greenhouse. The crew returned to their mats for the night with terrible thoughts racing through their minds.

For *Grenadier*'s skipper, the torture was terrible. The knives shoved under his fingers caused excruciating pain, and Fitzgerald lost fingernails.[29]

> The pain caused by the pencils between the fingers on the right hand was so great that I did not realize my left hand was being stabbed with a knife. Only when I saw the blood rushing out did I realize what had happened.
>
> I was beaten severely by a club or two clubs as the mood struck the Japs. Simultaneously, two Japs would arrange themselves on each side of the victim, taking turns to see who could drive the hardest. Usually, one would be knocked down in short order, twenty or thirty blows doing the trick.
>
> I was then tied to a bench with my head hanging over the edge. The Japs would elevate the bench to such an angle that my feet were on a plane of thirty degrees above my head. They would then start pouring tea kettle after tea kettle of water down my nose, holding a hand over my mouth in the meantime. Every time I'd move my head to try for some air, a heavy fist would

bounce off my chin.

Following this, I would receive another club beating until I passed out. Upon coming to, they would try to get me to talk; if not, more beatings.

Fitzgerald recalled that "to the best of my knowledge Knutson, J. S., RM1c, and I were the only ones to receive the water treatment." In spite of the abuse being dealt out, "I think the men held up remarkably well." His beatings made him so sore that "it was almost impossible to move, let alone change position from standing to sitting or reclining even if able to get away with it. The three pieces of chewing gum I happened to have in my pocket went a long way to stave off the hunger, which was becoming more acute day by day."[30]

The crew received two hardtack biscuits on their second day of interrogations. By early afternoon, five more men from each classroom had been taken. A new, older guard with two gold teeth joined the rotation this day. He became known as "Gold Tooth Maize." Another smaller, younger guard became known as the "Snake." This youngster walked softly but could suddenly turn and strike a man with his stick whom he had not even been looking at.[31]

Just before dark this second day of interrogations, the guards delivered a bucket of sticky brown rice to the enlisted men and an after-dinner cigarette. The two classrooms had slowly emptied as men were interrogated and then moved into another room. Late in the day, eleven men were moved from one classroom into the other. In the ensuing whispering, the men figured that the third classroom must now be full and that they were the only ones who had not been questioned yet.[32]

The next day, Al Rupp was the third man taken from this room. In the interrogation room, he was slapped and beaten when he said his submarine was the *Goldfish* and that she operated from Pearl Harbor. After hearing more lies, the Japanese guards placed short, pencil-thickness sticks between Rupp's fingers. A cloth was placed around his hand, knotted, and a stick shoved under the knot. By turning this stick under the knotted cloth, it drew the victim's fingers tighter like a vice closing. The pencils began to separate Rupp's fingers between the third joint and knuckle. "By the third turn, I was sure my fingers would break." As the guards continued to rotate the stick, Rupp decided to answer questions with what he believed they wanted to hear. He was finally hauled back to the different classroom with throbbing fingers, a swollen face, and bloody scalp.[33]

When Bill Cunningham's turn came, one of the Japanese said that he was from the *Grenadier*, which he denied. His interrogators believed that a submarine sailor could do any job on the boat, including that of the skipper. Cunningham found that their phrase was, "Submarine sailor knows all." The Japanese beat him when they did not like the answers they received. Cunningham told them that his ship's deck gun fired 1,500 yards, but found that a gunner's mate had said it fired 15,000 yards. Pharmacist John McBeath said the submariners fired junk from the torpedo tubes during depth charge attacks to fool the destroyers, but Cunningham told his interrogators this was nonsense. "Everybody gave conflicting stories," he said.[34]

The men with higher ratings generally received more abuse. Chuck Ver Valin, *Grenadier*'s fuel king, was larger in physical size than some of his crewmates and received extra attention.

> They would take a piece of bamboo a little bigger than a toothpick, just fatter than a wooden match. They put it up my nostril about a third of the way up, about a half inch up into the flexible end of my nostril. The guy would put it up your nose and then snap it out hard toward his body. The pain from it—damn! After two or three times of him snapping the stick out of your nose, it would usually bleed. You'd get this awful, excruciating pain up through your nose, up past your eyebrows and alongside your head.
>
> For the fingernail treatment, they used some kind of piece of bamboo. One of the guards would grab your hand and hold it down flatly on the table. He would just shove that bamboo slowly right up under your fingernail. Things would hurt so bad that the next thing you knew, they'd knock you right over backwards out of the chair. It would daze you, but they brought you right back and sat you back up in that chair.

The guards placed milk, cookies, and coconuts in front of Ver Valin and said, "You want food? Talk." He was questioned thoroughly on his submarine's armament. "What the hell could we tell them?" he thought. "They had better pictures of submarines than we'd ever seen."

Ver Valin tried to lie his way through the questions. "I told them it was the first submarine I'd ever been on, which was a damn lie. I was on the *Gudgeon* for four runs. I just sure as hell didn't want to tell them that we'd sunk seven or eight of their ships." The Japanese called him a liar. Although Al Rupp and Lt. Sherry had also served on *Gudgeon* previously, Ver Valin knew they would not have given out such information. The interrogators likely surmised that a first class petty officer must have served on other submarines. "They didn't get nothing out of our crew," Ver Valin later stated, "not a damn thing. We had guys that were beat to hell but they wouldn't talk." After his round, he was taken to another classroom with other shipmates. "They'd haul your ass back there and leave you sobbing and hurting," Ver Valin said.

The Japanese also took great delight in abusing another of the big men, MoMM2c Pappy Shaw, a husky Texan who weighed about 230 pounds when first captured. On one occasion, he was beaten in the face 165 times with a bamboo pole. Shaw later related in September 1945 that he actually begged the Japanese guard to just kill him after the beating broke out his teeth. The guard instead slugged Shaw again, breaking his jaw. He was finally handed a toothbrush and bar of soap 45 days later to clean up his mouth wounds.[35]

Gordon Cox professed ignorance to some questions. "I didn't want them to know that I was on another submarine or had been in the Navy a year and a half or that I was at Manila when the war broke out," he recalled. For any answer they refused to believe, the guards struck him with a club on the arm between his shoulder and elbow. "This would paralyze the arm for a while," Cox wrote.[36]

While the interrogations proceeded, the two guards known as Snake and Gold Tooth worked the rooms. One of Snake's favorite forms of entertainment was making crewmen do what they came to call "The Devil Stance." The man was made to stand with his feet about 24 inches apart, go into a half knee bend, raise his arms over his head straight up, palms facing each other, and raise up on the balls of his feet. Snake circled him, tapping him with the stick on his calves when the bend was too shallow. Each time a man's heels touched the floor, he was swatted. After a short time, the nerves in a man's thighs and arms began to react and his body would tremble from stress. Snake would then administer several blows and knock the man to the floor. He then picked a new victim and repeated the process.[37]

This painful crouch always ended when a man's leg muscles simply could not hold out. "It was funny sometimes," seaman Gordon Cox remembered. "When they told you to stand straight, the muscles in your legs would start jerking and you would look like you were doing a dance. But it was very painful and turned out to be one of the Japs' favorite forms of torture." The guards also picked one crewman to climb on top of a low table in the room. Other men were forced to lift the table and sailor over their heads for as long as possible. "When their arms started to give out, the Japs would start swinging their clubs, trying to force us to raise it up again," Cox related. "Soon, the whole thing would come crashing down. The Japs would have a whale of a party beating everyone."[38]

As the days of internment at Penang passed ceaselessly, the crew came up with a way to leave some indication of their presence. "During those terrible days of interrogation, as we were allowed to pass back and forth to the benjo or the water fountain, we scratched our names in the wall or post along the route," recalled yeoman Bob Palmer.[39]

On a wooden door, someone scratched the numerals 4/23/43, the day that the *Grenadier* crew had arrived at Penang. Below the date, Tom Courtney recalled that men began scratching their names with a belt buckle. The list began with E. A. O'Brion, Ralph Adkins, Thomas Courtney, Miner Pierce, Charles Roskell, Gordon C. Cox, and Al Rupp. Other men scratched their names into the door or the wall near a window as the days progressed.[40]

Chuck Ver Valin simply etched in "Chuck" on the wall. "You just carved with a rock, a sharp stick or whatever you could," he said. "We didn't have knives. If you had a watch or ring, they either took it away or beat you to death. If they wanted it, they got it from you—whatever you had."

The crew half expected their carvings to be discovered and removed by their Japanese guards. They would be stunned to find that more than 60 years later, their carvings are still visible in the door and walls of their Penang prison.

7
"We Became Terrific Liars"

Despite all the abuse the Japanese interrogators on Penang rained down on him, Lt. Cdr. John Fitzgerald never cracked. After abusing him for a week, his captors received orders to send the submarine skipper to Japan, along with *Grenadier*'s executive officer and communications officer. On the evening of 28 April, Fitzgerald, George Whiting and Kevin Harty were given a bath and ordered to wash their own clothing. "Regret to state that because [of] a paralyzed right arm, Whiting had to wash my clothes and assist me in my bath," Fitzgerald wrote.[1]

Some of the crew who made trips to the benjo were able to catch a glimpse of their skipper. "I saw him in the shower where they were allowing him to clean up," recalled Skeeter McCoy. "There wasn't a white spot on his body anywhere. He was blue, green, yellow, and every other color."

While he was in the shower room, John Fitzgerald was able to leave a message on the wall for his crew. He scratched, "Keep your pecker up!" McCoy later explained, "When we were in Australia, the locals had this saying, 'Keep your pecker up, mate.' It means keep your spirits up, keep moving on. And so, during our internment experience, that became our battle cry."

No one was sure of what Fitzgerald had used to scrawl his inspirational messages but many believed they were in blood. "Whenever the Captain went to the head he scribbled messages to the crew on the bulkhead, such as 'Guard the TDC,' 'Keep your heads up,' and 'Don't tell 'em anything.'" Gordon Cox recalled: "On the wall was scrawled in something red—'Keep your pecker up!' I figure the skipper used that Australian expression so the Japs probably would not get the meaning."[2]

Fitzgerald, Whiting, and Harty were blindfolded, handcuffed, and flown from Penang to Tokyo from 29 April to 1 May 1943. Fitzgerald believed that they stopped at Saigon and then either Shanghai or Formosa en route. They remained handcuffed during transit except when kept overnight in cells and were fed only sparingly. After arrival in Tokyo, the *Grenadier* trio was brought into Ofuna in the back of a tent-covered truck after a cold ride of about an hour and a half.[3]

Blindfolded and handcuffed as he was led out of the truck, Kevin Harty heard one of the guards say, "Good bye, my friends." The *Grenadier* survivors later learned that during the afternoon of 1 May, all Ofuna inmates except Australian aviator Geoffrey de Lempriere had been transferred to the other wing of the building to make room for them. Harty recalled that Lempriere, captured at Rabaul, was "a very important Aussie wool businessman who received visits from Japanese wool men while at Ofuna. They were trying to keep in the good graces of Aussie business, I guess."

Fitzgerald learned there were 19 men occupying about a dozen rooms, necessitating some doubling up in the cramped cells. Breakfast on 2 May consisted of the normal meal of soup and rice. "About a teaspoonful of soybean paste—"miso"— and a small bowl of rice, constituted the size of it," he said. As the day progressed, the *Grenadier* officers saw another American POW.[4]

He was Cdr. Arthur Lawrence Maher, the former gunnery officer of the lost cruiser *Houston*. Maher came rushing down the passage well ahead of his guard, and said quickly, "Maher, Gunnery Officer *Houston*, get data to you as soon as possible." With that, Maher simply went about his business. "He was acting as an interpreter in the camp, there being no Jap interpreter in Ofuna," wrote Fitzgerald.[5]

Later that morning, Fitzgerald saw Lt. Cdr. Dave Hurt from *Perch* across the compound. "We were later able to get a little information back and forth by means of messages scribbled on scrap bits of paper left in the toilet," he related. "Hurt gave me a line on what he had been feeding the questioning officers, which we learned to call the QKs, short for Quiz Kids."

The three *Grenadier* officers were quickly indoctrinated into daily life at Ofuna. Prior to the first of May 1943, scrubbing of the passageways occurred about once a week. Fitzgerald, Whiting, and Harty assumed the task of scrubbing these passageways and emptying the benjos daily. This collected waste was then carried to a farmer's cart to be used as fertilizer in the fields. "On occasion, a bucket rope would break," recalled Fitzgerald. "As a result, there was quite a mess to clean up. Needless to say, some of the fertilizer found its way to those of us doing the carrying."[6]

Harty, Whiting, and Fitzgerald began a regimented daily routine on 3 May. After folding their blankets, they were lined up for morning count and exercises. Those who fell behind during runs were beaten with clubs. After their exercises, the prisoners were allowed to wash up in a single open-air spigot. Each man received approximately one teacup of rice with a teaspoonful of soybean paste and a cup of soup three times daily, with only slight variations on certain days.[7]

Questioning of the *Grenadier* officers began on 3 May. Fitzgerald told his interrogators that *Grenadier* was out of Pearl Harbor instead of Sydney. Whiting, Harty, and Fitzgerald shared information as best they could, trying to avoid conflicting stories to the QKs. Fitzgerald wrote:[8]

Our chief QK's name was [Sanematsu], a commander from the Jap Naval Academy class of 1923. He was, prior to the war, in the Naval Attache Office in Washington, and had been touring the U.S. obtaining all the information he could gain; even spent a year or so at Princeton. His English was fair. The interpreter that worked with him had been in the embassy in Washington, and had attended USC during his years in the States. This man's name was J[ames] Sasaki, a Lt. Commander in the Naval Reserve.

Questioning continued daily for quite some time [on] areas, numbers of boats operating and where, number of subs sunk or badly damaged. We became terrific liars and usually got away with it. On matters of commercial design used on merchantmen or universally known and data which could be obtained from *Jane's Fighting Ships*, we told the truth, which I believe helped us when we were lying.

Kevin Harty felt the "guards at Ofuna were very brutal in their treatment of prisoners. Everything possible was done to make living unpleasant. Speaking was not permitted by prisoners. Men were frequently beaten." Harty found Hirabaya "was the worst of guards; was sadistically brutal in beating prisoners. Hirabaya-san was nicknamed 'Shithead.'" Kubiya, PO2c "was also brutal and sadistic."

When the *Grenadier* officers arrived at Ofuna, there were two wings to the barracks, each of about 15 rooms with two of them used for storage. During May, construction of wooden frame structures—typical Japanese barns—was started. The Ofuna prisoner capacity was increased to about 92 rooms. Fitzgerald recorded:[9]

A new quiz room was added, a new bath was constructed, new goats' office and kitchen [was] enlarged. The gochos or senior petty officers were known among us as "goats." From Ofuna there was no information in or out. Strictly silence, literally "out of this world." Dave Hurt did receive seven letters from the States during September and October 1943. Must have been a mistake because he was the only one to receive any mail at Ofuna.

On 19 May, camp commander Kakuzo Iida had his prisoners line up "to do double time around the camp compound," related Fitzgerald. "The distance we ran was approximately 4 miles. Numerous people, due to sheer exhaustion, began lagging behind, resulting in them being beaten by clubs. It was not until Lt. Whiting fell unconscious that the running was stopped."

The *Grenadier* officers were put to work building a concrete wall between two of Ofuna's structures. Fitzgerald, Whiting, and Harty were not allowed any relief during the entire project, while the non-submariners were spelled by other prisoners from time to time. Two Japanese guards, Shinoda and Hirabashi, "took delight in directing their attention toward both Whiting and Harty in particular," recalled Fitzgerald. Both of his junior officers "were struck several times with a shovel because they could not keep up with the fresher men turning the concrete."

Cdr. Al Maher from the cruiser *Houston* later testified, "On June 1, 1943, Fitzgerald of the *Grenadier* was beaten severely for talking to another POW. I was beaten when I talked with another POW and once when I didn't remove my shoes while in the washroom."[10]

John Fitzgerald noted that in June, fighter pilot Al Mead tried to step in for Lt. Carlton Howard Clark when Clark could not carry on his kitchen duties due to injuries. The Japanese guards did not believe Clark was truly unable to work so they beat him "unmercifully with a club in the presence of all other prisoners."

Kevin Harty recalled, "I got to know Dave Hurt, the skipper of the *Perch*, as well as the other officers. I especially remember one time after a particularly bad beating at Ofuna when I was feeling sorry for myself. Dave Hurt passed my cell and gave me a short comment that raised my spirits."

Two months after the *Grenadier* officers arrived at Ofuna, they were joined on 29 June by a shipmate, RM1c Joe Knutson. He had been taken from Penang about 3 May and flown to Surabaya via Singapore. "In Surabaya, he was questioned by German and Jap radio and radar experts," related Fitzgerald. "When he wouldn't "give," he was starved and hung by his thumbs for ten days." Knutson's abuse did not let up at Ofuna. In July, a guard named Shinoda caught him stealing a hat full of rice from the camp kitchen. Shinoda brought Knutson in front of the other prisoners and beat him 27 times with a baseball bat–sized club.[11]

On 3 September, a TBF crew from the carrier *Yorktown* (CV-10) arrived at Ofuna. They were Lt. James Willoughby "Pop" Condit, USNR, gunner AMM3c Kenneth Oscar "Ko" Kalberg, and radioman ARM1c Gordon Henry Marshall. Their TBF had been downed on 31 August 1943, while attacking Marcus Island. Kalberg suffered a broken arm during the ditching, and Condit was wounded in the leg and arm by shrapnel.[12]

Fitzgerald would later learn that the submarine *Sculpin* had been ordered to find Lieutenant Condit's downed air crew. When *Sculpin* was later lost, Lt. George Brown from her crew eventually made his way to Ofuna and encountered Condit. He told the aviator, "We were supposed to pick you up off Marcus, but I couldn't locate your boat. Anyway, mission accomplished, but a helluva place to find you and not be able to do anything about it."[13]

On 15 September 1943, 1st Lt. Louis Silvi Zamperini and his B-17 pilot, Capt. Russell Allen Phillips, arrived. They had spent 47 days in a rubber raft and some 40 days in the Marshall Islands in a Japanese cell. During his first days at Ofuna, Zamperini was punched a dozen times for examining food that was being brought into camp. When he was taken in for interrogation, Zamperini was confronted with James Sasaki, whom he had known well while attending USC pre-war. "I felt like I'd taken a sucker punch to the gut," he later recalled. Zamperini, a former Olympic runner who had competed in 1936 in the Berlin Games, endured the abuse at Ofuna just like all others.[14]

Other prisoners arriving at Ofuna in September included Italian naval officers and enlisted men. As fall 1943 approached, Lieutenant Commander Fitzgerald, Lieutenant Whiting, Lieutenant Harty, and radioman first class Knutson had no knowledge of what happened to their shipmates. On 12 October, they found out when 24 *Grenadier* enlisted men and the other five ship's officers were marched into Ofuna. As Fitzgerald wrote, "Their story was one of much hardship, trials and tribulations."[15]

Penang: May 1943

With the removal of three *Grenadier* officers, the ship's former engineering officer—Lt. Harmon Sherry—had become the senior American submariner held in Penang. The *Grenadier* officers continued to undergo questioning. "There was a daily routine of beating for no reason except to please the guards, and when we went to the questioning room, we were beaten until we passed out," Lt. Al Toulon recalled.

The other officers with Lieutenant Sherry—Toulon, Arthur McIntyre, John Critchlow, and John Walden—were kept separated from their enlisted men during this interrogation period. The men remembered Fitzgerald's scribbled words of support, "Keep your pecker up!" One of the guards actually remarked in front of seaman Tom Courtney that their captain was one of the bravest men he had ever met. "Quite a tribute from an enemy," thought Courtney.[16]

30 April marked the crew's eighth day at Penang. Yeoman Bob Palmer noted that the guards made them perform embarrassing stunts this day—"like sitting on deck, hands on knees and staring rigidly ahead. All men put into a circle with heads between legs of man next to him. Crawl about cement deck imitating train and animals until knees and hands were raw. No baths." Gordon Cox remembered "one guard had everyone crawling around on the floor, barking like a dog, grunting like a pig, clucking like a chicken." When this guard ran out of animals he could think of, he started the list over again. In one of the three rooms, Tom Courtney was told to stand and sing for his captors. "He straightened himself out,

stood erect and in a loud voice, he sang 'The Old Rugged Cross,'" Cox related. When he finished, "the guard had tears running down his face and walked out of the room."[17]

By his 14th day at Penang, S1c Al Rupp felt that time was slipping by. "The floor was getting harder or the mat thinner," he recalled. In the evening, there was the cigarette and rice. As men were shifted from room to room, their roll call number was changed, making it confusing. By mid-morning on 6 May, the Japanese interrogators had questioned the entire *Grenadier* crew. When the last interviewee returned, there was speculation that perhaps now the crew would be listed as prisoners of war. The answer came that afternoon when a corporal appeared, selected a sailor and led him off for interrogation. As before, those questioned were returned to another empty classroom so that they could not warn others of what had happened.[18]

The second rounds of interrogations stretched into the next week. Seaman Gordon Cox later wrote of the first weeks at Penang.[19]

> We were told that we were not prisoners of war, but were enemy, and wouldn't be POWs until we reached a regular camp. We soon learned which guards were the bad ones and the ones that were not.
>
> On the way to the toilet, we passed a flower garden and some trees. After awhile, there were no flowers left or leaves on the trees. The men passing by would grab them and hold them in their hand until in the toilet, then eat them. We all had lost a lot of body weight. If we had been a rough looking group when we left the ship, now we were terrible looking. No shaves, no baths, no haircuts. Some of the men had gonorrhea when we were captured and it was getting worse. Some also had crabs that had spread to everyone.
>
> One fellow that had a very heavy beard sat against the wall and continually pulled the hairs of his beard out on the right side of his face, which ended up almost bare. The other side was a heavy beard filled with crabs. They were even crawling in his eyebrows. He wouldn't talk to anyone. We thought he might be losing his marbles. Everyone was showing signs of the stress in different ways. Most withdrew within themselves. We had no training on how to react to this treatment.

The *Grenadier* sailors learned against turning on the guards. Al Rupp lost his cool one day with Gold Tooth, who struck him hard with his stick and forced Rupp to take on the awkward squat the men called the "Devil Stance." As he stood in the crouch, another guard punched him repeatedly in the face and head.[20]

During May, Bob Palmer recalled that the men were forced to eat "hedge blossoms, stems and grass. We ate Listerine toothpaste mixed with tobacco for Mother's Day." Dengue fever and beriberi started to break out among some of the men. Sometime around June 5, the guards moved their prisoners in groups of four and five out of the classrooms to smaller cells. "There were small cubicles on three sides, with a small court-type opening in the center," recalled Gordon Cox. The dirt floors of the little cubicles had been built up about a foot from the ground with wood. Cox was locked in a cell with CEM Charlie Whitlock, EM2c Judd Hinkson, and FC2c Orville "Pappy" Taylor.[21]

Sitting with their backs to the wall, the four or five men in each cell could touch the other wall with their feet. They could whisper freely but soon ran short of things to talk about. After more than six weeks at Penang, there was little new to discuss other than what happened each time a prisoner was led off for questioning.

That afternoon, the guards let the men wander about in an area between the cells that looked like a little meditation garden. They gazed at the coconut trees that grew up from the courtyard, noting some coconuts lying about on the ground near their cells. In the evening, there was the usual meal of rice, which did little to ward off the continual hunger pangs. At night, there were no lights in this area of the school, so guards had to check the prisoners with flashlights. The *Grenadier* prisoners watched for the guards making their rounds and talked in between rounds. Those caught watching out for the guards were taken out and beaten for good measure.[22]

Bill Cunningham sat each day in his cell with his "knees drawn up and hands hanging down in front with nothing to do but look at each other." Occasionally, one of the men would be called to stick his head through the door so a guard could flick his nose with a hard bamboo rod. "If no nose was forthcoming, the guards came in and beat the whole gang," Cunningham related.[23]

Cunningham shared a cell with Joe Minton and Lt. Harmon Sherry. "Where there was no officer in a cell, there were four enlisted men in a room," he explained. One of the few times they were let out of their cells was for bath time. Men often had their watches or rings stolen from them, "but an Academy ring was shown some respect." While washing, Sherry dropped his Academy ring in a trough. He turned and handed it to Bill Cunningham to hold for him. A guard came by, noticed the officer's ring on Cunningham and proceeded to beat both Cunningham and cell mate Joe Minton. "Sherry should have kept out of it," Cunningham said, "but he said it was his, so he was beaten, too."[24]

The men learned more about each other in their tight quarters. F1c Dempsey McGowan had been placed with Cunningham, Minton, Sherry, MM2c Joe Garza Ingram, and F1c Joe Price. McGowan—nicknamed "Angus" by engineman Chuck Ver Valin—learned that Ingram's nickname "Chili Bean" came from his Spanish heritage. He also learned that Bill Cunningham shared his exact same birth date. Both men turned 19 on 10 June while secluded in their cramped cell.

S1c Skeeter McCoy found some comfort that he was at least put into a cell with other sailors from his home state of Texas. The other Texans off *Grenadier* were

EM2c Ben "Steamboat" Fulton from San Antonio, mess attendant T. J. Trigg from Austin, EM2c Lester Barker from Brownsville, RM1c Lou Poss from Anson, S1c Thomas Rae from Franklin, and MM2c Joe Ingram from Pharr, Texas.

S2c Tom Courtney was locked into a cell with MoMM2c Lee Shaw from San Antonio, Texas, and TM3c John Leskovsky from Bellaire, California. He recalled that sergeant of the guard Gold Tooth Maize actually passed some of his time with the men. "He would unlock the cell door and sit down and talk with us," wrote Courtney. "I learned much Japanese from him."[25]

In this cell area, men were questioned and tortured daily. The sound of a cell door being opened in the darkness led to fear as they knew that someone else was making the dreaded walk to the Dragon's little interrogation area. "The pressure began to show on the men," wrote Gordon Cox. "Their nerves were getting frazzled and their weight was beginning to drop. Days and nights passed with the limited food, solitude in the cells, questionings, beatings, occasional cigarettes, and daily exercise time in the garden area. The ones coming back from the last questionings said the Japs had so much misinformation, they didn't know what to believe." Persuasive measures, such as jabs from clubs during the sessions, were common. "The genitals were not excluded; any part of the body was considered fair game," wrote Al Rupp.[26]

Cox passed his twentieth birthday in his little cell on 13 June 1943. "There wasn't much of a celebration," he recalled. "I'd managed to save a few pieces of hard tack that they had given us to feast on."[27]

Perhaps the biggest mental challenge was the sight of the fruit in the courtyard just outside their cells. While sleeping, the men occasionally heard a loud thump as a coconut fell from the trees onto the courtyard floor. "We couldn't get to them," fireman Virgil Ouillette stated. "You could see them out the window, but they were just beyond reach." The temptation proved to be too much. "We fooled around with our door and found the latch to hold us in was very flimsy," wrote Cox. "We could open it. Checking further, there was a door to our left where we could get outside."[28]

One crewman finally decided to sneak out for a coconut. Upon his return, he found it very difficult to husk the nut from its shell without being heard. Chuck Ver Valin later explained how they managed to open the coconuts.

> With the husk on, it is difficult to tear a coconut with your hands and then you make all kinds of noise when you pound it. So, we'd have guys in another room get in a fight. The Jap guards would go over there and kick the hell out of somebody while we're over there pounding like hell, breaking that coconut. We had an agreement. Nine guys would split one coconut whenever we got one. Then the next nine guys got it and then the next nine guys. Well, a lot of them never got any of it.

The Texans in Skeeter McCoy's cell found that they could loosen a small screen on their cell enough for one man to wriggle out and collect a coconut. "We found an old nail and used a rock to pound the coconut on the floor against the nail to get through the husk," McCoy related.

One prisoner was suffering terribly from gonorrhea. His testicles swelled to the point that he had to cut the crotch out of his pants to relieve the pressure. At one point, he even traded his prized gold ring to a Japanese guard for sulfa pills. The guard returned with unmarked white pills which had no curing effect, believed to be mere aspirin.[29]

One guard was known as Baseball Joe for his proficiency with a bat. Occasionally, he would call for 20 minutes of push-ups or two whacks from the bat. "Push-ups meant staying bridged, so whacks were usually simpler," recalled Bill Cunningham. "If you moved, you got an extra or until you stopped moving." Baseball Joe had MoMM2c "Pappy" Shaw and Cunningham spread from the table on their toes to the floor with their hands. If they sagged, they were whacked. "Shaw got the shakes and collapsed, but I would not give them the satisfaction of moving," said Cunningham.[30]

The malnutrition had terrible effects on the men's bodies. MM2c George Stauber set the record for about 48 days without a bowel movement. As loathsome a fact as it was to document, the lack of bowel movements was just one terrible detail that the *Grenadier* crew actually tracked. "I only managed 26 days," recalled Bob Palmer. Torpedoman Riley Keysor suffered through 28 days before his body could perform its natural function. Lou Poss was second to Stauber with 45 days.[31]

The Japanese finally brought in long, low tables for their prisoners to dine on. "When some of us, not too smart, decided to use them as benches to sit on and spend our leisure time, the Japs took a dim view of that," Riley Keysor later related. "I still have black and blue marks on my butt from that episode."[32]

The only break from the maggot-laced rice and soup was an occasional cup of stew. Bill Cunningham felt that it "was so peppered that tears ran as it was eaten. Made of rotten meat."[33]

The men who had been heavier-set at the time of their capture now had loose skin hanging in ripples from their stomachs. Unshaven and dressed in rags, they began to look something like scarecrows. The malnutrition led to sickness and high fevers in some cases. "One man was unconscious for 10 days. We all thought he was going to die," recalled Cox. "The Japs would not give us any kind of medical help. The man finally came around, but he died within a couple of years after returning to the U.S."[34]

Angus McGowan recalled that cell mate Joe "Chili Bean" Ingram's command of the Spanish language helped them. "Ingram noticed this one guard with a cross around his neck. He began talking to him and found that the guard could speak Portuguese," said McGowan. "Ingram was Spanish and he spoke both Spanish and Portuguese, so they got to be friends." The Japanese guard spoke freely with Ingram, explaining that he had learned Portuguese while stationed in Brazil at the Japanese embassy. "He had become a Christian down there, so he wasn't quite as rough on us."

Periodically, the Penang commandants criticized the entire group of *Grenadier* survivors for allowing themselves to be captured. By 31 July, Al Rupp was very weak. "I lost a lot of weight. My ribs now showed clearly beneath the layer of skin which covered them. My pants would have fallen from me had it not been for the piece of rope that was holding them."[35]

Looking at the little scratch marks he was scarring into his legs, Rupp was stunned to see the count. The date was 1 August 1943, but by his self-inflicted calendar, the number of days for internment at Penang for the *Grenadier* crew now stood at 101.

8
Hell Ships and Hard Times

During the early morning on 5 August, the 72 officers and men of the *Grenadier* crew still kept in the Catholic school at Penang could sense that something was up. Guards appeared with machine guns and they were taken outside onto the grass.

"They lined us up in formation in front of the rooms where we were originally imprisoned," recalled Gordon Cox. "We were facing the center compound where three manned machine guns faced us. Most of us figured this was it. They'd gotten all they can from us; now they're going to mow us down."[1]

Instead, the Japanese commandant gave another speech of what he planned on doing with his American prisoners. "We were the dirtiest, ragged, stinking bunch you could imagine, and far too weak to fight or run," stated Cox. After this speech, the U.S. sailors were marched through the school's gates and herded onto waiting trucks.

The trucks drove them through Penang down to the docks. They were marched out in two rows toward a small Japanese freighter, the *Hie Maru*. EM2c Ben Fulton later learned that *Hie Maru* was an 11,621-ton former supply ship built in 1930. They were led up the gangway and down into the forward hold. The cover was replaced and the hold quickly became hot and uncomfortable.[2]

After several hours, the ship's engines began rumbling and they began to move. They were not fed before leaving camp and received nothing the first day in the hold. "When the food ration came, it was much more generous than we had been getting, steamed rice with some barley," wrote Gordon Cox. "We gleefully gobbled it up."[3]

After eating this food, men asked to go to the benjo. They were led out on deck and many were beaten while topside. "Before long, more and more had to go," said Cox. "It became obvious we had all got diarrhea from the food. The guard had to give up and they brought a couple five gallon buckets for us to use."

The buckets were placed in one corner of the hold, but they soon became full. The men tried unsuccessfully to get the guards to let them empty the waste. As time passed, the roll of the ship grew greater and the human waste in the buckets began slopping over the sides. The sailors could no longer lay on the decks to sleep, as the waste ran from one side of the compartment to the next, covering the deck completely. By the end of the voyage, however, some did finally lay down or pass out on the filthy deck.[4]

Bob Palmer could only remember of his time in *Hie Maru*'s hold "that terrible darkness and those damn huge rats that ran across our bodies." During the second day of the voyage, the guards passed out cigarettes and placed a tin can in the hold for their butts. On 7 August, *Hie Maru* entered a harbor and the engines stopped. Movement on deck could be heard for hours before the hatch cover was removed and bright midday sunlight flooded the compartment. The guards shouted orders and the *Grenadier* crew was quickly removed from the hold.[5]

They were in a busy port, which they soon learned was Singapore. Guards led the POWs down a gangway to trucks for a half-hour ride to their new camp. They were lined up again, ordered to count off, and then were marched into a large, barbed-wire-fence-enclosed internment area. Al Rupp recalled the day of arrival as 7 August 1943, his 17th birthday. "What a birthday present! I was at last of legal age to be in the service."[6]

The men were led before thatched huts built on stilts, where an English-speaking sergeant explained the rules of behavior. There were threats of ten men being shot if one tried to escape. Guards were more scarce in Singapore than at Penang but the lack of sufficient food continued to be a grave concern. The Indian troops in a compound adjacent were receiving more food than they could eat, throwing away the excess, but they couldn't give it to the Americans. The men were warned they would be punished if they spoke to the Indian prisoners.[7]

Lt. Al Toulon asked for soap, razors, blades, clippers, scissors, and other basic grooming supplies. The prisoners were told they would cook their own meals. In front of each hut was an open fire pit for cooking. The officers and Chief of the Boat Buck Withrow organized the crew, assigning the highest rated enlisted man to be in charge of each hut. Around 1730, the sergeant major entered camp with guards and summoned Lieutenant Toulon. He needed men to carry the evening rice, buckets, bowls, and pots. They were given a bag of rice to last for a week, and a few vegetables. "The hardest part of this was not using up the food ration too quick," wrote Gordon Cox. The *Grenadier* cooks boiled the rice in one of the pots the guards had left.[8]

They were also given matches and chopsticks for eating. "We learned to use the chopsticks to pick the worms out of the rice," said Bernie Witzke. Al Rupp sat down with Bill Cunningham, trying to use his chopsticks. "After three or four attempts, I laid the chopsticks aside and used my fingers."[9]

Much to everyone's surprise, the Japanese guards returned with the requested toiletries, including shaving supplies. The officers and leading petty officers took charge, ordering the crew to boil their clothing and to shave all the hair off their bodies. Harmon Sherry was the first to have his shaved. Cunningham noted that in contrast to his tanned body, Lieutenant Sherry's white head now stood out.[10]

"Almost everyone jumped at the chance to be rid of the bugs, but as usual, there was one or two that had to be forced into it," related Gordon Cox. "After we were all cleaned up, we felt like new men. During the clothes washing and shaving, we had a good look at how emaciated and beaten up our bodies were."

Finally able to talk freely about their suffering at Penang, the men compared stories. One man showed his hands, where wooden slivers had been shoved under his nails and set on fire. Another told of the guards passing a candle close to his face, burning off his eyebrows and eyelashes, leaving burn marks on his face. Some had the pencil treatment between the fingers and others had bayonets pressed against their skin until slight punctures were made.[11]

That night, the men climbed into their respective huts, laid down upon straw mats and slept heartily for the first time in months. During daylight the men could use the head in a slit trench and could splash their faces from a water tap near the guard entrance. The guard truck returned in the morning and the mess cooks were sent to fetch their daily ration of rice. They soon realized that the previous evening's feast had actually been an entire day's ration.

The *Grenadier* crew was notified that half of their group would clean camp each day while the other half went out on work detail. They were instructed to talk to no other prisoners besides themselves, to salute the Japanese flag in the morning and evening, and to line up whenever guards arrived. For following orders, they would be given food each day. Warren Roberts recalled, "The food was a little better and we got fed three times a day with rice and fish and Australian and English canned goods."[12]

On the third morning, five men from each hut were selected and marched to the gate where two trucks waited. "The officers were excused from work, as were the cooks," remembered Gordon Cox. Work meant survival. "If we worked, we'd get some food," said Angus McGowan. The trucks took the crewmen to an abandoned horse-racing track where some were issued scythes and baskets to cut and collect the weeds on the badly overgrown track. The remaining men had to kneel and pull the stubborn weeds by hand. Within hours, the corporal of the guard began slapping faces and returned everyone to their starting point, mad that too many small weeds had been missed. There was no food at the track, but just a ten-minute cigarette break. By late afternoon, the men had only cleared a 15-foot section of the track to the guards' satisfaction. They were assembled, counted, and loaded back on the trucks.[13]

The track workers awoke the next morning with pains all over from raw fingers, knees, and legs. The working party returned to the race track and saw how little they had accomplished. Men's knees became raw from kneeling on the hard ground again, and soon bloodstains became common on the knees. Some were slapped or punched when their little basket did not seem full enough to dump into the larger one.

While using the primitive head in camp, crewmen were able to sneak brief conversations with Indian prisoners across the wire from them. Chief Buck Withrow was made aware of conversations his men had with one little Indian prisoner. They waited to see if he was a spy planted to trick them into talking to other prisoners, a forbidden activity. "He came several times, giving information that was transferred to our officers," Gordon Cox wrote. "They gave him a list of the names of the *Grenadier* crew, there in case we didn't make it."[14]

The track-weeding duty wore on the men. "Many were just little stubs sticking out of the rock hard ground," wrote Cox. "They gave us no tools to work with." Cox tried to perusade a guard to let him use a little stick to dig weeds with, but this was refused. "If you missed one, you got the old rifle butt treatment," he recalled. "It wasn't long before some of the fellows' fingers were bleeding. It soon became obvious that this was not a work party to get rid of weeds, but an exercise to degrade and humiliate us, breaking us down more." Tired of digging his fingers until they bled, Cox found a two-inch narrow rock that he used to dig out the small, stubby weeds and smuggled it back to camp. When the Japanese guards eventually found it, however, he received a beating.[15]

The only mental distraction while crawling about the Singapore track was watching the Japanese Army training and running races on the track's infield. The Japanese soldier who finished last was beaten by his fellow soldiers and forced to the track again. "This must have surely made him a better soldier," Cox wryly recorded.

The entire circle was a mile in length and about 30 feet in width. At the pace that was being kept in thoroughly pulling the weeds, the men realized that there would be new weeds grown back before they completed the first lap. During the second week at the track, one man from the south noticed a different, thicker type of weed. The prisoners stuffed these weeds into their pockets and delivered them to the camp cook that night. The next day Al Rupp thought: "The whole day seemed to have some purpose now." The men picked weeds and stuffed the better ones in their pockets. The guards inspected the first group of men who entered the truck. When they saw the smuggled weeds, they broke into laughter and allowed them into the truck.[16]

That night, the previous day's "greens" had been added to their rice dinner. The concoction proved to be terribly bitter. "We could not eat them," Cox related. "So much for adding to our diet." Most of the men scraped the bitter weeds from their bowls. "The crewman who declared the green broad leaf weed eatable was not very popular for the next few days," wrote Rupp.[17]

Some of the *Grenadier* men began scheming up wild ideas of escaping from Singapore. Chief Carl Quarterman and others tried to keep the idea quiet, but Lt. Al Toulon soon heard of it and joined the schemers. Chuck Ver Valin asked to join, although he was told to keep it quiet. With their prison camp basically being on an island, the men reasoned that they could use logs behind their barracks to float downstream through the jungles of Rangoon.

"Lieutenant Sherry got wind of this and he and Toulon got into an argument," recalled Ver Valin. "Sherry had seniority over Toulon. Sherry finally quashed the plan because the Japs would take it out on all the rest of those who didn't escape. Thinking about it now with clear heads," he admitted, "nobody would have made it."

The little elevated huts in the prison camp were tightly packed with prisoners. Ver Valin shared his hut with Carl Quarterman, Max Wilson, Robert "Sarge" York, Railroad Leslie, Robert Evans, Jewell Embry, and Charlie Erishman. "We could see through the cracks in the boards and see boxes stacked in the room next to ours," said Ver Valin. "The room at the end was not used by the Japs." Determined to find out what kind of supplies were being kept there, the eight submariners worked on prying up the boards with their fingers.

Ver Valin recalled, "Every board was about four inches wide and eight feet long. We worked the nails out but kept them where we could replace them when the guards came." The smallest man, York, finally wriggled through and found cans of Eagle brand condensed milk, stores captured from the British. Using nails to puncture the cans, the prisoners enjoyed some of the condensed milk. "We had to put the empty cans back in the box and cover them with good cans," said Ver Valin.

The days slipped into September as the *Grenadier* crew worked at the horse track. Around late September, the sergeant major appeared in camp after morning roll call and announced that the submariners would be given a two-day rest period and a pack of cigarettes each. Rumors spread that perhaps they were going to be moved from camp.

On the second rest day, the crew was lined up as three trucks appeared at the front gate. The sergeant major told them to collect all of their belongings and then form two lines for departure. EM2c Lester Barker, suffering from a badly infected throat, was left behind for medical attention. Fire controlman Pappy Taylor gave a homemade knife to Barker. Bob Palmer recalled that Taylor "made the knife on the grindstone brought in from the dump at Singapore, along with a couple of old fencing foils." Barker later told his shipmates that the Japanese guards caught "Gunga Din," the Indian man whom the officers had given a *Grenadier* muster roll. "The little Indian would not talk," Ben Fulton was later told. "Our crew was accused of passing the message and our little friend Gunga Din was executed."[18]

The trucks hauled the *Grenadier* crew to the harbor, where they boarded armed transport ship *Asama Maru*—the converted luxury liner that transported *Perch* and *Pope* survivors to Japan in October 1942. Gordon Cox recorded the date of their arrival aboard hell ship *Asama Maru* as 24 September. The crew had been in Singapore for 51 days.[19]

The men were placed into a small hold that included bunks for sleeping. To use the head, the prisoners had to be escorted topside by guards—who eventually began beating some men during their return trips below. Al Rupp recorded the sailing date in a tiny hidden calendar as noon on 27 September 1943. The hold was hot with very little air circulation. *Asama Maru* traveled at about 15 knots. Guards provided a ration of thick rice and drinking water the next morning, the first nourishment for the Americans since leaving the Singapore compound.[20]

About a week into the voyage, crewmen were allowed topside in groups of four for 20 minutes of exercise in the fresh air. "On that ship, the chow was just about nothing," said Bernie Witzke. "I was six foot, two inches tall, but I eventually got down to 98 pounds." After a few days of exercise privileges, some of the guards began singling out men for beatings. "They had found out that we were a submarine crew, which all Jap sailors feared and hated, so they would take it out on anyone they could get ahold of," recalled Gordon Cox.[21]

As men were abused while going topside to relieve themselves, some chose not to do so. When Seaman Cox had to urinate, he began going to the back bulkhead in the hold and aiming for a groove near the hull, where it ran under the bulkhead and away.

Asama Maru refueled in Formosa en route to Japan. A day or two after leaving Formosa—on about the eighth day after leaving Singapore—the crewmen were mostly asleep around midnight. They were suddenly awakened by the dull sound of four or five heavy explosions. "There was no mistaking that sound," wrote Al Rupp. "One or more ships in this convoy had been hit by a torpedo."[22]

Then the men heard the familiar sound of depth charges exploding. By the time the depth charging finally ceased, the men noticed that their guards were appearing edgy. "Their attitude told us something had happened," Cox recalled. Food rations were cut considerably. Early the next morning, all hell broke loose. Around 0300, four Imperial Marines bounded down the ladder into the hold with other *Asama Maru* sailors—all hollering and acting like they were drunk.[23]

The *Grenadier* POWs were herded up onto the landing hatch. One Marine was particularly muscular, standing at least six feet tall and weighing more than 200 pounds. He went to the stairs and removed an eight-foot piece of railing that was more than two inches in diameter. "They made the first man in line step up to the edge of the hatch and put his hands above his head," Cox related. "This Marine with the rail took a swing with it, striking him on the buttocks, driving him off the hatch and into the bulkhead five or six feet away. There were big cheers from the Japs. They kicked and beat him back onto the hatch for another lick with the rail. This time, when he hit the bulkhead, he fell to the deck."[24]

This sailor was clubbed and beaten back into the hold and another victim was selected. The Marine swung the railing hard in a 180-degree turn—impacting each sailor's lower back or buttocks, driving the sailor into the bulkhead. Watching one of the first victims, 17-year-old Al Rupp was terrified. "So powerful was the blow, he could not stand. He appeared to be paralyzed and only with assistance was returned to the place he was summoned from."[25]

Railroad Leslie found the beatings especially tough. "Being tall and skinny by nature, not to mention a few months on rice broth, the blows probably hit the bone a little harder in my case," Leslie commented. Bob Palmer related: "The torture inflicted on that beautiful liner was terrible. I watched a Japanese 'screw' body sores off Glen Fourre's body with a broken swab handle—the jagged end."[26]

Fourre, EM3c Charles "Johnny" Johnson, and several others who were suffering heavily from the malnutrition at Penang and Singapore had developed large boils on their bodies. "When the Japs hit them, that damn dark, purplish blood and the yellowish, white puss in the center of the boils would pop out and ooze right down their legs," related Chuck Ver Valin. "The blood looked like it was black instead of red."

"They worked us over good," Virgil Ouillette recalled. Ver Valin nervously waited for his turn with the big Japanese Marine. "He was drunker than hell," he recalled. Watching the guys ahead of him take their beatings was tough. "You're thinking, oh no, there's only four more and then it's my turn. Now, it's just three. Now, it's two," said Ver Valin. "That's a hell of a feeling!"

Ver Valin's first lick caught him "right below the cheeks of my butt. The reason was, I raised up a little. A couple of guys before me had been hit high and they were laying on the deck with their damn legs twitching, moaning and screaming." Numbed with pain, he knew that he had another lick coming. This time, Ver Valin raised up a little higher before the rail impacted him and he was hit a couple of inches lower on his upper legs—almost halfway down his legs. "My legs just went completely out from under me," he said. "I had no feeling whatsoever. I went right down on the ground."

Moaning and writhing, all he could hear was the Japanese Marine screaming, "Get up! Get up! Get up!" He could not understand the words but knew from the upward gestures of the guard's club that he was being waved back to his feet. Ver Valin was unable to move, however. The Marine kicked him in the ribs and stomach before moving to his next victim. He collapsed into a pile of shipmates.

"I've never in my life seen a whole group of people, that many people, all moaning, groaning, and sobbing at one time," Ver Valin stated. "I just dragged myself over to my bunk and lay there for another hour or so moaning."

Dempsey McGowan tried to deflect the blow with his hands but only managed to be hit in the back and wrist. "That was a mistake," he admitted. "They grabbed me and made me hold a rail and whacked me again." Gordon Cox's first blow struck the back of his legs and knocked him on his back. Heavy shoes and rifle butts pummeled him until he regained his feet. "I saw him start to swing again out of the corner of my eye, but I never did feel it land." Cox came to, lying in the corner as the guards proceeded to pound all 72 *Grenadier* officers and men.[27]

During these beatings, one *Asama Maru* sailor who spoke decent English made a remark about *Grenadier*'s past torpedo attack success. "So, you're from the submarine that sank the ship off the Pilgrim Island last April," he said.[28]

Pappy Taylor had been suffering from an ailment aboard *Grenadier* which Doc McBeath had been treating with antibiotics. Once captured, Taylor was relieved of his medicine bottle. After time in Penang without this medicine, his condition had deteriorated and his infected areas swelled horribly. The infection spread and Taylor lost his vision. The Japanese guards on *Asama Maru* clubbed the ailing Taylor mercilessly. One blow burst the swollen infected areas on his body, splattering the area and leaving Taylor writhing in agony. Gordon Cox noted that the beating sprayed "blood and puss all over" the deck.[29]

It was more than Skeeter McCoy could stand. Momentarily blinded with rage, he came off the deck and lunged for the guard. "It was really a stupid move on my part," McCoy later admitted. "It was one that very well could have cost me my life."

Fortunately for him, the guard retreated, apparently content with the agony he had created. McCoy and others tried to soothe Taylor—who would remain without vision for some time. Bob Palmer could only imagine "the terror he must have felt in the darkness" from his blindness. "We rigged some rope for him to get exercise" and to use to find his way to a toilet pail. In spite of his serious condition, Pappy Taylor's body slowly mended itself and his vision began to return in time.[30]

"Only one crewman sustained more than two blows. He was an expert athlete before entering the service and still was very strong willed," wrote Al Rupp. This crewman was S1c Peter Zucco. "He was a short Italian kid, but stocky as hell," Chuck Ver Valin said. "He had been a football player and wrestler. They beat the living hell out of him because he didn't flinch when they whapped him on the ass."[31]

Rupp counted five blows before Zucco collapsed. "They whacked him with the clubs and when he was down, they kicked him in the guts and in the face," Ver Valin said. Only when Zucco was motionless did the Marines move to their next victim. Lou Poss recalled, "When you sat down you were beaten and when you stood you were beaten." Bill Cunningham found this to be "the worst concentrated treatment" the *Grenadier* men had collectively undergone.[32]

It took time for the men to regain feeling in the lower portions of their bodies after the guards departed. Some had lost bodily control and urinated in their pants. Gordon Cox tried to assist a shipmate but found his nerves so damaged he could only drag himself across the deck. His shipmates told him to drop his pants so they could inspect him. As Cox began to lower his pants, he passed out and was carried to his bunk to recover.[33]

After the departure of the guards, Railroad Leslie produced some Japanese cigarettes and passed them around to his suffering shipmates. Bob Palmer could never figure "for the life of me how Railroad got that far with cigarettes." This at least provided some small comfort. "I wonder how we kept our sanity," S1c John Simpson reflected.[34]

The next day, there was no food or water until after noon and all exercise privileges were gone. That night, the four Japanese Marines appeared again and selected another crewman to beat with the handrail. One after another, the other *Grenadier* prisoners were ordered over to the hatch and were driven into the bulkhead by vicious blows. Al Rupp was literally propelled against the steel bulkhead and knocked unconscious by the force of the railing's blow. Gordon Cox, still collapsed in his bunk, could not even stand without wobbling. The guards forced him to hang on to the handrail and face the bulkhead. "Every time he would draw the rail back to hit me, I would jump out of the way," he recalled. The infuriated guard forced Cox to get in the center of the hatch in a push-up position. "He brought the rail down a couple of times, knocking me flat both times."[35]

Cox crawled back to his bunk, "dazed and shaken." While the rest of his shipmates endured more beatings, he passed out again. The men writhed in their pain through the night. When the next ration of water and rice was delivered later, some found it was all that they could do to stumble over and receive their meager ration.[36]

Fortunately for the *Grenadier* crew, they would not have to endure a third round of beatings with the rail. The hell ship *Asama Maru* arrived in port the next morning and the hatch was finally opened. Fresh air rushed into the hold to stir up the smells of foul air, body odor, and human waste. The ship had been at sea more than two weeks. Bob Palmer recalled that *Asama Maru* arrived at "Shimoda Saki 10 October 1943."[37]

The next morning, the crew was ordered to rise and climb the stairs single file to the main deck into the morning sunlight. "We were forced out on the hatch again and lined up as before, with a lot of screaming and pushing by the Japs," wrote Cox. The badly injured *Grenadier* officers and men were herded down a passageway toward the gangway. "All along this distance on each side, the crew of the ship and their Marines were lined up with clubs in their hands," Cox recalled.[38]

One at a time, the sailors were urged forward to the gangway through throngs of laughing, screaming Japanese who beat them every step of the way. Some men fell down and found it almost impossible to regain their footing as clubs whacked them from all sides. "Watching men go through the line, it seemed that if you tried to run, they would knock you down," recorded Cox. "Then they would all jump in, beating you more. If you went too slow, that would also draw their attention." He simply tried to keep a fast-paced walk, but was equally pounded en route from both sides.

Each bruised, battered, and freshly bloodied *Grenadier* man made his way off the terrible hell ship at long last. The much-abused American prisoners of war could only silently fear what next round of hell awaited them in Japan.

9
"The Castle" at Fukuoka

It was 10 October 1943 when the 71 officers and men of the *Grenadier* crew were marched off *Asama Maru* and onto the docks at Shimonoseki on the peninsula of the Japanese island of Kyushu. The final beating they had endured while heading for the gangway was their official welcome to Japan. Things would not improve. A dozen armed soldiers formed the crew in lines of three and ordered them to march. Anyone not marching in proper formation received a slap, kick, or rifle butt. The crew hiked more than two miles to the local marine training base where they were further organized for future transfers. The commander explained what his prisoners could expect while his right-hand man interpreted his speech.[1]

"He talked to us for a long time, telling us how good things were going to be for us if we followed orders and didn't cause trouble," recalled S1c Gordon Cox. They would be expected to bow at the waist to every Japanese soldier or salute him. They must also bow toward the Emperor both night and morning. Reminders were also given on how to properly count off in Japanese.[2]

"Of course, we would be treated well," Cox wryly recorded. "All of this was pretty hard to believe since we had just been almost beaten to death." The *Grenadier* men were black and blue on their buttocks, backs, and legs. Cox speculated that some of the Marines present may have been on *Asama Maru* during the voyage.

The interpreter briefed them on daily routines, washing, and that they were not to wander beyond their restricted area. A truck arrived and delivered to each man a bar of soap, a blanket, and a few loosely packed Japanese cigarettes. "They told us we would have to work, but didn't say when or where," Cox wrote.[3]

They were marched into a single-story building. They could see straw mats rolled up and evenly spaced along the right and left walls. The men were ordered to stand in front of a mat and then the guards left, closing the door behind them. Three crewmen were used to help deliver hot rice, fresh water, chopsticks, a tin cup for each man, bowls, and hot tea. The guards came back to collect the bowls and one crewman was ordered out to wash them. For the first time in weeks, the *Grenadier* men were able to wash out their filthy clothes. Reveille the next morning was at the crack of dawn. The men washed, ate their rice and tea breakfast, and then were ordered outside.[4]

After roll call, they had to learn proper assembly for the raising of the Japanese flag and the playing of the national anthem. The first day of bowing to the flag did not go well and interpreter Lieutenant Sato spent time teaching them how to properly bow. "He summoned the chief of the boat, questioning him about the men's refusal to bow," wrote Seaman Al Rupp. Buck Withrow tried to protest that it was against the Geneva Convention, but Sato was not impressed. Withrow convinced his *Grenadier* enlisted men "to cooperate at colors as they raised their flag. Think of it and see it as the Stars and Stripes," wrote Rupp.[5]

According to TM2c John Leskovsky, the *Grenadier* men "spent one day at the transfer camp" before being called out for some to transfer. On the morning of 12 October, the 71 men were mustered before the Japanese officials on the marine base. From a list, one of the officials began reading off names of people who were to step forward. A total of 29 names were called, including all five officers—Harmon Sherry, Al Toulon, John Critchlow, Arthur McIntyre, and John Walden—and another 24 enlisted men. "They took all the officers and most of the senior petty officers," recalled TM1c Al Albertson. The only chief petty officer not called was CEM Charlie Whitlock. Only a few of those called forward were not the highest rated: F1 Carlisle Herbert, F3c Paul Russell, and S1c Pete Zucco. Some figured that those selected were the men on duty when *Grenadier* was sunk. "I never knew for sure how they were picked," thought Cox.[6]

This group of 29 was moved away to the Ofuna Naval Interrogation Center on 12 October. The *Grenadier* crewman left ill at Singapore, Lester Barker, would eventually join those being sent to Ofuna. They joined the other submarine survivors already interned at the interrogation camp, the four men from *Perch* and the four from their own ship: Skipper John Fitzgerald, Exec George Whiting, Lieutenant Harty, and Radioman Joe Knutson.

Lieutenant McIntyre, *Grenadier*'s assistant communications and commissary officer, found that Ofuna was much tougher physically than Singapore had been. "Soon after arrival, we were forced to run," he related. "Those that fell out were beaten. Many suffered from beriberi, body sores, and could hardly walk. This let up after two weeks. We were locked in our rooms at night. Had to call guard to go to latrine. Beaten on the butt when disciplined."

Grenadier Crew Transfers in Japan: 12–19 October 1943

Transferred to Ofuna: 29 Men (30 with Barker)

Albertson, Norman A.	TM1	Poss, Edgar L.	RM1
Andrews, Davis J.	TM1	Quarterman, Carl O.	CQM
Barker, Lester L. *	EM2	Rae, Thomas J.	S1
Barrington, Clyde W.	TM2	Russell, Paul D.	F3
Clark, Lynn R.	SM1	Shaw, Lee C.	MoMM2
Critchlow, John N., Jr.	Lt.	Sherry, Harmon B.	Lt.
Erishman, Charles A.	CMoMM	Stauber, George F.	MM2
Herbert, Carlisle W.	F1	Toulon, Alfred J.	Lt.
Hinkson, Richard J.	EM2	Walden, John S.	Gunner
Landrum, James D.	EM1	Westerfield, Charles W.	CCS
Leskovsky, John	TM3	Wilson, Charles M.	MM1
McBeath, John J.	PhM1	Wise, William E.	GM2
McIntyre, Arthur G.	Lt.	Withrow, William C.	CTM
Palmer, Robert W.	Y1	Zucco, Peter	S1
Pianka, John K.	MoMM1	Zufelt, Fred	GM1

* Detained at Singapore and later transferred to Japan.

Transferred to Fukuoka: 42 Men

Adkins, Ralph L.	EM1	McGowan, Dempsey E.	F1
Courtney, Thomas R.	S2	Minton, Joseph A.	QM3
Cox, Gordon C.	S1	O'Brion, Elwood A.	EM1
Cunningham, William M.	S2	Ouillette, Virgil A.	F1
Doyle, Charles	MoMM1	Pierce, Miner B.	S1
Embry, Jewell C.	MoMM1	Price, Joseph T.	F1
Evans, Rex R.	RM3	Roberts, Warren E.	TM2
Evans, Robert E.	SC3	Roskell, Charles	F2
Fourre, Glen R.	EM2	Rupp, Albert J.	S1
Fulton, Ben H.	EM2	Rutkowski, Henry W.	S1
Garrison, Randolph J.	SC1	Sawatzke, Lyle L.	F2
Guico, Justiniano G.	StM1	Schwartzly, John F.	F1
Gunderson, John H.	S1	Shoemaker, Dean B.	TM2
Ingram, Joe G.	MM2	Simpson, John E.	S1
Johnson, Charles E.	EM3	Snyder, George W., Jr.	MM3
Keefe, William H.	RM1	Taylor, Orville A.	FC2
Keysor, Riley H.	TM3	Trigg, Thomas J.	Matt1
Leslie, Raymond G.	MoMM1	Ver Valin, Charles H.	MoMM1
Linder, Charles F.	MM2	Whitlock, Charles H.	CEM
Loftus, Irving C.	F2	Witzke, Bernard W.	F1
McCoy, Charles H.	S1	York, Robert F.	EM2

Fitzgerald recalled that these runs around the compound were usually three to four miles in duration. Laggers or those who fell were severely beaten with clubs and fists until they got up and ran again. The *Grenadier* skipper noted that guards

Akiyama and Asoma took the greatest delight in beating the fallen. John Leskovsky recalled of his first days at Ofuna: "Here, a Jap guard, Sergeant Watanabe, knocked my teeth out of my mouth for no reason at all. He beat up my face terrible."

Some of the older Ofuna inmates took notice of the large group of submarines who arrived. AMM3c Murray "Mick" Glasser and his VT-10 squadronmate ARM1c Tom Nelson had reached Ofuna in late November 1942. Both *Enterprise* Avenger airmen had been captured after bailing out of their blazing Torpedo Ten TBFs during the carrier battle of Santa Cruz in October. Glasser was picked up by the Japanese destroyer *Makigumo* and was forced to kneel on the deck as his captors threatened to behead him.

Now an old hand at the Ofuna camp, Mick Glasser noted with interest the arrival of a group of Italian naval prisoners and the rushed construction of a new barracks during the autumn on 1943. "Something was in the wind," Glasser thought. "It wasn't long before about 30 new POWs were brought in. We were to learn that they were part of the crew of the USS *Grenadier*, a submarine sunk with all the crew captured. Between the Italians and the *Grenadier* crew, some of the pressure was taken off us 'older' residents."[7]

Within one week of the arrival of the 29 *Grenadier* men, they experienced their first death at Ofuna. Anton Minsaas, an engineer from the lost Norwegian ship *Madrono*, had been seriously ill with beriberi and malnutrition upon their arrival. He died on 18 October 1943 from neglect. Fitzgerald recorded that commandant Iida had taken no steps to hospitalize the critically ill prisoner.

Y1c Bob Palmer recalled that he "was questioned by a Jap Naval 'Gunrabo' (Nip FBI), Commander Sanematsu. He was educated in the United States; a graduate of Palo Alto High School and of Stanford University. He boasted that he was an attache in Washington, DC, on December 7th." Palmer would find Lieutenant Commander Fitzgerald to be a role model for inspiration. "The Skipper's display of 'guts' pulled many a man through more than once." Bob Palmer later related that at Ofuna he would first face "another nine months of hell."

————————

Forty-two *Grenadier* enlisted men remained at the Japanese Marine base on Kyushu after the first 29 were called away to Ofuna. "When we got there, they gave us food and treated us pretty decent," recalled Chuck Ver Valin. "But when we began taking off our clothes for our first bath, the Japanese saw how everyone's ass, backs and the backs of their legs were all marked where they had beaten us. That did it, because from then on, they were taking their turns on us, too."

When the Ofuna bunch departed on 12 October, the Japanese picked five other *Grenadier* prisoners to go on work detail that day. "We were marched to what appeared to be an old riverbed. There was a bank on either side, about twenty feet high," wrote Gordon Cox. One guard stood at the top of the hole, while another shoveled gravel for the road bed that other prisoners were building. The remaining three took turns walking up planks to the top of the hole. Each man balanced a long pole on his shoulders that held full baskets of gravel at each end. "The pole was springy, so if you walked with a normal gait, the basket would begin to bounce," Cox related.[8]

One man caused the baskets to bounce so much that he fell from the planks back into the hole, gravel baskets, pole, and all. The guards at the bottom beat and kicked him until the baskets were refilled. "If the baskets weren't full and running over, he would get a whack with the rifle butt," recalled Cox.

Bill Cunningham recalled that work "on the rock piles was during the day from sunrise to dark. There was a fanatic on physical education at the camp who ran the men before breakfast and had them beaten if they dropped behind."[9]

"The food was pretty good since we ate the same as the rest. We had no medical attention. The treatment was pretty rough here. They ran us up and down the highway with no shoes on in front of people who threw stones as us," related torpedoman Warren Roberts.

"At the naval barracks, conditions were fair although there was some mistreatment," recalled S2c Tom Courtney. In a secret diary written on scrap paper, Courtney wrote that by the time he left this compound on 19 October, his weight was down to 125 pounds.[10]

The *Grenadier* sailors were lined up on 19 October after their rice breakfast and marched to a train. Anyone caught peeking out of the window blinds was beaten. The old train clanked slowly across Kyushu until after dark. They were ordered off the train and lined up to count off in what looked like a large railroad switching yard, filled with many guards. The prisoners had been moved to a special industrial work camp known as Fukuoka Branch Camp No. 3. "We were unloaded at what seemed to be a large mill with many people coming and going," recalled Gordon Cox. "They walked us away from the mill, through what seemed to be a residential district. Shacks were made of corrugated metal and other scraps."[11]

They marched more than a mile, up a steep hill prodded with rifle butts. They finally reached a white industrial building several stories tall. The *Grenadier* men quickly dubbed this large concrete building the "castle on the hill." Cox found it to be "an ominous-looking place. It turned out to be worse than that."

Inside, the men were issued clothing to replace their tattered rags. The Japanese handed each man a thin, light green pair of pants, a burlap-type jacket, a Japanese Army uniform and a large, heavy wool overcoat captured from the Russians many years before. For underwear, they were given traditional Japanese G-string cloths, to be tied around the waist with the cloth pulled up between their legs.

"They also gave us a couple of blankets, a razor with one blade, a toothbrush, and a small wooden box with a sliding lid that was our lunch box," recalled Cox.

They were also issued a type of tennis shoes that had the big toe separated from the other toes and were hooked in the back once the foot was slid in. "I couldn't get my foot in far enough to hook them," he wrote. "They were so tight they hurt my feet. I ran around for months with my heel protruding out the back."[12]

The *Grenadier* crewmen were ordered to climb to the fourth, top, floor of the "castle." At the top step, they faced two doors. Rupp felt a sudden anxiety before entering these doors. To him, it seemed very cold and different. "With that thought on my mind, I placed my first foot past the threshold into hell!" he related.[13]

The men were ordered to put on their Army uniforms and fall into formation outside of their cells. Their interpreter told them they were lucky for being allowed to live and work in the great country of Japan. "We were interviewed by a Japanese Army Major by the name of Rata," Warren Roberts said. "He told us we were prisoners of war and not to forget our social position; that we were brought there to work and work only. We were sent to work the day after we arrived."

Bill Cunningham found the first medical attention for each man consisted of "one tablespoon of cod liver oil to build him up." The uniforms included a patch sewn on to each to identify the prisoners. When the first Allied prisoners had arrived at Fukuoka No. 3, the Japanese began numbering at one. The *Grenadier* men realized that there had been at least 500 Allied prisoners in this camp before them. A Japanese soldier wrote an identification number on each man's patch—a number they were to keep throughout their stay. They were also instructed how to properly pronounced their designated number in the Japanese language.[14]

Charles Doyle was 513, Glen Fourre was number 516, Bernie Witzke was 520, George Snyder was 522, Chuck Ver Valin was 523, Railroad Leslie was 526, Gordon Cox was 528, Pappy Linder was 544, Dempsey McGowan was 546, steward's mate Justiniano Guico was 553, and so on. The newly arrived prisoners were dressed in their new heavy Army coats, which helped to hide their skinny frames, and their individual photos were taken for identification.[15]

In the compound, the men were placed into large cells along a long corridor on the upper floor. The floor's single benjo had a large circular wash sink and 11 stalls in working order. The first 22 men were put in a room that contained two racks built up about 30 inches off the floor. The racks, running the length of the room, were made of wood and contained woven straw mats. Eleven were assigned to each side. The rest of the crew was distributed in similar fashion in a room across the hall. Two men were assigned to fetch the evening meal of rice and warm tea.[16]

The interpreter had explained to the *Grenadier* prisoners that they would work every day unless the camp doctor declared someone too ill to work. The "castle on the hill" was packed with prisoners, ranging from the American submariners to captured Javanese. "Men started dying about as soon as we arrived there," recalled Gordon Cox. "They were continually bringing more people into the camp to keep the number at about 1200."[17]

The morning of 21 October was the first work day for the new *Grenadier* prisoners of Fukuoka No. 3. They would work at the Yawata Steel Mill some three miles away. They would receive morning rice, a lunch box for the noon meal at work and would get an evening meal. The work detail assembled in the courtyard in front of the guardhouse and was marched down the long hill to the steel mill. They marched past houses and shops, where people shouted at them in Japanese.

Upon arrival at the mill, each submariner was assigned to a work detail. Some worked outside in the weather, hauling coal. Bernie Witzke and F2c Lyle Sawatzke were put to work on a riveting gang in the Yawata factory. Sawatzke, a 22-year-old from Nebraska, was a powerful man who had received amateur boxing awards during high school and worked as a carpenter before joining the Navy.

Al Rupp, Tom Courtney, Bill Cunningham, Angus McGowan, and F1c John Schwartzly were assigned to work with five men from Java in the casting area. They were given a hammer gun and two chisels. Their foundry work involved forming ships' guns and various steel parts in large molds with molten metal. "We had to pour the steel in the molds and then they'd bake them a long time in the big oven," said McGowan. "When they brought them out, we had to chip the mold off to get down to the bare metal for machining it." McGowan found the smelting work was brutal. "We would stand up there in that heat and throw 60-pound weights of iron nuggets into the furnace to be melted down," he said.[18]

"I got what they called the pipe shop," recalled Gordon Cox, who found that he, Bill Cunningham, and about a dozen shipmates were at least fortunate to be working inside. "We were inside a large, galvanized metal building open on one end, but sheltered from the wind and rain. Usually, there was a small furnace or two going that put a little heat in the building."[19]

For lunch, the prisoners were allowed to drink water and eat their firm, cold rice balls. When their shift ended, the men returned their tools and were marched back to the concrete "castle" building. There, they were led to bathing tanks on the first floor and they stripped. There was a scum on the steaming water, but it was their first hot bath in six months. After bathing, they returned to eat their evening rice. At evening roll call, anyone who forgot his number was slapped in the face.

There was punishment at the factory for anyone who did not properly clean a casting or follow orders. The work could have been bearable if not "for the starvation that was with us continually and the cruelty," thought Cox. "The castle on the hill was such a horrible place that I hated to leave the shop and go back there at night. Every night as we came in from the shop, we had to pass in front of the guard house. There was always some poor soul there being beaten or on his knees with a stick behind them. I came to the conclusion that they always liked to have someone on display like that as a warning to everyone," wrote Cox.[20]

The Yawata mill guards, dubbed civilian pushers by the *Grenadier* men, were mainly ex-soldiers discharged due to injury or some other reason. During the second week, Al Rupp smuggled a pencil from the factory and days later he acquired some wrapping paper from a trash bin. "Not only could I make a decent calendar now, but I could also keep a diary," he wrote. With Bill Cunningham watching for guards, he would hide his little paper diary and calendar under his bunk space under a cross member that supported the decking.[21]

Seaman Tom Courtney managed to keep a little diary in a hand-made notebook measuring 2.25" by 2.5" in size. During his first two months at Fukuoka, his notes were brief, indicative of how little time he had to write without being caught:[22]

10/24	Received first candy
11/25	Mother's birthday
12/15	Moved to new barracks, chow damn low—men starving
12/24	Yasmay for Christmas—received 2 oranges—Chow lower, 10 men died

By the end of December, Courtney had dropped in weight to 115 pounds, a ten-pound loss in just over two months. When the first payday came in December, the men found that they were short-changed. "At 10 sen a day, I should have 4 yen 60 sen," wrote Al Rupp. He found that 60 sen had been deducted. In the camp store, he had enough to buy five packs of cigarettes and two powdered sugar cookies that looked like lady fingers. "Bitterly disappointed, I left and went to my room. The sweet taste of the cookies lasted just a few seconds," he wrote. "The gall in my throat caused by my disappointment cancelled any trace of their sweetness."[23]

Disgusted, Rupp slowly performed his work the next day. The civilian foreman summoned two civilian workers and ordered them to punish Rupp. "They beat me with their fists in the head and face area. After each one delivered several blows, the guard ordered them to stop and me to return to my work space," he wrote.[24]

Gordon Cox found that beatings were a daily routine, both at the Yawata mill and in the Fukuoka barracks. "One thing I did learn early was that if you showed the slightest bit of defiance, in your face or eyes, you were in for a beating," he wrote. "The Japs had been taught that they were superior to all other races."[25]

Chuck Ver Valin, quick to learn how to count off in proper Japanese, was appointed as a section leader for *Grenadier* workers. When the Japanese guards entered the barracks, they shouted for the men to line up and count off. "Sometimes, we were up for two or three hours at night because some jackass forgot his number," Ver Valin said. As soon as the count was blown, the guard would get in the guilty prisoner's face and scream at the men to start over again.

"Now, you know that guy's nervous at this point because he's got that guard blowing right in his face," he related. The count would sometimes be thrown off by a man going to sick bay or dying. If the prisoner whose number fell next failed to change his number to make up for the missing man, the guards were all over him.

"The guard would take his rifle butt and jam him right in the belly or wrap him upside the head with his fist," Ver Valin said. "As soon as the man got back up, the guard would holler to count off again. Guys would get mad at the guy getting hit because he couldn't remember his damn number."

As winter began to set in, other prisoners about the camp died from the conditions and malnutrition. "Every day seemed a week long," Cox recalled. "The cold seemed to penetrate right to the bones. Even the hot bath that we got was so hot it seemed to almost scald the skin, but didn't warm you all the way through."

The move to a new camp in mid-December did not improve conditions. The new facility, built specifically for the new prisoners, was not completely finished. "We were crowded into the barracks, with hardly room to lie down," Cox recalled. He learned that the Japanese Army furnished the mill guards, while Yawata Steel Mill provided housing, clothes, and food for their inmate workers.[26]

This camp, surrounded by a high fence, was built near a large coal-fired power plant with six large smokestacks standing on the edge of Moji Bay. A railroad ran in front of the camp. A wide street ran through the middle of camp, with four barracks to the left side and six to the right. Inside the barracks building's center aisle was a pot-bellied stove with a crudely built table on either side of the stove. A kitchen and bathhouse were at the far end of this street that ran through camp.

The bathhouse had two large tubs—one for Japanese guards and prisoner officers, the other to serve the needs of more than 1,000 POWs. "The other tub for the prisoners was rotated by barracks number, so if you were last in line, the water was so dirty you could almost walk on it," Cox recalled.[27]

If men working on the coal-mine detail bathed ahead of the others, the water was particularly filthy. The *Grenadier* prisoners soon became annoyed with some of the Indian prisoners, who abused the bath privileges. "Some of them washed their clothes in the tub," Cox wrote. "This was forbidden of the rest of the prisoners." Chuck Ver Valin recalled that the Indian prisoners "never took off their loincloths to bathe. They didn't want anyone to see their privates." When the submarine POWs became tired of this and their desire to wash their clothes in the community tub, a fight ensued with the Indian prisoners. "They wouldn't bathe with us anymore after that," said Ver Valin.[28]

At the mill's pipe shop, about 20 POWs hammered, cut, and bent pipes via the furnace heat. The civilian pushers were rough on their inmate helpers. Equally troublesome for the POWs were some Americans who cozied up to the Japanese for special treatment. Gordon Cox was beaten by a traitorous, heavyset prisoner one day for not working hard enough. "This guy was a civilian worker on Wake Island when he was taken prisoner in 1942," Cox recalled. "He had turned against his fellow Americans to suck up to the Japs for extra food. When I told him what I thought of him, he hit me as hard as he could. I got two black eyes and a broken nose. I didn't fight back. He outweighed me about 100 pounds."

With two Japanese guards present at the time of the beating, Cox later realized that "the traitorous rat had planned it that way to make himself look better in the eyes of the Japs." Back in camp, word of Cox's broken nose was delivered to a large, former North China Marine known as Moose. Moose delivered a message to the turncoat POW "that if anything like this ever happened again, he would not survive it. That was the end of it."[29]

Seaman Skeeter McCoy also worked in the pipe shop, filling the pipes with sand and packing them to be sent to the turn tables. He became friends with a shipfitter, SF2c Charles M. "Ripper" Collings from the cruiser *Houston* who was an experienced welder. "Tell them you can weld," Collings urged McCoy one day. "I can teach you the basics." McCoy took the offer and spent two weeks learning the fine art of welding. Collings told the guards that his buddy was a little rusty and needed some refresher training. In short order, the pair became the shop's chief welders, offering McCoy the chance to move into a more preferred work role, welding flanges onto pipes. "Purposefully, we would leave stops and carbon in some of the pipes so that they would fail inspection and be sent back for rework," McCoy recalled of their sabotage efforts. "We liked to throw a few wrenches in the machinery to hinder the Japanese war efforts."

The prisoners worked on Christmas 1943, but did find that the Japanese New Year was a major holiday. The factory shut down for one day and the prisoners enjoyed hot baths, a pack of cigarettes, and two sweets.

Without body fat, the *Grenadier* men found the winter of early 1944 almost intolerable. Tom Courtney was down to 108 pounds after four months at Fukuoka. Like the others, Courtney did what he could to improve his food rations, even finding that cough medicine helped flavor the bland daily rice. When men pleaded that more food would help them work harder, guards told them they did not care if the Allied POWs died or not. The inevitable illnesses such as beriberi set in during January. Large, ulcerous sores began showing up on men. Those severely ill were put into the hospital building at Fukuoka.[30]

Stealing from the Japanese became a way of life. Chuck Ver Valin recalled Skeeter McCoy was often punished. "He'd get caught stealing salt. He'd steal peanut oil," Ver Valin said. "McCoy got beat more than any other crew member in Japan. Anything he could get ahold of, he'd swap it for something."

Al Rupp went to great lengths to feign illness to get out of factory work. During January, he even intentionally broke his arm with a chisel at the mill's casting shop. In pain, he then climbed a ladder and faked a fall on that arm. Cradling his swollen left arm, he was marched back to Fukuoka to see the camp doctor. He was taken off work detail and he tried to stretch out his pain as long as he could to avoid duties.[31]

Bill Cunningham came down with a fever soon after Rupp "broke" his arm. Diagnosed with pneumonia, Cunningham lay in the hospital for eight days.

There, he witnessed a Javanese prisoner who had stabbed himself in the throat with a nail file, ripping his jugular vein. "He was put in the bed next to me and died in ten minutes, after an excessively bloody session," Cunningham recalled.[32]

About the time Cunningham was placed in the hospital, *Grenadier*'s officer mess attendant T. J. Trigg was put on sick leave with severe dysentery. He was a large man for submarine duty. "He was always the first target the guards picked on," wrote Rupp. "It gave them a sense of superiority when they could beat him to his knees, or humiliate him in any way."[33]

Rupp worked out a plan with this mess cook to steal extra bread rations. Guards, noticing that bread had been disappearing for a week, beat Trigg severely until he confessed that Rupp was stealing. They quit kicking and punching Trigg and beat Rupp in the head with a strap and fists until the sailor slumped to the floor.[34]

Even after revealing where he had hidden the bread under the benjo floor, Rupp's guards kicked his shins and others kneed his groin. He was clubbed until he soiled his pants. After shipmates helped clean and wash him, Rupp was taken to the guardhouse and made to kneel for two days with only one cup of water.[35]

While some tried to escape work by a variety of methods, most suffered through their daily ordeal as best they could. "I was on the sick list a couple of times, but I stayed and did my work," Chuck Ver Valin stated. "There was a time when I had a fever of 103.5 degrees and I had malaria, but I still went to work every stinkin' day. I had no desire to be in the hospital, sitting around feeling sorry for myself."

Ver Valin's bunkmate was EM3c Johnny Johnson, a husky, six-foot-one-inch-tall man of 190 pounds. During his ordeal at Fukuoka, illness and malnutrition caused him to drop nearly 70 pounds. He was concerned as the illnesses began to claim some of his shipmates. "They could tell you what was wrong with you," Johnson recalled, "but it always boiled down to the fact that you needed more food."

By February 1944, Fukuoka prisoners were dying on a regular basis from their illnesses and malnutrition. StM1c Justiniano Guico, the only Filipino officers' steward, was the first man from *Grenadier* to die from pneumonia. Weighing only about 140 pounds and standing about 5' 4", Guico at age 37 was the oldest crewman from *Grenadier*. In his diary, Tom Courtney recorded the date as 4 February 1944. Gordon Cox had talked to Guico on many occasions. "He told me he would live longer on this diet than the rest of us, as he was accustomed to it. His death really surprised me, as I had believed what he told me."[36]

Chuck Ver Valin was troubled by the abuse Guico received. "They beat the hell out of that guy because he had real high cheek bones and they used to call him 'Chink.' They said he was part Chinese, but he wasn't. Hell, he was Filipino."

With their rice ration cut, the camp prisoners were on a maximum of 700 grams per day. "In February of 1944 we were given a Canadian Red Cross package, each package to be used between two men," related Warren Roberts. The camp commandant finally released one Red Cross parcel to be split between every two men on 6 February. They contained canned meat, a chocolate bar, a tin of butter, spread, two packs of American cigarettes, salt and pepper, and other condiments.

"Taking a hot bath then going into a cold barracks was just inviting pneumonia," Al Rupp wrote. "There was never any fuel for the barracks stove, which would have done little to warm the place, even if there was fuel. Before the end of the month, we lost our second shipmate."[37]

Pappy Linder, who had been a leader aboard *Grenadier*, died less than three weeks later. "Pappy Linder upset me pretty bad when he passed away because he was a big, husky guy," recalled Gordon Cox. "He was the type of guy you thought could outlast everybody else and he was one of the first to go."

Some felt Linder had lost the will to live. "His biggest problem was that he was married and they had kids," Chuck Ver Valin stated. "He was so worried about who in the hell was going to take care of them while he was gone. He worried about it night and day." Ver Valin tried to alleviate his shipmate's concern about his Michigan family. "Look," he said, "if she's on welfare, she's living a thousand percent better than you and nobody's going to let her starve to death." Ver Valin felt his pep talk did no good, because Linder "had it in his mind and it was dragging him down. As a matter of fact, if you look at his POW picture, you can tell from looking in his eyes and face that he wasn't going to be around much longer."

Malaria, dengue fever, beriberi, and other ailments plagued the *Grenadier* POWs during early 1944. Fireman Virgil Ouillette became deathly ill while working at Yawata's foundry. "Men kept dying off until sometimes there were only three or four of us going to work at the foundry," he recalled. Ouillette found himself close to being pronounced dead. "They carried me off to head to the crematorium one day, but they brought me back into the hospital because someone said, 'He ain't dead yet.' I was comatose for two weeks. In the sick bay, there was probably about 50 prisoners at any one time. They called it the sick bay, but it was the place they took you to die. I laid in there until I guess they figured I was alive."

On 3 March, a new, more lenient major was put in charge of the Fukuoka POW camp. "Major relieved," Tom Courtney wrote in his little diary. "New one better. Slight increase in chow." Warren Roberts felt, "The major left and we got a new major by the name of Rikitaki. He gave us a little more food and broke out a little medicine and let some of the boys that were sick stay in a little."[38]

Even the release of some Red Cross packages was not enough to stop the illness and starvation. They even cut up and ate a whale that washed up on the beach of Moji Bay near their camp. The alarming death rate did not stop. Three weeks after Pappy Linder's death, motor machinist's mate first class Doyle from *Grenadier* died on 12 March. "Charles Doyle had been beaten the week before, but he was run down with malnutrition and he caught pneumonia," recalled Ver Valin.

"Things were looking bad," wrote Gordon Cox. "Three of our crew had died in a month. How long could the rest of us last?"[39]

10
S-44's Final Fight

The single blast of *S-44*'s diving alarm made CTM Ernest Arthur Duva leap straight out of his bunk. Instead of the normal two blasts to dive, "Tony" Duva knew that one blast was the pre-arranged signal to prepare for a night surface attack.

An old Navy hand from Altoona, Pennsylvania, Duva had been relieved from watch duty at 1800 on 7 October 1943 by CTM Harold Arvid Stromsoe. He headed to the galley for some supper and then retired to the forward battery compartment to get some sleep. Two hours later, the night surface attack alarm caused him to toss down his book, pull on a pair of shorts and race aft.

Duva reached his battle station in the control room, where he stood sentry over the Christmas tree panel of lights. Glancing at the clock, he noted the time was 2030. As the senior enlisted man aboard the 18-year-old *S-44*, Duva was chief of the boat. He held the all-important duty of monitoring the hull indicator lights, ready to make sure that all vents were properly closed should his boat be forced to make a crash dive to escape.

Locker doors banged open noisily as the gun crews grabbed 4-inch shells and scrambled topside to man their deck gun for the battle. The ship's two gunner's mates, GM1c Clarence Elmore Moss and GM2c Philip James Jaworski, would direct their fellow enlisted men on the main deck and 20mm bridge guns. They were joined by other gun crew members, including MoMM2c Holly J. Howard, MoMM2c John V. Rubits, EM1c Charles W. Smith, MoMM1c Nicholas A. Hugyo, and chief torpedoman Stromsoe.

It was a dark night topside, but *S-44*'s radar had contact on a small Japanese ship. Believing it to be an unescorted merchant ship, Lt. Cdr. Francis Elwood Brown, *S-44*'s skipper, closed in on the unsuspecting vessel. He decided that his gunners could work over the little maru with *S-44*'s powerful 4-inch deck gun. Brown stood on the bridge along with his executive officer, Lt. Robert Groves Quinn, and their battle lookouts.

S-44 was already the most famous S-boat of the Pacific fleet. Launched on 27 October 1923 in Quincy, Massachusetts, she was commissioned on 16 February 1925. In the spring of 1941, she had been sent back to the East Coast for an extensive overhaul that would carry into early 1942. *S-44* was then deployed to Australia and departed on her first war patrol on 24 April 1942. During the next three weeks, she made three unsuccessful attacks and approaches on enemy ships. Operating off the Solomon Islands, she fired four torpedoes on 12 May and scored with two, sinking the 5,644-ton converted salvage vessel *Shoei Maru*.

On her second patrol, she covered the area west and south of Florida Island, sinking the 1,051-ton converted gunboat *Keijo Maru* on 21 June 1942. It was during her third patrol that *S-44* achieved great recognition for one of the old "Sugar boats." Off New Hanover on 10 August 1942, *S-44* hit the 8,800-ton Japanese heavy cruiser *Kako* with four torpedoes and sank her. *Kako* was returning triumphantly to Kavieng, having helped inflict severe losses on Allied warships off Savo Island near Guadalcanal. *S-44* and her crew were widely photographed and praised as heroes for their destruction of a key Japanese warship of the Guadalcanal campaign.

On her fourth patrol off New Georgia, *S-44* damaged a destroyer on 4 October and survived a severe depth charge attack that sent her back to Philadelphia for an extensive overhaul. When *S-44* put to sea again from Attu in the Aleutians on 26 September 1944, she was one of the last S-boats to go on patrol. Enough new fleet boats had been produced that the S-boats could be retired or used as training boats. *S-44* had a new skipper, Lt. Cdr. "Frank" Brown, whose luck with the S-boats had not been good thus far in the war.

Described by one he commanded as "tall, slender, dark, and sporting a small moustache, Brown was a serious and intense type who had the same desire as any other skipper—to make a name for himself." A 1933 Academy graduate from Reno, Nevada, he had helped decommission *S-32*, served on the giant *Nautilus*, and then put in three years on *Seal*.[1]

Lieutenant Brown was given command of *S-39*, but the old boat suffered engine problems during her luckless fourth patrol. After extensive repairs, Frank Brown's *S-39* was making her fifth patrol when she ran aground on a reef off Rossel Island at 0200 on 14 August 1942. He was forced to abandon his ship and take rescue by an Australian naval vessel. Adm. Ralph Christie sent out aircraft to bomb the trapped submarine after her crew had been safely retrieved. Christie was impressed enough with his cool effort to save *S-39* that he gave Frank Brown another S-boat to command, *S-43*. He made one luckless patrol out of Australia in September 1942, after which she went to the West Coast for an extensive overhaul.[2]

Given his chance to redeem his loss of *S-39*, Lt. Cdr. Frank Brown was eager to destroy Japanese shipping when he took *S-44* out for her fifth patrol. *S-44*'s destination was the northern Kuriles, where shipping targets had been plentiful off Paramushiro. *S-44* departed Attu on 26 September 1943 and only one day out of port she had been forced under by a Japanese float plane which dropped two depth charges near her. On the night of 7 October, *S-44* made radar contact with what appeared to be a small merchantman.[3]

————————

From the control room, Tony Duva could feel the vibration as *S-44*'s big 4-inch gun roared into action. With the 1MC open for the men below to hear the action topside, he heard shouting on the bridge.

"What is the target?" Lt. Robert Quinn asked his lookouts.

"I don't know," one yelled back, "but it's something big!"

Skipper George Brown had conned his boat to a position only 200 yards away from the enemy vessel before he ordered his deck gun crew to open fire on the dark silhouette. Once *S-44* opened fire with her 4-inch and 20mms, the Japanese ship's deck suddenly opened with flame and a roar as he returned fire with a heavy gun. In an instant, those topside realized they had not stumbled upon a helpless merchant vessel but instead a Japanese man-of-war!

This warship was, in fact, the 860-ton escort destroyer *Ishigaki*—armed with three 12cm/.45-caliber guns and four 25mm anti-aircraft guns. Frank Brown shouted orders to his helmsman and gun crew during the opening moment of the duel. Shells were returned in anger from the startled destroyer crew. It was not a fair contest for a small submarine with only one heavy gun. If *Ishigaki*'s gunners could hole *S-44*'s pressure hull, she would not be able to dive.

"Gun crew below!" shouted Brown. "Stand by to dive!"

Clarence Moss' gun crew secured their deck gun and scrambled for the conning tower hatch. Just as the men were coming through the conning tower on their way below, *Ishigaki*'s 12cm guns began finding their mark. A shell smashed into the conning tower and shook *S-44*. Gunner Moss was hit and began streaming blood, but he managed to get down the ladder and make his way forward.

The next shell tore through the control room, puncturing *S-44*'s pressure hull below the waterline. The seas began spraying into the submarine's nerve center as the Japanese destroyer closed. At the same time, numerous 20mm shells hit the sub's pressure hull, further adding to the leaks. Another heavy caliber shell pierced *S-44*'s hull near the forward battery room.

The submarine was caught in a perilous situation. With her hull punctured in numerous places, she would head for the bottom if Lieutenant Commander Brown decided to dive her. "By the time the captain got to the control room from the bridge, the water was rising above the control room floor plates," recalled Tony Duva.

Clarence Moss, the wounded gunner's mate, was tended to by CPhM Tom Cleverdon, the ship's only medical person. Cleverdon was one of four brothers who joined the Navy to fight for his country. As *S-44*'s medic, Chief Cleverdon did what he could to comfort his wounded shipmate.[4]

In the confusion of flames, smoke, and fountaining spray, the S-boat rolled and lurched under the series of hits from *Ishigaki*'s guns. Skipper Brown sloshed forward toward the forward battery room to see how bad the damage was there. In the meantime, Chief Duva and the auxiliarymen managed to get the trim pump started to move water to the control room bilges.

The water was rising faster than the pumps could manage, however. A moment later, the captain's voice came over the 1MC from the forward battery, "Abandon ship!" *S-44*'s wounds were mortal. She could not dive and had no chance of fighting it out against the superior Japanese destroyer escort. Brown's only option was to allow as many of his men to escape as possible before his submarine made her final dive.

Lt. (jg) James Stephenson, the diving officer, ordered *S-44*'s main vents to be opened. By this time, all hands were making their way forward to the torpedo room, where an escape hatch was located. "I left my station, picked up a life jacket of the Kapok type, and went into the torpedo room," Tony Duva stated. "There was some more water coming into the forward battery compartment, and already a considerable amount in there, but I couldn't see where it was coming in."

There were already quite a few men packed into the forward torpedo room. TM1c Joe Albert Velebny climbed the ladder to the forward escape trunk and undogged the hatch but found that he could not raise it. Exec Bob Quinn replaced Velebny on the ladder and finally opened the hatch. As it was flung open, light filtered in from the "target" ship's searchlight.

"The target proved to be a destroyer about 300 yards on our port beam," Duva said. "The submarine was afloat, the attempts to dive having been stopped when abandon ship was ordered. The destroyer was still laying machine-gun fire across the deck and, consequently, no one was making any particular effort to get up the ladder."

The water was rising quickly, but no one was eager to face the gunfire above. "The submarine was pitching and heavy seas were coming down the hatch," said Duva. "At times, it seemed as though the bow would never rise again." Lieutenant Quinn gave orders to secure a pillowcase to the boat hook and he waved it out of the hatch in a vain attempt to signal surrender. Chief Duva, standing beneath the exec on the ladder, could not make it topside due to the throng of men crowding around the ladder and hanging onto him. Either the Japanese destroyermen failed to see the pillowcase in the night or they chose to show no mercy. Another heavy shell hit the torpedo room, its explosion knocking most of the men off their feet.[5]

Standing below Duva in the forward torpedo room was RM3c William Francis Whitemore, who had been born on August 31, 1919, in Morrison, Illinois. He completed three years of high school and was active in the Civilian Conservation Corps, which he joined full-time before completing high school. After the outbreak of war, he joined the Navy in 1942 and trained at Great Lakes. *S-44* was his first submarine. His brothers Allen and George Whitemore had also joined the Navy.[6]

Whitemore found that immediately after *S-44*'s guns had opened fire on the Japanese destroyer "all hell broke loose." When Lieutenant Quinn began waving the white pillowcase to surrender, Whitemore was standing on a torpedo skid rack. "A shell came through the overhead directly above me, about a foot from my head," he recalled. "I was burnt on the face and caught small shell splinters in my back. Then Duva finally got up."

Tony Duva scrambled out onto the deck and began waving his arms at the destroyer, hoping the firing would stop. *Ishigaki*'s gun continued to roar and machine-gun bullets chewed up the decking around the chief of the boat. "Luckily I was not hit," he said. "They kept right on firing."

Ishigaki's searchlight was right on Duva and the other *S-44* sailors who began coming up from below. "Heavy seas hit me at this time and knocked me under the deck gun, where I stayed," he recalled. "The firing was continuous and the 20mm and machine-gun fire was hitting the superstructure and pressure hull."

Bill Whitemore followed Duva up the hatch. "Seeing that they were still firing, I fell over backwards into the water," he said. As luck would have it, a heavy wave picked up the radioman and washed him back onto *S-44*'s deck. Whitemore scrambled over to the deck gun and lay down beside Duva to take cover. Two other shipmates, EM3c Patrick Carrier and F2c Lonzo Green, took cover with Whitemore and Duva behind the 4-inch deck gun.

As they watched, more of their shipmates came out on deck from the hatch. Close behind Whitemore was GM2c Phil Jaworksi, who had participated in the deck gun battle moments earlier. Jaworski, a 25-year-old from Maryland who had joined *S-44* in 1941, was the only submariner in his family although his younger brothers Joseph, Bernard, James, and Carl had all joined the Navy during World War II.

Machine-gun fire next cut down CTM Harold Stromsoe as he reached the deck. "I saw Stromsoe lying by the torpedo room hatch," said Duva. "He was bleeding about the head and I realized he had been hit. His hand was moving up and down. The Japs machine-gunned us. They had us right in the middle of the biggest searchlight I have ever seen or want to see."[7]

Whitemore and Duva saw several more men emerge from below, including EM3c William Ellis, Chief Tom Cleverdon, and MoMM1c Rhollo Fees. Including the wounded Chief Stromsoe, at least nine men made it to *S-44*'s deck as their submarine was settling fast below the waves. As she went under, some of the men jumped overboard or were carried away by the ocean. Some, including Cleverdon, were cut down by gunfire as they moved out on deck.[8]

"I climbed to the 20mm platform and just as I got there the platform was awash," said Duva. "Seas knocked me overboard on the starboard side. Her nose went down and the stern came up. She made her last dive sinking very quickly by the bow. I felt no suction or explosion, although I was practically over the spot where she went down."

Within moments of taking her first hit from the Japanese destroyer, the proud old *S-44* was gone. She took 49 officers and men with her to the bottom, leaving only eight men on the surface, some struggling to survive, some riddled with gunfire and shrapnel.

She took down a brave crew who had taken on Japanese warships valiantly with their 18-year-old submarine. F1c James Sloan, a young man from Rhode Island, had left a poem with his mother before leaving to join the Navy. Its final lines indicated Sloan's true desires for the war's end:

We fight like mad for our country dear,
So that no longer there will be fear
Of gaping holes and hellish fire
That rob us of our hearts' desire—PEACE.

Survival in the rough winter waters off the Kurile Islands would not be long. "The temperature of the water at the time the submarine went down was 47 degrees F," testified Duva. "I know because I was keeping the water injection log."

About a minute after *S-44* disappeared below the waves forever, *Ishigaki* extinguished her searchlight. "I couldn't see the destroyer but I heard voices in the water asking for assistance," recalled Duva. Bill Whitemore shouted at one man who was calling for help.

"Do you have a life jacket?"

"No," called the man, whom Whitemore and Duva said was William Ellis.

Whitemore then shouted toward Chief Duva, "Do you have a life jacket?"

"Yes," Duva shouted. He could not see the radioman in the dark, rough seas but soon heard him swimming toward him.

Whitemore finally reached Duva and hung onto his life jacket for support with one hand while paddling with the other. Whitemore turned to look back for William Ellis "but he was gone. He apparently had an attack with the cramps and drowned because the water was so cold, the temperature being 45 degrees." The

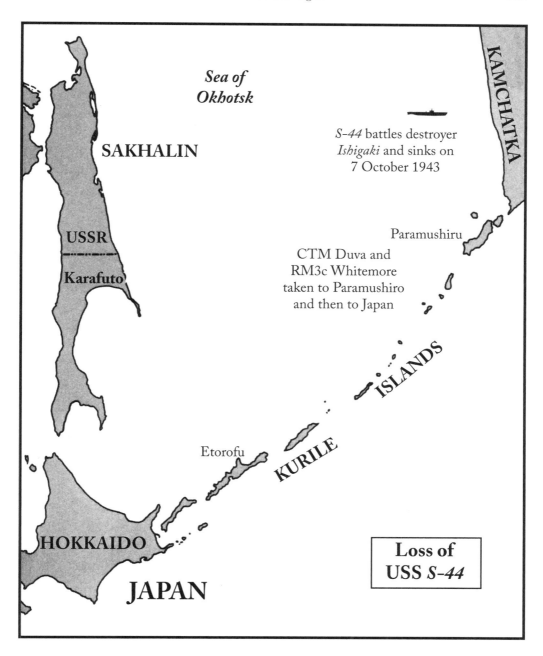

Sea of Okhotsk

SAKHALIN

S-44 battles destroyer *Ishigaki* and sinks on 7 October 1943

KAMCHATKA

USSR

Karafuto

Paramushiru

CTM Duva and RM3c Whitemore taken to Paramushiro and then to Japan

ISLANDS

Etorofu

KURILE

HOKKAIDO

JAPAN

Loss of USS *S-44*

survivors bounced about in the waves with nothing in sight. It appeared to them that the Japanese destroyer had departed.

More than ten minutes later, they saw the dark silhouette of a ship and started yelling at it. "The ship turned on her searchlight but trained it on an object on the opposite beam from us," said Duva. "The light stayed trained on this object for three or four minutes and then started sweeping. Apparently the object, whatever it was, sank from sight."

According to Whitemore, this "object" was EM3c Patrick Carrier. "They held the light on him for about five minutes while they were lowering a boat into the water, but before they could pick him up he apparently drowned."

The sweeping light finally trained on Whitemore and Duva. During this time, they could hear the voices of others still shouting for help in the cold ocean. The Japanese boat rowed over to the pair of bobbing submariners. Whitemore climbed aboard the boat while Duva grabbed onto a life ring and was hauled aboard.

"As soon as we were aboard the small boat, the searchlight on the destroyer went out," Duva recalled. Apparently, a couple of survivors to verify their kill was all that the Japanese skipper desired. "No attempt was made by the small boat to pick up any other survivors. It returned directly to the destroyer, about 300 yards away. When we were picked up by the small boat, I couldn't hear any other voices in the water."

Both men were certain that *Ishigaki* picked up no other *S-44* survivors. As soon as they were hauled aboard with the boat, the destroyer got under way, apparently fearful of another lurking submarine in the vicinity. "Duva and I were in the water about 25 minutes," related Whitemore. "We were told later that we were only supposed to last five minutes in that cold water."

Whitemore and Duva were quickly questioned and beaten as the Japanese tried to find what other submarines were in the area. "The Japs expressed surprise that Whitemore and I had survived in the water as long as we did," said Duva. "There were no other ships in the area as far as I could tell. I feel certain that the others who got out drowned. I don't believe they had a chance in the world to survive. The rubber life raft was never launched and I didn't see any debris in the water that would keep a man afloat."

The two *S-44* sailors were kept together as *Ishigaki* moved away. The destroyer reached Paramushiru about two and a half hours after picking them up. *Ishigaki* anchored in the harbor for the night and throughout the following day. "We were questioned that night and then questioned more the next afternoon," said Whitemore. On the morning on 9 October, Duva and Whitemore were taken from the destroyer and escorted over to a Japanese seaplane tender in the harbor. From Paramushiru, the tender made about a 36-hour voyage to the big island of Honshu in Japan. "There we were put on a train and taken to Ofuna," stated Chief Duva.

In short order, *S-44*'s only survivors would join other U.S. submariners at Ofuna. Unlike *Grenadier* and *Perch* previously, Admiral Lockwood's submarine force did not have to wait until the end of the war to learn of *S-44*'s loss. The codebreakers picked up the story and passed it to ComSubPac. Lt. Cdr. Frank Brown had the dubious distinction of becoming the only submarine skipper of World War II to lose two boats.[9]

Once *S-44* was sufficiently late for return, she was listed by the Navy as overdue and presumed lost. Tony Duva's brother and Bill Whitemore's parents received telegrams on 4 December 1943 that their loved one "is missing following action in the performance of his duty and in the service of his country."

The submarine veterans had become more plentiful at Ofuna during the fall of 1943. The longest tenured were those from *Perch*. Lt. Cdr. Dave Hurt had arrived in April 1942, along with *Pope* skipper Welford Blinn. Late that month, they had been joined by the other five *Perch* officers and her three radiomen. By the end of 1942, the four junior *Perch* officers had been transferred on to other camps, leaving only Hurt and radiomen Ted Reh, Ray Normand, and Robert Berridge.

After a full year at Ofuna, *Perch*'s four prisoners had been joined on 1 May 1943 by three *Grenadier* officers: Lt. Cdr. John Fitzgerald, Lt. George Whiting, and Lt. Kevin Harty. Next in had been RM1c Joe Knutson at the end of June. The next big arrival had been the 29 officers and men from *Grenadier* on 12 October 1943. The U.S. submarine POW count at camp Ofuna thus stood at 37 officers and men of the Silent Service by late October.

This count increased by two when *S-44*'s only survivors—chief torpedo-man Duva and radioman third class Whitemore—reached Ofuna during early November. The much-traveled sailors were placed into individual cells and subjected to lengthy interrogations during their first weeks. John Fitzgerald managed to get their story and the circumstances of *S-44*'s loss during their first few days in camp.

Newly arrived *Grenadier* yeoman Bob Palmer remembered that Fitzgerald, Lieutenant Whiting, Lieutenant Commander Blinn from *Pope*, and Geoffrey Lempriere had an intelligence system going. "Someone would steal the Japanese paper and get it to them. With Lieutenant Commander Blinn somewhat fluent in the Japanese language and with a daily map the Japanese included in each paper, the progress of our forces was very clearly marked on more elaborate charts kept under someone's tatami mats." Palmer recalled that when the Japanese later discovered his skipper's underground intelligence mapping, they "were more than a little impressed."[10]

A short time after the arrival of the *S-44* men, rumors circulated around camp on 22 November that the Japanese were preparing to transfer some prisoners. The previous sizable transfer had been in May, when ten were transferred to other camps and became official POWs. On 3 December 1943, about 30 more officers and men left Ofuna. Thirteen of the *Grenadier* enlisted men were among those transferred, including: Al Albertson, Davis Andrews, Lester Barker, Clyde Barrington, Jewell Embry, Carlisle Herbert, Judd Hinkson, Denny Landrum, John Leskovsky, John Pianka, Paul Russell, Lee Shaw, and Charles Wilson.

Among them were Lieutenant Commander Hurt from *Perch* and Lieutenant Commander Blinn from *Pope*, who had both been at Ofuna since April 1942. At 19 months, Hurt was by far the longest tenured U.S. submariner held at Ofuna. Also transferred on 3 December were Lt. Cdr. Al Maher of *Houston*, who had arrived at Ofuna just one week later than *Perch*'s skipper. "One can well imagine how glad they were to leave for another camp," Lieutenant Commander Fitzgerald later wrote. "This left me senior POW in Ofuna. Many headaches, as well as trying to fill the job of interpreter, then became my lot."[11]

Also among this transfer group were four other old-timers at Ofuna, naval aviators Ens. Al Mead from *Enterprise*'s VF-10, VT-10 aircrewmen Mick Glasser and Tom Nelson, and PBY pilot Carlton Clark. "Together with the *Grenadier* crew, we were walked to the Ofuna train depot and were taken to a regular POW camp at Omori, a suburb of Tokyo," Glasser recalled. For the three *Enterprise* aviators, this transfer marked the end of one year and nine days at the special camp at Ofuna.[12]

Torpedo Ten airman Tom Nelson was equally pleased to be leaving Ofuna with John Fitzgerald's transfer group. "Physical abuse varied from face slapping with a close fist to being clubbed with a hardwood tool handle from the middle of your back to the back of your knees," he later recalled. To survive, Nelson had even once struck a crow with a bamboo stick and brought it back into camp to bake. "Tasted like chicken to us," squadronmate Glasser stated. "Yep, we actually ate crow!"[13]

Two days after the transfer of Blinn, Hurt, and the other prisoners, the *Perch* radiomen, the remaining *Grenadier* officers and crew, and *S-44*'s two survivors learned the reason for the hasty removal of these men. The Japanese had captured another U.S. submarine crew. On 5 December, they arrived at Ofuna, just 21 survivors from another lost boat. Fitzgerald found them to be "barefooted, makeshift clothing—mostly cast off Jap undress blues—and in general a weary looking lot."

These new arrivals were the survivors of the proud submarine *Sculpin*. Their ordeal during the previous two weeks before reaching Ofuna was nothing short of amazing.

11
Sculpin's Last Battle Surface

Joseph Nicholas Baker Jr. would never forget his nineteenth birthday. The day would start with this New York City boy's submarine making contact with a Japanese ship shortly after midnight. Aside from the now-familiar call to battle stations, F1c Joe Baker's birthday on 19 November 1943, would become memorable in other ways—none of them pleasant.

Baker's boat was USS *Sculpin* (SS-191), launched in 1938 and commissioned on 16 January 1939. During her shakedown cruise four months later, *Sculpin* was ordered to search for her sister submarine *Squalus* (SS-192), which had sunk during a test dive off Portsmouth on 23 May. *Sculpin* located her sunken sister, established communication and stood by until a rescue ship arrived to help those trapped on the ocean floor make their escape. *Squalus* was later refloated, repaired, and recommissioned as *Sailfish*. Superstitious submariners dubbed her "Squailfish." *Sailfish* and *Sculpin* would continue to be intertwined throughout their wartime careers with a bizarre coincidence to be played out in due time.

When war broke out for America, *Sculpin* departed Cavite in the Philippines on 8 December 1941, to begin her first war patrol against the Japanese. America's "greatest generation" was turning out en masse to join the armed forces following the nation's "day of infamy" at Pearl Harbor. Billie Minor Cooper, a young man who lived near Chattanooga, Tennessee, was eager to help his country avenge the surprise attack in Hawaii. With his father on the road, he had to anxiously wait for his return to obtain the necessary parental signature.

Once he had his father's blessing, Cooper took his papers to Chattanooga only to find it would take him five days to be called. "I think every kid around Tennessee wanted to join the Navy after the Japs bombed Pearl Harbor," he said. "Some of 'em I don't think had ever even been to town before."

Bill Cooper volunteered for submarine service but found that the submarine schools were full. He eventually ended up as a relief crew member of the submarine tender *Fulton*, which he rode out to Pearl Harbor in June 1942. "After the battle of Midway, they sent the *Fulton* out to Midway to pick up survivors from the carrier *Yorktown*," he said. During the return trip to Pearl, one of *Fulton*'s old chiefs helped Cooper achieve a transfer to the submarine *Greenling* (SS-213). He became a qualified submariner during her highly successful second, third, and fourth patrols. He was later transferred to the tender *Sperry*. When the sister subs *Sculpin* and *Sailfish* entered Pearl from West Coast refits, Cooper asked to return to active war duty and was put aboard *Sculpin* prior to her eighth run.

Sculpin made eight patrols under Cdr. Lucius Henry Chappell, sinking two confirmed merchant ships during 1942. Following a short overhaul at Pearl Harbor, *Sculpin* made ready for sea again to conduct her ninth war patrol. She had a new skipper, Cdr. Fred Connaway, a 32-year-old from the Academy class of 1932. Having commanded *S-48* for two years, Connaway was stepping into huge shoes. His crew had great respect for their previous skipper and he was faced with a large number of new men reporting on board, including two new ensigns.

There were still many veterans left aboard. Nine men had made all nine runs on *Sculpin*: GM2c Robert Wyatt, EM2c Ellis Warren, EM2c John Swift, MoMM1c George Rocek, EM1c Arnold Moreton, CSM Weldon Moore, CMM Richard Hemphill, TM3c James Harper, and CMoMM Phil Gabrunas.

At the last moment, another officer came aboard *Sculpin*, Submarine Division 43's commander—Capt. John Philip Cromwell. He was put on board by Admiral Lockwood to form a coordinated wolfpack as deemed necessary, consisting of *Sculpin*, *Searaven* (SS-196), and *Apogon* (SS-308). Captain Cromwell had great knowledge of Lockwood's Ultra project for directing submarines via intercepted intelligence. He had also been fully briefed on all plans for Operation Galvanic, the planned Allied invasion of Tarawa and Makin in the Gilbert Islands. Lockwood had instructed Cromwell not to impart the Galvanic information to anyone, in order to avoid exposing the campaign if his submarine was sunk and prisoners were taken.[1]

QM2c Bill Cooper was familiar with Cromwell. The division commander had spent three days aboard his old boat *Greenling* while drilling the men on how to fight the war. With two commanders aboard, Cooper knew something big was up. *Sculpin* stopped at Johnston Island on 7 November to refuel before voyaging another 3,500 miles to the southwest toward Truk Atoll. *Sculpin*'s mission was to attack Japanese forces that sortied from Truk's northern gateway during the Gilbert Islands campaign. Fred Connaway had achieved no sinkings during his two years as skipper of *S-48*. Prior to taking command of *Sculpin*, he made a PCO run aboard *Sunfish*, which received wartime credit for three sinkings. With his own fleet boat, Connaway was eager for the chance to rack up his own kills.

He and *Sculpin* would find plenty of action off Truk.

———————

"Radar contact, sir," came the call from the conning tower. *Sculpin* had two men who primarily manned the SJ surface-search radar when the boat was surfaced—RT2c Edgar Beidleman and RM3c John Parr—and both were making their first patrol on *Sculpin*.

It was 0030 on 19 November. Skipper Fred Connaway and division commander John Cromwell were both on the bridge at the time, as *Sculpin* patrolled north of Truk. Lt. Joseph Rollie Defrees Jr. made his way topside to relieve Captain Cromwell as battle stations OOD. Son of an admiral and a fresh 1942 Academy graduate, Defrees was known for his enthusiasm for action. The torpedo and gunnery officer had a certain fondness for his ship: his mother had christened *Sculpin* back in 1938.[2]

The convoy appeared to be making 14 knots, so Commander Connaway commenced an end-around run at full speed to pull ahead of these ships. This convoy included prime targets: 5,160-ton Japanese submarine tender *Chogei*, the 6,280-ton light cruiser *Kashima*, and the destroyers *Wakatsuki* and *Yamagumo*, all of which had departed Truk on 18 November.[3]

As the dawn was beginning to break, *Sculpin* reached a satisfactory position for attack. Connaway dove his ship and sounded battle stations. Taking quick periscope observations, he made out what he believed to be a single freighter escorted by a cruiser and five destroyers.

Just as *Sculpin*'s crew was preparing to fire, a last periscope observation showed trouble. The Japanese convoy had zigged and was heading directly for the submarine.

"Down scope!" cried Connaway. "Emergency, two hundred feet!"

In the control room, the diving officer was New York–raised reservist Lt. George Estabrook Brown Jr., *Sculpin*'s third officer and an aggressive veteran of the old *S-40* and four prior *Sculpin* patrols. After two years at Yale, he had joined the Navy in 1940, first serving on board the cruiser *Chester* before entering sub school. Experienced in quick action, Brown flooded the boat's negative tanks and took her down fast. The ensuing noise of the negative tanks was likely picked up by the Japanese sonarmen. "I believe this outfit heard the *Sculpin* or were alerted, for the whole convoy speeded up," recalled Brown.

Fortunately, the convoy did not drop any depth charges. At 0730, Captain Cromwell and Cdr. Connaway decided that this maru must be an important ship to have such a large escort force. *Sculpin* must go after it, so they decided to surface and make another end-around on the *Chogei* force. Bill Cooper, the assistant navigator, had just left the conning tower and was sitting down to eat some breakfast in the galley. A duty messenger told him that the exec, Lt. John Nelson Allen, wanted him on the bridge, as the boat was about to surface again.

On the bridge, Cooper scanned aft in his area and reported all clear. Allen suddenly said, "What does that look like to you?"

Turning with binoculars, Cooper looked and replied, "That's a crow's nest right in front of us."

Just over the horizon, the upper works of a ship could be seen through their binoculars some 6,000 yards away. Unable to discern what type of ship it was, Lieutenant Allen called for the skipper and sounded the diving alarm to be safe.

As *Sculpin* went to periscope depth, Commander Connaway swept the surface with his scope and announced that a destroyer was bearing down on *Sculpin*. The Japanese convoy had apparently left this tin can behind as a "sleeper," ready to pounce on the American sub. The approaching warship was the 2,370-ton destroyer *Yamagumo*. At 388 feet in length and capable of 35 knots, *Yamagumo* was heavily armed with six 5-inch deck guns, numerous anti-aircraft guns, eight torpedo tubes and racks holding three dozen depth charges.[4]

Although some skippers would opt to shoot at oncoming Japanese destroyers with "down the throat" shots, Fred Connaway chose to run silent and run deep. If he could avoid this tin can, he might be able to get to the surface again for another shot at this important convoy.

Diving officer George Brown took her down to 300 feet as *Yamagumo* raced in. In *Sculpin*'s after battery compartment, S2c Edwin Karl Frederick Keller had manned the battle phones. A recent New London submarine school graduate, the lanky 19-year-old with the booming voice that earned him the nickname "Whispering Ed," had just reported on board *Sculpin* before her ninth run. He had never experienced a real depth charge attack. "The screws sounded like a freight train coming through a tunnel," Keller later said. Glancing around nervously, he saw S2c Tom Brown fall to his knees, blessing himself. A veteran of two previous *Sculpin* patrols, Brown knew what was coming from above.[5]

As *Yamagumo* raced overhead, *Sculpin*'s best sound operator, RM3c Grover Marcus, heard the splashes of ashcans hitting the water. The heavy, 600-pound charges tumbled to their prescribed depth and exploded with sudden violence. An exhaust valve in the after engine room was ruptured and the room started taking on water. Several sea valves were jarred off their seats and could not be made watertight. "The damage received by the first depth charges was not unusual but disconcerting," George Brown noted.

Departments called in their damage as Fred Connaway conned his boat away from the searching destroyer. *Yamagumo* remained above, carefully stalking her prey during the next hour. At 0830, sound reported the destroyer speeding up to make another attack. This time, *Yamagumo* dropped 18 depth charges. The concussions rocked *Sculpin* and caused more damage. In the engine room, fireman Joe Baker felt that these concussions "jarred holy hell out of us."

Lieutenant Brown recalled, "The hands on the depth charge gauge fell off in front of my face. The pressure gauges near the diving station commenced flooding." Weather conditions were perfect for the Japanese destroyer crew. "There was a straight line on the bathythermograph down to 300 feet," said Brown. "Our evasive tactics were next to useless on that day." Lieutenant Brown left his diving station momentarily and ducked into the galley, where he found one of the cooks and seaman Ed Keller.

"When do we lose these bastards?" Keller asked the lieutenant. To his dismay, Brown shot back, "We're not going to lose them. They have us."[6]

Yamagumo kept a vigilant guard over *Sculpin*, like a cat toying with a wounded mouse. It was around 0930—about an hour after the second punishing barrage—that the destroyer was heard to begin a third attack run. Once again, the submarine was rocked by a violent string of explosives. Although minor damage was added, *Sculpin* was still under control in spite of the fact that she had a large up-angle of 13 degrees or more and much weight in the boat from the extra water flooding in.

Grover Marcus picked up a rain squall on his sound gear and Commander Connaway ordered his helmsman to head toward it, submerged. With the aid of this surface squall, he was able to evade the sweeping destroyer for more than half an hour. Lieutenant Brown found that the trim pump would not take suction to help regain diving trim. He was ordered by Connaway to make a damage control inspection throughout the ship. Ens. Wendell Max Fiedler, a young reservist making his first war patrol, was detailed to take over the diving officer duties in his place.

Moving aft, Brown found the after engine room so flooded that further leveling the boat could be a problem. "We decided to bail the water forward to another compartment until we could trim the ship without endangering main motors," he recalled. Temperatures were approaching 115 degrees in this room.[7]

Skipper Connaway decided to come up for a periscope observation, normally a routine maneuver. At 200 feet, Ensign Fiedler began blowing the ballast tanks. The depth gauge moved to 180 feet and then to 170, where it stuck—unnoticed by all. Fiedler continuing blowing ballast, unaware that his ship was shallower than what the errant gauge was showing. Without warning, *Sculpin*'s bow suddenly broached the surface and created a heavy splash. On his battle phones, Ed Keller suddenly heard the man in the forward room scream, " The bow is out of the water!"[8]

The stuck gauge had caused the inexperienced temporary diving officer to bring the boat up too fast while George Brown was checking on the bucket brigade. "No one could be blamed for this as the depth gauge was stuck at 170 feet and the pressure gauges around the diving station were all flooded out," Brown offered. When *Sculpin* broached the surface, *Yamagumo*'s lookouts spotted her some 5,000 yards away and the destroyer raced for her position. Max Fiedler quickly flooded the negative tanks and took her back down as the alert destroyer came in to attack.

The first depth charge string was punishing. *Sculpin*'s radio transmitter was torn from the bulkhead and its receiver was smashed. Light bulbs burst throughout the ship and the torpedo tube valves in both torpedo rooms were severely damaged. This caused the ship to lose diving control and she dropped toward the bottom. *Sculpin* plunged past 500 feet and then surpassed the 600-foot mark. She was approaching crush depth by the time Lieutenant Brown charged into the control room to help.

Brown put a bubble in the bow buoyancy tank, releasing enough compressed air to stop the boat's downward plunge before she reached her limits. With the rush of compressed air, *Sculpin* lurched back toward the surface and he fought to keep her from broaching again.

The heat in the boat was intense. *Sculpin* had made a full power run the previous night and all the engine heat had since been sealed in the boat with nowhere to escape during the hours of depth charging. Having vented the negative tanks two or three times, and due to having so many leaks, the air pressure in the ship had exceeded five inches—twice the normal pressure.

In the forward engine room, MoMM1c George Rocek spotted salt water spraying out between the pipe flanges from the hull on the forward starboard side. A native of Cicero, Illinois, who had made all previous *Sculpin* patrols, Rocek had done his share of depth charge damage control. He was seasoned and lived the life of a typical submariner. While on patrol, he let his beard grow out full and thick. To his family, he was simply George, but shipmates always knew him as "Moon" Rocek.

F1c Joe Baker was with Moon Rocek in the forward engine room during the depth charging. "It was very severe," Baker later stated. "We were damn lucky to get out of the thing." Although this was only his second run on *Sculpin*, he realized what a terrific pounding his ship was taking. "The air was getting worse and the heat was horrific."

Connaway and Cromwell decided they should have their boat try to withstand at least one more depth charge attack. This came at 1230 and the damage was heavy once again. Both the forward and after torpedo rooms reported cracks around their torpedo tubes. The sound heads were driven up into the boat, shearing their holding-down clamps right off. This left *Sculpin* without sound gear to hear what action the Japanese destroyer above was taking.

Depth control could now only be maintained with more turns of the screws, 170 turns. A check of conditions revealed that *Sculpin* could no longer stay down.

The battery power was almost shot and it was still six hours until sundown. From the forward room, TM1c Herbert Thomas reported 184 pounds of pressure on the hull forward to the battle talker, Y2c Delbert Schroeder.

Connaway decided that the only course was to surface his boat and fight it out with the destroyer. While his gun crew was thus engaging the enemy warship, the rest of the crew could at least have a chance to abandon ship if events became so dire. "Things were looking damned rugged for the *Sculpin*," Joe Baker later stated. "They had dropped 52 600-pound charges, which is a lot of TNT. But the crew wasn't about to give up without a hard fight first."

Division commander John Cromwell and *Sculpin* skipper Fred Connaway had a difference of opinion about what to do next. "Commander Connaway had been so calm, resourceful, and perservering during the five hours of severe depth charging that it was hard for the crew to realize that the situation was as serious as it was," George Brown recalled. Connaway told his men that their boat could simply not withstand another close string of depth charges. He said that he owed it to his crew, who had fought so well, to give them at least a chance to abandon their completely shattered ship.

PhM1c Paul Todd witnessed the debate between Skipper Connaway and wolfpack commander Cromwell. "Captain Cromwell asked the skipper to keep the boat down," Todd recalled. By this time, however, the decision had been made and *Sculpin* was on her way to the surface. "The skipper wanted as many men as possible to escape." QM2c Bill Cooper also overheard the disagreement.

Cromwell told Connaway, "Keep her down! Keep her down!" He wanted *Sculpin* to try to ride out the last of her air until sundown before escaping. Cromwell also felt that the destroyer should be nearly out of depth charges.[9]

"No, we're going to battle surface," the skipper replied.

Diving officer Brown overheard these exchanges made by his skipper. "As he started up to the conning tower, he ordered me to make sure *Sculpin* was scuttled in case we lost the one-sided engagement with the destroyer. He still maintained his calm, collected, courageous manner."

Bill Cooper witnessed another exchange between the skipper and his chief of the boat, CSM Weldon Edward Moore, as *Sculpin* was preparing to battle surface. Possessing the best night vision as a lookout, Moore had been with the ship throughout the war. Known affectionately as "Dinty" Moore to his men, he had designed *Sculpin*'s battle flag during an earlier patrol.

"Don't you want to make ready the tubes?" Moore asked his skipper.

"No," said Connaway. "Just battle surface."

Cooper was stunned. He felt that this was simply giving up. "If we'd have had those tubes ready for that Japanese ship," he later said, "all we would have had to done was aim the boat at him and fire our torpedoes with about a one-degree spread. We were just sitting there dead in the water." The decision was clear that Connaway only planned to give his men a chance to escape. Some among the crew silently felt that their previous skipper, Lu Chappell, would not have gone out without at least firing his tubes.

"Stand by to battle surface," Yeoman Schroeder called over the 1MC.

The conning tower was packed as *Sculpin* prepared to surface. Connaway was there, ready to take the bridge for his final fight. Quartermaster Cooper was ready, hands on the wheel that dogged the conning tower hatch as the ship popped to the surface. "Skipper, permission to open the hatch?" he asked.

Standing near the ladder's base was TM3c James Harper, a plankowner who was part of the 20mm bridge gun crews. Sensing a delay in orders from the skipper, Harper cried to Cooper, "Give us a chance! Open the hatch."

As Cooper spun the wheel, seawater sloshed down onto the men who raced up the ladder. *Sculpin* surfaced about 1300 and the gun crews raced to their stations. Lt. Joe Defrees was out on deck directing the gun crews. Commander Connaway stood on the bridge, directing the ship into the best attack position. In the distance, *Yamagumo* appeared to be almost dead in the water about a half mile away on the port side of *Sculpin*.

In the conning tower, Lt. Nelson Allen relayed the skipper's orders to the helmsman and those below. Lt. (jg) George Embury manned the radar and relayed fire control data to the gun. A reservist not schooled at New London, Embury's background was in electrical and electronic engineering. A fellow officer who helped train him during *Sculpin*'s seventh patrol found him to be "eager to learn, bright and attentive."[10]

In the control room, George Brown had a group of men who were eager to know what they could do to help. "I ordered them to the torpedo room to make ready the tubes," he later related. In direct contrast to his skipper's desires, he later stated, "I intended to fire a spread from the control room." He was not even sure, however, that the damaged tube doors could be opened.

As the hatches opened, the gun crews raced to the 20mm cannon and their main deck gun. On deck, the 3-inch gun was manned by CSM Dinty Moore, TM1c Herb Thomas, TM1c Warren Berry, MoMM2 Duane White, GM2 Bob Wyatt, F1c Joe Baker, MoMM2 Edward Ricketts, and F1c Harry Milbourn. "Once and for all, we were going to fight it out," said Baker. "The day was a pretty one, with whitecaps coming up over the decks."

The gunners hoped that all of their practice drills would pay off now, under the direst of circumstances. Chief Moore took his seat on the left side of the gun. Herb Thomas served as site setter. A 24-year-old raised in northeastern Iowa, Thomas had joined the Navy in 1938 instead of finishing his schooling.

The 3-inch crew could not see the oncoming destroyer at first, but *Yamagumo* was soon spotted about 3,000 yards off. Joe Baker was serving as first loader, helping to manually place the 3-inch shells into the main deck gun. "We got the first shot in, which went over him," Baker stated. "The second fell short."

Seven other men manned the 20mms and light machine guns to fire on the Japanese: TM3c James Harper, S2 Eugene Arnath, TM2c Charles Pitser, S1c William Partin, GM2c John Rourke, MoMM1c Charles Coleman, and F1c Alexander Guillot. Bill Cooper noticed the gunners struggling to fire one of the 20mms aft of the conning tower. "Can I help you?" he called.

"Yeah," replied James Harper, who explained that one of the normal gun helpers had not showed up, likely caught up in the action elsewhere. Cooper assisted Harper with a jammed gun as the 20mms pounded away at the approaching destroyer.

Gunner John Rourke, a 22-year-old from New Haven, Connecticut, had been stationed in the forward battery during the depth charge attack. His station was not damaged and he now concerned himself with keeping the guns firing. "My station was repairs on 20mms and .50-caliber machine guns," he later stated. "I was trouble shooter on the guns in case there was any stoppage or misfire."

Yamagumo did not immediately open fire but instead maneuvered to get out of the line of fire of the submarine's deck gun. After *Sculpin* had fired her first two rounds, *Yamagumo*'s gunners opened up with their powerful 5-inchers. The first salvo straddled the sub, blowing geysers of seawater into the air.[11]

The destroyermen adjusted their fire and made their next salvo count. A 5-inch shell slammed into *Sculpin*'s conning tower, demolishing her main inductions and blowing shrapnel across the men on deck and on the bridge. In the conning tower, Exec Nelson Allen and radar officer George Embury were killed. On the bridge, Commander Connaway was mortally wounded and Lt. Joe Defrees, leading the gun crews' efforts, was cut down by shrapnel. In an instant, *Sculpin* had lost four senior officers.

Bill Cooper escaped serious injury from the direct hit. The young man beside him, torpedoman's mate third class Harper—friend of *Grenadier* POW Gordon Cox—was not so fortunate. "They got the first hit right in the conning tower. It knocked me off my feet when the shell hit the conning tower," Cooper said. "It also tore the left arm off the gunner's mate who was up there with me."

In addition to Defrees being cut down, others among the 3-inch crew were pierced by the shrapnel. "That shell blew the conning tower apart," said first loader Joe Baker. "I got hit in the leg with shrapnel, but we kept firing." F1c Alex Guillot from Louisiana was pounding away on one of the .50-caliber machine guns when *Sculpin*'s conning tower was hit. "The Japs made a direct hit on his gun and wounded him severely," said Baker. "I still remember how he looked with blood streaming from great rips in his chest, passing ammunition until he fell over the side."

James Harper, his left arm blown off, was seen by Ed Ricketts to remain at his 20mm gun even as *Sculpin* was torn apart by bullets and 5-inch shells. When the shells ripped apart the conning tower, GM2c John Rourke leaped overboard with his life jacket. Cooper and another seriously wounded 20mm gunner, Charles Pitser, both leaped from the wrecked bridge into the ocean.

Battered and bloodied, the surviving gun crew members kept ramming in shells and firing as *Yamagumo* bore down on *Sculpin*. As the range narrowed, the Japanese opened up with machine guns and small arm fire. Other crewmen were killed by machine-gun fire as they came out on deck to abandon ship. S1c William Henry Partin, a 23-year-old with a new son he had never seen, was cut down by the gunfire. SM3c Dowdey Shirley, according to gunner Bob Wyatt from Los Angeles, "died of bad shrapnel wounds" during *Sculpin*'s final fight.

Joe Baker, already wounded, was shot through the leg right above his ankle. "A lot of people didn't know that I'd been shot," he recalled. In the frenzied action, the gallant gunners maintained their fire in spite of their own injuries. MoMM2c Ed Ricketts had come topside from the engine room to serve as the third loader on the 3-inch gun. "We had time to get eight rounds off," he said, "but all went over the destroyer."

In the control room, diving officer George Brown quickly realized that *Sculpin* had been severely damaged. "I considered it unwise to wait longer for scuttling operations because the next shell might damage the hydraulic system, thus making it impossible to operate the vents," he recalled. Word was passed down to him of the loss of the ship's senior officers, which left him in command of the boat.

Calling back to the maneuvering room, Lieutenant Brown rang up emergency speed. When his order was acknowledged, he then ordered abandon ship over the 1MC. Watching the control-room clock, Brown tried to give his crew at least a fighting chance to make it topside before he flooded his submarine. Standing by his side was CMoMM Phil Gabrunas, one of the nine men who had been aboard *Sculpin* for every war patrol. With Chief of the Boat Dinty Moore topside leading the fight from the 3-inch deck gun, Gabrunas gallantly volunteered to stay behind and man the Christmas tree with the chief engineering officer.

When the call came to abandon ship, everyone in the after battery compartment scrambled for their life jackets. Ed Keller witnessed the new yeoman, Delbert Schroeder, race into the compartment in great distress because he had no life jacket and could not swim.[12]

Keller gave up his own jacket just as more shells were heard to slam into the water alongside *Sculpin*. With that, he raced toward the hatch, forgetting that he was still wearing his battle headset. Yanked back to the deck, Keller picked himself up and followed Schroeder and others toward the engine-room hatch. The first sailor up the hatch, S2c Robert Carter, was shot and fell back down the ladder.

The next man heading up was S1c George Goorabian, who noted that Keller was not wearing a life jacket.

"I'll wait for you on deck," he offered.

"For God's sake, don't wait for me!" Keller replied. As he neared the hatch exit, Keller saw that "Goorabian was hit and half his body was blown off. At that point, there was an explosion in the boat and I was blown out the hatch and over the side."[13]

When the order to abandon ship was issued, TM3c Harry Toney was in the mess hall, helping to pass the 3-inch ammunition topside. "We started out through the conning tower when we got word to go through the forward engine room hatch," Toney recalled. "I ran forward to the conning tower and remember seeing the destroyer standing by, firing dead away. Everyone was diving overboard, so I dove, too."

Lieutenant Brown sent two of his chief petty officers to spread the word manually in case the loudspeakers were out in any compartment. CMM Richard Hemphill ran forward through the boat while CMM William Haverland headed aft to pass the word. When the chiefs returned, Brown waited one additional minute, watching the clock.

Turning to Phil Gabrunas, the diving officer then ordered him to open all the vents, thus allowing the ocean to begin flooding into every ballast tank. Those still aboard knew all too well that *Sculpin* would be under the waves within the next moment and that she would never resurface.

Brown had informed Captain Cromwell, who was in the control room, of his plans and he was told to go ahead.

"I'm not coming with you," Cromwell said. "I know too much." He explained that the classified information he possessed could cause great injury to his shipmates at sea if the Japanese were to torture it out of him.

Ens. Max Fiedler, the young officer who had inadvertently broached *Sculpin*, also decided that he was not leaving. Some of the motor machinist's mates noticed him as they raced topside. "The boat was making 17 knots when she went down with the hatches wide open," recalled Ed Ricketts. "Ensign Wendell Max Fiedler, the commissary officer, grabbed himself a deck of cards and went into the wardroom to play solitaire." Chief Hemphill also reported to shipmates that he had seen Ensign Fiedler in the wardroom. The young officer was playing cards and chatting with one of the two Filipino mess attendants, Ck1c Eugenio Apostol.

"Come on, let's go," Hemphill urged. "We're scuttling the boat!"

"We do not choose to go with you," Fiedler replied. "We prefer death to capture by the Japanese."

With no time to argue, Hemphill headed for the control room, leaving Apostol and Fiedler to their elected fates. He relayed the conversation to diving officer George Brown.

Brown left John Cromwell behind and scrambled up the ladder into the conning tower, where he found the bodies of several shipmates who had been killed by the direct hits. "As I left the conning tower door, water was coming waist deep over the sill, and I am certain no one left the ship after me," he stated. Brown did see Chief Phil Gabrunas coming up through the conning tower hatch, but neither he nor Hemphill escaped *Sculpin*. They either became fouled in the jagged wreckage of the diving submarine or were cut down by Japanese gunfire because they were not seen again among the survivors in the water.

Motormac Moon Rocek reached the deck and immediately noted the bloody corpse of a shipmate. Seeing the approaching destroyer, he started for *Sculpin*'s port side when she was slammed by another direct hit. "I was momentarily stunned and numb all over," he recounted. "After seeing I was intact, I jumped over the side." Rocek had been peppered with shrapnel from the direct hit, which left many watch spring-shaped metal fragments embedded in his skin.

EM3c Eldon Wright—a Utah native who had completed only three years of high school before joining the Navy in late 1940—had been passing ammunition topside during the gun duel. When the abandon ship order was passed, he raced topside. "I started to go to the conning tower but just before I reached it, a shell hit it and I jumped over the side," Wright stated.

Dinty Moore and his deck gun crew remained at their gun until *Sculpin* started down. "We heard the vents being pulled, so off into the ocean we dove," recalled Joe Baker. "Many of the crew had already dove off before this."

Some of the crew made no effort to leave and rode their ship down. Others had been killed aboard ship. Herb Thomas remembered that his torpedo room boss, CTM Claiborne Weade—a veteran of many patrols aboard Fearless Freddie Warder's famous *Seawolf*—did not leave *Sculpin*.

Sculpin made her final dive for the ocean floor as her crew swam away from her. Heavy shells and machine-gun fire chopped up the ocean as the *Yamagumo* gunners fired on the disappearing American sub until she was gone. Their gunfire also raked the survivors, some already wounded, as they struggled in the water. "Her last dive was really a nice one," noted Ed Ricketts whose vantage point was in the ocean. "The last I saw was the radar mast going under," said Harry Toney. "She made a beautiful dive."

Five years and 115 days since she had come down the ways in Portsmouth, *Sculpin* was gone. Moments after she started her 5-mile descent to the ocean floor, the survivors felt a heavy concussion as her 252 storage batteries short-circuited and exploded. A half mile from the struggling survivors, they saw a giant waterspout announce the end of their proud boat.[14]

Radioman Julius Peterson—an 18-year-old from Idaho who had just joined the sub after serving two years on the tender *Holland*—called out to Ed Keller and they swam toward yeoman Delbert Schroeder, who had on Keller's life jacket.

Sculpin battles destroyer *Yamagumo* and is scuttled on 18 November 1943

41 members of *Sculpin* crew held as prisoners on Truk's Dublon Island from 20–30 November 1943

North Pass

Moen

Tol

Dublon

TRUK ISLANDS

Kuop Atoll

Loss of USS *Sculpin*

Keller had been blown out of his clothes when the explosion forced him out of *Sculpin*'s hatch. In the water, he rolled over and "saw the destroyer was very, very close. I was looking up at it. The bow was already by me and the after gunners were machine-gunning those in the water." When Peterson and Keller reached the yeoman, they saw that Schroeder was dead. He had been shot in the chest twice.[15]

Senior officer George Brown called out to his men, collecting the survivors into one large group in the water. "Those of us who were strong swimmers aided the wounded and weak swimmers," he said. Brown later cited Ens. Charles Smith, Ens. Worth Gamel, and Chief Weldon Moore for being "instrumental in saving many of those struggling in the water before being taken aboard the Japanese destroyer."

First loader Joe Baker, suffering from shrapnel wounds and a gunshot through his leg, selflessly tried to help support another shipmate in the water who had been more severely wounded. "He'd been hit quite bad. I tried to help him stay afloat, but it was just too much."

GM2c John Rourke was knocked senseless by the explosions. His life jacket helped support him but he would not have survived without the help of a friend. "I lost consciousness and only with the aid of a shipmate did I make it to the Japanese destroyer to be picked up," he recalled.

Herb Thomas, the sight setter on the 3-inch gun, offered his life belt to gunner Rourke and to S1c William Welsh. A young sailor striking for his quartermaster rating, Welsh had been badly wounded in several places by shrapnel from one of the shell explosions. "Though wounded, Welsh talked to me while in the water," Rourke recalled. After swimming for some time, however, Welsh was close to giving up hope as *Yamagumo* slowed to retrieve survivors. Thomas slapped Welsh in the face and told him, "Open your eyes. There's a ship and we're going to go on it."

The Japanese destroyer that had dealt *Sculpin* her death blows ceased machine-gunning the submariners after making a complete pass to ensure that the American sub was no more. Around 1500, *Yamagumo* slowed down and threw lines over the side to give the survivors a chance.

Many of the men were understandably reluctant to go aboard the *Yamagumo*. "When I first got into the water, it was my intention to swim away from the destroyer for I had heard of the torture that the Japanese gave to prisoners," said Eldon Wright, "but I decided to take the chance."

12
Ten Days on Truk

Bill Cooper regained consciousness as the Japanese destroyer approached. He had been knocked out by the force of the underwater explosion when *Sculpin* went down. "When I came to, I was under the water," he said. Wearing only shorts and sandals, he kicked for the surface, aware of a great pain in his back area. "They had these iron bars that were welded on top of the screws," Cooper recalled. He later believed that one of the explosions may have caused one of these pieces of metal to strike his back. Shaking off the pain, the quartermaster kicked away his sandals and started swimming for his only hope of rescue—the enemy destroyer. He encountered Chief Dinty Moore and another young sailor and together they swam. En route, Cooper saw shipmates die as machine-gun bullets sprayed the ocean surface.

Seventeen-year-old S2c Mike Gorman from California had been so eager to join the war effort in October 1942, that he had to convince his parents to sign forms allowing him to enlist in the Navy. Fresh from boot camp and torpedo school in San Diego, Gorman was one of the youngest hands on board when he joined *Sculpin* prior to her ninth patrol. As he peered up at the Japanese sailors on the destroyer's deck above him, he knew that only his strong faith could get him through whatever was in store for him.[1]

As many as a dozen aboard *Sculpin* had been killed by *Yamagumo*'s 5-inch shell explosions during the gun duel. Several other members of the 84-man crew had elected to go down with the ship. More than two dozen others were killed as they exited the hatches or were machine-gunned while in the ocean. When the shooting finally ceased, *Yamagumo* only brought on board 42 survivors of *Sculpin*'s original 84 men.

Ed Keller and radioman Julius Peterson climbed the destroyer's rope ladder together. Men with rifles motioned them to go forward to the bow. Keller panicked, thinking back to the movie *Black Swan* he had seen in *Sculpin*'s forward torpedo room. It told the story of a sailing ship on which illegal slaves were tied to the anchors and dropped overboard to avoid discovery by the British.[2]

"They tied our hands and feet together and sat us on the steel deck on topside, up in the bow," said Joe Baker. Eldon Wright was stunned by the loss of another shipmate. "Seaman first class Welsh, weak from loss of blood resulting from a chest and shoulder shrapnel wound, fainted on the deck of the destroyer." This was apparently enough to make the Japanese decide Welsh was not worth keeping. "Pharmacist's mate Todd told me several days later that he had a good chance of survival if he had been given proper treatment," Wright related.

Herb Thomas had tried to help Welsh in the water and once he was up on the destroyer's deck. "He had a triangular chest wound and as he breathed, that triangular piece of flesh wavered in and out." Thomas laid Welsh out on deck. "Blood was running down his legs but the Japs couldn't see his chest wound. They thought it was coming from his legs."

Bill Cooper grabbed his young quartermaster striker and called for assistance. Ens. Charles Smith came to his aid. "We were so crowded aboard *Sculpin* that when this new ensign came aboard for the last run, they put him in the forward torpedo room to sleep with us," Cooper recalled. "I got acquainted with him pretty good. We were the only two on the boat from Tennessee. I grabbed Welsh around the chest and Smitty grabbed him around the legs," said Cooper. "We started forward and got about halfway there when this Jap officer stopped us and made us lay him down on the deck."

Although identified as Claiborne Weade in some accounts, this man was seaman William Welsh, "a kid from St. Louis," according to Cooper, Harry Toney, Herb Thomas, and Ed Ricketts. Welsh had been wounded by shrapnel in the chest, in the arm, and above his eye. "He could have been saved," Ricketts said. "He was brutally thrown over the side," RM2c Julius Peterson later stated. Thomas later testified of Welsh's death, "Since the captain of the [*Yamagumo*] was present at the time, it is presumed this was done on his orders."[3]

Gunner John Rourke had been helped to *Yamagumo* by a shipmate. He had swallowed a good deal of salt water and collapsed on the deck. In addition to swallowing salt water, Rourke "had sustained shrapnel cuts on my toes and my back and was vomiting." After tossing Welsh overboard, the Japanese decided that Rourke might be too injured to keep also. The sailors picked up the wounded gunner's mate and carried him to the quarterdeck. "Here they proceeded to swing me with the intention of throwing me over the side," Rourke recalled. "On the third swing,

---

Sculpin Survivors Picked Up By Destroyer *Yamagumo*

Anderson, Edward Niles	SC2	Milbourne, Harry Smith, Jr.	F1c
Baglien, Jerome Warren [1]	RM3	Moore, Weldon Edward [1]	CSM
Baker, Cecil Eugene	F2	Morrilly, Robert Michael [1]	EM3
Baker, Joseph Nicholas	F2	Murphy, Paul Louis	F1
Barrera, Maximo [1]	Ck1	Murray, Leo Joseph	MoMM1
Berry, Warren Rawling [1]	TM1	Parr, John [1]	RM3
Brannum, Bill Clifton [1]	F1	Peterson, Julius Grant	RM2
Brown, George Estabrook, Jr.	Lt.	Pitser, Charles Earl [1]	TM2
Brown, Thomas Vincent [1]	S2	Ricketts, Edward Forest	MoMM2
Carter, Robert William [1]	S2	Rocek, George	MoMM1
Cooper, Billie Minor	QM2	Rourke, John Paul	GM3
DeLisle, Maurice Simon [1]	F1	Smith, Charles Gold, Jr. [1]	Ens.
Elliott, Henry Leonidas [1]	F1	Taylor, Clifford Gene [1]	RM3
Eskildsen, Leo Aage	F1	Thomas, Herbert Joseph	TM1
Gamel, John Worth [1]	Ens.	Todd, Paul Allen	PhM1
Gorman, Michael Thomas	S2	Toney, Harry Ford	TM3
Haverland, William Herbert	CMoMM	Van Beest, Henry [1]	S1
Keller, Edwin Karl Frederick	S2c	Welsh, William Henry [2]	S1c
Kennon, John Bowers, Jr. [1]	SC3	White, Duane Joseph [1]	MoMM2
Laman, Harold Dewitt [1]	MoMM2	Wright, Eldon	EM3
McCartney, James William [1]	EM3c	Wyatt, Robert Orlin	GM2

[1] Rescued according to http://www.subvetpaul.com/Sculpin.html. This research of Paul W. Wittmer's accessed on 5/5/08. Other confirmation of survivors' names from various survivor statements, interviews, and in 1948 war crimes testimony of John Rourke and Cecil Baker.

[2] Thrown overboard to his death.

I kicked loose. By that time, they thought I was still alive and they gave me a thorough beating for one hour. They brought me back to the forecastle, [and] tied my hands and legs."

George Brown, the senior surviving *Sculpin* officer, later testified of the initial abuse on *Yamagumo*.

> Upon coming on deck, my crew were stripped of any excess clothing they had, all personal effects and jewelry. We were then ordered forward through two rows of Japanese enlisted men who lined the deck, with small paddles, clubs and sticks who pounded us on the head and the body and legs as we passed forward. Upon arrival in the forecastle, the Japanese made us face forward in a crouched position.

> The Japanese officials took one of my enlisted men around behind a gun turret and worked him over to get information about the submarine and about our destination and home port. When they were through questioning the enlisted man they called me and proceeded to beat me

with their fists and a small club for having given them false information about the name of the ship, the skipper and the tonnage.

They questioned me concerning the date of sailing and destination. When I refused to answer, they again beat me with their fists and told me the answers they received from the enlisted man.

Of the 41 *Sculpin* survivors remaining on *Yamagumo*, many had been wounded by machine-gun fire and shrapnel. "There was blood all over the place," said Ed Keller. A shipmate asked him how bad he had been hurt. "I said I wasn't hurt," he remembered. "But then I looked down at my chest and saw blood everywhere. It was dry, but right then I thought I was going to die."[4]

As he lay tied up, George Brown recalled how Captain Cromwell had tried to get *Sculpin*'s skipper to keep the boat down for one more attack. Cromwell had believed that *Yamagumo* must be running low of depth charges. Sure enough, the survivors found that the destroyer had only three more ashcans left in her racks as she covered the 200 miles back to the west to reach Truk.[5]

That evening, the survivors were given a few hard crackers and a few eight-ounce cans of water to share. It was their last food or water for days. "Little had been done to help any of the wounded," said Joe Baker, who had his own bullet and shrapnel wounds. "There were guys with all kinds of wounds imaginable, and were losing valuable blood. That night, we were all left on deck. Our hands and feet [were] tied, with only a piece of tarpaulin stretched over all 41 of us for protection in a hard rainstorm against a raging sea."

Long before dawn on 20 November, *Yamagumo* began steaming into the anchorage of Truk. By gunner Rourke's estimation, it was about 0100. *Yamagumo* docked at Dublon Island, a busy seaplane and submarine base within Truk's lagoon. At Pearl Harbor, the submarine command was aware of what had happened to *Sculpin*. On 19 November, code breakers intercepted *Yamagumo*'s signal to Truk. The destroyer radioed: "At 1304, sank enemy submarine with gunfire. Have 41 prisoners. Will send action summary later." The next day, another message was intercepted, this one indicating that the prisoners would be turned over to Base Force Commander at Truk and *Yamagumo* would commence refueling.[6]

After *Yamagumo* dropped anchor in the harbor, blindfolds were placed on each man before they were prodded toward the little boat. "Being blindfolded and our hands still tied made things complicated as all hell," said Joe Baker. "This is where some of us received our first slugging because we were curious and tried to see from beneath our blindfolds."

The Japanese did not want them to see the super battleship *Musashi* and other key warships anchored in Truk Lagoon. Once the launch reached shore, the *Sculpin* prisoners were moved toward a waiting truck. "I was blindfolded, barefooted and the only clothing I had was a pair of torn underdrawers," recalled Lieutenant

Brown. "We were forced to walk across a coral beach barefooted with a Jap guard prodding us with rifles." With their hands secured by ropes, the *Sculpin* men were beaten and poked with bayonets. Many were suffering from various wounds and found walking difficult. One man's arm was nearly severed from wounds received on the submarine and another was losing blood from his calf being torn nearly from his leg.[7]

Their journey in the bouncing truck took them to the other end of Dublon Island to a small, fenced detention compound at the foot of a 1,500-foot peak. The compound's size indicated that it had been made to handle a small number of prisoners but it was now to become home to 41 U.S. sailors.

The survivors were taken to a wooden outdoor prisoner compound, an area of about 30 square feet which had three cells on one side. The men were shoved into the cells, each of which had a hole in the floor to serve as a toilet. No food was offered on the first day. Worst of all, their hands remained bound and many had been stripped naked. The *Sculpin* survivors were forced to eat, sleep, and even use the benjo with their hands tied.

Fireman Cecil Baker was placed into the first cell on the left side of the compound with 13 other shipmates. As to its size, "our estimate was around seven feet by five feet. The interior of the cell had a dirty wood floor [with] maggots and ants crawling over it," Baker later testified. "There wasn't even anything to sit on. We had to sit on our haunches with our hands tied. Some of the fellows had to sleep inside the head in order to make room for all of us to even get our elbows down beside us." The men in the first cell with Cecil Baker included MoMM2c Ed Ricketts, S1c Mike Gorman, S2c Ed Keller, GM2c Bob Wyatt, RM2c Julius Peterson, and TM3c Harry Toney. Seven other men were crammed into the first cell, including "a couple of new fellows I didn't know then."

Ed Keller later recalled that any conversations ended when a hand reached through their window with a bat that was swung against the prisoners. "I got hit in the shoulder and head," he said. "You learned to put your hands over your head and turn to protect yourself." Keller said that cell mate Baker occasionally yelled out, "I need water! I need water!" With the cries, "that hand with the bat would reach in and whomp! whomp! whomp!"[8]

Joe Baker, who had been shot and wounded by shrapnel during *Sculpin*'s gun battle, was packed into the middle cell with 13 others. He recalled that "the ventilation within each cell consisted of one window protected by wooden bars." In addition to Baker, four others in the middle cell were severely wounded. TM2c Charles Pitser, RM3c Jerome Baglien, and F1c Henry Elliott—a six-patrol *Sculpin* engineman known to his shipmates as "Rebel"—had each been shot or terribly wounded by *Yamagumo*'s shells. "We all took turns standing to allow more room for them," said cell mate Moon Rocek, suffering from less severe wounds. Others in the center cell included gunner's mate second class Rourke (also wounded by shrapnel), RM3c John Parr, S2 Robert Carter, TM1c Warren Berry, Ens. Charles Smith, TM1c Herb Thomas, and MoMM2c Duane White. Rourke recalled the conditions in this crowded cell.

> One man named Baglien with severe .50-caliber wounds was one of the occupants. I saw his legs, though blindfolded, by working the blindfold up from my nose. They were maggot-ridden and he was in severe pain all the time I was with him. Because of the cramped quarters, at least three men had to rest in the head.
>
> At times Baglien was laying down. I wouldn't say completely down but we tried to help him as much as we could. He was severely wounded and always in pain.
>
> While making room for the wounded, we had to crouch and often to relieve the strain on our legs we would stand up. We had to take turns at doing this because when we would stand up the Japanese proceeded to work our heads over with a stick a little bit bigger than a two by four. The guard also chose to bring us out of the cell and make us crouch with our hands on our knees and smack us in the back with the stick for standing up.

F1c Paul Louis Murphy, a 20-year-old from New Castle, Pennsylvania, was placed into the third cell with EM3c Wright, CSM Dinty Moore, Ens. Worth Gamel, PhM1c Paul Todd, Lieutenant Brown, and four other shipmates. "We couldn't wash, shave or brush our teeth," Murphy recalled. "The only toilet facilities provided here was a hole in the floor in the same room we were confined to."

Eldon Wright related, "I was confined with ten other members of the crew of the *Sculpin* in a cell. We were interrogated separately and beaten with a wooden club on our hind quarters when we failed to answer questions to the satisfaction of the Japanese naval officers present."

QM2c Bill Cooper later stated that he, SC2c Edward "Andy" Anderson—a prewar cook from California who was the oldest man from *Sculpin*—and two others were packed into a little closet near the three cells. "They put the rest of them out in three little brigs out behind the office," said Cooper. Desperate for water, Cooper literally begged for it from his little closet. "I had been on the wheel for eight of our last hours, hand steering the boat," he recalled. "When you're hand steering, it would take a hundred turns on that wheel to change from left rudder to full right rudder. I had sweated so much that I was thirsty when I left the boat." Although he begged for three days, the guards would not give Cooper a drop of water. "They just laughed at me."

Lieutenant Brown was only in his cell for about ten minutes before he was again blindfolded and led across the coral to a little table set up in the compound yard. Behind it, "a Japanese Rear Admiral and five or six other ranking officers of the

Japanese Navy were seated. They proceeded to question me through an interpreter." The admiral sought information on *Sculpin*, other U.S. submarines, operating bases, code and communication information."

When the admiral did not like Brown's answers, he nodded to two Japanese enlisted men to apply four or five blows to the American officer's back and legs with long clubs. "At one time during the questioning, the force of the blows were such that they lifted me off the ground and across the table and I fell upon the Japanese admiral," Brown related. "I was then dragged off and severely beaten for daring to attack a Japanese admiral."

Following this questioning session, Lieutenant Brown was led blindfolded to a pillbox and made to stand at attention for 48 hours. This time was "broken only by intervals of questionings and beatings. At any time that I relaxed from a position of rigid attention, the guard would drop his rifle on my bare foot or kick me in the shins and beat me over the head with his rifle butt."

After two straight days of alternately standing at attention, being beaten and being interrogated, George Brown was hauled back into the cell block with his men. During this time, the other *Sculpin* men had been undergoing their own interrogations out of sight of the foxhole where Brown was standing.

No food or water was offered to any of the *Sculpin* men during their first days at Truk. Rebel Elliott was in severe pain from a shell hole through the palm of his hand and Jerome Baglien writhed in agony from holes in his thighs. During one of the harassment sessions, Joe Baker became angry when the Japanese guards began poking at shipmate Charles Pitser with bamboo poles. Pitser's arm had been blown almost completely off at the shoulder and the torpedoman could not defend himself. "He was about 235 pounds, 6 feet, 2 inches in height, had long black hair, a big round face, and was tattooed on both forearms," Baker said of his friend Pitser. "I tried to protect my colleague," he related, but he was removed from the cell by guards. "Two of them beat me unconscious with clubs and closed fists."

———

The Imperial Japanese Navy officials on Truk were intent on learning as much as possible from the 41 U.S. submariners. In addition to Lt. Brown, all *Sculpin* men were interrogated at least once and often numerous times. Eldon Wright was questioned as to the number of submarines the United States had, how many were based at Pearl Harbor, and on the names of American battleships and carriers.

John Rourke was questioned only once, during his first day on Truk. "I was beaten again and again by the guard for not coming to attention," he related. "As the guard called attention in Japanese it wasn't until the interpreter told me what he was saying that I received no more beatings from the guard." He was questioned just outside of the brig, where his blindfold was removed as he stood before an officer seated at a little table. "He asked me where my submarine was operating," Rourke later stated. "When I told him I didn't know, the guard gave me a couple of more whacks. Not satisfying the questions, I was returned to the hut."

"Many of us took some hard beatings," said Joe Baker. Julius Peterson later described the lead interrogator as a man who "seemed to be the 'big shot' of the camp. He was a little larger than the average Japanese and had gold in his teeth." Ed Keller was led naked and blindfolded outside of his cell, where he was stood in front of five officers in white fatigues. After giving out his name, rank, and serial number, Keller was addressed as "Edwin" during his 20-minute interrogation. When asked if the sunken U.S. battleships were still on the bottom of Pearl Harbor, he replied that he had not seen them. "I was rapped one time in the groin with a stick between the legs," Keller related.[9]

Torpedoman Herb Thomas gave the Japanese false information to try to ward off the beatings. He considered it a wonder he and others were not paralyzed by the blows that often landed high above their tailbones. "When that club hit you too high, it would just jar the shit out of you," he said. Thomas found that "men accidentally gave answers and the Japs compared notes. I gave them nothing truthful whatsoever." He told his interrogators that the U.S. subs were refueling at a secret island between the Gilberts and Truk. When the Japanese thrust an ancient chart in front of Thomas, he could not help them find the mystery island. Back in his cell, Thomas whispered the ruse to his buddies. "The men were subjected to constant questioning. It appeared that the officers received the worst treatment, with the radar men being the next in line."

Ed Ricketts recalled, "Thomas spread the bum dope upon questioning that American subs were refueling at a secret island between the Gilberts and Truk. They dragged out charts from back in 1820 but couldn't find anything. Thomas gave us the word and we repeated the story."

During his interrogation, George Rocek was blindfolded and led to the little desk with the senior interpreter. He learned to stall for time by saying he could not understand the question. "The Japs had their own interpreter and he couldn't speak English too well, so I was able to get away with it sometimes." When Rocek's answers did not suit his captors, "this guy would nod his head and those seamen would whop you across your rear end with that big bat," he said. "It hurt like hell, especially when he hit you a little high in the tailbone." During interrogations, Joe Baker was "hit with clubs and baseball bats, mostly on the bottom of my spine."

TM3c Harry Toney stated, "If they were asked for water, they hit you with a club. I was beaten and slugged by one guard until I was bleeding." Bill Cooper, already suffering from a back injury, was hit "across the back right above the butt with a club as big as a ball bat."

On his third day at Truk, Cecil Baker was shown a map and learned that they were on Truk. He was questioned about his sub, its operating base and on other

U.S. subs operating in the vicinity. Baker was eventually taken out for questioning three times, resulting in "numerous sores and bumps on my back and shoulders and numerous headaches."

The three officers—Lieutenant Brown, Ens. Charles Smith, and Ens. Worth Gamel—were beaten more than the enlisted men during their interrogations. Although the enlisted men did not witness the ordeal of George Brown, they could often see the results. "He would come back under guard each day from these interrogations black and blue from head to foot," Joe Baker testified.

Lieutenant Brown's class ring was stolen on one occasion by one of the Japanese guards. When Brown complained to the interpreter, the guard was called forward by the interpreter to be searched. According to John Rourke, however, this was "not before the guard had slipped the ring into Ensign Smith's trouser pocket. The guard himself searched Ensign Smith, and finding the ring he himself placed there, showed it to the interpreter."

Smitty was thus falsely accused of stealing his fellow officer's ring and was sentenced to punishment by the interpreter. "He received a terrific beating on his buttocks," related Rourke. "They kept knocking him down and forcing him up again."

When it became apparent that the Japanese wanted to know who the radar officer was, Brown and his fellow officers took steps to protect the only surviving radar operator, RM3c John Parr. Four radiomen—Parr, Julius Peterson, Cliff Taylor, and Jerome Baglien—were held at Truk. Of them, only Parr had regularly served on the radar watches, but he had just joined *Sculpin* for her ninth run. The other two members of *Sculpin*'s radar and sonar gang, RT2c Edgar Beidleman and RM3c Grover Marcus, had been killed in the conning tower or while swimming. "The officers informed all of us he was to be considered a gunner, not a radarman," said Ed Keller.[10]

Although every effort was taken to protect Parr, the Japanese came into his cell one day and called him out by name and rank. He was taken for an intense round of questioning on the secrets of radar. "He was gone several hours," said Keller. "When he came back, he was beaten badly in the shoulders and arms." Parr told his shipmates his interrogation group included a group of officers under a tree.[11]

"Upon his return the first time, he told me that they asked him about radar. He was taken out quite often during the day and night," recalled John Rourke. After his second round of abuse, Rourke noted that Parr was "kind of dopey, like he had been beaten up too much. He wasn't the same person he was aboard the submarine. He was semi-conscious. On the submarine, he was the type who would joke, but here he kept to himself. They would keep him out for a half hour, put him back and an hour later take him out again."

Radioman Julius Peterson felt that John Parr, Ensign Gamel, Lieutenant Brown, Ed Keller, Bob Wyatt, and Eldon Wright "were beaten the most severely" during the first days at Truk. "The Japanese seemed to enjoy the suffering of us prisoners," Peterson added. "The guards would point their guns at us, take out the clip, put it back, and suddenly pull the trigger. We would not know whether the guns were loaded or not."

When food rations were finally offered to the *Sculpin* men, Moon Rocek said it consisted of "one rice ball a day and a few ounces of water. We were let out of our cells twice a day for about ten minutes, an event to which we gratefully looked forward to." This short time only offered minor relief. "Being so cramped inside, when we did get out we could hardly straighten our legs and stand up straight," said Paul Murphy.

"At about 1630 each day, a guard would bring in a platter of boiled rice and give each man a rice ball about as big as the palm of one's hand," related Joe Baker. "During mealtime, the doors of the cells were open and we were allowed to obtain water from two bottles." To do so, the *Sculpin* prisoners were lined up outside their cells and made to cup their hands or open their mouths. When Cecil Baker and a couple others were brought out for water, the guards "made us kneel on the ground and they poured water down our throat and nose out of a bottle." John Rourke added of one guard, "When you choked, he would get a big kick out of it. It was his intention to try and choke us."[12]

After the first days of confinement, the *Sculpin* men were weak from hunger, dehydration, and their beatings. While they were allowed out of their cells during one of the short periods, their guards found new forms of entertainment. "As another form of mistreatment, they would make us get into a squatting position, our knees partially bent and hold our hands up in the air," stated Murphy. "Some of the fellows fell over from the intense heat here and were beaten until they got up again."

Beatings were frequent during the "recreation" periods. "Ensign Smith was out in the compound talking to one of the guards," recalled Cecil Baker. "The guard kept telling him about how the Japanese planes were going to bomb the United States. Ensign Smith said the Japanese would never get that far but that American planes would bomb Japan." The guard became enraged and beat Smitty severely in front of his shipmates.

The Japanese finally allowed the men to clean out the filth, blood, and human waste from their cells one day. Water was brought in and the prisoners were forced to scrub the floors of their cells. While doing so, John Rourke tried to get a drink of the water. One of the guards caught him and he was "subjected to a thorough beating." Three others—Duane White, Warren Berry, and Jerome Baglien—were also beaten with fists and clubs for drinking the filthy cleaning water.

"While they were washing the huts they would look around to see if any guards were looking and they would take a drink of this water and they were caught," related Cecil Baker. He also recalled that guards nicknamed Ed Ricketts "Monkey" and continued calling him a monkey "when they noticed his resentment." Sensing the anger Ricketts expressed at this name-calling, the guards removed him from his cell and beat him severely in the open section of the compound.

"Three guards used baseball bats, clubs and their fists on Ricketts, working him over from head to foot, but hitting him mostly on the bottom of his spine, his back, shoulders and face, until he was unconscious," said Joe Baker. He saw them throw Ricketts' unconscious body back into his cell. On a separate occasion, Baker watched the guards beat John Parr unconscious "in the same manner as they did Ricketts, but this time they left him in a corner of the compound still unconscious. Later, the guards threw this man into his cell after he had regained consciousness but would not give him any food that day or night."

Herb Thomas learned to dread the Japanese punch he and his shipmates dubbed "the haymaker." Using their clenched fists, Japanese guards would wind up and swing with great speed. "It was like being slapped across the face with a closed fist," Thomas explained. "This way, they could hit you with haymakers and cause great pain. If they would have just kept punching us straight on in the face repeatedly, they would have killed us."

Lieutenant Brown complained forcefully to the Japanese about the poor conditions of his shipmates, trying to signal various needs via crude sign language. He asked repeatedly for help for the three most seriously wounded sailors. After the fifth day, 24 November, their wounds were beginning to stink as gangrene set in. Joe Baker found "it a living hell for everyone concerned with the ants, maggots, flies and mosquitoes pestering the wounded and getting into their wounds." Since the Japanese had removed their clothing, the injured simply had no way to cover up their wounds. "Pitser's arm wound was gangrene and it was really getting terrible," recalled cell mate Herb Thomas.

On the fifth day, the little compound was visited by a group of well-dressed Japanese officers. Ed Keller said, "They could smell the gangrene. The leader asked us who was in charge."[13]

Brown announced himself as the senior officer and answered questions.

"Who are the wounded?" he was asked.

"Just about everyone," Brown answered. He told the officers that none of his men had been treated or even given an aspirin for their serious wounds. Keller, watching the exchange, recalled, "The officer then turns and rants and raves at another officer. To punctuate the comments, he punches him in the face and knocks him backwards."[14]

Within hours, the first treatment offered to the prisoners was crudely handled by a Japanese Navy medical corpsman. He looked over the various wounds and, according to Joe Baker, he "wiped off dried bloodstains with a very dirty rag using some sort of liquid from a green bottle. No attempt was made to take out the bullet which I had in my leg."

Following this corpsman's visit, the most severely wounded *Sculpin* survivors were offered the opportunity to visit the local hospital on Truk. Eight men with the most serious gunshot and shrapnel wounds were ordered out of their cells. "We were blindfolded with a line around our waist to the man in front of me and behind," said John Rourke, who went to have medical attention for the shrapnel wounds to his toes. Among those who were herded from Rourke's cell were Moon Rocek, Robert Carter, Rebel Elliott, Charles Pitser, and radioman Jerome Baglien.

En route, Baglien struggled to walk. Baglien, forward of Rourke in the tie-line, stumbled and fell, pulling Rourke down with him. "He had fifty caliber wounds, large wounds in both legs in his thighs, which crippled him to a degree that he could hardly walk. We were then subjected to a good beating by the Jap guards escorting us," said Rourke. The guards worked over the wounded with bat-sized clubs until they could regain their feet. After finally reaching the medical office, the men's treatment was no better.

George Rocek, suffering from shrapnel wounds in his legs, found that wounds were treated with fish oil and bandages, but no medicines were administered. John Rourke's blindfold was removed and fish-oil bandages were also applied to his wounds—a shrapnel wound in his back and two lacerated toes. The Truk doctor crudely probed his most severe open wound with a wire-like metal instrument. "Every time he put it in the place where I was cut, they would get their laugh when I was in pain," Rourke later testified.

Rocek, Rourke, and the three other less seriously injured were then returned to their prison while the three most seriously wounded remained at the medical office. Bridge gunner Charles Pitser was suffering from an arm that had been badly injured by the first shell hit. Although *Sculpin* pharmacist Paul Todd knew that an operation could save it, Pitser's arm was cut off by the Japanese in the crude facility. Rebel Elliott had a silver-dollar-sized hole in his hand. Unwilling to operate on him either, the Japanese restrained him while it was removed. The Japanese also sawed off one of radioman Jerome Baglien's legs in a similarly horrible fashion.

"One man had his hand amputated and the other, his arm," said Moon Rocek. "They told us the amputations were done without any anesthetic and they were questioned at the same time." Ed Ricketts testified that "Elliott was shot in the hand, but could move all his fingers, and our pharmacist's mate said it was o.k., but the Japs amputated his hand at the wrist." Cecil Baker later stated that there were "three amputees who had their leg, arm and their hand amputated."

Baglien, Pitser, and Elliott remained secluded away from the other survivors at the medical office for several days before being returned. Julian Peterson stated in 1948, "The wounded were left uncared for until several men lost good limbs." War crimes testimony from the trial of Vice Adm. Seisaku Wakabayashi, Commander of the Fourth Base Force, would show that three *Sculpin* men had been given amputations without anesthesia.[15]

Following this first round of "treatment" offered by the Japanese, no other *Sculpin* man was willing to receive medical attention again. "The next time they asked for men who wished to obtain medical treatment at the hospital, I didn't answer up," said Rourke. Cecil Baker had suffered a ruptured eardrum during his second interrogation. After hearing about the beatings his shipmates had endured en route to the medical office, "I decided not to tell them about my ear."

After the senior Japanese officers visited, conditions improved for the other submarine survivors in terms of food and water. After ten days on Truk, the *Sculpin* survivors were herded out of their cells on the morning of 30 November and the Japanese shaved off all of their hair. Each man was issued a set of Japanese Navy undress blues to wear and was given a flat, square, wooden block with Japanese writing on it to wear around his neck like a dog tag. "We were all naked until now," stated Joe Baker. He said they were "told that we were going to Japan, where we would be kept until the end of the war." The men's hands were tied and they were blindfolded for the ride to the harbor.

One day after the 41 *Sculpin* prisoners had been delivered to Dublon Island, an important task force of warships had arrived from Yokosuka to help deal with the American invasion of the Gilbert Islands. The arriving warships had included the 12,950-ton light carrier *Zuiho* and two 17,830-ton escort carriers, *Unyo* and *Chuyo*. *Chuyo*, originally the transport *Nitta Maru*, had been converted to an aircraft carrier during 1943 following Japanese carrier losses at the battle of Midway.[16]

Vice Admiral Mineichi Kogo ultimately decided not to send his three carriers against the superior U.S. carrier task forces in the vicinity. The carriers would return to Japan with the captured American submariners, who would be grilled for more information on the Pacific offensive.

The *Sculpin* prisoners were marched toward the water while blindfolded. Their ropes were removed so that they could walk with their hand on the shoulder of the man in front of them. "On the way to the dock, I was repeatedly struck with a club when I fell or did not walk fast enough," said John Rourke. Cecil Baker found that if anyone stumbled or could not walk fast enough, "guards would come up from behind us and beat us with the club they carried." The Americans were loaded onto landing barges and transported out on two small whaleboats to aircraft carriers. According to George Rocek, they could only look down. When someone dared to look up, "the Nips would clobber the hell out of us with bats. One shipmate of mine had gotten a glimpse and said that we were heading for a Japanese aircraft carrier."[17]

John Rourke later stated, "I know it was a carrier because I inched my blindfold up and I could see when we were alongside the ship." They were all loaded aboard *Unyo* as the fleet prepared to sail for Japan on 30 November—one and a half weeks after arriving at Truk. The Japanese ultimately sorted the survivors into two groups and moved 21 of the 41 men over to the carrier *Chuyo*.

Lieutenant Brown and 19 enlisted men remained locked in a hold below the waterline on *Unyo*: Andy Anderson, Cecil Baker, Joe Baker, Bill Cooper, Leo Eskildsen, Mike Gorman, William Haverland, Ed Keller, Harry Milbourne, Paul Murphy, Leo Murray, Julius Peterson, Ed Ricketts, John Rourke, Herb Thomas, Paul Todd, Harry Toney, Eldon Wright, and Bob Wyatt.

Chief Dinty Moore, Ens. Charles Smith, and Ens. Worth Gamel were transferred to the carrier *Chuyo*. The most seriously wounded—including amputees Baglien, Pitser, and Elliott—were moved with this group. Twenty-one *Sculpin* men were packed below decks aboard *Chuyo*, the other 15 being: Maurice De Lisle, Maximo Berrera, Warren Berry, Bill Brannum, Tom Brown, Robert Carter, John Kennon, Harold Laman, James McCartney, Robert Morrilly, John Parr, Moon Rocek, Cliff Taylor, Henry Van Beest, and Duane White.

The Japanese carriers sailed on 30 November, heading for Yokohama, some 2,000 miles distant. The carriers were escorted by the heavy cruiser *Maya* and destroyers *Akebono*, *Urakaze*, *Sazanami*, and *Ushio*, the latter of which had contributed to the submarine *Perch*'s destruction in 1942.

Admiral Lockwood's staff became aware of the voyage of this Japanese convoy and sent out Ultras to submarines along the intended path. It was *Chuyo*'s 13th voyage along that route since the previous December. As fate would have it, *Chuyo*'s 13th voyage would prove to be quite unlucky due to the alerted American submarines.

Fate also dealt an unusual hand in that *Sailfish*—the former submarine *Squalus*, whose sister sub *Sculpin* had helped after her sinking—played a leading role in the drama that was to unfold for the unfortunate *Sculpin* survivors.

USS *Perch* (SS-176): Lost 3 March 1942

USS *Perch* (SS-176), seen at sea before the war. Her entire crew was picked up by a Japanese destroyer on 3 March 1942 after they scuttled their badly damaged submarine. *Photo courtesy of Charles H. McCoy.*

Lt. Cdr. Dave Hurt *(below)*, skipper of *Perch*. *(Right, top)* Lt. Beverly Robinson Van Buskirk, *Perch*'s second officer, from his Academy photo. *(Right, lower)* Lt. Kenneth George "K.G." Schacht, *Perch*'s fourth officer.

RM2c Joseph Raymond Normand, one of *Perch*'s three radiomen who were sent to Japan.

TM1c Samuel Ford Simpson was in charge of *Perch*'s forward torpedo room.

S1c Thomas Moore, an orphan before the war, was *Perch*'s battle talker on her last patrol.

(Above, left) TM3c Robert Wayne Lents celebrated his 20th birthday on 10 October 1941 by having this picture taken in Manila in the Philippines. *Courtesy of Robert Lents.*

(Center) Lt. (jg) Jacob Jay "Jake" Vandergrift was *Perch*'s junior officer. *Courtesy of Charles Hinman, USS Bowfin Museum.*

(Above, right) TM2c Warren Ingram Atkeison joined the Navy at age 17 from Mobile, Alabama. *Courtesy of Bill Atkeison.*

(Right) EM3c Ernest Virgil Plantz from West Virginia was one of the *Perch* enlisted men who spent the rest of the war as a POW at Makassar, Celebes. This view of Plantz with his sister Arnette was taken in September 1940 during his leave from boot camp. *Courtesy of Ernie Plantz.*

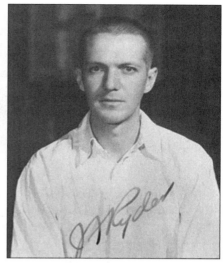

POW propaganda photos were taken and distributed by the Japanese in hopes of showing that their Allied prisoners were receiving proper care.

(*Above*) Captured U.S. officers were photographed together in this 1943 Zentsuji photo. *Left to right are:* Lt. (jg) Jake Vandegrift of *Perch*, and Lt. Robert V. Bassett Jr. and Lt. William R. Wilson of the destroyer *Pope*.

This photo of *Perch*'s engineering and diving officer, Lt. John French "Jack" Ryder, was taken in 1943 at the Zentsuji POW camp in Japan. *Photos courtesy of Lee K. Ryder.*

The 16,975-ton armed transport ship *Asama Maru* was the "hell ship" that transported some of the *Perch* crew to Japan in October 1942 and most *Grenadier* survivors from Singapore to Japan in late September and early October 1943. This view was taken after her 1929 launching, when she was a luxury liner. Aboard *Asama Maru*, the *Grenadier* POWs were beaten and tortured. *ONI-208J.*

This photo was taken of the *Perch* survivors aboard the Japanese destroyer *Ushio* en route to Malaysia on 3 March 1942. The photo was later found by a member of the Submarine Force in the radio room of a Japanese submarine. The Japanese writing on the back of the photo was translated as, "Enemy personnel picked up by our ship the day after Naval engagement off Surabaya."

In the right corner of the photo, looking toward the camera wearing a white sailor's cap is EM2 Jesse Robison of *Perch*. Two men beyond Robison, capless and looking directly toward the camera, is MM1 Tom Byrnes. Directly behind Byrnes' head is S1 Gordon Clevinger, also capless. To Clevinger's right, smoking a cigarette, is CMoMM Albert Newsome. The top of the head (partially obscured) with white sailor's cap (to Newsome's left) is EM3c Ernie Plantz. Beyond Plantz, the bearded sailor with white cap clearly seen against *Ushio*'s bulkhead is MM2 Charles Brown. The Filipino officer's cook sitting cross-legged and looking back toward the camera is CK1 Macario Sarmiento. The *Perch* sailor with crossed arms just beyond Sarmiento is TM1 Glenn Taylor. Neither Brown nor Newsome survived his POW captivity. *Courtesy of Robert Lents.*

(Left) CEM Houston Ernest Edwards of *Perch* died in 1944 in the Makassar camp. *Photo courtesy of Charles Hinman, www. oneternalpatrol.com website.*

(Right) EM2c Paul Richard Richter Jr, one of the *Perch* sailors who survived three and a half years of captivity. Richter, seen here at his home in San Antonio before the war, also survived a crude appendectomy shortly after arriving at the prisoner camp at Makassar. *Courtesy of Frances Richter Swinny.*

USS *Grenadier* (SS-210): Lost 21 April 1943

USS *Grenadier* (SS-210), seen leaving Portsmouth on 27 December 1941 for the war zone. She was severely damaged on her sixth patrol and her crew was forced to scuttle the boat to avoid it falling into Japanese hands. *Photo courtesy of Gordon C. Cox.*

Lt. Cdr. John Allison Fitzgerald *(above)*, the skipper of *Grenadier*, bravely endured much abuse as a POW. *Courtesy of Charles H. McCoy.*

Lt. Kevin Dennis Harty *(above)* was *Grenadier*'s communications officer at the time of her loss. He and the submarine's two senior officers were the first of their crew to be taken to Japan for interrogation. *Postwar photo courtesy of Cdr. Kevin Harty, USN (Ret.).*

Lt. Cdr. George Harris Whiting *(left)*, *Grenadier*'s executive officer, was making his eighth war patrol at the time of his ship's loss. Lt. Alfred Joseph Toulon Jr. *(center)* was *Grenadier*'s fourth senior officer. Toulon had joined the submarine at the beginning of 1943, just prior to *Grenadier*'s fifth patrol. Lt. Harmon Bradford Sherry *(right)*, *Grenadier*'s diving officer, had made four prior patrols on *Gudgeon*. *Courtesy of Charles Hinman, USS Bowfin Museum.*

(Right) Lt. Arthur G. McIntyre was new to *Grenadier* at the time of her loss. *Courtesy of Charles Hinman, USS Bowfin Museum.*

 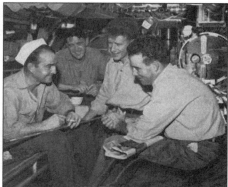

Grenadier pharmacist's mate John McBeath helped sew a sail after the ship lost all power. McBeath *(second from right, above)* is seen postwar with crewmates in *Amberjack*'s forward torpedo room. *Photo courtesy of Veronica Mayo.*

Grenadier crewmen in photos taken before their ship's loss. *(Left to right:)* TM1c Norman Arthur "Al" Albertson, S1c Gordon Charles Cox, and MoMM1c Raymond Grant "Railroad" Leslie. *Courtesy of Norman Albertson/Gordon Cox.*

Three views of the Penang Catholic girls' school where *Grenadier* survivors were held for more than 100 days. *(Center)* The greenhouse building where Lt. Cdr. John Fitzgerald was tortured. *(Bottom)* The interior rooms and courtyard where the submarine prisoners were kept in small cells. *Photos courtesy of Gordon Cox.*

(*Left*) MoMM2c Lee Clifford "Pappy" Shaw in his whites. Shaw was among the *Grenadier* crewmen later transferred to Ofuna and Omori. He would also be the only U.S. submarine POW survivor to go aboard the battleship *Missouri* at war's end for Japan's surrender. *Courtesy of Pat Havel.*

At Fukuoka, the *Grenadier* POWs were tagged with a number and photographed in heavy overcoats, which masked their thin bodies. Shown in late October 1943 are: EM2c Glen Fourre (*top left*), MoMM1c Raymond "Railroad" Leslie (*top center*), S1c Gordon Cox (*top right*), MM2c Charles "Pappy" Linder (*second row, left*), S1c Al Rupp (*second row, center*), and F1c Bernie Witzke (*second row, right*). At right is MoMM1c Chuck Ver Valin. Pappy Linder did not survive his internment in Japan. *Photos courtesy of Gordon Cox and Chuck Ver Valin.*

(Right) The Catholic sisters who still run the girls' school in Penang have preserved the areas where the *Grenadier* crewmen scratched their names. Others scratched their names into doors.

(Below) One of the Penang classrooms where the *Grenadier* crew spent its first months in 1943.

Photos courtesy of Chuck Ver Valin.

USS *S-44*: Lost 7 October 1943

The most successful old "Sugar boat," *S-44* is seen here *(above)* at the start of the war. This wartime publicity photo *(below)* shows *S-44* returning from patrol on 8 February 1943. Her kill claims of four marus and four men-of-war are recorded on her conning tower. On the bridge *(left to right)* are: Lt. Cdr. Frank Brown, SM1c George F. Smith, Lt. (jg) R. Fox, and Lt. C. W. Flenniken. Two of these men, Captain Brown and Smith, would be lost with *S-44*. *Photo courtesy of Submarine Force Library and Museum, Groton, Connecticut.*

CTM Harold Arvid Stromsoe points to the Rising Sun in his torpedo room for sinking the heavy cruiser *Kako*. Stromsoe escaped *S-44*, but he was not rescued. *Courtesy of Charles Hinman, USS Bowfin Museum.*

The two *S-44* survivors picked up by the destroyer *Ishigaki* were RM3c William Francis "Bill" Whitemore *(left)* and CTM Ernest Arthur "Tony" Duva *(right)*. Both men were taken to Paramushiro before being transported to Japan. *Courtesy of Robert Whitemore.*

(Left) CPhM Tom Cleverdon was killed as he tried to escape from *S-44*. *Courtesy of Jamie Hulsey.*

S-44's gun crew following her fourth patrol. *(Left to right:)* CGM O. V. Johnson, MoMM2c Holly Jackson Howard, MoMM1c Donnovan, EM2c John Walden Emerick, GM3c Philip James Jaworski, EM1c Charles Wayne Smith *(training the gun)*, MoMM1c Nicholas Andrew Hugyo, and CTM Harold Stromsoe *(seated at gun)*. Bill Whitemore was standing behind *Life* photographer Ralph Morse when this photo was snapped. Stromsoe, Hugyo, Smith, Jaworski, and Howard were lost with *S-44*. Emerick was lost with *Corvina* (SS-226) one month after *S-44*. *Courtesy of Robert Whitemore.*

USS *Sculpin* (SS-191): Lost 18 November 1943

USS *Sculpin* (SS-191), seen leaving Mare Island Navy Yard in May 1943, was known throughout the fleet as the submarine that helped save the crew of her sister sub *Squalus* in 1939. Severely damaged during a depth charge attack, *Sculpin* went down fighting in a gun battle with Japanese destroyer *Yamagumo* on 18 November 1943. *Official U.S. Navy photo.*

Cdr. Fred Connaway, skipper of *Sculpin*, was killed in action on her bridge.

Capt. John Philip Cromwell, division commander aboard *Sculpin*, chose to go down with the ship versus being captured by the Japanese.

Lt. Joseph Rollie DeFrees Jr., the gunnery officer of *Sculpin*, was also killed in action during the gun battle. *Photos courtesy of Charles Hinman, USS Bowfin Museum.*

Sculpin engineers in a photo taken in 1943 at San Francisco *(left-right)*: Lt. George Brown, CMM Paul A. Bachofer, and CMM Richard E. Hempill. Brown was the only officer to survive the war from *Sculpin*'s last patrol and Hemphill died during *Sculpin*'s sinking. *Photo courtesy of Carl LaVO.*

(*Left*) MoMM1c George "Moon" Rocek and CMoMM Philip Joseph Gabrunas. Rocek survived the sinking of *Sculpin* and the carrier *Chuyo*, but Gabrunas was lost while scuttling *Sculpin*. *Courtesy of Carl LaVO*.

S1c Edwin Karl Frederick Keller (*above left*) and S1c Michael Thomas Gorman (*above right*) were among the 21 *Sculpin* sailors who would survive the war. *Photos courtesy of John Keller and Maxine Gorman*.

TM1c Herbert Joseph Thomas (*right*) helped man the 3-inch deck gun during *Sculpin's* last fight. This photo was taken on 11 February 1943, during his last Stateside leave. *Photo courtesy of Herbert J. Thomas*.

(*Above*) QM2c Billie Minor Cooper was on *Sculpin's* bridge during her final fight and survived the war as a POW. *Photo courtesy of Bill Cooper*.

Sculpin chief of the boat CSM Weldon Edward "Dinty" Moore (*below right*) with shipmates St1c Carlos Tulao and Lt. Corwin Mendenhall in 1943 with the *Sculpin* battle flag he designed. *Photo courtesy of Carl LaVO*.

CK1c Eugenio Apostol (*below*) opted to go down with *Sculpin*. *Photo courtesy of Charles Hinman*.

RM3c Jerome Warren Baglien *(left)*, EM3c James William McCartney *(second from left)*, Ens. John Worth Gamel *(third from left),* and RM3c John Parr *(right)* were among the 20 *Sculpin* sailors later lost with the Japanese carrier *Chuyo*. Baglien's leg was amputated at Truk. *All photos courtesy of Charles Hinman, www.oneternalpatrol.com website.*

F2c Bill Clifton Brannum *(left)*, CK1c Maximo Berrera *(second from left)*, TM1c Warren Rawling Berry *(third from left)*, and F1c Henry "Rebel" Elliott *(right)* were also lost during *Chuyo*'s sinking. Elliott's hand was amputated at Truk.

RM3c Clifford Gene Taylor *(left)*, MoMM2c Duane Joseph White *(center)*, and S1c William Henry Welsh *(right)* were all picked up by the Japanese destroyer *Yamagumo* after *Sculpin*'s loss. Welsh, badly wounded, was thrown back into the ocean. Taylor and White later perished during *Chuyo*'s sinking.

Ens. Charles Gold Smith *(left)*, F1c Maurice Simon DeLisle *(center),* and SC2c John Bowers Kennon Jr. *(right)* survived Truk but were lost with *Chuyo*.

EM3c Robert Michael Morrilly *(left)* went down with the carrier *Chuyo*. Ens. Wendell Max Fiedler *(right)* was the junior diving officer who opted to go down with *Sculpin* rather than attempt to escape. *Courtesy of Charles Hinman, www.oneternalpatrol.com website.*

Fearing the Japanese could torture classified intelligence from him, wolfpack commander Capt. John Cromwell elected to stay in *Sculpin*'s control room and go down with the ship. For his gallantry, Cromwell was posthumously awarded the Congressional Medal of Honor. *Painting by Fred Freeman, copyright 1949.*

USS *Tullibee* (SS-284): Lost 26 March 1944

Only one man, GM2c Clifford Weldon Kuykendall *(below left)* survived the loss of *Tullibee* *(seen above)*. Senior officers at the time of *Tullibee*'s loss were Cdr. Charles F. Brindupke *(right upper photo)* and executive officer Lt. Cdr. Greer A. Duncan Jr. *(right lower photo)*. *Courtesy of Cliff Kuykendall.*

USS *Robalo* (SS-273): Lost 26 July 1944

Robalo, seen above under way on 19 November 1943, struck a mine off Palawan Island on 26 July 1944. At least four, and as many as six members, of the crew swam to shore and were captured by the Japanese. *Photos courtesy of Charles Hinman, www.oneternalpatrol.com website.*

Robalo's skipper was Lt. Cdr. Manning Marius Kimmel *(above)*, the son of Admiral Husband E. Kimmel and a nephew of Admiral Thomas Kinkaid. Naval intelligence indicates that Kimmel was shot and killed after being captured on Comiran Island.

Four other *Robalo* survivors are known to have been taken in 1944 from Palawan to Manila, where they disappeared from the records. Three of these *Robalo* POWs were Ens. Samuel Lombard Tucker *(below, left)*, EM2c Mason Collie Poston *(below, center)* and SM3c Wallace Keet Martin *(below, right)*.

USS *Tang* (SS-306): Lost 24 October 1944

USS *Tang* (SS-306) is seen returning to Pearl Harbor after her second war patrol with 22 rescued aviators on her deck. In addition to this famed rescue, *Tang* was officially credited with sinking 24 Japanese ships for 93,824 tons before she was struck by her own circling torpedo off Formosa on 24 October 1944. *Official U.S. Navy photo.*

Tang officers shown at the boat's commissioning 15 October 1943 *(left–right)*: Lt. (jg) Henry James "Hank" Flanagan, Cdr. Richard Hetherington "Dick" O'Kane, Lt. Cdr. Murray Bennett Frazee, Lt. Frank Howard Springer, Lt. William Walsh, and Lt. (jg) Fred Mel Enos. Frazee and Walsh transferred off *Tang* before her fifth and final run. Dick O'Kane was washed off the bridge as *Tang* sank and was picked up by the Japanese. Frank Springer perished in the flooded conning tower. Hank Flanagan and Mel Enos both led escape attempts from the forward torpedo room as *Tang* lay 180 feet below the surface, but Enos did not make it to the surface. *Courtesy of William R. Leibold.*

Photos on this page courtesy of William R. Leibold unless otherwise noted.

CBM Bill "Boats" Leibold *(left)* on liberty on Oahu in 1944. Scheduled to take over as *Tang*'s chief of the boat, Leibold was one of the few survivors from the bridge.

(Right) MoMM3c Clayton Oliver Decker became the first American to survive an unassisted ascent from a sunken U.S. submarine.

(Below) RT1c Floyd Merle Caverly *(right)* and his boss on *Tang*, Lt. Edward Huntley Beaumont—in a photo taken in September 1944. Caverly escaped the conning tower after the torpedo hit, but Beaumont did not.

(Below) RM1c Edwin Bergman tried to escape *Tang*'s flooding conning tower with Lt. Larry Savadkin, but Bergman did not survive. This photo, and those of Caverly and White seen on this page, were taken with Caverly's camera just before *Tang*'s fifth and final war patrol.

Three of the topside lookouts who did not survive *Tang*'s sinking. *(Below left)* GM3c Darrell Dean Rector, who had survived a submerged appendectomy aboard *Seadragon* in 1942. *(Center)* RM2c Charles Andriolo. *Courtesy of Charles Hinman. (Below right)* GM1c James Milton White. *Courtesy of William R. Leibold.*

This 1949 illustration depicts the *Tang* survivors gathered in her forward torpedo room. They are donning their Momsen lungs to try and make an escape out the torpedo escape hatch. *Painting by Fred Freeman.*

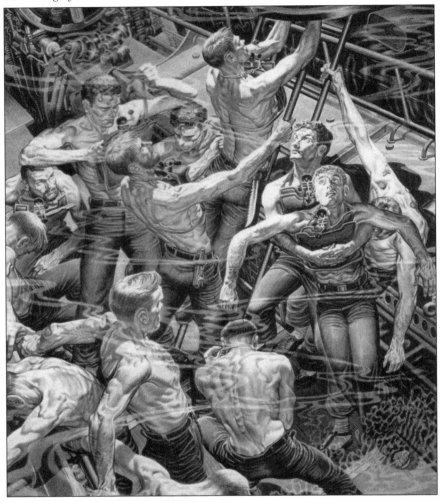

Ens. Basil Charles Pearce *(left)*, MoMM1c George Zofcin *(center)*, and MoMM1c Robert Vance McMorrow *(right)* all survived the *Tang*'s sinking but did not successfully escape their sunken submarine. *Courtesy of Charles Hinman, USS Bowfin Museum.*

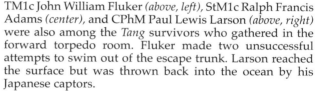

TM1c John William Fluker (*above, left*), StM1c Ralph Francis Adams (*center*), and CPhM Paul Lewis Larson (*above, right*) were also among the *Tang* survivors who gathered in the forward torpedo room. Fluker made two unsuccessful attempts to swim out of the escape trunk. Larson reached the surface but was thrown back into the ocean by his Japanese captors.

CTM William Franklin Ballinger (*left*), *Tang*'s chief of the boat, escaped from his sunken submarine but died shortly after reaching the surface.

Photos courtesy of Charles Hinman, www.oneternalpatrol.com website.

Tang crew photographed on deck by Dick O'Kane following his ship's first patrol. (*Front row, from right moving left*) Division engineer, Lt. Murray Frazee, Ens. Mel Enos, CTM Bill Ballinger (head turned). (*Rear row, from right moving left*) Lt. (jg) Hank Flanagan, Lt. Bruce H. Anderson, and Lt. Frank Springer. Ballinger, Enos, and Flanagan were among the 13 men who swam out of their sunken *Tang*. Enos did not reach the surface. *Courtesy of William R. Leibold.*

(Above) Sculpin, S-44, Grenadier, and *Tullibee* POWs worked in this Ashio mountain mine during 1944 and 1945. The Watarase River and the foot-bridge over it are seen in the foreground.
(Below) The Ashio POW camp postwar in a view taken from the camp's entrance gate. *Photos courtesy of Carl LaVo.*

LEGEND

Barracks:

1-3.	Dutch Navy
4-9.	British Navy
10-13.	British Army
14.	Cooks
15-16.	U.S. Navy
A.	Watch
B.	Cells
C.	Officers, Office
D.	Barbers, Tailor
E.	Engineers
F.	Vegetable Garden

G.	Doctors
H.	Galley
J.	Pigpens
K.	Gudang
L.	Tobacco Gudang
M.	Library
P.	Lavatory
Q.	Refuse
R.	Tengko
S.	Palm Bed

HOSPITAL:

I.	Sick Bay	VII.	Surgery
II.	Ward	VIII.	Pharmacy,
III.	Ward		Laboratory
IV.	Ward	IX.	Morgue
V.	T.B.C. Ward		
VI.	Dys. Ward		

MAP OF DUTCH ARMY CAMP, MAKASSAR

Drawn by Adrian Borstlap, 1989, courtesy of *Perch* survivor Robert Lents.

(Below) Photo of the jungle camp constructed by the POWs and inhabited from June 1944–September 1945.

These sketches of the Makassar camps were drawn from memory by *Pope* survivor Philip R. "Shorty" Nagele 20 years after the war.

(Top) The POWs were forced to drag a huge cement pillbox over the soft beach sand to a new defensive position.

(Center) The POWs pulled tree stumps out of the ground by hand while building their new jungle camp.

(Bottom) This Nagele sketch depicts the *Pope* and *Perch* crews standing at attention in their Makassar camp while guards beat one POW and dump a bucket of water on another man.

Sketches courtesy of Turk Turner and Bob Lents.

Grenadier crew photographed at Fukuoka Camp No. 3 on 15 September 1945. Camp is in background near coal fired power plant. *Rear row (l–r):* TM2c Dean Shoemaker, EM2c Ben Fulton, SC1c Randolph Garrison, S1c Miner Pierce, S1c John Gunderson, and F1c Bernard Witzke. *Center row:* RM1c William Keefe, F2c Charles Roskell, S1c Henry Rutowski, RM3c Rex Evans, F2c Lyle Sawatzke, CEM Charles Whitlock, and EM3c Charles Johnson. *Front row:* QM3c Joseph Minton, S1c John Simpson, TM3c Riley Keysor, F1c Virgil Ouillette, and Matt1c Thomas Trigg. *Courtesy of Chuck Ver Valin.*

Omori POWs wave home-made American, British, and Dutch flags as their rescuers arrive. *Grenadier's* Dennis "Slim" Landrum is holding the American flag with shipmate Al Albertson standing to the left of him. *Tang's* Clay Decker is on the left side of the photo in front, standing above the second pier post with his arms in motion. *Courtesy of Gordon Cox.*

This aerial view of the Omori camp was taken by a Navy carrier plane in August 1945. The prisoners have marked the barrack roofs to indicate their prisoner of war camp. *National Archives photo.*

Note the starved condition of these two Omori prisoners. The man on the right is Lt. Daniel Galvin, a *Hornet* pilot shot down over Guam in June 1944. *National Archives photo.*

This photo, taken inside the Omori barracks on liberation day, shows two of the *Tang* survivors. The man circled in the lower right is MoMM2c Jesse DaSilva. The man circled above and left of DaSilva with his left arm upraised is MoMM3c Clayton Decker. *National Archives photo.*

Grenadier survivors and other POWs mill about the main street in Fukuoka Camp No. 3 as Allies arrive to liberate them in 1945. *Courtesy of Chuck Ver Valin.*

This view shows the inside of the prisoners' barracks in Fukuoka Camp No. 3. The hole in the floor indicates where a stove was intended to be installed for the men. *Courtesy of Chuck Ver Valin.*

When Hellcat pilot Lt. Sam Hibbard of USS *Bataan* discovered the Ashio POW mountain camp on August 29, 1945, he dropped this scribbled note to the POWs. Lt. Cdr. Dave Hurt, former skipper of USS *Perch*, kept Hibbard's note of encouragement until he returned to the United States. *Courtesy of David A. Hurt Jr.*

Grenadier survivors Chuck Ver Valin *(left)* and Charles "Skeeter" McCoy in California in September 1945 before going home to see their families. *Courtesy of Chuck Ver Valin.*

Liberated *Sculpin* sailor Mike Gorman waves his cap in celebration while straddling a Japanese Betty plane at Kisarazu Airfield in Japan. *Courtesy of Maxine Gorman.*

Sculpin's only surviving officer, Lt. George Brown *(far right)*, seen on 6 September 1945, just released from prison camp. He is showing officers of USS *Rescue* the samurai sword presented to him by the Mitsubishi Prison Camp No. 2 commandant. *Courtesy of Carl LaVO.*

The POWs were freed from their camps after a U.S. Navy fleet anchored in Tokyo Bay at the end of August 1945. On 2 September, the Japanese officially surrendered aboard the battleship USS *Missouri*. *Courtesy of Pat Havel.*

Grenadier survivor Lee "Pappy" Shaw *(below white arrow)* watches the Japanese surrender ceremony aboard *Missouri. Courtesy of Pat Havel.*

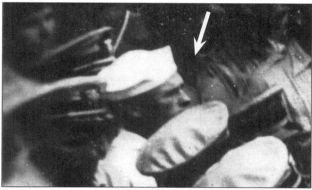

Four freshly liberated U.S. POWs were allowed to board the USS *Missouri* for the surrender ceremonies. Seen here *(left to right)*, they were: Lt. William F. Harris, USMC, of Lexington, Kentucky; MoMM2c Pappy Shaw of San Antonio; Lt. James "Pop" Condit of Washington, DC; and Cdr. Al Maher from Chicago. Shaw's smile had become closed-mouth style due to losing many of his teeth at Penang. *Courtesy of Pat Havel.*

Some of *Perch*'s enlisted men were repatriated from Fukuoka Camp No. 6 on Kyushu, Japan, after three and a half years as POWs. This photo, taken 15 August 1945, shows MM1c Joe Foley *(upper left)* with two buddies wearing Army uniforms given to them by their liberators. *Photo from Joann Foley Schwarz, courtesy of Charles Himan, USS Bowfin Museum.*

Liberated *Perch* electrician's mates *(left to right)* Ernie Plantz, Ansil Winger, and Jesse Robison taken at the Plantz home in Cheshire, Ohio, in 1945. *Courtesy of Ernest Plantz.*

TM3c Bob Lents of *Perch (left side of table, front)* enjoys a beer with *Pope* POW buddies F1c Harley McCoy *(right front)* and EM3c Bill Seward *(right rear)* during their first liberty in New York City. *Courtesy of Bob Lents.*

Perch and *Pope* survivors are debriefed on Palawan Island in September 1945. *(Left to right are)* S1c Joe Sisk, S1c Tom Moore *(head on chin)*, CBM Richard "Wolf" Sperandio, and S2c Thornton Singleton. *Courtesy of Tom Moore.*

MoMM2c Joseph N. Baker Jr. with Adm. Chester Nimitz after being pinned with Bronze Star Medal in May 1947. Baker was cited for his heroic action as a member of *Sculpin*'s gun crew during her last battle on 19 November 1943, where he was wounded in action and later taken prisoner. *Official U.S. Navy photo, courtesy of Joe Baker.*

Sculpin survivor Joe Baker at age 83 in 2008. *Courtesy of Joe Baker.*

Tullibee's sole survivor Cliff Kuykendall enjoys happier times back home in Texas after the war. *Courtesy of Cliff Kuykendall.*

Rear Adm. John Fitzgerald, badly tortured on Penang and held for 15 months at the secret interrogation camp at Ofuna, was believed by some of his crew to have been worthy of the Medal of Honor. *Courtesy of Gordon Cox.*

Grenadier survivors in 2001. *(Left to right)* "Sarge" York, Charles Johnson, Gordon Cox, Riley Keysor, Bernard Witze, Chuck Ver Valin.

Grenadier reunion in Nashville, 1975. *Front row (l–r):* Al Albertson, Rear Admiral "Fearless Freddie" Warder, Mays, Rear Admiral John Fitzgerald, and Joe Minton. *Rear row (l–r):* Gordon Cox, Irving Loftus, Lynn Clark, Carlisle Herbert, and Ray "Railroad" Leslie. *Courtesy of Gordon Cox.*

Another *Grenadier* reunion group photo from 1975. *Front row (l–r):* Lou Poss, Randolph Garrison, John Fitzgerald, George Stauber, and Gordon Cox. *Rear row (l–r):* Al Albertson, Charles "Tim" McCoy, Charles Johnson, Charles Westerfield, Lynn Clark, Joe Minton, Mays, Denny Landrum, N. W. Jones, and Ben Fulton. *Courtesy of Gordon Cox.*

Grenadier survivors and their wives at 17 September 1981, Sacramento reunion. *Back row (l–r):* Buck Withrow, Paul Whaley, Bob Palmer, Elwood "Pat" O'Brion, Gordon Cox, Art Coleman, Don Langer, Al Albertson, Lynn Clark, Ben Fulton, Janice Cox, Bernie Witzke, and John Leskovsky. *Center row (l–r):* Millie Withrow, Barbara Lee Palmer, La Vaughn O'Brion, Mrs. Art Coleman, Eleanor Langer, Laura Wise, Betty Albertson, Joann Clark, Millie Witzke, Virginia Jones, and Chuck Ver Valin. *Front (l–r):* Al Rupp, Bill Wise, N. W. Jones, and Vern Atha. *Courtesy of Charles H. McCoy.*

Cdr. Dick O'Kane receives the Congressional Medal of Honor from President Harry Truman in March 1946. *Official U.S. Navy photo.*

On the anniversary of the *Tang's* loss in 1986, Adm. Dick O'Kane speaks at the dedication of a memorial in Palatka, Florida. This Mark XIV torpedo is mounted above a USS *Tang* Memorial plaque and another which lists the boat's final crew. The memorial is maintained by the Basil Pearce Chapter of Submarine Veterans of World War II. *Courtesy of W. G. "Doc" Sweany.*

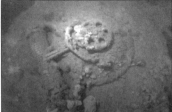

A team of international divers discovered the sunken *Perch* in 190 feet of water off Surabaya City in 2006. These photos by Kevin Denlay show: a close-up of a conning tower plaque with the name USS PERCH; a view of the forward hatch; and a ladder. *Copyrighted photos used by permission of Kevin Denlay.*

Recently liberated American POWs eagerly await the ladder to the four-engined Skymaster airplane so that they can plant their feet on U.S. soil again. *(Seen left to right are)* Lt. Cdr. Fort H. Callahan, USN, Major Donald W. Boyle, USMC, Lt. Cdr. Dave Hurt of USS *Perch,* and Cdr. Al Maher, USN. These four were flown from Tokyo and are seen landing on 12 September 1945 in Oakland, Ca. *Official U.S. Navy photo.*

Lieutenant Commander Hurt of *Perch (below, right)* is reunited with his oldest son Dave Jr. in Washington, DC. *Courtesy of David Hurt Jr.*

Perch reunion. *(Front row, l–r)* Gordon "Sleepy" Clevinger, Sam Simpson, and Roger "Shaky" Evans. *(Rear row, l–r):* Dave Hurt Jr. (the skipper's son), Earl "Bud" Harper, Marion "Turk" Turner, and Ernie Plantz. *Reunion photos courtesy of Robert Lents.*

(Left–right) Elmo "Snuffy" Monroe, Bob Lents, Ernie Plantz, Turk Turner, and Bud Harper of *Perch.*

(Front l–r) Ernie Plantz, Dan Crist, and Turk Turner of *Perch.*
(Rear, l–r: Jesse "Robbie" Robison, Bob Lents, Victor Pederson, and Bud Harper.

Seven of the nine *Tang* survivors at a 1988 reunion. Adm. Dick O'Kane presents a copy of his book *Clear the Bridge!* to Bob Thicksten, superintendent of the Palomar Observatory. *(Left to right are)* Larry Savadkin, O'Kane, Floyd Caverly, Bill Leibold, Thicksten, Jesse DaSilva, Pete Narowanski, and Clay Decker. *Photo courtesy of William Leibold.*

One of the 21 *Sculpin* survivors, Edwin Keller, in a photo taken beside a submarine model in his New Jersey home in 1984. *Photo taken by Carl LaVO.*

Sculpin survivors Mike Gorman (left) and George Rocek pose for a photo aboard USS *Silversides* in 1984. *Photo taken by Carl LaVO.*

Five *Sculpin* veterans at a mid-1980s *Sculpin/Squalus/Sailfish* Association reunion. *(Left–right)* Bill Cooper, George Brown, Ed Keller, George Rocek and Julius Peterson. *Photo courtesy of Sam Swisher.*

13
Chuyo's Sole Survivor

Joe Baker knew that he and his *Sculpin* shipmates were being transported in a prime target ship. American submariners could find no greater glory than sinking a Japanese aircraft carrier. The carrier *Unyo* and her escorts successfully dodged the submarines that Admiral Lockwood laid in their path during the first few days out from Truk.

Baker said that *Unyo* was not "out of the harbor very long before they were dropping depth charges on one of our subs. We really began to sweat, expecting to get hit with a fish at any moment. We were three decks below, just about even with the waterline. We had been told that should the carrier be torpedoed and sunk, we would be obliged to go down and visit Davy Jones' locker."

En route to Japan, the carrier task force was on high alert and battle stations sounded often. "On board the carrier, we were given better treatment," said Paul Todd. "They asked us if we wanted anything and we told them food, tobacco, and medical attention and in turn we received some of each. They tried to teach us the Japanese language for they figured we would need to learn it as we were to be prisoners in Japan for a long period of time."

Ed Keller recalled that key phrases were "the words for attention, permission to go to the bathroom, and how to say thank you and good morning." The prisoners' compartment was well ventilated on *Unyo* and the men were treated fairly during their voyage.[1]

For Bill Cooper, the daily rice balls and ample supply of water on the carrier was a godsend. "I didn't care much for rice, but under the circumstances, I figured that I'd better eat it." Although he continued to drop weight, Cooper felt that the Navy men "respected us and treated us better than the Army soldiers had."

The 21 *Sculpin* prisoners aboard the carrier *Chuyo* endured a completely different treatment. "Conditions were bad," said motormac Moon Rocek. "Food was available, but very little water. We only received a few ounces a day per man. The compartment was crowded and the ventilation was practically non-existent." The Americans were kept in what was originally a valuables vault on the middle deck of the old *Nitta Maru* before she was converted to an aircraft carrier. According to *Chuyo* sailor Takuji Azuchi, the carrier had no room for POWs so the former vault was chosen as a convenient area to lock and guard. Food was passed down through a small hatch near the ceiling and the men slept on straw mats.[2]

By 3 December, the *Chuyo* and *Unyo* convoy was approaching Japan when it encountered a typhoon. The ships were battered by heavy waves and winds in excess of 50 knots. "We could feel the ship rolling and could hear waves outside and something thrashing about," said Keller.[3]

The violent seas and winds were so heavy that the Japanese convoy commander opted to suspend evasive maneuvers. Certainly, he reasoned, no American submarines could attempt a torpedo attack in such extreme conditions. *Sculpin*'s survivors would soon find that this decision was deadly wrong.

Admiral Lockwood's submarines were on high alert from the moment the carrier convoy departed Truk. Cdr. Gene McKinney's *Skate* had been the first to attack on 30 November. He closed in for a shot at the carrier *Zuiho* but the convoy zigged at the last moment, forcing him to fire and miss. The ensuing depth charging that Joe Baker recalled shortly after leaving port was the result of *Skate*'s failed attack.[4]

Gunnel was the next U.S. sub to attack the Japanese carriers. Her skipper, Lt. Cdr. John Sidney McCain Jr., picked them up during the late morning of 2 December, north of Iwo Jima. *Gunnel* also tried to attack *Zuiho*, but the convoy's maneuvers forced him deep to avoid a collision. Although McCain fired four bow tubes, all again missed the lucky *Zuiho*.

The last of Lockwood's submarines lying in wait off Japan was the old *Sailfish*, making her tenth war patrol. This boat was formerly the *Squalus*, which sunk in 1939 and had been raised, repaired, and recommissioned as *Sailfish*. Sister sub *Sculpin* had played a significant part in locating and standing by the sunken *Squalus* until her crew could be rescued. In an ironic twist of fate, four years later the *Sailfish*—referred to as the "Squailfish" by some submariners—was about to cause great grief for many of the *Sculpin* men.

Ed Keller had hoped to get aboard *Sailfish* back in the previous November, but he had instead been assigned to *Sculpin*. *Sailfish* was under command of Lt. Cdr.

Robert Elwin McCramer "Bob" Ward. From Pearl Harbor, Cdr. Dick Voge sent out an Ultra on the three Japanese aircraft carriers and moved *Sailfish* into an intercept position. Bob Ward surfaced on the evening of 3 December in a raging typhoon with tremendous seas whipped by 50-knot winds. It was anything but desirous weather for a torpedo attack, but radar picked up the carriers near midnight.[5]

Ward closed to 2,100 yards and fired four torpedoes from radar depth at 0012 on 4 December, at one of the largest radar pips in the convoy. He and his crew heard two distinct hits but could not verify the ship's destruction. A Japanese destroyer raced in to deliver 21 depth charges, forcing *Sailfish* to lie low for two hours.

Just after midnight on 4 December, *Sailfish* hit *Chuyo* with one torpedo in the port bow magazine. The 21 *Sculpin* prisoners aboard the Japanese flattop cheered the success of their fellow submariners in torpedoing their carrier—even though they knew that they would likely die if *Chuyo* sank.

Moon Rocek, seated at this moment in the prisoners' compartment several decks below the flight deck, recalled, "A few of us were sitting on deck. When the torpedo hit, we flew straight up about two or three feet in the air. We could sense she had lost power and smoke filtered into our compartment." The prisoners could hear the Japanese frantically attempting to shore up the bulkheads with timber. Their efforts were nullified by a heavy sea and soon the bulkhead below was heard to collapse. Rocek heard water pouring into the compartment below him as more ocean entered *Chuyo*.

"As the water rose to our compartment, we yelled and pounded on the locked hatch," he said. "We undogged the hatch but it was locked on the outside and we couldn't break it open." They removed a three-foot long metal pump handle from the head and used this as a pry bar. "We all pushed and pulled and on the second try, the hatch broke open," Rocek stated. "If you were on an American ship, you could never do that because the American ships are built a lot stronger."

While Rocek and his companions struggled for their lives, the other 20 *Sculpin* prisoners were listening to the sounds from the third deck on *Unyo*. "We heard three loud explosions, which scared the hell out of all of us," said Joe Baker. "One thing we did know was that something had been hit."

Chuyo was damaged but continued on as the prisoners fought to escape. *Sculpin* chief of the boat Dinty Moore organized the survivors as they struggled to find their way topside. "Moore designated one of the men who had served on a service craft to lead," related Rocek. "He thought he would have the best chance to get us topside." The *Sculpin* survivors held hands, keeping amputees Charles Pitser,

Jerome Baglien, and Rebel Elliott near the front, as they stumbled through dark, smoky passages. More than once, the Americans were forced to backtrack when they reached a dead end in the smoky corridors below.[6]

During this time, Lieutenant Commander Ward's *Sailfish* had returned to the surface in the violent ocean and was driving in for another torpedo attack. At 0552, *Sailfish* fired three more torpedoes. Ward saw a puff of fire from one explosion and a brilliant fireball from a second hit before he dove *Sailfish* to reload her tubes again.

Two of *Sailfish*'s torpedoes slammed into *Chuyo*'s port engine room, stopping the carrier dead in the water. With three torpedo hits, the ship could go down at any time. "Frenzied Jap damage controlmen ignored us and we finally reached topside," Rocek related. In a small compartment, the *Sculpin* men found and donned life jackets that had once been used for *Nitta Maru* passengers. For amputees Baglien, Pitser, and Elliott, these would offer their only real chance of staying afloat. The survivors also found *Chuyo*'s galley, where they hastily looted food and bottled soft drinks.[7]

Beyond the galley, they found a ladder leading to the flight deck. "A Jap officer pulled us out of the line and escorted us to the flight deck, where we were stripped of our life jackets," said Rocek. *Chuyo* sailor Azuchi later wrote that this officer was angry at the Americans for wearing the life jackets, something most Japanese sailors did not do. He considered the life jackets "unbrave" and felt the POWs were already "cowardly" for allowing themselves to be taken prisoner in the first place. "They started to tie us. In the confusion, however, only eight men were tied and the others quickly freed them," Rocek related.[8]

A short while later, a heavy internal explosion rocked the carrier. Sensing the end, the Japanese began passing out stores of candy, beer, canned goods, and rice. Even the prisoners managed to sneak their share in the chaos. In spite of the high winds and internal explosions, *Chuyo* defiantly remained afloat. Bob Ward ended *Chuyo*'s survival hopes, however, when *Sailfish* fired three stern tubes at 0940.[9]

On *Chuyo*'s flight deck, the *Sculpin* survivors were rocked again as *Sailfish*'s torpedoes slammed home. *Chuyo*'s port list immediately became more pronounced. As *Chuyo* started sinking by her bow, George Rocek and Dinty Moore held onto a portable searchlight on the carrier's port side about 30 feet above the water. Their other shipmates went to the higher starboard side. Rocek sadly recalled, "That's where we lost just about all the rest of the *Sculpin* crew. When she went down, the guys on the high side were in the water a hell of a lot faster than me and Dinty."

As *Chuyo* nosed under, Rocek hollered, "Let's go, Dinty!" Letting go of the searchlight, Rocek slid down the flight deck and plunged deep into the ocean. "I just about gave up. I could no longer hold my breath and began taking in water. At this point, my whole life flashed before me, even details that I normally never recalled before. It was an eerie and serene sensation." Just as he was gulping in ocean water, Rocek looked upward and saw light. He later believed that an air pocket helped push him closer to the surface.

He swam for the nearby raft, which was crowded with survivors clinging to it. Among them, he found two familiar American faces—Ens. Charles Smith and *Sculpin*'s Filipino mess cook, Maximo Barrera. "The seas were awfully heavy and we were holding onto that raft. What I did was jam my hand and wrist as far as I could between the lashings," related Rocek. "I didn't think I would be able to last very long the way the seas were. But I hung in there."

Fearful of the lurking American submarine, the Japanese destroyer *Urakaze* circled the life rafts for about five hours before finally picking up survivors. "She came by with one Jacob's ladder and a number of lines trailing over the side," recalled Rocek. "When you grabbed the lines and the ship rolled, you slid right back into the sea. Your best chance was one Jacob's ladder."[10]

As *Urakaze* came alongside their raft again, Rocek, Ensign Smith, and Barrera lunged for the lines. Rocek grabbed the Jacob's ladder while his *Sculpin* shipmates grabbed lines. "A Jap officer stepped and crawled over me, forcing me under," said Rocek. "I was very weak by now, but luckily a huge swell pushed me onto the Jacob's ladder again. I threw my arm through the ladder and latched onto my wrist with the other hand. They pulled the ladder and me both topside."[11]

Smith and Barrera were unable to scale the destroyer's dangling lines. Rocek sadly watched as Japanese sailors jabbed them with poles to knock them back into the ocean. "That was the last time I ever saw any of my shipmates from the carrier *Chuyo*," he recalled. Captain Okura Tomasaborou and 1,250 officers, men, and passengers went down with the carrier. *Urakaze* rescued only 160 Japanese crewmen and one American, MoMM1c George Rocek, from the stormy, winter ocean.[12]

Being clothed in Japanese undress blues, he believed that some of the sailors figured him to be a Japanese survivor. Rocek was left lying on the deck, exhausted and unable to move. "Then four sailors picked me up and carried me to the fantail," he related. "I was sure they were going to throw me overboard but [they] then must have been ordered to return me amidships." The American survivor was placed in *Urakaze*'s laundry compartment while rescue operations proceeded.

————

Aboard *Unyo*, the other 20 *Sculpin* survivors felt the explosions and knew that American submarines had torn into the convoy. "They didn't abuse us after the carrier sinking," recalled Bill Cooper, "but they sure didn't treat us as nice as they had before."

Surviving carriers *Zuiho* and *Unyo* continued on at high speed and entered Uraga Bay off Yokohama on 5 December. The 20 *Sculpin* prisoners were rustled from their compartment. "We were taken up to the hangar decks and lined up in two ranks," said Joe Baker. "We weren't tied down, only blindfolded. The Captain told us not to worry at all, to take good care of our health and good luck to all of us."

Unyo's Sculpin prisoners were loaded onto a motor launch and headed for the shores of Yokusaka on 5 December 1943, one month after they had left Pearl Harbor. "The weather was pretty damned cold and here we were barefooted and nothing but old third-hand Navy blues covering our bodies," said Baker.

They saw no signs of their other 21 shipmates who had been herded aboard the other Japanese carrier.

Moon Rocek grew so cold in *Urakaze's* laundry compartment during the night that his body shook. He crawled into a metal tank filled with lukewarm water, keeping only his head above water. The next morning, a Japanese chief who smelled of alcohol visited him several times and alternately "slugged the hell out of me" and talked.[13]

A kinder engineman visited the American and slipped him two crackers, Rocek's only food aboard the destroyer. "It took me a long time to eat the crackers because I couldn't work up any saliva." *Urakaze* entered port at Yokohama the next morning, where Rocek noted many damaged merchant and naval vessels. Hours later, he was led to the gangway with tied wrists and taken ashore in a small craft.[14]

Rocek was led through the city, able only to peek downward through his blindfold. "I could see the women's shoes and bottoms of their kimonos," he recalled. "I felt a little funny at first, because the seat of my uniform was torn out from sliding down the carrier flight deck."[15]

He arrived at a railroad station and was seated on a bench, where one of his guards removed his blindfold momentarily to impress a young Japanese lady. "She was a doll and dressed stateside with a short skirt and high heel shoes," he noted. Rocek was packed aboard a crowded commuter train and he stood for the two-hour ride from Yokohama to Ofuna. When Rocek's guard herded him off the train, he insisted that Rocek run down a stony road toward camp wearing only some slip-on sandals.[16]

Moon Rocek realized that he was the lone American survivor from *Chuyo's* sinking. He had no idea whether his other 20 *Sculpin* shipmates had survived their carrier voyage.

14
"No One Knows You're Alive"

The other 20 *Sculpin* survivors from the carrier *Unyo* were prodded blindfolded through the Tokyo suburbs toward an uncertain future. According to Joe Baker, "People threw sticks and things at us, whatever they could get their hands on."

They rode an electric tram southwest of Yokohama and marched the last five kilometers to Ofuna barefooted on frozen ground. "It really gets cold there in December!" recalled Ed Ricketts. Shipmate Baker's first impression of the Ofuna countryside was "it seemed to be shut off from the rest of the world."

Like 41 captured U.S. submariners before them, Lt. George Brown and the 19 enlisted men from *Sculpin* who entered Ofuna on 5 December found that they were never officially listed as POWs. The veteran Ofuna men slipped data to Brown and his shipmates to prevent conflicting statements to the QKs. Former *Grenadier* skipper John Fitzgerald was pleased to hear from Brown that the submarine command had compiled a list of 55 known survivors from *Grenadier*—men who had been transferred to camps aside from Ofuna.[1]

The new *Sculpin* arrivals received new clothes upon arrival and were placed in the Sanku barracks. "Each of us was put into a separate room. Our first meal was a bowl of rice, two small baked fish heads—guts, bone, and all—and a couple of spoonfuls of soy sauce," said Joe Baker. "The barracks we were in was full of *Sculpin* survivors," said torpedoman Herb Thomas. "In the other barracks were the men from another submarine that went down, the *Grenadier*. There were also two prisoners captured from an S-boat."

Ed Keller heard one guard proclaim, "You have survived the sinking of a submarine. No one survives the sinking of a submarine. No one knows you're alive." He said that they would answer questions or be shot for refusing. If they were killed, no one would ever have known they had survived. "I was scared," related Keller. "But I didn't think it was the end of the world. We had survived Truk Island after all."[2]

Australian pilot Geoffrey Lempriere helped the new *Sculpin* arrivals learn the ropes. "While interpreting the Japanese questions, he sandwiched in information to me," related Lieutenant Brown.

In his new cell, Bill Cooper was in agony from the long barefoot hike to Ofuna over frozen ground. "Buddy, when they started thawing out, they like to killed me. They hurt so bad that I started crying. Somebody told George Brown about me and he came down there and helped rub my feet."

Also arriving at Ofuna on 5 December, separately, was Moon Rocek, the only *Sculpin* prisoner to survive the *Chuyo* sinking. "George Rocek came into camp all black and burned as if he had been in a fire," Joe Baker recalled. In addition to smoke and soot, his Japanese Navy blues were covered in fuel oil.

Upon arrival, Rocek was questioned by two guards. When he said he was a survivor from the sunken Japanese carrier, the guard became indignant. " I told him I was off the *Sculpin*," Rocek said. "He apparently knew what had happened because he didn't say anything more and led me into a bath."[3]

To his great surprise, Rocek found two *Sculpin* shipmates in the bath. He was unable to talk to them but crawled into the warm water, which relieved the pain of his injured legs. "I almost fainted since it felt so good, so warm and relaxing." The 21 reunited *Sculpin* survivors were dressed in fresh clothes and escorted back to the barracks. During the early morning hours, Rocek was able to whisper details of the *Chuyo*'s sinking to his shipmates in neighboring cells.[4]

After 0530 wake-up, the submariners folded their blankets and were marched into the compound. "We lined up in two ranks, facing the Emperor's palace and had to bow to the Emperor," said Joe Baker. "This was done every morning, rain or shine." Many Ofuna prisoners made a habit of spitting as they bowed to show their indignity toward the Emperor.

"Treatment here was rather bad," said Eldon Wright. "Men were beaten severely for stealing a raw onion." The men could not help but to steal. "We were fed very sparingly on fish heads, potato tops, and some kind of vines that were boiled in plain water," F1c Paul Murphy related. "Women barbers would come in from the village every two weeks to shave us, using cold water, salt water soap and very dull razors."

"You were generally quizzed pretty continuously for the first two or three weeks," related Joe Baker. When Murphy refused to answer some of the questions, he was "beaten severely." Herb Thomas found that the "interrogators' English was better than mine. I assume they were in Washington at one time." Moon Rocek and his shipmates lied, saying that *Sculpin* had been on her first patrol when she was lost. "We filled in with bullshit on our time in the Navy until the sinking," he later stated. "The only thing we had to make sure we did was answer each question quickly. If you started stumbling around, they would feel you were trying to lie to them."[5]

Lieutenant Brown was given the worst treatment. He was put on reduced rations, threatened with death, and beaten regularly. Allowed to consult *Jane's Fighting Ships*, Brown gave out only the information contained in the book.[6]

Brown, suffering from a severe cold, chronic diarrhea, and no medical attention, was treated worse than his enlisted men. During his frequent interrogations, Brown gave "no information which would prove of military value to the Japs." Joe Baker—suffering from two gunshot wounds to his left leg—soon found help in Christmastime Red Cross packages and an Army doctor captured in the Philippines. "This doctor suggested that we heat one of the packages of Argentine bully beef from the Red Cross stuff," Baker said. "I heated it and stuffed some of it into my wound. Many doctors have since said that was the only thing that saved my leg because the maggots got in there and they killed all the germs."

John Rourke's shrapnel wounds in his toes and back gradually improved at Ofuna. Shrapnel wounds in Moon Rocek's legs hobbled him as they festered. Even though he was given a fish oil ointment and one set of bandages, the wounds became infected and began turning gangrenous. Rocek, remembering advice from his dad to urinate on a wound if he was unable to seek treatment, called on buddy Ed Ricketts for help. "It didn't bother him at all because he was a hunter and fisherman himself and had heard that urine could heal wounds," Rocek recalled. "He did it every day. Every one of the wounds healed up after that except for one on my shin bone in my left leg."[7]

Herb Thomas received more of the dreaded closed-fist haymaker punches during his sessions at Ofuna. "The guards would swing from way back. You'd try to relax but you would grit your teeth because you knew it was coming. You'd keep your neck relaxed but it still hurt and gave many of us chipped teeth."

Grenadier's chief commissary steward, Charlie Westerfield, was put to work in the Ofuna galley in December 1943 for months. "During this period, we got a total of 45 pounds of meat, some rotten, some good," he related. "Rice ration was 4 ounces per person per meal for two months."

As Christmas approached, some men were spending their second holiday season as captives. John Fitzgerald helped orchestrate a Christmas program which included "various scripture readings, appropriate songs and prayers. In the afternoon, a track and field program was carried out, the QKs in attendance. Prizes in the form of baked sweet potatoes and cigarettes were given to the winning contestants." Everyone received a few apples and tangerines that day. "Conversation among the older prisoners in Ofuna, to a limited degree, was permitted for that day."[8]

On New Year's Eve 1943, Lt. Kevin Harty rushed in from the benjo about 1700 whispering something about a truckload of Red Cross boxes. Fitzgerald chided Harty that "he must be crazy, or in need of glasses. No such thing would ever be given [to] any of us in Ofuna."[9]

Guards soon called for POWs to help unload a truck with 72 cases, each of which contained cartons of Canadian Red Cross food. "Excitement ran wild," Fitzgerald recalled. He wrote that the POWs were like "small children anticipating the arrival of Santa Claus." Two cartons of the new Red Cross food were contributed to a food bank for new POWs that would arrive during the year—a plan he caught some flak for creating. The other boxes were carefully rationed, with specific dates for when they could be opened.[10]

"Apparently, the Nips did not know that each box contained eight small boxes," recalled *Grenadier* gunner's mate Bill Wise. "In order to save face, they said we could only eat one box per week." Yeoman Bob Palmer found that during his stay at Ofuna "the one bright light was the Red Cross aid. We never got any mail."[11]

Although the new *Sculpin* and *S-44* submariners had taken the brunt of interrogations since their arrival in late 1943, the others each had their return trips. Lieutenant Commander Fitzgerald was hauled back in on 6 January. "They have been at me every month since my capture off Penang," he wrote.[12]

Grenadier's Palmer recalled that some of Ofuna's more tenured prisoners were in poor shape by this time. Famed Olympic runner Lou Zamperini "was the largest walking skeleton I have ever seen," Palmer wrote. "His huge barrel chest formed a grotesque upper bone pile on top of the thinnest legs you ever saw. His face was hollow and brown skin hung over him like loose cloth over a pile of sticks. He had grit."[13]

Sculpin's Ed Keller became familiar with which guards were the ones to avoid. One guard nicknamed "Fatso" would offer a prisoner a lit cigarette while he stood outside his cell. "When he felt you had smoked enough, he'd take it from you, snuff it, and then hit you," Keller related. John Fitzgerald struck Keller as an enthusiastic, happy-go-lucky, natural leader. "He would come over and smile and talk with you. Because he was the skipper of a submarine, it made your day a little better."[14]

Grenadier's Al Albertson quickly learned what missteps would produce a beating at Ofuna. "Every morning, they would take us out on the parade ground and run us around," he said. "They'd chase you around with a club and the last guy would get beat up."

Snow fell over Ofuna on 6 January, the first that many of the Navy prisoners had seen in years. The barracks were very drafty and the Japanese picked this day to give the prisoners a haircut and shave, leaving their closely cropped skulls even colder. CQM Carl Quarterman remembered "walking around that circle in the compound with Buck Withrow and other members of the *Grenadier* crew in order to keep warm." George Rocek found that even warming in the sunlight had its consequences. "If you were sitting there soaking up the sun and feeling good and closing your eyes, the guards would draw their bayonets and put them right up to your eye," he recalled. His fellow prisoners developed a system. By applying leg pressure to the man whose eye was being threatened with a bayonet, that man knew not to move suddenly and cause himself eye injury. "The guard would finally move away," said Rocek. "The guy next to you would cough and you knew it was okay."[15]

By 19 January, Ofuna held 82 prisoners. Those in the worst condition were Ens. William Wells, USN, who was very sick with malaria, and 2nd Lt. Fred Francis Garrett, an Air Force B-24 pilot who had had his leg amputated before his arrival at Ofuna. Garrett's crew had been executed at Kwajalein. When his ankle injury became badly infected due to neglect, the Japanese had amputated his leg above the knee using an ordinary crosscut woodsaw without anesthesia.[16]

On 23 January, there was an uprising about some of the men opening the fourth Red Cross box ahead of the prescribed schedule. A few of the men were slugged by the senior Gochyo and the offenders had their rations removed. The schedule prescribed had been one Red Cross box per week. "Looks like the best thing to do is eat them up and not try to make them last out winter months as was planned," Fitzgerald wrote in his diary.[17]

On 24 January, another big prisoner transfer took place and 21 men became POWs, officially. They were: four non-submariners; John McBeath, Lou Poss, George Stauber, Bill Wise, and Pete Zucco from *Grenadier*; and twelve *Sculpin* survivors: Cecil Baker, Bill Cooper, Leo Eskildsen, Mike Gorman, Ed Keller, Harry Milbourne, Paul Murphy, Ed Ricketts, Moon Rocek, Harry Toney, Eldon Wright, and Bob Wyatt. The *Sculpin* men remaining at Ofuna were George Brown, Andy Anderson, John Rourke, Herb Thomas, Paul Todd, Joe Baker, William Haverland, Leo Murray, and Julius Peterson.[18]

"They said we would be registered as prisoners of war," said Ed Keller. "That meant a lot to us. We knew everybody back home thought we were dead. They had been told we were presumed lost at sea."[19]

"Men whom the Japanese thought had the most information were kept for questioning," said Paul Todd. "They kept one from each branch and rate," explained Joe Baker. "We were really disappointed we weren't going, but that's just the breaks."

The departing Ofuna prisoners were allowed to take only opened Red Cross boxes with them. "We were ordered to fall out with what gear we had and the remaining Red Cross boxes went with us," Bill Wise remembered. "It just so happened that Lou Poss had eaten a good three-quarters of his total box. I had foolishly only eaten one stinkin' candy bar out of next week's box." He was greatly disappointed when the guards then forced the transferees to give up their Red

Cross boxes they had planned to take with them. Wise was left with a new POW motto: "Eat it when you get it."[20]

The transferees were blindfolded, marched to the train station and transported north to Tokyo where they were kept overnight at the Omori prisoner camp. Returned to a steam train the next day, they were moved into the mountains northwest of Tokyo to the mountain mining village camp of Ashio.

Following this transfer, rations at Ofuna were cut even further because of the Red Cross boxes. "The tobacco situation is becoming very acute," Fitzgerald wrote. "Looks like we might all become non-smokers in a couple of days." Lt. (jg) Stephan Albert Nyarady, a U.S. Navy prisoner, was punched in the face repeatedly by the senior guard for urinating in a tin can instead of going to the benjo during the night on 27 January. Fitzgerald and George Whiting were interrogated again on 30 January. "Many times we would be told that our crews were very dumb," Fitzgerald wrote. [21]

Chief Charlie Westerfield surprised his skipper by sneaking in to hand out a hot cup of coffee and cigarette an hour before reveille on 2 February. Westerfield had found a moment to slip out of the camp kitchen while the duty guard was toasting his feet by the kitchen stove. The following day, in honor of the Japanese cook's child turning one year old, Westerfield collected powdered milk from Red Cross rations and he helped the Japanese cook make doughnuts, three for each prisoner. "How about coffee and doughnuts in a prison camp?" Fitzgerald penned.[22]

Seven aviators came in on 13 February, six from Capt. Wilbur Leroy Morris' B-24 Liberator crew and one man from the sub tender *Canopus*, who had escaped Corregidor with 1st Lt. William Frederick Harris, son of Marine Corps Gen. Field Harris. A B-24 pilot, 1st Lt. Harold H. Van Wormer, was brought in on 16 February. Enough snow fell during the month to cover trees and buildings in the valley.[23]

Sleet, rain, and snow mixed with high wind at Ofuna in early March. "We went through a cold winter with no extra clothing," said Joe Baker. "They also kept our hair shaved bald all the time. The only time you got warm was for a few minutes in the bath on Wednesday and Sunday afternoons."

Another Navy pilot arrived on 3 March, Lt. George Clough "Red" Bullard from *Intrepid*'s VF-6. Bullard's Hellcat had been shot down on 17 February during carrier air strikes on Truk. Seven more prisoners, Australian and American aviators, came in the next week, the most notable of these on 7 March being Marine Maj. Gregory "Pappy" Boyington. The skipper of VMF-214's Black Sheep squadron was shot down on 3 January 1944 over Rabaul. Before he was downed, Corsair ace Boyington scored his 26th kill, tying the year-old record held by Marine ace Joe Foss. Painfully wounded, the Corsair pilot was picked up by a Japanese submarine and eventually made his way to Ofuna. It was not until press releases of the loss of the fabled aviator and the subsequent push in the United States to award him the

Congressional Medal of Honor that the Japanese began to realize just who they had captured.[24]

One of Greg Boyington's cell mates was Joe Baker from *Sculpin*. "Here I was this 19-year-old kid with this ace. He was a real tough-guy," said Baker. Although the major was only about seven years older than him, he was a bona fide war hero whose name was known. Years later, Baker would be disappointed when Boyington failed to mention his cell mate in his famous autobiography, *Baa, Baa Black Sheep*.

When the Japanese heard of the Medal of Honor movement, Boyington was badly beaten. "They made us all line up in the compound and they beat the hell out of him," Baker recalled. "Men were often beaten," said *Sculpin* radioman Julius Peterson. "The Japanese were continually questioning us." *Grenadier*'s Lieutenant Harty said the "acting camp PhM was very sadistic in treatment of prisoners, and insanitary and ineffectual in medical treatment. Lieutenant Toulon was beaten with fists when he was sick." *Grenadier*'s Lt. Arthur McIntyre related, "The Japanese orderlies were very unsanitary. They gave us very little sulfa and zinc ointment for sores. There were no anesthetics."

Treatment of Pappy Boyington's leg wounds came as a result of rumors that he was slated to receive the Medal of Honor. "Ko Kalberg and I were summoned," recalled *Grenadier*'s Bob Palmer. "We were somewhat stronger than the others in that we were working in the kitchen. The two of us were to be the anesthetic for the Major, while that wild, four-eyed Conga Cho [Kitamura] cut his leg open well up on his thigh."[25]

Kalberg and Palmer watched the Conga Cho grope through Boyington's wound. Told not to let the Marine scream, they instead found that Boyington smoked a Japanese Cherry cigarette to keep his mind off the pain. "He calmly smoked and talked to us all the time the moron cut and probed his leg." Pharmacist Kitamura cut away the flesh around the wound area, probing until he popped out the shrapnel. "The Conga Cho never even stitched him up," Palmer related. His wound tied with a dirty cloth, Boyington "hobbled back to his cell on that home-made crutch he had, cussing all the way."[26]

On 14 March, the Japanese moved out men to prepare for some new arrivals. From *Grenadier*, Lieutenant Harty and Gunner John Walden were called to leave. The others were non-submariners who were crippled—such as amputee Fred Garrett—or suffering from beriberi or malaria.

"Have missed five drafts out of here so far," wrote Fitzgerald. "Maybe the next time—I hope."[27]

———

Makassar: 1943–1944

The majority of the *Perch* crew detained at Makassar on Celebes would never have the option of being transferred and becoming official POWs.

On 2 October 1943, an officer's draft was pulled from the Makassar camp and sent on a ship to another camp in Batavia. *Pope*'s exec, Lt. Dick Antrim, was among those departing, leaving only eight officers in camp. The senior American POW became Lt. (jg) Allen Jack Fisher, the only *Pope* officer remaining at Makassar. Camp strength was reduced from more than 2,000 men to a total of 1442 with this transfer, including 167 enlisted men from the *Perch* and *Pope* crews.[28]

The five *Perch* officers, three radiomen and eight machinist's mates who had been taken to Japan were the only men of the crew to become registered as POWs. As winter turned into spring of 1944, despair set in among some as they approached their second year anniversary as unregistered prisoners of Japan. "We knew what the date was," recalled EM3c Ernie Plantz. "In some cases, we scratched it on the walls. Others of us got together and made calendars out of scraps of paper."

SK3c Bill Penninger, a 23-year-old *Pope* sailor from Fort Worth, Texas, kept a secret diary to record dates and events. "When I went out on my second working party from Makassar we were working in an abandoned Dutch home. In a drawer, I found a lady's little pocket notebook which was about 3 by 4 inches in size," he said. Penninger slipped the tiny notepad in his shoe and used it for making notes throughout his internment.

Yoshida, the most hated of the Makassar guards, only occasionally ventured into the prisoner's barracks to single out men for beatings. "For the most part, the guards would leave us alone once we were in our barracks," said Turk Turner.

The camp quarters were crowded and unhygienic, particularly due to improper footwear. The Makassar prisoners worked in rainstorms and broiling sun, laboring with shovels and picks regardless of the weather. During early 1944, work began on a new prisoner camp about a mile outside of Makassar. "At one period, the men worked 90 consecutive days, and sick men were often forced to work," recalled Lt. (jg) Fisher. "POWs on working parties were treated in a slavelike manner."[29]

Treatment in the Makassar hospital was little better than nothing at all. "I went into the hospital once with malaria," related Fireman Alabama Arnette. "After that, they didn't put me in the hospital again because they didn't have enough bunks for us there. I had malaria three times and the other two times I just had to suffer it out in camp." Although his family back in Perdido, Alabama, had no knowledge of his survival, they were still holding out hope. "I guess I was a very fortunate person," claimed Arnette. "I had a lot of people back home praying for me. I figure the Good Lord got me through it."

Dental problems were treated in the most rudimentary methods. "I was cutting my wisdom teeth and the darn things wouldn't come through the skin," said Ernie Plantz. "So they sat me down in the chair, took a knife and cut the gum away from the tooth. They didn't have anything to give you for pain."

The *Perch* men supplement their starvation rations with illegal trading. During the spring of 1944, American planes started bombing Celebes and morale soared.

"It was the most wonderful experience when they started bombing that place," Alabama Arnette said. "Whenever you came out of the bomb shelters, you made sure to never laugh or smile."

One bombing raid hit a Japanese warehouse filled with rice straw cigarette paper. After extinguishing the warehouse fire, the Japanese salvaged many partially burned bundles of the cigarette paper. Much of this water-damaged paper was given to the Allied prisoners in a rare act of "kindness." Ernie Plantz said, "We scattered it out on the line in the hot sun and it dried out in minutes. We found that this paper was better than money for trading with the local natives for food. The natives couldn't get cigarette paper."

A short time later, the Japanese caught a Chinese merchant who possessed a significant quantity of this salvaged cigarette paper. "They beat the hell out of him and made him confess where he'd gotten it," Plantz said. "He said he got it from the American prisoners." The Japanese marched the battered Chinese merchant into the Makassar camp and had the Americans fall into ranks for his inspection.[30]

The merchant picked out two *Pope* survivors and two from *Perch*—TM1c Glenn Taylor and S1c Robert Osborne. The Japanese then told the merchant they needed one more man. "The Japanese made us put our hats back on," said Plantz. "I happened to have a native woven straw hat that was frayed around the edges. I put that hat back on and that doggone Chinaman pointed to me and said, 'He was the other one.'"

Plantz, Taylor, Osborne and the *Pope* prisoners were locked in a brig for days while the Japanese tried to discover any other Americans who had been trading. For good measure, the other prisoners were routinely lined up and beaten to try and extract confessions.

In the brig, Ernie Plantz found that

> Food rations were practically nothing. They'd slap us around a bit and threaten us. We were there about a week. In the morning, we got all the rice we could eat with soybean paste they made from fermented paste. At noon, we got the same thing. Come evening time, we were beginning to get a bit worried. We had been told if you ever got in trouble where they had to execute you, the day they chopped your head off, they'd give you all you wanted to eat. That wasn't a good feeling.

After nearly a week of confinement, the five men were released. Several dozen new Japanese guard recruits were brought into the Makassar compound to help with the punishment. The entire camp contingent of 168 American prisoners was called to quarters on 1 May 1944. The Japanese claimed they knew other men were involved in trading the cigarette paper. "If everyone who sold didn't confess, they said they would chop our heads off," Plantz related. "I think all of the Americans came forward and said we all did, thinking there was safety in numbers. A whole bunch of them beat the hell out of them. They broke arms and cracked heads and did just about everything they could do."

The five "guilty" men were then brought before the rest of the camp and leaned forward on the end of "beating tables." Each new guard was given the chance to practice his beating technique on the buttocks of the five men, swinging clubs or baseball bats. "I was first," said Plantz. "Two Japs beat me with clubs. I wouldn't fall down and I wouldn't holler. They just beat me until I dropped."

After absorbing an incredible 75 blows from the clubs, Plantz was left to suffer as the guards selected another American. Glenn Taylor and Robert Osborne from *Perch* were both beaten with as many as 25 licks before the guards determined them to be sufficiently remorseful.

For good measure, the guards also worked over each of the American prisoners to serve as notice about future stealing. Bob Lents remembered that for his crew 1 May 1944 "was a significant day. Everybody at the barracks was beaten from 15 to 75 times across the buttocks with baseball bat sized clubs." Lents felt that the health of the Makassar inmates dropped steadily after this mass beating.

Helped away by *Perch* shipmates, Plantz said "my butt was swollen out about three inches larger than normal and was just as black as it could be." This camp beating went a long way to curb the desire for future illegal trading. Ernie Plantz was thereafter held in high esteem by his fellow prisoners for enduring 75 licks, a single-day camp record for punishment at Makassar.

15
Tullibee's Sole Survivor

"Wake up Kuykendall. You're wanted on the bridge."

The young quartermaster nudged the sleeping sailor in the forward torpedo room. "We're making an approach," he said. The duty messenger handed the groggy sailor a pair of night vision goggles and proceeded back to the control room once he was certain the man was awake.

It was 0245. GM2c Clifford Weldon Kuykendall had grown accustomed to these odd-hour wake-up calls. As a veteran submarine sailor, he knew to catch what little sleep he could when the opportunity presented itself. His boat, the USS *Tullibee* (SS-284), was making her fourth war patrol and had since established a regular attack party when it came to making torpedo approaches. Kuykendall had been selected to be one of the battle station lookouts for surface torpedo attacks due to his keen night vision.

A young man from Wichita Falls, Texas, he was already an old-timer on *Tullibee*, his first submarine assignment. Kuykendall had gone into the Navy right out of high school, attended submarine school, and then was assigned to new construction in Mare Island, California. *Tullibee*, the very last of the *Gato*-class boats, was launched on 11 November 1942, and commissioned on 15 February 1943, with Cdr. Charles Frederick Brindupke in command.

She had departed from Pearl Harbor on her first war patrol on 19 July 1943. During her first three runs, *Tullibee* earned three battle stars. Officially, she was credited with sinking three Japanese ships and damaging three more. During her third patrol, she had participated in a U.S. wolfpack. *Tullibee* sank a small 500-ton net tender and packmate *Haddock* had heavily damaged the Japanese aircraft carrier *Unyo*. *Tullibee* returned to Pearl Harbor for refit and her crew went ashore to the Royal Hawaiian for a much-enjoyed R&R stint.

Commander Brindupke's boat sailed from Pearl on 5 March 1944 on his fourth command patrol. His destination was the area north of Palau and his assignment was to take part in "Operation Desecrate," a carrier air strike at Palau that was scheduled for 30 March. Japanese shipping targets were expected to be rich in the area. *Tullibee* stopped briefly at Midway en route to top off with fuel and departed on 14 March, never to be seen again in an American port.

Tullibee reached her assigned station on 25 March and began hungrily patrolling the area. During the night of 26 March, she made radar contact on a convoy around 2000, consisting of a transport, two medium-sized freighters, two anti-submarine vessels and a destroyer. The skipper called his tracking party and plotted the convoy's course and speed to intercept. Brindupke tried twice to move in to firing range as the night rolled into the early morning hours of 27 March. He had to withhold fire because of a blinding rain that hampered efforts on the bridge.[1]

The Japanese escorts were fully alerted and began using their searchlights while running around and dropping between 15 and 20 depth charges. *Tullibee* tried to set up for a third approach, but again was prevented from completing her torpedo attack.

Fred Brindupke wanted his best battle lookouts topside to overcome the weather obstacle, and Cliff Kuykendall was considered something of an eagle eye. Once he had rolled out of his bunk, he knew that he had to obtain the battle goggles to give his eyes the customary fifteen minutes to adjust before he went to the bridge. Strolling forward to the galley, he found that the cooks on duty, SC2c Lionel Blanchard and SC1c Edward Dzik, had the coffee brewing and snacks ready for the men of the approach party. Kuykendall chose to sip a couple of cups of hot chocolate, never suspecting that it could be his last.

He hoped that this approach would give the ship another kill to add to the battle flag. Just that prior afternoon, Kuykendall had strolled into the forward torpedo room as the torpedo gang was servicing the Mark 14 fish. TM3c Lomon Crane was a buddy that he had made leave with between patrols.

"Hey, Cliff," Crane called. "Come paint your girl's name on one of the fish." During the war, torpedomen frequently painted their girlfriends' names or some foul message to Admiral Tojo on their torpedoes before they were loaded into the tubes. Seizing the chance to have a little fun, Kuykendall painted the name of the last girl he had dated on one of the Mark 14s. Crane's crew then loaded this fish back into the No. 2 forward tube.

As Kuykendall made his way toward *Tullibee*'s bridge, he wondered if his torpedo would be one of the ones to sink a Japanese ship this night. Moving forward into the control room, he noted his friend Dave Butler had assumed the duties of diving officer. Ensign Butler, a Navy veteran who had climbed the ranks from seaman to warrant officer, was a "mustang." Famed skipper "Fearless Freddie" Warder had promoted him aboard *Seawolf*, the boat on which Butler made seven historic runs in 1942. A Silver Star recipient, he had been assigned to *Tullibee*, where he served as the assistant engineering officer to Lt. David Spencer Wilson. Near Butler, Kuykendall noted the chief of the boat, CGM Thomas Morris Delaney, keeping vigil at the Christmas tree.

As he paused in the control room, a lookout who was coming down from the conning tower handed him a life belt that he had been wearing around his waist. The sailor removed his inflated belt and said, "Here, Cliff, take this."

Kuykendall replied instinctively, "I don't need that."

"Go ahead and take it," the lookout said, "You might need it."

Shrugging, Kuykendall took the life belt and fastened it to his waist and forgot all about it. "This was the first time I had ever worn a belt topside, and I had been in very stormy weather before," he later recalled. "Anyone going topside on *Tullibee* wasn't required to wear a life belt. I later wished I could thank that guy."

Kuykendall finished his hot chocolate and climbed the steel rungs of the ladder that led to the conning tower. There, he found his direct boss, gunnery officer Lt. Henry Taylor Irwin Jr., seated at the TDC with his assistant, FC2c John Grosz, to input the firing data for the ship's torpedoes. Forward, on the wheel as battle helmsman was QM2c John Barcoozy. Serving as the skipper's assistant approach officer and manning the periscope was the ship's XO, Lt. Cdr. George Assheton Duncan Jr. Standing by as his assistant was the senior quartermaster, QM1c Don Arnold. RT1c Allen Nopper from Oklahoma City monitored the radar and was calling out distances on the approaching Japanese ships.

Kuykendall also noted chief commissary steward Walter "Rocky" Schoenrock in the conning tower having a conversation with Duncan and Arnold. Schoenrock and Arnold had both served on the old *S-39* and were with her when she ran aground off Australia and was lost. The entire crew was rescued. Schoenrock, whose hair was receding with his age, had a passion for tattoos. He and fellow cook Ed Dzik, who had served on the old *Dolphin*, were the oldest men on *Tullibee*.

Kuykendall had seen this scene before and passed through the conning tower team just like any other night when he had been called to the bridge for a battle approach. The time was 0300 on 27 March 1944, and he never even considered that he had just glimpsed these men for the last time in his life.

"Permission to come to the bridge," he called up to the OOD.

"Permission granted," Lt. (jg) Richard Hermal Peterson called back down.

Kuykendall popped through the conning tower hatch, noting Peterson and Commander Brindupke both on the bridge, directing the ship's approach. In the darkness and light mist that was falling, he did not pay particular attention to who his fellow lookouts were that were being relieved.

"Kuykendall, take the starboard aft position," Lieutenant (jg) Peterson directed. The other lookout handed him his heavy pair of binoculars and Kuykendall put the strap over his neck as he climbed up. He duly took his perch on the after periscope shears platform and made a sweep with his binoculars.

"We were flooded down on the surface," Kuykendall recalled. "Our decks were almost awash as we were approaching this Jap convoy. We were lining up on a big transport."

Tullibee's fourth attack approach on the Japanese convoy proved to be more successful than the first two attempts. Kuykendall and his fellow lookouts kept the officers apprised of the distance and position of the three Japanese escort ships as their submarine made ready to fire. The torpedo tube doors were opened forward and as the range came down to about 3,000 yards, Commander Brindupke called, "Fire one!"

The boat was loaded with both the new Mark 18 electric torpedoes and the older Mark 14 steam torpedoes. The after room had been loaded with the Mark 18s and the 14s had gone forward. *Tullibee* shuddered as the first Mark 14 torpedo left its tube. Seconds later came the call, "Fire two!" *Tullibee* belched forth her second warfish, set to run just deep enough to rip into the fat transport's vulnerable belly.

On the bridge, Cliff Kuykendall heard the words of one of his fellow lookouts. It was the forward starboard lookout, S1c Paul Ray Abnet from Georgia, whose Southern accent punctuated his statement, "There they go. We'll see what happens now."

Less than 30 seconds after firing, *Tullibee* had an answer for Abnet's query. The range was long for the torpedoes but the angle was good. One of the torpedoes, however, began curving back around after it had only traveled partway to the enemy ship. In the darkness, the lookouts and officer on *Tullibee*'s bridge could not see the deadly menace that careened into a circular run toward its firing point. Without a chance to dodge it, the submarine was slammed by her own errant torpedo. From the time of firing until "a terrific concussion shook the boat" was less than one minute.[2]

WHAM! The torpedo struck *Tullibee* with a deafening blast and violent explosion that rocked the ship. The concussion was forceful enough to literally blow the topside men from their positions on the conning tower. From his after starboard shears perch, GM2c Cliff Kuykendall was suddenly airborne.

All I can remember is a crimson flash before my eyes and being blown high up through the air. Somehow, I caught a fleeting glimpse of the ship's stern. It looked to be going under the water. I arched myself with my arms outstretched before I hit the water. I was knocked unconscious. The next thing I know, I was under the surface and my binoculars were long gone. I came to, kinda dazed and badly bruised. I swam upward and finally broke the surface, gasping for air.

Kuykendall found that he was not severely injured but dazed and in a state of mild shock. Conducting a self-inspection, he found that his upper lip was bleeding from a nasty gash and that his teeth were shattered. Three teeth on his upper left and two on the upper right side of his mouth were either completely broken out or chipped off. He figured that the heavy binoculars had smashed into his face from the force of the explosion.

He heard other voices crying out in the water, likely those of Commander Brindupke, Lieutenant (jg) Peterson, and the other lookouts. Kuykendall was able to manually inflate the life belt he had been handed before going on watch. "There was a very thick oil slick covering the water around me," he later testified. "Ten minutes after I regained consciousness in the water, all the yelling ceased, and everything was quiet."

Shortly after reaching the surface, Kuykendall saw *Tullibee* about 75 yards distant from him. "It was going down by the stern and the after part of the conning tower was sinking below the waves when seen," he recalled. "A large, dark, low rain cloud came between the sub and myself and I didn't see the sub again or see it go down. All this happened between 0300 and 0315."

He swam through the dark night alone without hearing any further voices. By dawn's first light on 27 March, he could not see a soul as he bobbed in the ocean. There was nothing but a "thin oil slick on the water" as he swam along, supported only by his life belt.

Around 1000, an escorting destroyer approached from due west at about 6,000 yards and then began circling him. "At about 3,000 yards, the vessel turned sharply to starboard, traveling a distance of about one mile, then made sharply to port," he recalled. "When due south of me, he sighted me and began circling."

Kuykendall's worst fears came true as the warship's port machine guns opened fire on him. The destroyer made a full 360-degree circuit around him, spraying the water with bullets the entire time. Fortunately, they were either lousy shooters or only intended to intimidate him. Still, Kuykendall's flesh was ripped in five places by bullets or fragments that grazed him.

The Japanese destroyer finished its circle before moving in to pick up the lone American survivor. Kuykendall was hauled aboard and immediately came face to face with an English-speaking officer. The officer swung a large club against his head and knocked the American sailor unconscious.

When he came to, Kuykendall found that his captors were at first confused as to where exactly he had come from. He found out later that they were completely unaware of *Tullibee*'s loss, adding certainty that his ship had not been lost due to Japanese efforts.

The English-speaking officer who had clubbed him was joined by another who spoke broken English. Together, the Japanese officers interrogated Kuykendall. They wanted to know the name of his submarine, the captain's name, where his ship was operating from, and all details of his sub—including length, dimensions, the types of guns aboard, and the names of his fellow crewmen. Once the destroyer men realized they had captured a U.S. submariner, things went downhill for Kuykendall. They accused him of sinking one of their transports. "You are the one that sank the maru ship," he was told in broken English. "You die."

His captors struck him again and prepared to execute him with a sword.

Two Jap Navy officers beat me and said they were gonna behead me. One had a saber as tall as he was. I was waiting to die for sinking their maru.

They had a Jap sailor on each side, holding me up. That Jap officer was waving his saber around, swinging the sword over his head. Every time he got ready to aim for my neck, those other Japs would turn loose of me and jump to the side, one to port and one to starboard. I would fall to the deck. That saved me several times. He swung his saber over my head five or six times. Each time, it passed over the top of me because I would collapse to the deck when they turned loose of me.

Then, a Jap officer up on the bridge started yelling down at them in Japanese in our direction. Those two Jap officers left and the others took me down into the forward deck house.

Injured and terribly frightened, Kuykendall was laid upon a mat in the destroyer's deckhouse. He would later find out how fortunate he truly was. "I didn't have any broken bones or serious internal injuries," he stated. "As I would later learn, they would probably throw you overboard if you had serious injuries. I also learned that if you survived your first day after being picked up by the Japanese, your odds were better on surviving."

The hardest thing he soon came to realize was that he was the only man picked up by the Japanese this day. "I've tried to figure out why I was the sole survivor of the *Tullibee*," he later wrote. "It was impossible. I couldn't. I realized if I continued to try and figure it out, it was impossible and I would never be happy."

Kuykendall was questioned throughout the day as the tin can made for Palau. He stuck to the basics, though: name, rank, and service number. In return, the English-speaking officers beat him with clubs, rawhide thongs, rifle stocks, and even hit him alongside the head with the barrel of a pistol.

Kuykendall later found out that the destroyer that picked him up was named *Wakatake*, a 22-year-old destroyer of 820 tons. She was in company with two escort vessels, *Patrol Boat 39*—the 750-ton, renamed old destroyer *Kiku*—and the submarine chaser *CH 6*, a 270-ton vessel. After picking up the American submariner,

Wakatake and the other ships made their way to Palau, where Task Force 58's carrier air strikes would soon find them.[3]

Wakatake arrived at Palau around 1630 on 27 March. The ship anchored in a harbor between two of the islands. "After arriving in port, I was questioned on deck and beaten some more," Kuykendall later testified.

A whaleboat from a pier came alongside *Wakatake* and he was blindfolded. As relieved as he felt to be alive and ashore, Kuykendall was apprehensive of where he had been taken. "I knew the air strike was coming on March 30–31," he later related. "The *Tullibee* crew was informed when we were north of Wake Island, after leaving Midway on patrol."

After what he had endured on the Japanese destroyer, young Kuykendall was not afraid of the Japanese killing him on Palau. "When we got ashore at Palau, they put me in a car and took me to what looked like some headquarters building," he stated. "I was in a bad way, being weak, so I laid down on the mat in this room under a mosquito net and immediately went to sleep."

Kuykendall guessed that he slept at least ten hours before he awoke to sun shining brightly through an eastward-facing window. As he opened his eyes, he became aware of a Japanese guard with a rifle watching him closely. Soon after waking up on 28 March, he was taken to an office and put in a chair in front of a desk. An English-speaking Japanese officer confronted him. "He got up, walked around in front of me, leaned over and stuck a finger in my mouth," Kuykendall said.

"Lost a few teeth, didn't you?" the interrogator asked.

The young American asked if he could see a dentist about his broken teeth, but he was informed that prisoners received no such treatment.

"You are a coward anyway," the officer told him.

"Why am I a coward?" asked Kuykendall.

"To let yourself be captured," he replied.

Kuykendall explained that he had been swimming for his life and had been picked up by the Japanese destroyer.

"You should have drowned yourself instead of letting yourself be captured," the interrogator stated.

He likened some of the green dungaree-uniformed Palau soldiers to Marines, noting that they were much larger in stature than the Japanese destroyermen he had previously encountered. Kuykendall only had vague ideas of how to handle the next round of questioning. "I'd been told if I was ever captured by the Japs that if I had to lie to them, be sure not to tell a lie that I couldn't back up," he recalled. "I also never smiled at them. I was told that if I smiled at them they felt I was making fun of them."

The Japanese wanted to know what caused Kuykendall's sub to be lost.

"There was an explosion," he said. "I guess we must have hit a mine."

Through his limited English, the Japanese interrogator scoffed at this comment.

He told the confused submariner that the water was far too deep for mines in this area. It was at that time that Kuykendall realized that his ship had most likely been struck by her own torpedo. "They had no idea how *Tullibee* had been lost," he recalled. "They hadn't fired on us."

Another realization struck Kuykendall. The forward tubes had fired the last two fish that morning, meaning that the Mark 14 he had hand-painted the previous day with an old girlfriend's name in tube No. 2 may have been the one that had sunk his ship. "I never knew that old girl would come back to haunt me like that," he later related.

After his first round of interrogations, GM2c Cliff Kuykendall was taken back to the store room where he was being kept. The following day, 29 March, he was moved to a brig, which he found out later was closer to the beach.

The morning interview that day was relatively short and he was not mistreated. In the afternoon, he was returned to the interrogator. The questions started up again: What is the name of your ship? Where did it sail from? What was the weight of your ship? How many men were on it? What was the commanding officer's name?

"I just gave my name, rank and serial number," Kuykendall recalled. "I reminded him of the Geneva Convention. He stated that Japan did not sign the Geneva Convention."

When the afternoon questioning ended, a guard motioned for him to follow him back to his cell. As he turned to leave the office, the Japanese interrogator warned, "When you are returned, if you don't answer my questions, you will be tortured."

Gunner Kuykendall was placed in the brig again and was able to sleep again that night. His worries about being tortured at the next morning's interrogation were interrupted by the unmistakable sound of aircraft engines overhead in large numbers. The Palaus soon became a mass of antiaircraft fire, smoke, explosions, and burning ships. Task Force 58's Operation Desecrate 1 was under way, and the carrier pilots pounded the Japanese fortress mercilessly. On the morning of 30 March, *Wakatake*—Kuykendall's rescue ship—was traveling through the channel west of Babelthuap with *CH 6* and *Patrol Boat 39* when they were attacked by aircraft from the carriers *Yorktown* and *Enterprise*. Both smaller vessels ran themselves aground but were blasted by the carrier aviators. *Yorktown* pilots torpedoed *Wakatake* and cameras captured the old destroyer's final moments off Palau. In the end, the American carrier pilots sunk 32 Japanese ships at Palau. A Japanese source lists six additional vessels sunk or damaged beyond salvage. Due to this fleet's devastation, it is unknown what ship *Tullibee* might have hit with her torpedo.[4]

As devastating as the American air strikes were against Palau's shipping, Cliff Kuykendall was in grave danger. Held in a barracks on Arakabesan Island, he could hear the whine of the Hellcat fighters, Avenger torpedo bombers and Dauntless dive bombers that strafed and blasted everything Japanese on the islands. "Bombs began falling and fighters began strafing the area I was in," he said. In the face of the carrier strikes against the Palaus, it is incredible that the Japanese forces there did not retaliate by killing their American submariner. "Overall, I enjoyed the strike hammering the Japs," he said, "but I could have been hammered, too."

A bomb blast destroyed much of the building Kuykendall was being held in. The concussion of the blast was enough to destroy his cell and the window it contained. "After the window was destroyed, I could see our own planes dive bombing and strafing the island and the other island across the bay," he testified. Japanese soldiers pulled him from the rubble and moved him into another building during the first day's air strikes. "Outside the window of this building, the Japs had an anti-aircraft gun," he recalled. "Three Japs manned it and they were peppering away at the low-flying planes."

A strafing F6F Hellcat soon took down the AA gunners. Starved and dehydrated, Kuykendall noted that a large water barrel was mounted above his cell. During the F6F's strafing run, a bullet pierced the water barrel above him "and I got a good drink."

Once again, the bombers destroyed the building Kuykendall was being held in. Strafing fighters ignited an ammunition dump, which blew with enough force to completely destroy the damaged brig. Fortunately, he escaped serious injury once again.

I was dragged out from under it by about three Japs, and we ran down a long slit trench. The Hellcat had six .50-caliber machine guns and most of them at Palau carried bombs under the front end of their fuselage. There must have been at least 50 Japs in that trench standing up—shooting at the Hellcats with rifles. Three Japs tossed me into a bunker at the end of the trench and came in behind me. At least one Hellcat was still flying low, strafing. One Jap knelt at the bunker entrance working the bolt on his rifle, making machine gun firing sounds. Every once in awhile, he'd look over at me and point the rifle at me.

I felt it was just a matter of time before they shot me.

Eventually, the attacks quieted down for the day and the Japanese removed Kuykendall from the bunker. They then led him to a hilltop on Arakabesan Island and tied him up. "I constantly felt they were going to kill me," he stated. "I can honestly say I was never scared. I guess I was in a state of shock. I figure the only reason they didn't kill me is because they had orders from higher up not to. They wanted me in Japan for interrogation."

Kuykendall remained tied to the tree "for about 55 hours," throughout the balance of the American air strikes. "I was not given water or food during this time."

He worked at removing the ropes that bound him, thinking of how he could escape Palau if he could untie himself.

At night, it was pitch black. I could hear things crawling around, but I don't know what they were. Off to my right, there was a Japanese house on stilts. Finally, I did untie the ropes and I was going to untie my ankles. I started fantasizing about stealing a boat and rowing to New Guinea. The Palaus were due north of New Guinea, about 500 miles away. Then I fantasized, no, I'll steal an airplane! I couldn't even fly, though.

Although he had managed to free his hands, he did not have time to work the bindings on his feet free before the Japanese returned that evening. A truck parked about 50 yards from him and two Japanese officers approached. Kuykendall thrust his hands behind his back and tried to pretend that he was still fully bound.

A Japanese officer noted the loose ropes and said simply, "Hhhmmm."

They untied the U.S. submariner's ankles and dumped him onto the hay-covered floor of their military truck. Kuykendall was driven down to a house near the beach on Arakabesan and pushed into a small, dark dugout behind the main home.

This little dugout might have been an air-raid shelter. It had flaps at the bottom, like behind a beer tavern. I couldn't stand up in it and I couldn't sit down. I just had to sit there with my chin almost touching my knees.

I crawled out to the entrance and made a motion to the guard that I wanted water. He smiled, went off and came back with a small teacup full of sweet tea. One evening, a Jap stuck his head in the entrance and stated, "Tell me the name of your submarine and I'll bring you a cover." The nights were cool in that small dugout on those slats. I didn't answer him. He left and I never got a cover.

One afternoon, two young Jap girls came out there looking through the little hole in the shelter. They looked at me and just giggled and left. They kept me in there about three days and nights.

On the morning of his fourth day in the shelter—5 April by his recollections—a car arrived and Kuykendall was led to it. He was driven down to a pier that jutted into Arakabesan's bay. His blindfold was removed and he was confronted by a naval officer.

The kind officer offered the American POW a bunch of Japanese rice crackers he called "kanippas," which he had wrapped in newspaper. The officer could speak fair English and he talked with the young American for a while. Presently, the drone of aircraft engines announced the approach of a large four-engine Emily

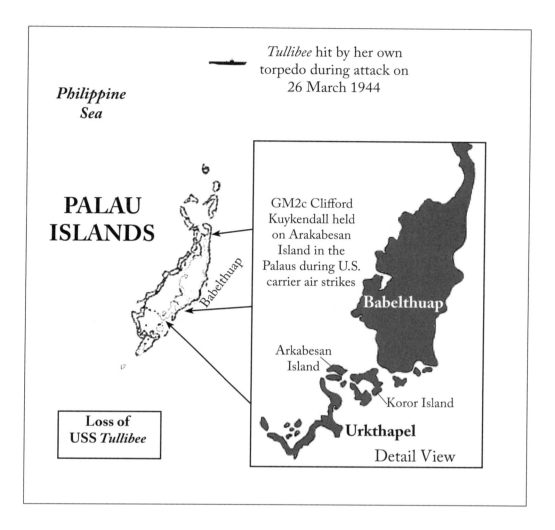

Tullibee hit by her own torpedo during attack on 26 March 1944

Philippine Sea

PALAU ISLANDS

Babelthuap

GM2c Clifford Kuykendall held on Arakabesan Island in the Palaus during U.S. carrier air strikes

Babelthuap

Arkabesan Island

Koror Island

Urkthapel

Detail View

Loss of USS *Tullibee*

flying boat. The seaplane landed in Arakabesan's bay and taxiied through the clear tropic waters to a point several hundred yards from the little pier.

"There you are," the officer said. "You're heading for there."

"Thank you, sir," Kuykendall replied. "Good luck to you."

"Thank you. I'll need it," was the officer's surprising reply.

Clutching his little package of Japanese crackers, Kuykendall was placed into a small motorboat and taken out to the seaplane. "They loaded me in through the hatch on the starboard side of the Emily," he said. "As soon as they got me in the seaplane, that starboard waist gunner on that plane took my crackers from me and threw me over in the corner."

The Emily taxiied around and climbed into the sky. As the aircraft reached high altitude, the temperature in the seaplane plummeted. "It got cold," Kuykendall said. "That gunner came over and threw a tarp over me. I will give him credit for that."

Kuykendall's journey, as he would later learn, first included a stop at Tanapang Harbor in Saipan on 5 April. He was taken to a Navy brig at Garapan, where he would remain for two days. One of the Japanese sailors at Saipan took his dog tag. His treatment on Saipan was good in comparison to his time on Palau. "I got all the water I wanted," he said. "It was given to me in a Jap green beer bottle."

From his cell in Saipan, Kuykendall could watch a Japanese naval officer sitting behind a nearby desk. He noted how such officers treated their own young recruits. When young Japanese sailors stood at attention before him, the officer would yell at them and strike them in the faces with the flat of his fists. "If he knocked them down, he'd kick them, and they would get back up and stand at attention. While doing this, he'd look over at me as if to say, 'This is the way we discipline our men.'"

On 7 April, he was on the move again. "They loaded me up on another four-engine seaplane, a Mavis, and flew me to Yokusaka," he said. His air transport was more luxurious this time. Kuykendall had a Japanese escort who spoke perfect English and he was seated on the starboard side forward near a window.

Quite a while into the trip, the young American was able to look out the window and see some islands. "I remember looking down and seeing a pork chop-shaped island with an extinct-looking mountain volcano at one end," Kuykendall related. After the war, he would fly over this island again and learn it was the bitterly con-tested island of Iwo Jima.

Once past Iwo Jima, Kuykendall was blindfolded for the final descent into Yokusaka, Japan. In Japan, he was moved to Ofuna. The sole survivor of the submarine *Tullibee* and a survivor of the carrier strikes on Palau, Cliff Kuykendall knew that he was fortunate to have been allowed to leave those islands alive.

16
Loss of *Robalo*

Routine harassment of the prisoners was the protocol at the secret Ofuna camp during the cold months of March 1944. Lt. Kunichi "James" Sasaki, born in Japan but educated in the United States, was the senior interpreter for the inmates. He spoke excellent English and dressed sharp with Oxford shoes and fancy suits, which earned him the nickname "Handsome Harry" behind his back.[1]

Grenadier's skipper, Lieutenant Commander Fitzgerald, was quizzed by Handsome Harry and Ofuna's commandant, Warrant Officer Iida, concerning the Aleutians headquarters. He was also told of intelligence the Japanese had received of specific U.S. submarine losses of 25 boats including *Wahoo*, *Grenadier*, *S-44*, *Sculpin*, *Perch*, and others.

"When will I be able to get out of this place?" Fitzgerald asked Sasaki.[2]

He was told that he was in a good place and should be happy. Fitzgerald replied that the lack of letters from back home was not a good thing. "There was no reply to this statement," he logged. "Looks like I'm here for the duration."

Ofuna's compound received yet another American submariner on 7 April, *Tullibee*'s GM2c Cliff Kuykendall. Arriving barefooted and weary from his journey to mainland Japan, he was placed in a cell in one of the barracks. Being the only survivor of his ship and having survived the U.S. carrier attacks on Palau, Kuykendall was apprehensive about what to expect next. During his first afternoon in confinement, he was approached by another American.

"Red Bullard was an F6F pilot who had been shot down in the first carrier raid on Truk," Kuykendall said. "He sneaked over in the room next to me and called to me through the walls." The pilot introduced himself as Lieutenant Bullard. He explained to the newly arrived prisoner, "Commander Fitzgerald, the commander of the *Grenadier*, is in charge of all POWs of the Japs. He wants to know your name and whether you're a submarine man or an aircrewman."

Kuykendall carefully replied, "Well, I don't know who you are. You might be a spy."

"Oh, no," Bullard tried to calm him. He explained that he was a fighter pilot who had been the executive officer of *Intrepid*'s VF-6 squadron. With four previous kills to his credit, Bullard's Hellcat had been forced down by AA fire just beyond Truk's reef. Before he could be rescued, Japanese gunners took him prisoner.[3]

After listening to the Hellcat pilot's story, Cliff Kuykendall replied, "Well, I'll think it over. I need more information. I have to be careful who I talk to."

Red Bullard left to confer with John Fitzgerald. "He came back about 15 or 20 minutes later, and we talked some more," said Kuykendall. He briefed the *Tullibee* survivor on what he could expect during his upcoming interrogations. "Commander Fitzgerald says it's all right to talk some," Bullard explained. "Give 'em your name, rank, and serial number, but don't tell 'em much of anything else."

Only when Kuykendall was comfortable did he relate the loss of *Tullibee* and his subsequent ordeal in finally reaching mainland Japan. When his questioning sessions began at Ofuna, he found that at least one English-speaking Japanese officer was always present. "Interrogators questioned me about all details of submarine operations and war patrols, bases of operation, and other naval vessels," he later testified. "Was questioned on rules and regulations of the United States Navy."

Gradually, Kuykendall had the chance to meet George Whiting and John Fitzgerald from *Grenadier* and the two *S-44* survivors. "They put me in a room by myself and I wasn't supposed to talk to other prisoners," he recalled. "If they caught you talking to them, they'd beat you up. But I did get to talk to quite a few of the other guys on the fly."

The Japanese camp cook Hata—known as "Curly" to the prisoners—became quite wealthy on selling extra prisoner rations. During early April, the rice rations were cut an extra 25 percent. On 8 April, Navy prisoner Lt. (jg) Stephan Nyarady—caught stealing four onions—was given six cracks with a bat and no rice at lunch.

On 9 April, the Ofuna prisoners had a nice Easter service conducted by Geoffrey Lempriere complete with the hymn "Onward Christian Soldiers." Lieutenant Commander Fitzgerald celebrated the holiday by eating a can of sardines and one strip of chocolate that he had been saving for the occasion. SSgt. Carl K. Cannon was brought into camp on a two-wheeled cart in very poor condition on 15 April. During the week, the rice ration took another 25 percent drop. "It's said that rice is now short but more later," wrote Fitzgerald. "If so, how about the truck which backed up to the kitchen last night and hauled several bags of it away?"[4]

Fitzgerald, Lt. Bill Harris, RAAF officer Noel T. Quinn and another prisoner confronted the Gochyos for a conference on the food situation on 17 April. They were told that rations throughout Japan had been cut. For the Ofuna prisoners, they had been cut to 213 grams a meal and 520 grams of vegetables per day. "It looks like tightening the belt and forget it!" Fitzgerald wrote.[5]

The dump at Ofuna became more atrocious in the warmer weather. Flies swarmed by the hundreds about the waste. Y1c Bob Palmer from *Grenadier* stated that the prisoners could earn cigarettes by killing flies. "I recall sitting around that garbage dump with [*Princeton* pilot Lt. (jg)] Charlie Bransfield, [2nd Lt. Edwin Jr.] Carl Kalbfleish, John Critchlow, Lou Zamperini, Pappy Boyington, Lt. Sherry, and a lot of others," he wrote. "We all had a palm frond cut to the shape of a fly swatter. We had a small match box that was to receive the flies that we killed with the palm frond." When the matchbox was filled, Palmer and his companions took their haul to the leading guard. "We bowed several times as we approached," and then presented their kills, in exchange for a cigarette.[6]

Sculpin's Lieutenant George Brown remained a steady interrogation target. "The seamen guards seemed to derive great pleasure and satisfaction from working over and torturing American officers," he related. "I was made to perform tasks even considered undignified by the Japanese, such as emptying the latrines, cleaning latrines, scrubbing the guards' clothes and doing manual tasks for the Japanese enlisted men." On several occasions, Brown volunteered to wash out filthy bandages that Ofuna pharmacist Congacho refused to clean. He was often beaten severely for endeavoring to instill Congacho with some sanitary practices. "I noted the Japanese pharmacist's mate treat one man for piles and use the same tweezers to treat another man for an infected throat," recalled Brown.

22 April 1944 marked the first year of being a prisoner for the *Grenadier* crewmen. The guards singled out some of the prisoners for humiliation in front of the others the next day. On 1 May, Fitzgerald marked his personal one-year anniversary at Ofuna. Four new B-24 aviators arrived this day from the air crew of Lt. Harold Van Wormer, captured in February. Van Wormer had been in the camp for more than a month, but the others of his crew brought the number of U.S. prisoners at Ofuna to 64.[7]

On 7 May, 2nd Lt. Glen A. McConnell was brought in. He had been shot down over Hong Kong on 18 April. "McConnell was a big, tall, blond-headed guy from Hollywood, California, and he was only the second prisoner I know of besides me who arrived at Ofuna barefooted," recalled Cliff Kuykendall.

Commander Sanimatsu, the visiting senior Japanese interrogator, kept up his questioning of George Whiting, trying to find out how they thought General MacArthur and allies would try to take the Philippines. Whiting told Sanimatsu he had no idea how the Allies would take over Japan, but that Russia might even get involved.

Another of McConnell's crewmen, Air Force SSgt. Tony M. Spadafora, came in with his leg in a cast, bringing the camp list of prisoners to 67 men. John Fitzgerald noted a swing in the general treatment the prisoners received in late June. Treatment was good on some days, "but when it's bad, it's really a bit of hell around here." Australian officer Noel Quinn had his eardrum broken in a beating with a club on 23 May. Fitzgerald thought of home on 4 June, wishing he could be there for his son Jack's ninth birthday. "If fate and luck be with us, I have hopes of being present for his 10th," he wrote.

On 6 June, Ofuna received four U.S. Air Force survivors of a B-24 from the Seventh Air Force which had been shot down on a mission over Saipan on 25 May. The pilot, Capt. Loren A. Stoddard, was a former college roommate of fellow Ofuna prisoner Wilbur Morris. The camp number was now at 71 men.

One of the B-24 airmen, 1st Lt. Ernest F. Peschau Jr., was suffering from a badly injured right leg and internal injuries. "I could see that Peschau was in critical need of immediate medical attention," wrote Fitzgerald. The seriously wounded airman was instead put into a small shack behind the prisoner barracks. "I was put in the shack to stay with him," recalled Cliff Kuykendall. "He moaned and groaned all the time, day and night. I couldn't help him. The Japanese pharmacist, Congacho, had very little medicine. If you were badly injured, you either recovered or you died." At night the Japanese guards would circle outside the little shack, moaning and groaning and mockingly saying, "Kendall. Kendall." According to Kuykendall, "They couldn't pronounce my name. They kept us in pitch dark in the shack."

Lieutenant Commander Fitzgerald was questioned by a naval jg on 8 June on his war patrols aboard *Grenadier*. "Mostly a pack of lies on my part and they seemed to be trying to shake out a new story and so get me across the well known barrel," he wrote in his secret notes. "They sometimes get their English a little mixed up and some of their statements are amusing."

That night about 2100, Lieutenant Peschau died from his wounds, apparently from severe internal injuries from his crash. Louie Zamperini recalled, "After he died that night the guards staged a mock bayonet drill using the corpse as a target." On 10 June, the Ofuna prisoners were allowed to hold a small service for him. The Japanese decided to inoculate their prisoners on 20 June, giving them each a shot for typhus, cholera, and dysentery. The effects were various aches and pains in muscles and joints, plus many light fevers. Captain Stoddard, however, became gravely ill and fought off death for nearly a month.[8]

New prisoners continued to trickle in, including a P-38 pilot on 23 June. The following day, Ofuna took in Lt. Daniel Terry Galvin and ARM3c Oscar Doyle Long from the carrier *Hornet*. Their VB-2 Helldiver had been shot down on 12 June during an attack on Guam. On 29 June, six more prisoners arrived, bound, handcuffed and looking to have been badly beaten. With the prisoner count now up to 79, the Ofuna men knew the next transfer of prisoners was imminent.

A Japanese admiral of the Yokosuka District inspected the camp on 1 July and the following day the Ofuna prisoners received a rare change in diet. *S-44* survivors Bill Whitemore and Tony Duva had been pressed into service as kitchen workers and POW cooks. They prepared small pieces of steak this day, along with boiled onions, gravy, rice, and barley.

Duva was most frequently used for the kitchen detail, along with former Grim Reaper pilot Al Mead. Lou Zamperini found that Mead and Duva maintained "impressive physical" condition because they "could always sneak an extra mouthful. Sometimes Duva and Mead would walk by my cell after dinner and throw me a rice ball, knowing the serious trouble they'd catch if caught."[9]

On 4 July, Japanese guards lined up the prisoners to harass them over one of eight washbasins not being cleaned that morning. The prisoners were in the Ofuna crouch with their knees half bent and arms in the air for 20 minutes. The Americans were thrilled when the air raid siren went off during this harassment. Lt. Pop Condit called out, "Hell, boys, that siren is music to the ears. Hope those bastards are catching the works! We can stand like this all day to that tune."[10]

The next prisoner transfer came on 10 July, when 30 men were marched out of Ofuna around 0800. This group included: Lt. John Critchlow, Lynn Clark, Bob Palmer, Charlie Erishman, Carl Quarterman, Buck Withrow, and Charles Westerfield from *Grenadier*; Paul Todd, Joe Baker, Herb Thomas, Ed Anderson, John Rourke, William Haverland, Leo Murray, and Julius Peterson from *Sculpin*; Ko Kalberg and Gordon Marshall from Pop Condit's *Yorktown* Avenger crew; and 14 other Army and Navy men.[11]

This left 49 prisoners remaining at Ofuna. This included six Army enlisted men and eight Navy enlisted men: *S-44*'s Duva and Whitemore; *Tullibee*'s Kuykendall; *Grenadier*'s Joe Knutson and Fred Zufelt; and *Perch*'s radiomen Robert Berridge, Ray Normand, and Ted Reh. Also remaining were three Merchant Marines, three Marine officers (including Pappy Boyington), 12 U.S. Navy officers (including Lieutenant Brown, Lieutenant Whiting, Lieutenant Commander Fitzgerald, Lieutenant McIntyre, Lieutenant Sherry, and Lieutenant Toulon), 14 Air Force officers, and three Navy Reserve officers.

A new prisoner, Ens. William Loughlin Connell, came in on 11 July. An SB2C dive bomber pilot from the carrier *Hornet*, Connell had been shot down over Chichi Jima on 4 July 1944. His gunner did not survive, but he was taken ashore on the island and lashed to a tree while American carrier planes pounded the island with bombs all day. Badly beaten and tortured, Connell was eventually flown out to Japan. He is believed to be the last American aviator to leave Chichi Jima alive during the war. Another American flyboy, ARM2c Lloyd Richard "Dick" Woellhof of *Hornet*'s VB-1, and an Army B-24 airman who had been captured were stabbed repeatedly and beheaded. One month after these murders, a TBF pilot from the carrier *San Jacinto*—one Lt. (jg) George Herbert Walker Bush—was also shot down during a carrier strike on Chichi Jima. Fortunately for the future President of the United States, George Bush was plucked from the sea by a lifeguard submarine, *Finback*.[12]

On 12 July, Greg Boyington was caught smoking in the benjo and was given eight hits across the buttocks with a club by guard Yamazaki—known as "Swivel Neck." "They really worked old Boyington over," recalled Cliff Kuykendall. *Grenadier*'s skipper, John Fitzgerald, watched out his cell window as two guards beat the Congressional Medal of Honor winner. The next day, the prisoners were told that if someone else smoked without permission, there would be no punishment to anyone else if the guards were alerted. If someone was caught smoking again and he was not ratted out to the guards, everyone would be punished. Pop Condit recalled, "Boyington never batted an eye. The punishment didn't stop him from smoking."[13]

Later that morning, one of the Japanese guards on duty was seen to go in and out of several prisoners' rooms three or four times. The guard stole laundry soap from the prisoners and framed *S-44* survivor Bill Whitemore by hiding a large piece of soap in his boot. The POWs were threatened with a clubbing but Fitzgerald was able to bring order to the situation without Whitemore or anyone else being punished for this injustice.[14]

On 14 July, Ofuna's prisoners were rearranged, with the 15 newer arrivals being kept in barracks No. 1 (Ichi). The kitchen and bath workers were quartered in No. 2 (Ni), while the remainder, including the longest tenured *Grenadier* prisoners, being moved into Barracks No. 3 (San).

Two large work groups were used during the month to dump water from a small canal via buckets into the adjoining rice paddies to help with the lack of rain. Some of the guards took exception in late July to Ofuna prisoners who failed to properly salute and bow deeply to the guards. The prisoners were lined up on 29 July in the Ofuna crouch while one guard slugged John Fitzgerald and Marine Bill Harris. Lt. Stephen Nyaraday was beaten with a bayonet and jabbed in the left leg with the bayonet's point. In the end, other senior Japanese chastised this guard and even gave him a few blows to the face. Fitzgerald saw this as a sign of hope. "Those with some intelligence along the matter realize that this country is losing and I think are a little more concerned about post-war conditions internationally."[15]

Intelligence trickled in that the Allies had taken Saipan and Guam. On 5 August, George Whiting was told by camp cook Curly that because of certain losses and rat infestations that food would be cut back again, including vegetable intake. The prisoners, however, could clearly see an outflow of their food departing on trucks in the illegal food sale carried out by some Japanese leaders. Three days later, they witnessed about 200 pounds of potatoes and onions leaving camp, along with a similar amount of rice. "Someone must be opening up a store and really getting set up in business," wrote Fitzgerald.[16]

The air raid sirens went off more frequently in early August. During the interrogation sessions, some of the prisoners received hope that they might be home in time for Christmas 1944, but few believed it.

––––––––––

Fukuoka: April 1944

Forty-two survivors from *Grenadier* had been sent to Fukuoka Camp No. 3 in October 1943. By the first anniversary of the sinking of their ship—21 April 1944—three of them had died from the poor conditions.

The prisoners were allowed one day off per month from working at the Yawata Steel Mill. During their "free" time, they washed clothes, cleaned barracks, and endured shakedown inspections from Japanese guards. During one search, a guard found a pencil stub that seaman Gordon Cox had found on the ground. With it, he had made some notes on Japanese words and their English translations.

"They got excited and called the interpreter," Cox recalled. "When I explained that I was trying to learn Japanese, they took my pencil and note, and whacked me over the head a couple of times, saying that was no good. I gave up trying very hard to learn Japanese."[17]

The deaths of three shipmates left a heavy gloom in the air for the other *Grenadier* POWs. The men began to realize a pattern about the deaths. Men became sick with amoebic dysentery—spread wildly by the Japanese use of human waste for fertilizer on their gardens—draining all of their strength. Once so greatly weakened, the men's bodies became subject to pneumonia. Once a man became so deathly ill, he was put into the camp hospital. "Most that were put there generally came out in a wooden box, to be hauled to the crematorium, where they were reduced to a much smaller box and returned to the camp," Cox wrote. "These little boxes were set on a shelf where we could see the number of boxes grow."[18]

The Allied POWs of Fukuoka became starved, scrawny skeletons of men who lined up for factory work detail each day. Fireman Angus McGowan was taken off work detail at the foundry one day and sent to the infirmary due to heavy swelling on his knee from a work injury. A Dutch and American doctor agreed that McGowan had gangrene in the knee. "So, they cut it open right there with a razor blade," he said. "No pain killer. Nothing. They sewed me up and I had to take a piece of sheet to wrap around my knee to keep it in place." After only two days to recover, McGowan went right back to the steel factory. "If you didn't work, you didn't eat," he said.

Skeeter McCoy was often punished for the chances he took in stealing food. On one occasion, he was abused for someone else's misdeeds. "The guards had a shakedown in the barracks and they found stolen goods stashed under my bunk that another guy had stolen," he said. *Grenadier* mess attendant T. J. Trigg had stolen food from the Indian POWs' barracks and hid it under McCoy's bunk, although his shipmates did not rat him out.

The Japanese guards strung up McCoy in front of the guard shack for five days and left him on public display for the other prisoners who filed in and out of camp going to work. "They only gave me a ball of rice and a teaspoon of water each day while I was strung up," he said. Left tied to a cross each day, McCoy could only think, "When I get out of this mess, Mr. T. J. Trigg and I will have a little get-together!"

When the guards felt that he had had enough punishment and starvation, they returned the *Grenadier* sailor to his barracks. "When I had the opportunity, I grabbed Trigg's dogtags around his neck and nearly choked him to death," McCoy stated. "I had gotten into enough trouble with the Japanese without his help!"

A sign of encouragement came in mid-June 1944, when Fukuoka's air raid siren went off in the middle of the night. "We began to hear the sound of bombs falling," related Gordon Cox. "What a feeling! The guards were running around screaming, causing a commotion." This was the first B-29 bombing attack—each plane carrying two tons of bombs—on Japan proper that the *Grenadier* men had experienced. "As I learned later, they came from Chenqtu field in China to destroy the coke ovens of Japan's largest steel plant at Yawata where we worked," Cox recalled. "It produced one-fourth of Japan's rolled steel." Upon returning to work the next day, the prisoners were disappointed to find that the American bombing efforts had caused very little noticeable damage at the Yawata steel plant. "We went to work as normal," he added, but found that "some of the guards were more surly than before. The Japs we worked with never mentioned the raid, and we were afraid to."[19]

The Fukuoka camp commander began holding drills for air raids and made the prisoners dig air raid shelters near the factory. Al Rupp, still recovering from his self-imposed injuries, was put on softer work detail working with others on an experimental farm within the compound. The prisoners spread "fertilizer" from the benjo tanks and little vegetables began growing during the summer. Rupp turned 18 on 7 August 1944, his second birthday as a POW. While working the experimental garden, he found comfort in occasionally seeing an American photo reconnaissance aircraft—dubbed "Photo Joe"—that began appearing on a more regular basis.[20]

The decline in pneumonia deaths was replaced in the summer by a severe outbreak of bed bugs and fleas in the Fukuoka barracks. The men slept on straw mats in two-tiered bunking areas. "If you slept on the lower tier as I did, bed bugs rained down on you all night," Gordon Cox recalled. "Our clothing was also full of body lice. Men sat around picking them out whenever there was a free minute." In the pipe shop, Cox and some of his companions were allowed to occasionally boil their clothing near a furnace to kill the bugs. Upon returning to their filthy barracks that night, however, their efforts would immediately be nullified by the onslaught of swarms more bedbugs, lice, and fleas.[21]

Hope was renewed with another big B-29 daylight bombing raid on 20 August. Fire and explosions filled the area as the prisoners fled the steel mill. "We had no air raid shelters," recalled torpedoman Warren Roberts. "We were put up on a second story of a pipe shop. Shrapnel was constantly beating down on this shop. Then they let us go down and get into a hole."

Gordon Cox found this attack to be "a very exciting display. Jap fighters went up to them and there was lots of ack-ack fire. A check on the raid showed the Americans lost fourteen B-29s and 95 men died or missing." Several downed airmen were brought into Fukuoka and isolated for days. "They were beaten and tortured for the time that they were there," wrote Cox. "We could hear the screams and sounds of the beatings that went on all night. We got a glimpse of them when they were brought into camp, but they must have been taken out at night, for we never knew when they left."[22]

The air raid alarm at the factory periodically sounded when incoming American bombing raids were spotted. "Sometimes there was enough time for them to move us to the tunnel that we passed through every day going to work," said Angus McGowan. "They would put us in a train and pull us back into the tunnel. We would worry that if they ever hit that tunnel, that would be the end of us." The air raids only added to the daily prisoner abuse. "They consistently told us that because we were submarine men they were getting their revenge on us," Warren Roberts recalled.

The men noticed a different attitude about their civilian guards at the Yawata mill after the second round of bombings. Some took out their anger on their prisoner workmen. Cox was pulled from his duties in the pipe shop one day and stood before two guards who held bayonets at his back. One of the young civilian Japanese guards punched him in the face until he was too tired to swing any more. "I got the impression he was trying to knock me down, so I moved my feet apart a little and tried to roll as much as I could with the blows. My nose was broken again," Cox said. "The next day both eyes were swollen almost shut. The rest of my face was so swollen my friends didn't recognize me."[23]

The presence of Photo Joe over the next weeks was encouraging. Some of the men, who had been officially registered as POWs upon being assigned to Fukuoka, received pieces of mail. Tom Courtney received his first letter from home on 12 September, which included a photo of his mother. Others would go their entire ordeal without a word from home. "My family never knew I was alive," related Virgil Ouillette.

The meager food rations ensured that sickness remained with the Fukuoka inmates. "There were always wheeler-dealers that took the chance of getting caught to get more to eat," said Cox. These prisoners created their own black market within the Fukuoka compound to improve their chances of survival. "They would get something in camp that they could trade to Jap civilians on the job for extra food," he added. "That was normally soybeans. Then they would have to parch them if they were not already parched. To get the beans into camp they had to get them through the shakedown entering camp."

These wheeler-dealers would collect enough soybeans to fill a pill-bottle-sized cylinder, which was then traded with another prisoner for a future food ration. "Starved as we were, the beans tasted like peanuts," Cox stated. The fact that local civilians had been deprived of clothing and necessities due to the war effort in Japan helped the wheeler-dealer POWs acquire the beans. According to Cox, these black market dealers considered the camp "as a dog-eat-dog business. They were getting more to eat, making them stronger than the average POW. Their customers didn't want it known that they were weak-willed enough to trade off their own future food."

The risk of a beating for being caught with the beans was worth the chance. One of those who dealt in this black market was MM3c George Snyder, who became very ill from the meals he traded off. "He got caught going through the garbage cans trying to do anything to get food," Cox recalled. "The Japs beat him badly several times. When it came to the notice of the rest of our submarine crew, it was too late for him. George could not understand why the Japanese beat him. I tried to tell him that they didn't need a reason, but he continued to worry about it."[24]

Snyder became very ill in September to the point that he could not get out of his bed. "He had big ulcerated sores on him, one on each hip that was the size of a donut," Cox recalled. "He was so thin you could see each of his bones standing out. I used to go talk to him. The last time he thought he was back home and was talking to his mother."

Snyder—a tall, good-looking young man—was reduced to a shriveled, comatose frame of a human by his beatings and starvation. "They rolled him over one day and his back was just all raw and opened up," said Chuck Ver Valin. "Each day he grew weaker," recalled Al Rupp. "On the 13th day of this illness, he slipped into a coma, and on the 14th day, he was gone."[25]

Snyder passed away on 23 September 1944 and his body was taken to the crematorium. His death bothered his shipmates greatly—such as bunkmate Skeeter McCoy—as some began to lose hope. In their first year at Fukuoka No. 3, four *Grenadier* sailors had died. As the Allied war efforts were being noticed more frequently in Japan, the silent prayers were that the war could end before more men passed away.

As American POWs were moved from outlying camps to mainland Japan aboard hell ships, there were inevitable losses as the war progressed. Famed skipper Dick O'Kane and his hot boat *Tang*—operating in the Yellow Sea during June 1944—had an incredible sinking feat recorded during the late night hours of 24 June. Firing all six forward tubes into a Japanese convoy, *Tang* managed to sink four merchant ships, including the 6,780-ton *Tamahoko Maru*. While this was the single best U.S. submarine attack of the entire war, it was later found to have been one of the deadliest for Allied POWs. When *Tamahoko Maru* sank, 560 of 772 POWs aboard that ship were killed, including 15 American soldiers and sailors, as well as 13 merchant mariners.[26]

Shortly after this unknown tragedy, another U.S. submarine was added to the list of those "overdue and presumed lost." From Australia, Admiral Ralph Christie had sent Cdr. Manning Marius Kimmel's *Robalo* on patrol to Indochina via the maze of islands and waterways of Balabac Strait.

Manning Kimmel, son of Adm. Husband Edward Kimmel and nephew of Adm. Thomas Kinkaid, had made six war patrols on *Drum* and *Raton* by early 1943. After two runs as her executive officer, Kimmel left *Raton* to join the PCO pool. His chance for command came in early 1944, when he was given the new boat *Robalo*—whose skipper was replaced after his first disappointing patrol. Assigned to the South China Sea, Kimmel's first command patrol during April 1944 was aggressive. He fired 20 torpedoes in four attacks and *Robalo*'s periscopes were badly damaged by the bombs from a Japanese plane.[27]

Setting out on his second command patrol, Lieutenant Commander Kimmel was familiar with the dangerous Balabac Strait. He had already maneuvered through them during his first command patrol in April. Admiral Christie's code-breakers had intercepted at least four messages regarding minefields in Balabac Strait, the details of which had been specified in the operation orders of outgoing submarines such as *Robalo*. Manning Kimmel's boat made the passage through this strait on 3 July, and received an Ultra dispatch that night.[28]

A *Fuso*-class battleship was reported to be in the area and *Robalo* moved to intercept it. Kimmel sent off a contact report soon thereafter, stating that he had spotted the battleship, two escorting destroyers, and air cover just east of Borneo, but he did not state whether he had attacked the battlewagon or not. Postwar records do not show any successful attacks for *Robalo* during the next weeks off Indochina. On the night of 26 July, Kimmel set course back toward Australia, returning on the surface via Balabac Strait.[29]

Tragedy struck *Robalo* as she moved through the strait. The boat apparently entered shallow waters and encountered one of the Japanese mines with deadly results. A violent explosion ripped the submarine apart, blowing the men topside into the ocean in a similar fashion to what Cliff Kuykendall had experienced when his *Tullibee* was destroyed by its own torpedo.

Although extant records are unclear as to how many *Robalo* men survived the mine's explosion, evidence points to the fact that six men and perhaps more remained alive as their ruptured submarine sank swiftly. Skipper Manning Kimmel, Ens. Samuel Lombard Tucker, QM1 Floyd George Laughlin, SM2 Wallace Keet Martin, EM2 Mason Collie Poston, and one unknown man are believed to have survived.[30]

The six survivors swam through the night and reached shore on Comiran Island. According to intelligence later obtained, the men made their way through the jungle up the east coast of Palawan in search of friendly guerrillas known to operate there. During the war, Christie's staff told the Kimmel family and spread the word officially that he had gone down with *Robalo*. The unannounced fact remained, however, that Christie's staff heard other stories.[31]

Just three weeks after *Robalo*'s loss, another U.S. submarine, Cdr. John Daniel Crowley's *Flier* (SS-250), struck a Japanese mine on 13 August. *Flier* was transiting Balabac Strait on the surface when she struck a mine less than 50 miles from where *Robalo* had been lost. The submarine was gone in less than a minute, leaving only 14 officers and men fighting for their lives. Only Commander Crowley and seven others survived 18 hours in the ocean and a swim of about 12 miles to the nearest small island. The *Flier* survivors constructed a raft and worked their way to Palawan Island, where the submarine *Redfin* (SS-272) rescued them on 31 August with the help of Allied guerrillas.[32]

While on Palawan Island, Commander Crowley encountered Sergeant Pasqual de la Cruz of the Philippine Army, U.S. Army Forces Far East, on August 21 at the guerilla outpost at Cape Buliluyan. Cruz informed Crowley that he had made a reconnaissance trip to Balabac Island "to verify a rumor that some Americans had been captured there." Cruz learned from "different sources" various stories that no less than four *Robalo* submariners had been captured on the beach on Comiran Island. Cruz's testimony, presented in a top-secret inquiry held on 14 September 1944 by the orders of Admiral Ernest King, shows these *Robalo* survivors to be "the commanding officer, Ens. Samuel L. Tucker, Martin, Wallace K., signalman third class, and the identity of the fourth was not known."[33]

Sergeant Cruz told Commander Crowley that *Robalo* sank on 3 July 1944, while 40 miles west of Balabac Island. Four of her survivors were surprised on the beach of Comiran Island and two (Lieutenant Commander Kimmel and an unknown submariner) were shot and killed. Due to conflicting stories from natives, Cruz was unable to determine if Kimmel and his crewmen were shot while attempting to escape or if these two were shot at a later date after all four had been taken prisoner. The two surviving prisoners, named by Cruz as "Lieutenant Tucker" and "quartermaster Martin," survived and were being held in a Japanese POW camp at Puerto Princessa, Palawan, as of late August.[34]

A different account made it into Allied hands that Skipper Kimmel and one of his submariners were murdered on Palawan. Japanese military police found the six *Robalo* survivors in a small bario northwest of the Puerto Princesa prison camp on the island. The Americans were taken to the camp, where they were held as

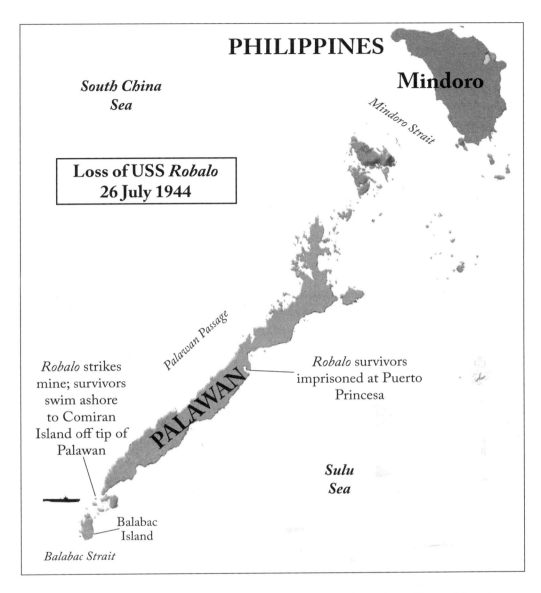

spies rather than prisoners of war. A few days after being placed into this prisoner camp, one *Robalo* man dropped a note from a window to a U.S. Army prisoner who was on work detail outside on 2 August. The note said that *Robalo* had gone down on 26 July, two miles off the west coast of Palawan. The note stated that the men believed their boat had suffered an explosion of the after battery and it named the four survivors being held in that part of the prison: Ensign Tucker, Signalman Second Class Martin, Quartermaster First Class Laughlin, and Electrician's Mate Second Class Poston.[35]

The Army prisoner turned the note over to a U.S. Navy POW, Y2c Hubert Dwight Hough, who later made contact with the wife of a guerrilla leader. Her husband, Dr. Trinidad Mendosa, in turn relayed the word of the *Robalo* survivors to Admiral Christie in Australia. Intelligence reported that when some Allied aircraft attacked Palawan, the Japanese became enraged, "went into a frenzy, pushed Kimmel and some other POWs in a ditch, then poured gasoline into the ditch and set it on fire." According to this story, Kimmel died in this blaze. In relation to the story told by Sergeant Cruz, it is feasible that Kimmel and another *Robalo* man were shot while trying to escape this blaze.[36]

Another account relates that the Palawan prisoners were made to dig three trenches, each 150 feet long and 4 feet deep. The men were told that they were air raid shelters and were made to practice scurrying into them during drills. On 14 December 1944, a U.S. convoy was sighted. It was heading for Mindoro but the Japanese on Palawan thought it was coming to invade their island. They sent the Americans into the trenches, poured gasoline in and set them on fire with torches and grenades. Any POWs trying to escape were bayoneted or shot. Still, some 30 to 40 Americans escaped the massacre. Most were hunted down along the shore or in the jungle and killed. Some accounts have it that at least two submariners were shot by Japanese forces on Palawan. Ten men survived by swimming across the bay and finding shelter with the inmates of Palawan's penal colony. According to Sergeant Cruz's 21 August intelligence given to Commander Crowley, Manning Kimmel and his *Robalo* crewmen had been previously executed.[37]

Radio intercepts indicated that four submariners named as "Rafuin, Posuton, Maten, and Taika" were not on Palawan for the massacre. These were Laughlin, Poston, Martin, and Ensign Tucker. They were placed aboard *Takao Maru* on 19 August and the light cruiser *Kinu* on 22 August 1944. *Kinu* left Palau on 19 August and made her way to Manila via Cebu and Palawan. The cruiser took the four *Robalo* survivors to Manila on 25 August, and from there they disappear from the record. They may have been killed on board or taken to one of the secret camps in Japan, where some pilots and submariners were killed.[38]

Robalo was listed as "presumed lost." Unlike the other lost boats of World War II from which POWs were taken by the Japanese, the half dozen *Robalo* survivors simply disappeared from history with little evidence as to their final fates.

17
"All Hands Were on Edge"

Makassar: 1944

After months of slaving in the hot jungles outside of Makassar's main city, the *Perch* and *Pope* survivors were transferred to a new camp on 5 June 1944. Located one mile south of the city, it was situated on a jungle peninsula in the remains of an abandoned native village. "It was a swampy, malaria-ridden area, and sanitary conditions were poor," said torpedoman Bob Lents.

The new camp area, located about 500 yards from the bay, had been a village of island natives who were run out by the Japanese during the war. Located about 500 yards from the bay, the area had a sufficient water source. "We had a well we dug ourselves," said Turk Turner. "The water table was so high that we were able to use the well for bathing."

The prisoners cleared brush and timber to help build the new camp. There were occasional fistfights when disagreements arose over work details. On one occasion, Sam Simpson was leading a 15-man party charged with carrying coconut logs out to a brush pile. The logs required as many as six men to move. One prisoner who refused to follow directions from Simpson caused confusion among the other log haulers and became belligerent when given directions. "He got pissed about it and called me a son of a bitch," Simpson recalled.[1]

"It takes one to know one!" Simpson shot back. The two squared off in camp that night and Simpson hit him in the mouth with a left jab. "The fellow went wild, backed off, and ran full speed into me and gave me an uppercut which knocked me out for ten minutes." Although he spent many weeks planning on how to get even with this man, Simpson eventually let the episode pass and the two got along fairly well thereafter.

There was one latrine for the Americans, two for the British, and four for the Dutch. Without proper toilet facilities, it was necessary to wash one's self with water from a bottle or other container. "Our bathroom was just two stones that you put your feet on to squat down and do your job," recalled Turner. "There was no toilet paper." There was a 1,000-gallon tank next to the latrines that was filled up for the prisoners to use for cleaning. Bathing consisted of throwing water over one's body with a container, soaping up, and then washing off.

"The buildings were made of bamboo with brick decks," recalled electrician Dan Crist. "The camp was in a restricted area. During rainy season, water covered half the camp and ran through the buildings. We were given very little clothes."

"All of the water had to be boiled to drink," said Lents. For the first months in this new camp, there were no eating utensils, forcing the men to rely on their fingers alone. Senior American prisoner Lt. (jg) Allen Fisher from *Pope* detailed conditions at Makassar's new "bamboo camp."[2]

> Beginning in August 1944, Allied bombing became quite heavy and was followed by a marked deterioration of camp conditions. Food was reduced to an even more dangerous minimum, POW work was increased both in hours and heaviness, and the general attitude of the Japs toward POWs became more vicious. An accumulative effect of these conditions caused an extremely low state of health with a corresponding rise in the number of sick. The rainy season of 1944–45 was very heavy and of long duration, and with it a particularly toxic type of dysentery broke out in epidemic proportions. Coupled with it, malnutrition diseases were felt in varying degrees by all hands, namely beriberi, pellagra, and oedema. In addition, all except five men were suffering from repeated attacks of malaria. The Japs were unwilling to supply proper foods or required medicines to combat this frightful condition, and from 8 January 1945 to 25 July 1945, almost 300 POWs died, including 28 Americans.

Ernie Plantz later described their new bamboo barracks. "It had a sand floor with bricks just laid over the sand, with open windows and open doors. Unfortunately, it was an area fairly contaminated with cholera and malaria. The Japs didn't know any better—or maybe they did." Cracks in the barrack floors allowed bedbugs to invade the sleeping areas and other jungle animals prowled the new camp at night. "There were rats as big as a small opossum," recalled Sam Simpson.[3]

"We could handle the physical abuse," seaman Ben Clevinger stated. "The worst was the lack of medical treatment and decent food. Dysentery, pellagra and beri-beri were rampant as conditions grew worse."[4]

Seaman Tom Moore was perpetually on the prowl, looking for things to steal for bartering to eat. He recalled one guard nicknamed "Kentucky" because of the way he marched around with his rifle cradled in his arm. "Kentucky caught me four times, but let me go with little or no consequences." When Moore explained that he took extra chances because he was hungry, Kentucky took him to the galley and fed him an egg and an extra bowl of rice. "I was in heaven," he recalled.[5]

Moore promised the guard that he would not steal or barter again but it was only a short time later that he was caught doing the same. Out on a work party, he was buying gumdrop-like candy from natives and concealing it in his pants. The guilty prisoners were lined up and beaten with a bamboo cane. "When he got to me, he gave me 20 hits," Moore stated. "My butt looked like a couple of basketballs when he finished beating me."[6]

Machinist Stephen Orlyk received severe lacerations from a beating with three-foot rattan sticks after being caught accepting cookies from the natives. "I was operated on by a Dutch doctor who died while he was in camp. He did a 22-piece skin graft," said Orlyk.[7]

Dan Crist noted that medical supplies were only "brought in every three months. There wasn't enough to last a week. The food was getting less. The work was getting harder." Crist found the hours ran from "0700 to 1900 with one hour off for dinner if you were lucky. Many of the men were forced to work making war weapons, hand grenades, trench mortars, and others."

Giant concrete bomb shelters were literally dragged from the bay shores hundreds of yards away by manual labor, dozens of men tugging on ropes to move the massive shelters to their final positions in camp. Other labor included work on radio towers, railroad tracks, and pulling weeds by hand.

"It was ungodly what they would think up to keep you busy or to harass you," related Turk Turner. "The mosquitos were so bad that we had to kill a quota of them every day and show the guards. We also had to catch and kill a quota of flies per day." Sam Simpson explained, "That was no small job. Sometimes there were none. When you have to turn in a hundred or so flies and mosquitoes a day, it's a problem." CBM Richard Sperandio, the unofficial leader of the *Pope* and *Perch* enlisted men, begged others to help him reach his quota. "Sperandio at one time was the Asiatic Fleet wrestling champion," recalled Simpson. The Japanese loved abusing the burly chief when he did not reach his quota. Fortunately, the fly and mosquito requirements were liberal—"anything with wings on it passed." The Americans beat the system by taking grease from the axels of work carts and smearing it on tin can lids. "One would go into the yard and fan the grass to catch mosquitoes, flies," wrote Simpson.[8]

As time progressed, the prisoners created new ways to smuggle food and vitamins into camp. The loot bags in their pants were modified into smaller belt bags around their waists. The Americans found their British counterparts were the ones eventually caught by the Japanese while they were smuggling items into camp. "Every time we thought of some new way to bring things back into camp, the Limies always fouled it up," said Turner. The Americans even created false bottoms on their soup tureens that could be filled with contraband—until this invention was also discovered.

The survivors from *Perch* and the destroyer *Pope* grew close to each other during their first two years of captivity. "During the time we were held captive, there was talk of a reunion of our crews in years to come," recalled *Perch*'s EM2c Paul Richard "Rick" Richter Jr. Characterized by his family as an upbeat, optimistic young man by nature, Richter had a strong will to survive. He had suffered through a crude appendectomy performed by a Dutch doctor shortly after the *Perch* crew reached Makassar. He helped regain his strength while on work parties by scavenging duck eggs, cracking them, and swallowing whole the raw contents.[9]

Paul Richter, who followed his father's footsteps by joining the Navy pre-war, was a tall, muscular man who had played high school football while growing up in San Antonio, Texas. The small-statured Japanese guards often put him to work in the galley because they were impressed with the ease in which the strong Texan could lift 100-pound bags of rice. In the new jungle camp, Richter used scrap wood to build a makeshift shelf so that he could sleep above the wet floor. When the guards discovered his new bed, they ripped it apart and gave Richter a public beating.

Ernie Plantz recalled that rising water during heavy periods of rain would creep up into the buildings due to the unlevel ground. "In the lower end, there would be maybe a foot of water inside the building. What we slept on was wooden boards with a straw mat on top. The guys would have to wade through the water to get in their bunks. It was a wonderful breeding place for mosquitoes."

The prisoners ate their evening meals in camp at a long table. Alabama Arnette learned the hard way not to complain. "We were sitting at the table one evening, and I don't know why I said it, but I said, 'I'm not gonna eat this shit.'" Unfortunately, one of the guards who spoke fluent English heard this insult. Arnette was ordered to stand so the guard could punch him several times in the mouth with his fist. "He made me sit down and eat the rest of it. I kept my mouth shut after that."

CPhM Loyd Raymond Coggins from *Pope* did what he could to help the sick and injured at Makassar. The Dutch maintained control over all medical stores during the early period of their internment and only allowed supplies to be used on Dutch prisoners. Before the Japanese allowed some medicine to be used on the American prisoners, Coggins conducted systematic raids on their storerooms to provide for the *Perch* and *Pope* survivors.

Illness claimed men at the new Makassar jungle camp as the malaria, beriberi, and dysentery ran rampant. CEM Houston Edwards was stricken severely with all three ailments and was hospitalized during early July 1944. He died from his illnesses on 10 July and his death was sorely felt among the *Perch* crew.

Turk Turner was one of the few Americans in camp who avoided catching malaria. As one of the few qualified blood donors for Edwards, he twice gave his chief blood transfusions—but his efforts were not enough. Turner had great respect for Houston Edwards.

> He was a fine man. He was the type of guy that when you had work to do he believed in doing it and getting it over with. If your work was done and your records were up to date, you could sit on your duff until something came up. He believed in work but he believed that he didn't have to try and go find you factory work.

Chief Edwards was the first man from *Perch*'s crew to die at Makassar. Including the loss of another shipmate in Japan previously, the 59 survivors had dropped to 57—and the war was far from over.

Ofuna: September 1944

Grenadier skipper John Fitzgerald went to great lengths to secretly document the abuse that he and his fellow Allied prisoners endured in the secret interrogation camp at Ofuna. In almost all cases, the punishment received was for very minor offenses or for things trumped up by the guards. On Labor Day, 4 September, the prisoners of Building No. 3 were lined up for a beating, accused of urinating behind Building No. 4. A number of the guards had been spotted coming out from behind this building, buttoning their flies, but this did not prevent the false charges and the beating. "I tried to get the punishment stopped only to be placed in line with the rest of the prisoners to receive my four licks across the buttocks," recalled Lieutenant Commander Fitzgerald.[10]

One of the guards, Seaman Third Class Murata—known as the "Termite"—decided to beat *Sculpin*'s Lt. George Brown to impress two of his civilian guests on 5 September. Brown was aroused from the room in which he was sleeping and given six licks from the club. "This is carrying the humiliation end a little far," Fitzgerald wrote in his diary.[11]

The food rations at this time were at least back to a full bowl of rice for the first time in many weeks. On 9 September, Marine Lt. Bill Harris and Navy pilot Red Bullard were caught talking in Bullard's room. Harris had acquired a week-old newspaper that Louie Zamperini had stolen from "the Mummy" when the warrant officer fell asleep and was trying to break down some of the headlines. He was able to decipher that the Americans had taken the island of Kwajalein and now used it as an advanced base. Lt. Harmon Sherry of *Grenadier* looked over a map in the paper and made a rough sketch of Allied troop advancements. Zamperini disposed of the newspaper but Harris hid the sketched map in his barracks. When Japanese guards searched the prisoners' quarters, they discovered Harris' map.[12]

After supper, the prisoners were called to attention by the Congacho. Harris and Bullard were called out in front of everyone and severely beaten. "The Quack called Harris out and started punching him, then grabbed a heavy cherrywood bludgeon and hit him repeatedly," recalled Zamperini. "We all wanted to jump in and stop the sadistic medic, but the guards had their rifles ready."[13]

Harris crumpled to the ground where Kitamura kicked him in the body and face until he could stand again. He was then beaten until again falling, where Kitamura proceeded to kick him further. The guards forced two American prisoners to then hold Harris upright so that Kitamura could punch him in the face repeatedly. "Harris' beating was the most severe I've seen since my Penang days. Harris had a lapse of memory for about three days." Fitzgerald wrote. Zamperini recalled, "The Quack kept jumping on Harris as he lay helpless on the ground. Had it been possible, I would have torn the Quack to bits with my own hands."[14]

The next night, Lieutenant Commaner Fitzgerald was able to have a meeting with Commander Sanematsu and Handsome Harry the interpreter to discuss the poor treatment of the POWs. "All was favorably received and I have hopes that we'll see its effects in a favorable light for us," he wrote. "They assured me that such would be the case. They also said they'd come here more frequently for a check-up on conditions."

Upon being returned to his room, however, Fitzgerald was visited by two of the worst guards, who appeared irate that he had gone to complain about the conditions. Fitzgerald told the guard that perhaps they should go see the "Gunrabo," who had been present for part of the meeting with Sanematsu. En route, the camp commanders stopped the guards and pulled Fitzgerald aside. The senior POW explained the situation in his best broken Japanese and then was told that it was not necessary for the guards to know the substance of the earlier conversation. Fitzgerald was sent back to his room. Irritated, these guards returned to visit Fitzgerald later. They were grumbling and threatening him with beatings. "I didn't at the time take much stock in his statement and paid no attention to him or them. Needless to say, all hands were on edge and everyone's nerves were as taut as a bass fiddle."[15]

The camp was hit with an extensive blackout on 12 September, with drills and sirens breaking up the monotony over the next few days. The random violence still occurred. Noel Quinn was knocked flat by one of the guards who witnessed him saying "good morning" to one of his fellow prisoners.[16]

During September, Pappy Boyington was serving as a cook's helper. He arose before dawn to start the fires for the big wood-burning ovens that were used to cook food for both the guards and prisoners. During the few breaks that he was allowed during each 16-hour workday, Boyington sipped tea and smoked the butts of cigarettes thrown onto the ground by the Japanese guards. When the opportunity presented itself, he would also sneak cooking ingredients, such as from the big lard tub. For a starving man, the fat "tasted like honey," so Boyington would "scoop out a big handful of this stinking lard."[17]

The camp commandant decided to stage a track meet one afternoon, featuring his prisoner Lou Zamperini, the former Olympic runner. The Japanese brought in a local runner and a foot race was run around the Ofuna compound. Zamperini let the Japanese runner keep the lead until the finish line loomed ahead. "Then I stretched out and passed him; I couldn't resist," he recalled. "I woke up on the ground. Someone had hit me on the head from behind with a cherrywood club."[18]

By late September, Ofuna's prisoner count had climbed back to 57, forcing a transfer of 27 prisoners on 30 September. The prisoners were marched through Ofuna's wooden gate and down the narrow dirt road toward the train station. This group included three British prisoners, one lieutenant from New Zealand, and the rest Americans, including Lt. Pop Condit from the *Yorktown* Air Group and First Lieutenant Zamperini. From *Grenadier*, departing were Lt. Harmon Sherry, Lt. Al Toulon, Lt. Arthur McIntyre, and GM1c Fred Zufelt. These three *Grenadier* officers were briefly detained at the Omori camp near Tokyo before being moved on to other camps. This left only Skipper Fitzgerald, Exec George Whiting, and radioman Joe Knutson at Ofuna from *Grenadier*. The two senior officers were marking their seventeenth month at Ofuna and Knutson his fifteenth month. Three other submariners were included in this draft: Cliff Kuykendall from *Tullibee* and Tony Duva and Bill Whitemore from *S-44*.[19]

Dejected at missing yet another chance to move on and become an official POW, John Fitzgerald at least found solace in the extra rice portion and soup the remaining 30 Ofuna inmates had for breakfast. "The treatment has vastly improved and frankly, under the conditions, can expect no more from the guards. I hope it lasts," Fitzgerald wrote. By the first of October, Ofuna's camp was split into two sections by a newly erected fence. The guards took extra steps to split up some of the prisoners, preventing the more tenured *Grenadier* prisoners from talking to newer arrivals. Ikku barracks was the place for special prisoners and those who were new arrivals. Prisoner beatings were often related to Allied victories during 1944. B-24 pilot Glen McConnell—who reached Ofuna on 7 May—stated that after a terrible loss, guards slammed "us around, banging people. Every time our troops would invade another island, we'd get another round of punishment."[20]

By 9 October, the camp count was back up to 42, including six downed B-29 aviators who were placed in solitary confinement to be tortured without witnesses. Air Force 2nd Lt. William A. Dixon, who arrived at Ofuna on 6 October, said, "They enjoyed frightening us American POWs." Camp pharmacist Kitamura "carried a black book with him at all times," making notations of infractions. Once a month,

Dixon said that 15 men were called from Kitamura's black book. Lined up before their fellow prisoners, these 15 selected men were then severely beaten.[21]

Rice rations were scaled back as the camp count increased. Four new prisoners came in on 20 October, including two *Wasp* aviators. Rumors were that another Red Cross parcel shipment was due to arrive before Christmas—offering hope to some prisoners that new clothing would be included in this delivery.[22]

Before any hopes of this delivery could be enjoyed, the Ofuna prisoners witnessed a flurry of activity on the evening of 3 November. Escorted by 23 guards, nine U.S. Navy prisoners were marched through the main camp gates. John Fitzgerald and his camp mates would learn that they were from another lost American submarine. They were the remaining men of one of the most successful U.S. submarines of World War II.

18
Tang's Tragic Twenty-Fourth

Unlucky enough to be a day late to make it on USS *Tang*'s official launching roster, Floyd Caverly and Bill Leibold were at least lucky to be caught together again in the right place to both survive their submarine's last moment.

Their sub was the hottest boat in the U.S. Fleet by the time she fell victim to her own hand. Just as *Tullibee* had been caught by one of her circling torpedoes, *Tang* (SS-306) was sunk by a boomeranging Mark 18 on her fifth run.

Tang was a product of the Mare Island Navy Yard, christened and launched on 17 August 1943. Those officially assigned were aboard her as the fanfare ensued. Standing atop the building ways, other workers watched Mrs. Antonio S. Pitre swing the bottle of champagne against *Tang*'s stem as the submarine was christened. "I stood there and watched her get christened," recalled radio technician Floyd Merle Caverly. "I hadn't had a drink in six months as I watched this captain's wife knock a bottle of champagne against *Tang*."

Caverly had volunteered to join *Tang*'s crew and was part of the "*Tang* detail" at Mare Island already. He and four others had arrived at Vallejo as people were hanging bunting and decorations for the launching ceremony. Living at the sub administration barracks, the men of the *Tang* detail had arrived just too late to have their names added to the official printed program for the launching of the Navy's newest fleet submarine.

Born on March 1, 1917, Caverly was raised in Minnesota, where his World War I veteran uncle convinced him to join the Navy. "He told me that if it ever looks like we're going to get in a war, join the Navy," he recalled. "He had been in the infantry, sleeping in the mud and slop in those trenches in France for about 90 days without a bath or any good rations." Listening to President Franklin D. Roosevelt give a radio address after the *Reuben James* was sunk, he heard Roosevelt sign off with, "Mother England, we will not let you down."

Caverly said to himself, "Mother England, I'd better get in that damned Navy while I've got a chance. I knew we were going to war."

Joining the Navy in December 1940, he was on a four-stack destroyer when the war broke out at Pearl Harbor. After three rounds of advanced schooling, 26-year-old Caverly had volunteered for *Tang*'s construction and arrived one day too late to stand on her decks as she rode down the ways on 17 August.

Another of the "*Tang* detail" who just missed the list was 20-year-old BM1c William Rudolf Leibold. When the war started he was serving on the light mine-layer *Pruitt* (DM-22), a ship converted from a destroyer which his future *Tang* skipper had also served on. When *Pruitt* suffered heavy damage from a typhoon near the Aleutians, Leibold was offered an on-the-spot promotion and his choice of duty for his damage control performance.

With that, Bill Leibold had earned his first-class stripes and his desired ticket into submarines. "At the time, by and large, submarines really didn't rate a bosun's mate," he recalled. "The old V-boats—*Nautilus*, *Argonaut*, and *Narwhal*—had them, but most fleet boats did not." Sent to submarine administration at Mare Island, "Boats" Leibold was dejected to find that they wanted to keep him around as a master at arms.

While delivering mail to the submarine *Grayback* at Hunter's Point in late July 1943, Leibold struck up a conversation with her skipper, Lt. Cdr. Johnny Moore. "Hey, Boats, you've really got a soft job," Moore kidded him.

"It's only temporary, sir," Leibold replied. "I'm going to submarines."

Moore offered to try and get him aboard *Grayback*, but Leibold told him that he was going aboard a brand-new boat being built at Mare Island, *Tang*, that he had become familiar with.

A young lieutenant asked, "Do you have orders to the *Tang*?"

"No, sir," Leibold admitted. "But I'm going to serve on her."

The lieutenant, Murray Bennett Frazee, introduced himself to Leibold and stated that he had orders to report to *Tang* as her executive officer. About ten days later, Boatswain's Mate First Class Leibold met Lieutenant Frazee and *Tang*'s prospective commanding officer, Lt. Cdr. Richard Hetherington O'Kane. "They questioned me for a while and looked at my records," he recalled. O'Kane then announced, "Well, you're going to come to the *Tang*, then."

Elated, Bill Leibold soon received his papers but—like Floyd Caverly—just missed being aboard when *Tang* was launched. Dick O'Kane, the former exec of Dudley "Mush" Morton's famed *Wahoo*, had helped her burn up the Pacific. *Wahoo* boldly stalked enemy convoys under O'Kane and Skipper Mush Morton, using her torpedoes and deck guns with equal fury. By the time Dick O'Kane received orders to report to new construction as a PCO, *Wahoo* had sunk 16 confirmed enemy ships plus a charging destroyer. During *Wahoo's* fourth patrol, Morton and O'Kane set the record by sinking an incredible nine Japanese ships for 20,000 tons. This single patrol record would not be surpassed—until O'Kane himself with his new boat *Tang* later topped *Wahoo*.

Tang's first patrol was the fifteenth best of the war, with five ships sunk for 21,400 tons. During her second run, *Tang* served as a lifeguard submarine off Truk where she instead turned in the second highest number of U.S. aviators rescued on a single patrol—22 naval flyboys shot down at Truk. The *Honolulu Advertiser*, followed by *Life* magazine, made Dick O'Kane a celebrity with their articles and oversized photos of the rescued aviators on *Tang's* bridge.[1]

On *Tang's* third patrol, O'Kane turned in the best patrol of the war in terms of ships sunk, ten confirmed for 39,100 tons. On his fourth run, Dick O'Kane was given wartime credit for sinking another six ships for 31,000 tons, although JANAC chopped this claim to two ships. In more recent years, Cdr. John Alden's research shows that *Tang* put four ships under.[2]

During these patrols, Boats Leibold earned the Bronze Star. Knowing that after his fifth patrol he would likely be transferred, O'Kane intended to make his last 24 torpedoes count. *Tang* departed Pearl Harbor on 24 September 1944 for Formosa Strait. Between 10 and 23 October, she slashed into Japanese convoys, sending at least six ships to the bottom and damaging others.

O'Kane headed toward mainland China to dispatch his remaining 12 torpedoes. Admiral Lockwood sent word on the night of 24 October that a large convoy was proceeding north along the China coast. *Tang* raced to intercept and soon sighted convoy MI-23, which consisted of seventeen ships.[3]

Tang charged into the convoy during the early morning hours of 24 October (25 October local time), firing ten torpedoes. Half a dozen ships took torpedoes and two large tankers headed for Davy Jones' locker as *Tang* raced away to load her last two torpedoes into the forward tubes. By 0125, all was ready and Commander O'Kane moved *Tang* back in toward the battered Japanese convoy to finish off some of her cripples.

Lt. (jg) Henry James Flanagan wanted to insure that his last two torpedoes performed as intended. He headed for *Tang's* forward torpedo room with the communications officer, Lt. (jg) Fred Melvin Enos Jr. Both officers had been with *Tang* since her commissioning. Enos, a reservist graduate of the University of California and submarine school, was new to submarines when he joined the boat but had proven to be an excellent officer during *Tang's* first four runs.[4]

Tall, rugged Hank Flanagan was a mustang, a former enlisted man who had earned his way into officer's country after 15 years at sea. He had been promoted up to chief torpedoman's mate during seven patrols on *Tambor* and another on *Thresher*. Qualified like few others to serve as torpedo officer, he oversaw the loading of forward tubes 5 and 6 with Mark 18 Model-1 electric torpedoes after his torpedomen had thoroughly checked each.[5]

At 4,000 yards to the nearest ship, Dick O'Kane called his crew back to battle stations and continued his approach on the surface. Shortly after 0200, Floyd Caverly on the SJ radar announced that the nearest crippled ship was only 1,500 yards away. On the bridge, Commander O'Kane ordered his boat slowed to 6 knots as he conned her in for an attack on a derelict transport ship that his submarine had torpedoed earlier. *Tang*'s bridge was heavily manned with the men most trusted by the skipper for night surface torpedo attacks.

The battle stations OOD was Lt. (jg) John Henry Heubeck. A Baltimore native, Heubeck was making his first patrol on *Tang* but had proven himself under fire thus far. Stationed on four sides of the periscope shears were trusted battle lookouts RM2c Charles Andriolo, GM1c James Milton White, GM3c Darrell Dean Rector, and F1c Lawrence Hall Erickson. Starboard side lookout Rector had extensive submarine experience and had survived an emergency appendectomy operation during *Seadragon*'s fourth patrol early in the war.[6]

Also on the bridge as special assistants to the captain were CQM Sidney William Jones and CBM Bill Leibold. Both men were plankowners and Jones had worked his way into the position of assistant navigator to the executive officer. "I was lined up to relieve the chief of the boat, CTM Bill Ballinger, after this patrol," Leibold recalled. "During surface attacks, Sidney Jones and I were there to assist the CO. Each one of us took one side of the bridge and watched the targets. We kept the skipper advised on our targets, in addition to the regular complement of lookouts we had on the bridge. I was stationed on the port side, forward on the bridge."

As O'Kane prepared to fire his last two torpedoes, he was still hobbling somewhat from a nasty fall through an open hatch he had taken earlier in the patrol. The ship's new pharmacist's mate, Paul Lewis Larson, diagnosed that the skipper had broken his foot. Chief Larson straightened the bones and fashioned an oversized tightly laced sand shoe for O'Kane to wear for the rest of the patrol—the best medical work available on a wartime submarine.[7]

From the conning tower below, Lt. Frank Howard Springer called up, "Right on at zero." As *Tang*'s exec, Springer served as the skipper's assistant approach officer. Another plankowner, he had served as the TDC operator on *Tang* until Murray Frazee had received new orders before the fifth patrol.

Springer directed the efforts of *Tang*'s able conning tower fire control party. In this tight compartment, another eight men were diligent in their assignments. Starting forward at the wheel was O'Kane's trusted battle stations helmsman,

QM2c Robert Welch, a plankowner. To starboard, keeping the Quartermaster's Notebook, was SM3c John Accardy. Lt. (jg) Paul Wines and Lt. (jg) Richard Kroth were helping to plot the converging ships' course at the little chart desk aft and assist with the TDC's angle solver. Along the port bulkhead, Lt. Lawrence Savadkin sat at the TDC. Radio technician first class Caverly was manning the SJ radar as the electronics officer, Lt. Edward Beaumont, supervised. Nearby manning the sound gear was RM1c Edwin Bergman, another *Tang* plankowner.

"I gave the bearing and range of the nearest destroyers to the Old Man just before we fired out the last two torpedoes," Caverly recalled. "Bergman was on the sonar. Beaumont did most of the mike work to the bridge and below to the plotters in the control room."

With *Tang* lined up for a zero-angle shot, Commander O'Kane called out, "Fire!" The range was 1,100 yards as Frank Springer hit the firing plunger in the control room. The time was 0230.

Continuing forward at 6 knots, *Tang* shuddered as her 23rd Mark 18 torpedo sped toward its target. "Stand by below!" O'Kane called down to his fire control team as the ship moved within 1,000 yards of the derelict ship.[8]

"Ready below, Captain," Springer called back.

"Fire!" O'Kane called again.

Tang shuddered again as her 24th and final warfish whooshed out of its tube with a rush of compressed air. With a range of a mere 900 yards, it was expected to hit in about 60 seconds.

Lieutenant Savadkin on the TDC heard someone yell, "Let's head for the barn!"

"The first torpedo ran hot, straight, and normal," said Boats Leibold. "Of course, it was pretty dark, so we couldn't see." The second torpedo, however, went astray almost immediately after departing its forward tube. Leibold said that it "broached shortly after it left the tube, so you could see the splash. It made a hard turn to the left and you could see it splashing as it came about." Port side lookout Charles Andriolo called out a warning.

"All ahead emergency!" shouted O'Kane. "Right full rudder!" Below, helmsman Welch spun the wheel to throw *Tang* into a quick fishtail maneuver to try to dodge the torpedo's turning circle. In the case of *Tullibee* months before, those topside did not have time to try and dodge her boomeranging torpedo.

"In less than ten seconds, it had reached its maximum distance abeam, about 20 yards," related Commander O'Kane. "It was now coming in. We had only seconds to get out of its way."[9]

"Left full rudder!" the skipper shouted down to Welch.

The engineers used emergency speed as *Tang* now twisted hard in the opposite direction, attempting to spin her 311-foot length out of harm's way. "The problem was akin to moving a ship longer than a football field and proceeding at harbor speed clear of a suddenly careening speedboat," wrote O'Kane.[10]

The speeding torpedo slammed into *Tang*'s port side, abreast the after torpedo room. "It hit well aft on the port side," Boats Leibold said. "It just looked like a large ploom of black smoke. I think what it really was was a big plume of water from the explosion. It was just a large black splotch back there."

The water cascaded down onto the after deck as the officers and lookouts tried to regain their footing. Below decks, the explosion was violent, whipping the boat about. Numerous personnel as far forward as the control room received injuries. The immediate result to the boat was to flood the after three compartments together with No. 6 and No. 7 ballast tanks. No one escaped from these three compartments and even the forward engine room was half flooded before the after door could be secured. The force of the explosion and the ensuing flooding claimed the lives of at least 20 men aft. In CEM James Culp's maneuvering room, CMoMM Albert Hudson's after engine room, and TM1c John Foster's after torpedo room, all hands perished.

In the conning tower, the ship's recorder, signalman John Accardy, was thrown from his feet and he plunged head first down the ladder into the control room, breaking his arm in the fall. As *Tang*'s stern plunged toward the bottom, the men fell aft. Floyd Caverly could hear the skipper shouting orders from the bridge. "He didn't realize how bad we were hit. He was trying to estimate the situation and how he was going to get us out of here. He didn't want to dive the boat right away."

With the bridge speaker working as a microphone, those regaining their footing in the conning tower and control room could hear Commander O'Kane's voice clearly. "He was telling us to shift the rudder and nobody would give him any information because we didn't have a mike that would talk back to him," said Caverly. "He couldn't hear us."

"Radar, I want information on those two destroyers and I want it right now!" O'Kane shouted.

The exec, Frank Springer, had moved forward to assist James Welch with the helm wheel, which was frozen in place. They could not guess how severely damaged *Tang*'s after section was from the torpedo explosion. Caverly raced to the conning tower ladder and tried shouting up to the skipper to answer his question. He then hollered up a request to come to the bridge. "Springer put his hand on the back of my shirt and the other hand on my butt and said, 'Get up there. Go on!'" Caverly recalled.

The radio technician raced up the ladder, less than a minute after the torpedo explosion. "God, I thought he was shoving me up to my death!" Caverly recalled. "I thought this is the end of me right here. What was I going to hang onto when that damn sub went down?"

As he reached the bridge, Caverly realized that his sub was going down fast. "I didn't even get a chance to talk to the Old Man because the water was coming up around my knees," he said.

Just as Caverly cleared the hatch, O'Kane shouted, "Close the hatch!"

O'Kane's "heart went out to those below and to the young men topside who must now face the sea. Our ship sank by the stern in seconds, the way a pendulum might swing down in a viscous liquid. The seas rolled in from aft, washing up from the bridge and shears, and of small consolation now was the detonation of our 23rd torpedo as it hit home in the transport."[11]

O'Kane, Lt. (jg) Heubeck, and Caverly were washed overboard as *Tang*'s stern plunged for the ocean bottom. "All of a sudden, she just dropped," said Bill Leibold. "With that, the people on the bridge, for the most part, went down with her—at least in my case."

Leibold could not escape the rapid plunge nor the ensuing suction of his submarine heading for the bottom. He caught a glimpse of the lookouts struggling to free themselves from the guardrails around the lookout platform. He distinctly recalled Charles Andriolo clutching the rails with a death grip as they were both sucked under the ocean with their boat. During her descent, he recalled "a very distinct jolt" that he assumed was *Tang*'s stern slamming into the ocean bottom below. "With that jolt, I started back toward the surface."

Popping to the surface, Leibold could hear lookouts Dean Rector and Sidney Jones calling out to one another somewhere in the darkness. In the blackness, he also spotted OOD John Heubeck swimming by in "a beautiful Australian crawl," heading for *Tang*'s bow, which was still jutting up above the surface. Heubeck was never seen again.[12]

––––––––––

Larry Savadkin was standing at the TDC beside soundman Ed Bergman. He heard the order to close the hatch and then O'Kane called down to ask if *Tang* had any propulsion. With insufficient time to close the hatch, water gushed through the wide opening into the conning tower. Savadkin started forward to check the pit log just as the lights went out in the compartment.

As the ship's tail end plunged down, he hung on by leaning against the No. 2 periscope shaft, which was down. "With the sudden downward angle of the boat, men and loose gear were bumping and falling by me with the rush of water," Savadkin said. "I apparently rose up along the periscope shaft. Things then quieted down." The conning tower was now completely flooded and men drowned. Lieutenant Savadkin poked his nose and mouth out of the water into an air bubble that formed in the overhead of the conning tower where the No. 2 scope penetrated through the hull to above.

"For some reason, I thought the boat was upside down," Savadkin related. "I had a fear of going up the periscope well and being caught in the pump room." He found another large air bubble in the forward end of the conning tower. Savadkin, realizing that he must exit quickly while he still had air, located the ladder. He went through the hatch which opened up underneath the bridge cowling where air was trapped. When Savadkin popped up again into this air pocket, he startled another conning tower survivor.

"Who is it?" a voice inquired.

"Mr. Savadkin," he said. "Who are you?"

"Bergman," the sonar operator answered. "Do you know where we are?"

"I think we are under the bridge," Savadkin answered.

The lieutenant said they had better try to head for the surface.

"Can I come with you?" asked Bergman.

"Sure."

Savadkin told Bergman to grab his legs as he swam out of the pocket and toward the surface. The officer pushed out and headed up. En route, however, he felt Bergman release his grip and did not see him again. Using both hands, Savadkin pushed hard toward the surface. "I wanted air and lots of it," he thought. Savadkin estimated later that *Tang*'s bridge was roughly 50 to 60 feet below the surface of the water when he tried to lead Bergman to safety. He was dressed in long trousers, a shirt, skivvies, and socks as he burst to the surface. Somewhere along his escape, he lost his watch and leather sandals.

He broke the surface gasping for air and saw *Tang*'s bow sticking out of the water ahead. Savadkin tried swimming for the submarine but he found the current to be too strong. In order to find new energy, he took off his shirt, trousers, and socks, tying all around his waist. "Then I began to get cold and began to shiver uncontrollably. When I began to shiver, I swallowed water," Savadkin related. "I felt alone—screamed bloody murder—no answer. I got the impression that I was the only person who had gotten off the boat."

Recalling his training days at San Diego, the lieutenant decided to use his pants as a life belt, blowing air into the pant legs and tying them off. He had to refill the air about every fifteen minutes, but found the floats to be sufficient to help his buoyancy. "I lay on my back and stomach. I knew there was an island about 10 miles away and I knew that we were near the China coast. Thought if I could stay afloat until daylight I could make it."

Some distance away in the ocean, other *Tang* survivors also struggled to stay alive through the night. Boats Leibold was thrilled when he came across Floyd Caverly, a poor swimmer. Leibold convinced him to just float to conserve energy. Not knowing who else might still be alive, the pair of *Tang* survivors drifted with the swells. Daybreak would certainly show them if anyone else were still alive.

19
Escape From 30 Fathoms

Pete Narowanski was thrilled as *Tang*'s 24th torpedo swooshed from tube No. 6. The 25-year-old torpedoman from Maryland vented the tube and stepped from between them.

"Hot dog, course zero-nine-zero," he sang out, as he slammed his fist into his palm with joy. "Head her for the Golden Gate."[1]

Torpedoman's Mate Third Class Narowanski knew that *Tang* could now head for the West Coast and her anticipated refit. He had completed his second patrol on *Halibut* when he received 30 days leave in San Francisco. Upon returning to Pearl Harbor, Narowanski learned that *Tang* was due to return to San Francisco for an overhaul after her fifth run. When he met a *Tang* sailor who wanted to trade duty, Narowanski arranged a swap. "He was a lookout who didn't want to go out again," Narowanski recalled.[2]

His Navy career had started aboard the troop transport *Hugh L. Scott*, which was torpedoed out from under him by a German submarine off Casablanca. He next served on the battleship *Alabama*, where he was "getting tired of shoveling snow on deck" when he volunteered for submarines. After two runs on *Halibut*, Pete Narowanski never expected to be aboard another torpedoed boat.

Narowanski was one of ten men present in *Tang*'s torpedo room when the last torpedo was fired. The other nine men were torpedo officer Hank Flanagan, senior torpedoman Leland Weekley, TM1c John Fluker, TM2c Hayes Trukke, FC3c Ralph Knapp, and the rest of the torpedo reload crew. No sooner had Narowanski uttered his "head her for the Golden Gate" cry than he was knocked flat to the deck as *Tang*'s last torpedo slammed into her after compartments. Arizona native Hayes Oliver Trukke, making his second patrol on *Tang*, related, "We knew we'd been severely hit. We lost our forward motion in a few seconds. The boat took on a slight angle as the stern seemed to drop to the bottom."

Trukke helped others close the watertight door between the forward room and the forward battery to secure their room. Although the lights remained on for about five minutes, Chief Weekley turned on the emergency lights. The bow plane rigging and tilting motor, tripped by the force of the explosion, began running and burning even though Ralph Knapp tried to stop it.

Muscular Chief Weekley climbed the ladder up into the forward torpedo room's escape hatch and opened the lower hatch. "Since it was quite possible the conning tower might be flooded and we were sure the after torpedo room was, that left only the forward torpedo room for escape purposes," related Hank Flanagan. "Therefore, we couldn't escape without waiting for everyone left alive to get to the forward room."

Some of the ten survivors discussed the possibility of leaving the ship through the empty forward torpedo tubes. They decided against this because of the depth charges which could be heard and the possibility that the ship's exposed bow might be shelled as they were attempting to crawl out. Lt. (jg) Flanagan decided to head back for the control room and assess the damage.

MoMM2c Jesse Borges DaSilva was out of place when *Tang* was struck by her own torpedo. A 19-year-old from Los Angeles, he had joined the submarine after her second patrol. His duty station was the after engine room, but he found little to do as his shipmates loaded the last two torpedoes. DaSilva asked for permission to grab a cup of coffee and was given an affirmative nod. "I never really liked coffee," he said, "but that's one coffee break I'm glad I took."[3]

When the explosion rocked *Tang*, DaSilva grabbed for the ladder under the after battery hatch and held himself as the ship whipped violently. "Someone dogged down the watertight door between the after and forward engine rooms," DaSilva recalled. "*Tang* was settling quickly by the stern. I clutched a ladder to keep from being pitched off my feet."

Water began pouring in from the open door that connected the crew's mess to the control room. DaSilva and others put their weight against the door and closed it with great effort to cut off the water flow. Once the sound of depth charges above ceased, he and the 20 other men present "knew that our one chance of escape was in reaching the forward torpedo room. This meant opening the control room door [again] and for all we knew, it might be flooded. Yet, we had to risk it."

Looking through the eye port to the control room, the survivors could see that water was already rising to the port. One of the men cracked the hatch and water immediately gushed into the ship's after compartments. DaSilva opened the lower deck freezer locker to act as a sump for the flooding while other men climbed atop the mess tables to keep from being swept away. He found that the water rose quickly around their legs before eventually subsiding.[4]

In the control room, DaSilva and company found that the water was knee-deep. Lt. (jg) Mel Enos and Ens. Basil Pearce were in charge, joined quickly by torpedo officer Hank Flanagan from the forward torpedo room. Flanagan noted that Enos was bleeding about the head from being slung against a solid surface by the torpedo explosion. Others were also wounded. Signalman Accardy had a broken arm from his fall from the conning tower and the chief commissary steward, John Parker, had suffered a broken leg in the control room.

Personnel in the control room succeeded in closing the conning tower's lower hatch but it had been jimmied in the explosion and it leaked badly. At the time of the explosion, MoMM3c Clayton Oliver Decker had been serving as the battle stations bow planesman along with MoMM2c George Robertson on the stern planes. Born in 1920, in Paonia, Colorado, Decker had left his wife Lucille and their two-year-old son Harry against his wife's wishes and entered boot camp.[5]

Tang's stern was resting on the ocean floor. CMoMM Marvin DeLapp, standing duty at the air manifold, had been thrown from his feet. Chief of the Boat Bill Ballinger—a veteran of all five *Tang* patrols and five others on *Tunny*—had been standing watch at the Christmas tree in the control room when the torpedo hit. His head bloodied from slamming into the controls, Ballinger called, "Deck, we aren't going to be able to get forward unless we get her level."[6]

"It was apparent that the ship must be leveled off before the mechanical lungs could be used through the escape trunk," Clay Decker recalled. He climbed atop the chart table in the control room to reach the lever to the main ballast tank vent No. 2. As Decker pulled the lever down, water rushed into the tanks and *Tang* sank until she "rested on the bottom at 30 fathoms."[7]

Still swimming on the surface, Lt. Larry Savadkin watched as *Tang*'s bow began sinking out of sight. He estimated it to have been at least 15 minutes after he had escaped from the flooded conning tower.

Once *Tang* settled at 180 feet, the control room men moved forward. Motormac Decker attached himself to Bill Ballinger and followed the veteran chief forward. In the officers' quarters, they found Mel Enos burning the ship's code books in a metal trash basket. The ensuing smoke made breathing difficult, so Ballinger convinced the young officer to instead destroy all classified publications by dropping them into the top openings of the batteries in the forward battery compartment.[8]

Those with broken limbs and severe injuries were wrapped in blankets and escorted forward. The 15-man group escaping from the control room included the injured John Accardy and Chief Parker, Doc Larson, Hank Flanagan making his return, Lt. (jg) Enos, Ens. Basil Pearce, Chief Ballinger, Chief DeLapp, Clay

Decker, officers' stewards Howard Walker, Rubin Raiford, Ralph Adams, and three others. The three mess attendants were the only African Americans on *Tang*. Raiford, a husky man from Charleston, West Virginia, was making his first war patrol on *Tang* but had made four prior patrols on *Spearfish*. New Jersey native Ralph Adams was making his first war patrol. Howard Walker, a Kentuckian who loved to gamble, was Dick O'Kane's favorite attendant and had put *Tang* in commission.[9]

When the group opened the door to the forward room at about 0245, the air pressure difference between the compartments literally blew the men into the forward room. The forward room was now crowded with about 25 *Tang* survivors.

Following this party were the 20 men who escaped the crew's quarters and mess hall. "We filed into the control room and destroyed all secret devices," said Jesse DaSilva. "I noticed at this time the depth gauge was at 180 feet."

DaSilva's party reached the forward torpedo room hatch about 0315—some 45 minutes after *Tang*'s torpedo hit. Opening this door was a dangerous task. The high pressure air lines to the forward room had been severed in the explosion, while the rooms aft of the torpedo room were still pressurized.

Inside the torpedo room, Hayes Trukke realized that the great difference in air pressure would be enough to blow the door wide open once again. Calling to steward Rubin Raiford to help, Trukke "tried to get them to open the door only a little till the pressure equalized gradually. But the men in the forward battery thought we were trying to keep them out. Since they didn't understand our signals, they forced the door open."[10]

The door was flung open violently by the force of the pressurized air. The door caught Raiford squarely in the face, splitting his lips open, breaking and flattening his nose to one side, and blackening his eyes shut with heavy swelling. Pharmacist's Mate Larson comforted Raiford as best he could as the steward writhed on the deck in pain, bleeding profusely. Larson used the first aid supplies in the forward room to treat Raiford, Accardy, Parker, and Enos' wounds as best he could.

Chief Weekley's forward torpedo room was now packed to the bulkheads with 40 to 45 men, all who were still living aboard the sunken *Tang*. The men discussed their situation. "We knew the boat would never run again but were confident we could escape," said Trukke.

The total survivor group included at least a half dozen torpedomen, ship's cooks John Parker, John Key, and James Roberts, at least a dozen firemen and motor machinists, the three officers' cooks, radiomen Homer Ijames, Robert Lee, and Lindley Llewellyn, several yeomen, fire controlman Ralph Knapp, several quartermasters, three officers, and a handful of electrician's mates.

The time was now a little after 0315. Momsen lungs were passed out to everyone and talk turned to escape attempts. "The air was foul and breathing was difficult," recalled Jesse DaSilva. Hank Flanagan and Bill Ballinger gave a crash course on use of the lungs, as they found that about half the men did not remember how to

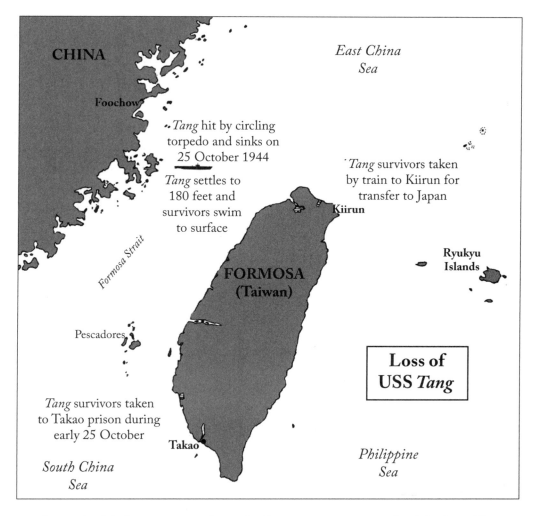

CHINA

East China
Sea

Foochow

Tang hit by circling
torpedo and sinks on
25 October 1944

Tang survivors taken
by train to Kiirun for
transfer to Japan

Tang settles to
180 feet and
survivors swim
to surface

Kiirun

Formosa Strait

FORMOSA
(Taiwan)

Ryukyu
Islands

Pescadores

**Loss of
USS *Tang***

Tang survivors taken
to Takao prison during
early 25 October

Takao

Philippine
Sea

South China
Sea

use them. At this inopportune time, the Japanese escort vessels picked up *Tang* on
their sonar and began making depth charge runs. They dropped about ten ashcans, which shook *Tang* but did no real damage.

The patrol boats moved on in a short while and the silence was again broken by
talk of how to escape from the bottom of the ocean. Some lay in the bunks, debat-
ing their odds of survival. Some disagreement ensued on what to do next. Lt. (jg)
Mel Enos decided that there might still be a chance to blow the boat to the surface
to make it easier for everyone to escape. He decided to lead a party of six men back
to the control room to reach the air manifold. When Enos' party started to open
the watertight door to the forward battery, however, a terrific blast of black smoke
poured into the room. A fire was raging in the forward battery.

Although the door was only cracked for a second, black smoke from burning
rubber and insulation filled the forward room. Men began gagging and vomiting.
Flanagan instructed them to take breaths through their Momsen lungs when the

irritation to their throats became too severe. Pete Narowanski said, "In general, most of the men were excited, scared and didn't know what to do."

The smoke motivated the men to proceed with an escape attempt from 180 feet. With foul air and lights failing from seawater seeping into the batteries, they knew their time was limited. "The conversation of the men at first was about our chances of escape and if we did, what we would do then," said Lt. (jg) Flanagan.

Clay Decker recalled, "With the number of guys we had in the forward torpedo room, we figured we had only about four or five hours of air left. We had to do something within that period of time or we'd all die."[11]

Leland Weekley had opened the escape trunk's lower hatch. Although accounts from the men who ultimately survived the sunken *Tang* differ, two men appear to have left the ship before any formal escape party was organized. According to Decker, it was Chief Weekley and MoMM1c Robert McMorrow who "scooted out" while Ballinger was organizing the first escape. He felt both were overeager to escape. "They didn't have a Momsen lung or a Mae West on," Decker related. "They just flooded the escape chamber, opened the hatch, and went out on their own." Weekley and McMorrow were never seen again after their free emergency ascents. Decker said that by looking into the chamber through thick glass, he could see the escape lever was *down*, indicating that the outer escape door was *open*.[12]

As is often the case with piecing together the exact order of events following a crisis, stories sometimes conflict. The testimony of Hayes Trukke just as clearly states that Weekley was part of the second formally organized escape party. In ComSubPac's report, McMorrow is not discussed but there is the brief statement, "CTM Weekley presumably left the trunk and was not seen again."[13]

Following the ill-fated exit of these first two men, the groups that left *Tang* thereafter were formally organized into escape parties. "Lt. Enos, though wounded by several deep cuts on the head, took charge and led the first escape," said Trukke. "I explained the use of the Momsen lung and operation of the escape trunk, operating the device until my escape."

"It seemed to take a long time to get the first escape started," recalled Narowanski, "but under the conditions a minute was just like an hour." Around 0330, Lt. (jg) Enos climbed up into the escape trunk with two other men, Chief Torpedoman Ballinger and TM1c John Fluker. Instead of bringing along a fourth man, they squeezed a rubber life raft into the chamber with them.

The hatch below them was closed and securely dogged down. Inside, Enos, Ballinger and Fluker wore their Momsen lungs and prepared to flood the chamber. The plan was to release a buoyed ascending line to the surface and open the hatch to the outside once the chamber was flooded. The last man out was to tap on the hull to signal those below to begin draining the chamber. Those still in the torpedo room could close the exterior door with an interior lever, drain the trunk into the bilges, and then reopen the chamber for the next escape party.

Inside the chamber, Enos and his party immediately began arguing over the proper use of the escape trunk. Preparing himself for whatever resistance he might encounter once on the surface or ashore in China, Lt. (jg) Enos had entered the chamber wearing bandoleers of ammunition, two pistols, and a bayonet. The sea pressure increased sharply as the trunk flooded. The men's voices became high-pitched and squeaky as the temperature and pressure rose. The trio had difficulty getting the life buoy attached to the reel of line and Enos decided not to wait.

Hayes Trukke, operating the escape trunk controls, waited for 40 minutes without hearing any signals from inside the trunk. Finally, "I closed it anyway and drained the trunk. We knew there were men in it before it was drained, but decided to find out from them what had gone wrong." When the water was drained, Trukke opened the door. The men found Ballinger, Fluker, and the rubber boat. Mel Enos—wearing ammunition, guns, and bayonet—had dived out the door without waiting to rig the escape line and was never seen again. His armament may have entangled him in *Tang*'s superstructure during his botched escape. Ballinger was near exhaustion but said that he was willing to try another escape attempt. Fluker climbed down and stated that he did not want to try it again. Both men stated that the life raft was too heavy and bulky to squeeze out the opening safely.

Trukke later stated "there were two attempts made before the first [successful] escape and after that at least one person left the trunk on every attempt." Pete Narowanski testified in a similar fashion: "About two attempts were made before the actual escape was successful." These two statements are in line with Clay Decker's firm recollection that McMorrow and Weekley scooted out together in the first unsuccessful attempt—followed by Mel Enos' second party (considered by most as the *first properly organized* escape group).[14]

It was now about 0415 and Lt. (jg) Flanagan decided that he would lead the next escape attempt. Three men had thus far left *Tang*, but none of them had survived. The life boat was pulled back down into the torpedo room and volunteers climbed the ladder to join Flanagan. Behind him, Chief of the Boat Ballinger entered for his second attempt, along with MoMM3c Clay Decker and an unknown fourth man.

As he prepared to climb the ladder, Decker spoke to his close friend, MoMM1c George Zofcin. Decker pleaded with Zofcin to come with him. Their wives shared the same apartment back in Richmond, California. Zofcin inspected Decker's Momsen lung and removed a wire packaging clip on the lung's discharge valve. In spite of Decker's pleadings, Zofcin refused to join the escape party. He did not know how to swim. Decker insisted that he could use his lung as a flotation device. Zofcin remained pessimistic, saying as he turned away, "Maybe I'll try later."[15]

Inside the trunk with the three others, Flanagan decided that without the boat there was room for a fifth escapee. Ensign Basil Pearce volunteered and crawled up into the trunk. The hatch was closed and the men inside began flooding the chamber. Hayes Trukke, again standing sentry over the controls, began to worry after

40 minutes passed without a signal. "I listened close to the hatch. I could distinctly hear moaning but nothing else."

Once again, things had gone wrong. Chief Ballinger had taken control as the water began flooding in. When the water reached shin level, he had Decker go under and test his Momsen lung. Decker then began releasing the escape buoy, counting knots on the soccer-ball-sized float as it headed for the surface above. He was certain that there were 30 knots, spaced one fathom apart—which would have been 180 feet to the surface.[16]

Decker felt the buoy reach the surface, tied it off on deck fittings and ducked back into the trunk to get a final breath of air. As the buoy shot toward the surface, the line pinned Hank Flanagan against the trunk's side. Once the buoy hit the surface, Ballinger gave Decker the go-ahead to make his ascent. With his mouthpiece in place, Decker exited the side door and began going up the line smoothly. He climbed the knotted rope, pausing at each knot to inhale and then exhale slowly before moving up—hoping to avoid the bends or an air embolism.[17]

As Decker approached the surface, the water grew lighter. He wiped blood away from ruptured blood vessels in his nose and cheeks that burst from the pressure change. He finally broke the surface and held onto the buoy to await the others. The fourth man to leave *Tang*, Clayton Oliver Decker had unwittingly become the first American sailor to have escaped on his own from a sunken U.S. submarine. Prior to his successfully reaching the surface, no U.S. combatant had made a submerged escape using self-contained equipment. Swede Momsen had tested his lung 16 year earlier but it had not seen actual use in a crisis. Prior to World War II, a small number of British, German, and Danish submariners had successfully escaped from their sunken boats.[18]

Decker saw Bill Ballinger break the surface in mortal agony, bleeding and screaming with pain. Ballinger's nose clamp was off and his mouthpiece was out. Decker stayed a few feet away from the chief of the boat, who thrashed about in agony. Zofcin had noticed that Decker's Momsen lung discharge valve was pinned shut. He believed that Ballinger's might have also been pinned shut, which probably resulted in a lung embolism. Decker believed that Ballinger suffered the "bends," a terribly painful condition caused by the body absorbing nitrogen into the bloodstream under high pressure. The effects on Ballinger's body were excruciating and he did not survive long on the surface.[19]

In addition to Decker and Ballinger, an unknown sixth man swam out from *Tang*'s escape trunk. Trukke again drained the trunk and found Ensign Pearce "in a stupor as we took him down." Lt. (jg) Flanagan, pinned to the bulkhead by the buoy's line, was cut loose and lowered down. Doc Larson and others wrapped him in blankets, put him in a bunk, and tried to comfort him. Basil Pearce had had enough. "The ensign said he would not attempt another escape but that there was no reason why every other man in the compartment shouldn't escape," Trukke said. Pearce was a graduate of the New London Submarine School and had successfully made the 100-foot escape in the tank.

Discipline began to fray as men watched the two officers being pulled from the chamber around 0500—two and a half hours after *Tang* was torpedoed. Japanese escort ships could now be heard again making another depth charge attack on *Tang*, but were judged to be about a mile away. The explosions, although distant, played heavily on the men's frazzled nerves.

The *Tang* survivors sat silently, conserving oxygen and praying that they would not make sounds which the enemy sonarmen could pick up. Acrid smoke continued to seep into the forward torpedo room from an unsuspected source—through the sink in the forward room. Oxygen was bled into the room several times to help relieve the feeling of suffocation. The use of the CO_2 absorbent was considered but the consensus was that the room was simply too crowded for it to be effective.

The best remedy was escape and a third formal escape party made ready to leave as soon as the escort ships faded away. This group consisted of torpedomen Pete Narowanski, Hayes Trukke, John Fluker making his second attempt, and a motor machinist's mate who was unknown to the torpedomen. Trukke had made only one prior patrol on *Tang*. Narowanski knew even fewer of the motormacs; he had been aboard *Tang* for a little over a month.

"We took a life ring with us to use as a buoy," recalled Trukke. This ring had been captured from a sunken merchant ship, *Yamaoka Maru*, that *Tang* had sunk on a prior patrol. When Trukke tried to charge his Momsen lung from the manifold, he found that there was no oxygen. "This worried the other men even though I explained they could blow the lungs up with their own air and it served the purpose. I felt very exhausted—like I couldn't get any oxygen into my lungs and began to get dizzy, so I knew I had better get out while I could. It took me about 15 minutes to rig the trunk including preparing the life ring as a buoy."

Close to passing out after rigging the trunk, Trukke exited and ascended the line while holding onto the maru's life ring. The seventh man to depart *Tang*, Trukke breathed through his Momsen lung while Narowanski held the line he was riding up. About 20 feet up, Narowanski attempted to pull back and slow Trukke's ascent. In the process, Trukke lost his lung and simply continued up without it, exhaling all the way up, trying his best to equalize the pressure. When he popped to the surface near Clay Decker, he was exhausted, sick, and vomited for half an hour.

The other three men in the trunk—Fluker, Narowanski, and the motormac—decided against making escape attempts. The forward torpedo room survivors once again closed the hatch and began draining the escape trunk. By this point, things were getting critical. The lights were noticeably dimmer and with the smoke that had seeped into the room, it was almost dark in the compartment.

A short while later, a fourth group entered the trunk to start the process again. Hank Flanagan entered again to make his second attempt, as did Pete Narowanski.

When Flanagan called for another man, MoMM2c Glen Haws declined but his buddy Jesse DaSilva decided to give it a try. The name of a fourth man in this escape party was not recalled by the eventual survivors.[20]

Some men crawled into the bunks and talked weakly about family and loved ones. Others had given up all hope. Survivors recalled StM1c Howard Walker—one of Dick O'Kane's favorite crewmen and a regular gambler during shore leaves—accepting his fate quietly. Walker sat calmly near the torpedo tubes, making no attempt to escape. He stated to others, "You guys had better stop talking and do some praying."[21]

The four men in the trunk found the lower portion of the bulkhead between the compartments to be so hot that the paint was peeling off. "I felt at ease using the lung and knew it would work after I tested it under the water before leaving the trunk," Flanagan stated. "I had made a 100 foot escape before."

Flanagan was the eighth man to depart *Tang*, followed three minutes later by Narowanski. Deciding it was time to go, DaSilva ducked his head under the water and swam out three minutes after Narowanski. DaSilva wrapped his feet around the line and "slowly let myself up 10 feet at a time, stopping and counting to 10 each time. About a third of the way up, breathing became difficult but soon the problem went away and the water became lighter and suddenly I was on the surface." Nearby, DaSilva found four other men clinging to the buoy, with mainland China visible in the distance. The fourth man in the trunk also departed but he was never seen again.

"As I reached the surface, my physical condition was a series of dry heaves and I was very weak," said Narowanski. "I did not hold myself back while making the ascent." On the surface, Hayes Trukke found the three newest escapees to be "very exhausted but all right otherwise."

Hank Flanagan related, "There was a Jap freighter's bow sticking up about 500 yards from the buoy. We decided to wait till the tide changed, then salvage a boat or raft and make for the coast under cover of darkness."

Lt. Larry Savadkin had spent the night floating on his back and reinflating his "life belt" trousers. He tried swimming west for the coast by using the stars but finally conceded that "I didn't know enough about them."

After dawn, he set out again for the distant Chinese coast, but found that the strong current only moved him around in great circles. Later in the morning, Japanese patrol boats appeared in the distance. Some passed fairly close by and occasionally dropped depth charges. After feeling the effects of the first depth charge explosion, he learned to anticipate the others by floating on his back and arching his back up out of the water as they exploded.

Savadkin realized that his only real hope of living was in being picked up. He began yelling and splashing water when the next ship came in his direction. Around 1000, one of the escorts approached. Shivering from hypothermia, he yelled and splashed until Japanese escort vessel *P-34* spotted him and hauled him on board.

Some distance away, Boats Leibold and Floyd Caverly were still swimming after eight hours in the ocean. About 30 minutes after picking up Lieutenant Savadkin, *P-34*'s crew spotted them. Leibold and Caverly were hauled aboard a pulling boat and placed in the bow section. One of the Japanese sailors asked a question that contained the word, "Deutsche." Caverly, quickly deciding that the Japanese figured them for Germans from one of the convoy ships, replied with, "Heil, Hitler."[22]

"They pulled us out and then on the way back to their ship, they ran across O'Kane," said Leibold. "He was kinda floating on what looked like a big door." As *P-34*'s whaleboat pulled alongside Commander O'Kane, Chief Leibold joked, "Good morning, Captain. Do you want a ride?" Understanding the word "captain," the Japanese sailors placed O'Kane in the stern of the whaleboat—his identity given away to his captors.

The boat was pulled up to the main deck of the patrol craft. Stepping aboard, Caverly looked at a petty officer's wristwatch to check the time. "He reached over and kinda twisted his arm so he could see the watch," Leibold recalled. "That's when he got his first knuckle sandwich."

Caverly reeled to the deck as the petty officer's fist smashed into his face. The time of his capture was left permanently impressed into his memory: it was 1030.

––––––––––

The five Americans clinging to their buoy were becoming uncomfortable. The cool water caused their bodies to shiver. Hours after Clay Decker had reached the surface, the *Tang* survivors saw a distant Japanese escort ship circling the area. *P-34* approached to within 100 yards of them and began sweeping in a circle.

During this time, Pharmacist's Mate Paul Larson popped to the surface with blood streaming from his nose and mouth. Yet another group of men had obviously begun the escape process from *Tang*'s forward torpedo room below. Hayes Trukke swam over and pulled Larson to the group, "as he was evidently unable to keep his head out of the water." Decker hung onto the pharmacist as Jesse DaSilva tried to get him to cling to the buoy. Lt. (jg) Flanagan said that "Larson was practically unconscious when he surfaced. His condition grew worse."[23]

Five minutes later, officer's cook Rubin Raiford—the thirteenth man known to have exited *Tang*'s forward torpedo room—came to the surface about 50 feet away. He had apparently lost the line during his ascent. He did not appear to be wearing a lung, due to the smashed face he had received from the forward hatch.

"None of us could possibly have reached him," stated Flanagan. "After struggling a few seconds he drowned, floating off with his head still visible but under the surface," said Trukke. Pete Narowanski felt "it was apparent something had gone wrong." Of the eight who had struggled to the surface, only six men stayed afloat. "Some men might have lost their lungs and some were too excited to come up slowly. Some missed the buoy line and were stuck in the superstructure of the submarine."

P-34 made another circle and then stopped a short distance away, turning its guns toward the *Tang* sailors. "Well, this is it," thought DaSilva. "They are going to shoot us." The Japanese instead lowered a small boat.

When the *P-34* sailors hauled the Americans into their life boat, the boat's coxswain cut the life ring free from the ascending line—still attached to *Tang*—and brought it along, as well. "It was from the *Yamaoka Maru* and so may have spurred some wonderment within Japanese intelligence," Dick O'Kane wrote.[24]

The Japanese hauled aboard Larson, Narowanski, Trukke, Flanagan, Decker, and DaSilva, the only ones still alive of the eight men who had reached the surface. "Larson stopped breathing before we reached the destroyer and while the Japs were tying us up on deck, I saw some of them attempting to revive him by slapping and kicking him," said Trukke. "He never moved and we didn't see him or his body again." When the whaleboat reached the side of *P-34*, the Americans began climbing on board. Clay Decker, the last man up, looked back in time to see the Japanese throwing Doc Larson's body overboard. He was unsure whether the unconscious pharmacist's mate was alive or not.[25]

The other five made it aboard *P-34*. "They tied our hands behind us and made us sit on the metal deck," said DaSilva. "I was surprised to see four other members of our crew on board. This made a total of nine that survived." *P-34* had already hauled in Dick O'Kane, Lieutenant Savadkin, Chief Boatswain's Mate Leibold, and Radio Technician First Class Caverly.

If others tried to escape from *Tang*, they were either not successful or simply were not picked up by the Japanese. "The smoke undoubtedly killed every man in the compartment not long after the Japs picked us up," Narowanski stated. O'Kane later wrote, "It is felt that [the after torpedo room door's] gasket blew out, either due to the pressure or an ensuing battery explosion, and that the remaining personnel were asphyxiated."[26]

Hank Flanagan, in the last surviving group to come up, said there were "13 who left the escape trunk." At least three—Ballinger, Raiford, and Larson—died after reaching the surface. The five picked up by *P-34* were the only Americans to have ever escaped on their own from a sunken submarine who lived. Another 30-odd men remain on eternal patrol at 30 fathoms in *Tang*'s forward torpedo room.

Aboard *P-34*, Boats Leibold noted Pete Narowanski climb aboard wearing a pair of brown swim trunks he had pulled on before his escape from *Tang*. On the sub, he had donned a flowered red and white pair at first. "Then he decided they were too flashy so he pulled on another pair that was brown."

The submariners were ordered to sit on the main deck of the ship, broiling in the mid-90s heat of midday as survivors from Japanese ships sunk by *Tang* were picked up. Everyone became badly sunburned. Hayes Trukke was seated beside Boats Leibold, who was sitting next to Skipper O'Kane. Aboard ship, he had managed to keep long blond hair, which he kept slicked back. "O'Kane was strongly opposed to mustaches, beards, and long hair," recalled Leibold. "Trukke's hair was hanging over his face and O'Kane asked me who that was sitting beside me."

"Trukke," Leibold replied.

"Was he on my boat?" the skipper exclaimed, puzzled by the long-haired man.

Commander O'Kane was taken away for special interrogations, since the Japanese had heard him referred to as "Captain." When he realized the abuse he and his shipmates received was being "administered by the burned, mutilated survivors of our own handiwork, we found we could take it with less prejudice."[27]

Jesse DaSilva recalled, "When it was my turn, they took me to another part of the ship and had me sit down between three of them." Although he was offered a ball of rice, he refused to eat it. A Japanese sailor who spoke English carried a bat-sized club and another carried an electrical device. "He would jab me in the ribs with this and I would twitch and jump," said DaSilva. "They thought this was very funny."

As the interrogation proceeded, DaSilva was slugged with the club when the Japanese did not like his answers. "After some time, when they figured that I wasn't going to tell them anything, they took me back to the others."

Leibold found the mood of *P-34*'s sailors worsened with each group of Japanese survivors that they hauled aboard. "The skipper got worked over pretty well on this Jap patrol craft," he stated. "When these people realized they had people from a submarine that had sunk them, they weren't too friendly. They stuck a cigarette out on my neck. They did the same thing to our skipper."

Caverly found the treatment equally brutal. "At first, they couldn't figure out who in the hell we were or where we had come from. But then they picked up the buoy out there with our other fellows, so they decided to kick the hell out of us and grind a few cigarette butts out in our ears." Savadkin recalled that Skipper O'Kane's neck was used to snuff out cigarettes. "I don't know if he bore to his death the scars on his neck, but that seemed to be something they delighted in doing."[28]

Floyd Caverly learned from two older, English-speaking Japanese men pulled from the water that they were skippers of two of the merchant ships sunk by *Tang*. "They didn't mistreat us like the other guys did, but they didn't stop any of the other guys either," Caverly said. "They couldn't. They were civilians." *P-34*'s sailors gave the *Tang* officers an especially hard time. "Flanagan was the torpedo officer and the Japs gave him a pretty bad time on that destroyer," Caverly said.

"They cracked him over the skull with a sword. He later developed a brain tumor from getting his skull cracked."

At dusk, the *Tang* survivors were moved to a small deckhouse bathing room aboard *P-34* and locked in. "It was so small that only two or three of us could lie down and the rest had to stand," recalled DaSilva. "It was very hot and had only one small porthole for air which they would not let us open."

"While locked in the very small 'hot bath,' we were able to exchange information concerning the sinking of *Tang*, conditions in the boat and escapes," Leibold recalled. "The total number of personnel who were known to escape was fixed at 23—that is nine from the bridge, one from the conning tower, and 13 from the forward torpedo room, of whom five survived."

After some time, the submariners convinced their guards to let them return to sitting on the deck in the fresh air. When *P-34* approached Takao, Formosa, a black cloth hood was placed over the prisoners' heads as the ship entered the harbor. "Our arms were securely bound to our chest at the bicep area with small line like marlin and hands were bound in front of our bodies at the wrist," stated Leibold. The Americans were herded onto a truck and driven to some buildings.

Inside, Japanese officials removed their hoods but kept the *Tang* survivors securely bound while they were inspected. "We were separated and placed in small rooms, where our arms, still bound, were pulled above our heads and tied to a ring in the wall," Leibold recalled. Unable to defend themselves, they were preyed upon by mosquitoes. "I was taken to a small room with no floors, just dirt and gravel," said DaSilva. Leibold was secured in a room beside Floyd Caverly, both of whom were warned, "No speak."

The food later brought in to them was barely edible. Guards questioned and beat some of the enlisted men during the night. After sunrise, the *Tang* men were lined up outside and again inspected by the Japanese officials. Dick O'Kane recalled, "Trukke had somehow managed to keep long blond hair, but now all of the slickum had washed away, and his hair bounded down all around to the level of his mouth, giving him the exact appearance of Hairless Joe in Al Capp's comic strip." The Japanese onlooker laughed and pointed at Trukke until O'Kane felt that the whole affair took on for the Japanese "the nature of a circus parade."[29]

The *Tang* men were blindfolded, followed by a little clubbing before being sent on a forced march. "We were actually in a procession, escorted by screaming, spitting, slugging riff-raff," recalled Leibold. "Our destination was the train station and we all still had our heads, despite being threatened with their loss."

Aboard the train, the prisoners were seated with a number of Japanese guards. "Once on the train, the blindfolds were removed," said DaSilva. After leaving the station, the shades were lifted and they could see the Formosa countryside going by. "It was like going back 100 years," thought DaSilva. "The only thing I ever saw were people working in the fields with hand plows pulled by oxen."

After a full day's trip, the train arrived at the other end of Formosa at the port city of Kiirun. The *Tang* men were marched to a jail controlled by the Japanese Army. "I was put with two or three others in a jail cell which had a raised wooden floor and large wooden bars," stated DaSilva. The toilet was a hole in the floor, but the food was better. "At dusk, to our surprise, generous balls of hot rice and fish wrapped in cane husks were pushed through the scuttles for each of us," Dick O'Kane wrote. "Within an hour everyone received a blanket, and after kindly dubbing our prison the Kiirun Clink, we got our first shut-eye since the tragedy."[30]

Before dawn, a Kiirun guard slipped popsicles to Larry Savadkin for the Americans, whispering, "I am a Christian." On 29 October, the *Tang* prisoners were herded onto a charcoal-fired bus, each man with his own guard. After traveling only a short distance, the engine quit and most of the guards got off to help push start it. "All of the guards carried a rifle and the ones that got off to push left their rifles on the bus," related Boats Leibold. "When the driver stopped his running bus to retrieve the guards who were now chasing it, they all got on board and started laughing and pointing to their rifles and their prisoners. It was funny."

The six enlisted men were put aboard a light cruiser and placed into a forward hold with two guards. The *Tang* officers were taken aboard Japanese destroyers, where Larry Savadkin and Hank Flanagan were each kept in the wardrooms.

Commander O'Kane was escorted to the Japanese destroyer captain's cabin, where he was kept under armed guard. He was provided meals, shoes, and clothing. The Japanese skipper joined him after dark and discussed naval tactics and literature. From his bookshelf, he produced a copy of *Gone With the Wind*, saying, "You recognize Mitchell's *Went With the Breeze*?" His opinion was that war could have been avoided if more influential adults had read the book.[31]

Bill Leibold could feel that the cruiser was moving at a high rate of speed. "During this transit, we were not mistreated and the officers indicated that they were treated well on the destroyers," he said. "There was a steady stream of Jap sailors coming into the hold we were in, where they would punch a hole in a sack and fill small bags with the sugar. That is how we learned what the cargo was."

The two destroyers and cruiser made port at Nagoya, where the naval base of Kobe was located on mainland Japan. O'Kane was ordered to return his borrowed clothes and shoes. Thanking the destroyer skipper for his kindness, O'Kane asked why treatment had been so rough on *P-34*. The skipper explained that the escort ships were not part of the Japanese Imperial Navy.[32]

The *Tang* prisoners were taken in a sizable motor launch for a lengthy trip to Kobe, where they were marched through a training center. "The weather was wet and cold as we marched from the boat landing toward some buildings," Leibold related. "A large group of recruits were drilling with rifles and fixed bayonets, doing a lot of shouting." The submariners were lined up alongside a fence outside of one of the buildings, where they stood in the rain and sleet waiting for inspection.

A tall Japanese rear admiral looked the *Tang* men over, and he stopped in front of Boats Leibold, whose teeth were chattering from the cold. "None of us had any significant clothing on," recalled Leibold. "I had on a pair of undershorts and a shirt. They had us up against a fence outside at Kobe. It was raining and cold." The Japanese admiral stepped up to the shivering sailor and asked in good English, "Are you scared?"

"No, I'm cold," Leibold replied.

The admiral looked and said, "Of course, stupid, no shoes!"

Leibold recalled, "O'Kane just thought that was funny as all get out."

They were taken into a building and waited for their next transfer. The submariners were later placed aboard a train and traveled a long time toward Yokohama. As they disembarked, Dick O'Kane noted the booming factories and bustle of wartime construction. A bus moved them an hour's ride from Yokohama to Ofuna. "It was cold and rainy as we were marched on a dark, muddy road to our new home, Ofuna prison camp. All of us were muddy," said Leibold.

"When I had made my escape from *Tang*, the only piece of clothing I had on was a pair of pants, so all the time we were walking, I was very wet and cold," said DaSilva. "When we reached camp, my feet were numb from the cold."

Although *Tang* was officially declared overdue and presumed lost, Admiral Nimitz's codebreakers knew the truth. They intercepted enough Japanese dispatches to figure that *Tang* had caused incredible damage and shipping loss on her last patrol. *Tang*'s former executive officer, Murray Frazee returned from leave in California and heard the news at Pearl. "*Tang* had been sunk, only nine of the eighty-seven-man crew survived, and O'Kane was a prisoner of war," he was told. A friend of the O'Kane family, Frazee wanted desperately to tell Dick's wife, Ernestine O'Kane, that her husband was alive.[33]

"All I could do was bite my tongue," he recalled. The Ultra secrets and the codebreakers' important work would be compromised if news leaked out in the States that Dick O'Kane was known to be alive. "So Ernie O'Kane . . . had to suffer."

The news of her husband's "loss" was devastating to Ernie O'Kane. "When you get that telegram, it's just the saddest thing you could get," she later stated. "A neighbor took the children for the rest of the day. You just try to get on your feet and decide what you want to do next. I decided to drive home to my folks."[34]

It would be many months before Mrs. O'Kane received any indication that her husband might actually still be alive.

20
"God Help Us"

Ofuna: November 1944

During their Ofuna introduction, the new *Tang* arrivals at least received some better clothing. Motormac Jesse DaSilva escaped *Tang*'s forward torpedo room wearing only a pair of shorts. With the onset of winter, he received a shirt, pair of pants, and tennis shoes "three sizes too small. This was all the clothing I ever received the whole time I was a POW."

Floyd Caverly and Boats Leibold were sent with a guard to fetch buckets of food for the new prisoners. The buckets contained a rice, barley, and vegetable mixture the *Tang* men came to call "all-dump." At their first morning quarters, "we learned that we were captives, not prisoners," wrote Cdr. Dick O'Kane. "Since this was a work camp, our ration would be reduced by one-quarter. On the nicer side was word that we would start learning Japanese on the following day." O'Kane saw the positive side that "at least we had a chance to live."[1]

Tang's crewmen were initially separated from other prisoners and were not even allowed to talk to each other. Three days after their arrival, they got their first glimpse of another American submariner, *Grenadier* skipper John Fitzgerald, at a disciplinary demonstration. "They told us that we were going to get a lesson in Japanese," recalled Leibold. "A bad day!" was how Fitzgerald noted 6 November in his diary.

With Commandant Iida present, the guards lined up eight veteran prisoners for punishment who had been found "guilty" of various offenses against warrant officer Taicho and other guards. Seven of the men—B-24 pilot Lt. Glen

McConnell, Air Force 2nd Lt. Charles Kaufman, Lt. Red Bullard, ARM3c Oscar Long, General Field Harris' son, 1st Lt. Bill Harris, Lt. Dan Galvin, and *Sculpin*'s Lt. George Brown—were pulled for talking, complaining, making derogatory comments, or working slow. Fitzgerald was the eighth victim, "probably for trying to get people out of trouble and sometimes disagreeing with the guard."[2]

The guards and the Japanese pharmacist's mate beat three of these men, including Fitzgerald, with a round club in front of the *Tang* survivors. Harris and McConnell passed out during the beatings. "We averaged 15–18 licks," wrote Lieutenant Commander Fitzgerald. "After watching this, I knew what could be expected if we didn't do what we were told," thought Jesse DaSilva. Dick O'Kane felt that Fitzgerald and the other two prisoners were "walking skeletons. We watched the largest guards, three at a time in rotation, club these men into unconsciousness while other guards held them up so the beatings could continue," he wrote. "Caverly was as tough as they come and had even been a professional boxer, but this sight made him vomit." As the *Tang* prisoners were led away, they saw the guards kicking the limp bodies of Fitzgerald and the first two victims before they moved on to their other five victims. "We believed them dead," recalled O'Kane.[3]

Tang's survivors were also introduced to the awkward Ofuna crouch. They stood with bent knees on the balls of their feet with arms overhead for hours. Any individuals who toppled after a long period in this stance were brutally clubbed. Like the others at Ofuna, they were put on a starvation diet that averaged no more than 300 calories per day.

Ofuna's QKs went to work on the new American submariners. Dick O'Kane told the QKs that *Tang* sank only five ships. When news of the loss of *Tang* and her famous captain reached Ofuna, the Japanese broke some of O'Kane's teeth. Sometime later, a Japanese officer produced a news clipping which related how *Tang* had been presented the Presidential Unit Citation for sinking 110,000 tons of Japanese shipping. Enraged at the officer's lies, the guards knocked O'Kane from his stool and beat him.[4]

Lt. Larry Savadkin gave vague answers to the basic questions and lied about more specific queries about *Tang*. Lt. (jg) Hank Flanagan gave false information when he was quizzed by QKs on American torpedo details. He and other *Tang* survivors tried to anticipate the questions and deliver similar responses. Savadkin later stated, "We all took Captain O'Kane's advice."[5]

According to Motormac Clay Decker, O'Kane told his shipmates, "I'm the guy they're after." He advised his men to give some kind of non-informative answers to questions versus refusing to answer the interrogators. When asked about *Tang*'s diesels, Decker explained that his sub had Fairbanks Morse engines. The interrogators then pulled out a factory catalog with complete descriptions on Fairbanks Morse engines. When asked how many ships were in Pearl Harbor, Decker replied that he had no idea since his submarine had no portholes and he worked below decks.[6]

When DaSilva was taken, he found that the Japanese officer spoke excellent English. "He would offer me a cigarette and ask me how everything was. He would ask me the same questions over and over, as I would give him the same answers he would not accept." DaSilva was only interviewed a few times. "I guess he figured I didn't know anything."

As a leading radio technician, Floyd Caverly was of more interest. "They tried to brainwash us and tell us that the Americans were no damn good," he said. "We actually started the war and all this sorta stuff." The Japanese often started the interview sessions by offering him a cigarette or some tangerine peelings. "This was supposed to soften you up and make you think that they were pretty good guys after all," Caverly recalled. Each interrogation started with a few refresher questions from his previous interviews.

"It seems to me you were the electrician repair man, right?" the interpreter asked.

"Yes, sort of," replied Caverly. "I changed all the light bulbs in the submarine and kept them going all the time so it would never be dark in there."

When asked how he repaired all the radio and electronic equipment, Caverly created tall tales. He claimed that he had a little tester he would use to check all the fuses and replace those that were bad. When the Japanese brought out some electronics books to get more detailed information, Caverly claimed that only electronics officer Ed Beaumont knew that information. "Beaumont was lost with the sub, so I claimed anything I didn't know was something that he knew. We learned to juggle these guys."

Caverly particularly fed misinformation to the Naval cadets who were brought in to witness the proceedings. "They were just real young kids," he said. "They all spoke very good English but they didn't know a damn thing. You could tell them something and their eyes would get big. They would just look at you and mutter. We told them the damndest lies about one thing or another."

The interrogators quizzed Caverly on *Tang*'s JK-QC sonar set. The JK's amplifier stack was attached to the sound head, which went down through the bottom of the submarine for listening. "On the side of that sound head, there were electrical magnets and on the other side was a chemical called Roshell salt," he related. During a detailed session on this radar head, Caverly insisted that his ship instead used Morton salt.

Unfamiliar with this brand of American table salt, the Japanese were duped by Caverly's story. "You could get away with this with these young fellows," he recalled. When asked about whether he went to school, Caverly proudly declared, "Oh, yeah. I got a good education. I finished fifth grade. My father only went to school to the third grade." He proceeded to tell the story that down in Arkansas, "we didn't have the good schools they had on the East Coast." Caverly's story began to fall apart when one of the more educated interrogators said, "You know, Mr. Caverly, I spent two years in postgraduate work at the University of Arkansas."

Searching, Caverly replied, "Well, I was just over the hills a little way back from Little Rock."

During the night, guards worked on the new prisoners' psyches. "In your cell, you would sometimes hear a scratchy sound on the door, like someone making a mark with a piece of chalk," Bill Leibold said. "It wasn't long before we knew what that meant. That night, we were going to get it." Caverly would never forget "these bastards sneaking in my cell at night and walloping the hell out of us with a club. They hit you from your shoulders down to your knees. They would just stand there and beat the hell out of you. There was no place you could go in that little cell, so you just took it as best you could."

During the next week, the guards had the prisoners begin digging an air raid shelter across the street. As mid-November passed, word was received that another Red Cross ship had arrived in Kobe, offering the Ofuna inmates some hope of new packages arriving soon. On the night of 22 November, packages containing 100 cartons of U.S.A. Red Cross boxes were delivered to Ofuna. "Again all men much excited, jovial and happier," penned John Fitzgerald.[7]

The following day, the prisoners were allowed to enjoy one package of Red Cross food. A barter system quickly ensued as prisoners traded one another for the items they most desired. Thanksgiving 1944 was celebrated with more raiding of the Red Cross goodies. This greatly helped the normal supply of food. "We were generally given a bowl of this milo maize," recalled Boats Leibold. "Sometimes there was some barley in it. We got some of that and usually a bowl of soup that was like a type of broth. We never did get any water but we did get a cup of tea with each meal."[8]

On 3 December, all hands except those with colds were inoculated again, their first shots since June. Winter was setting in and the season's first freeze was felt the following night. As the weather grew colder, the guards would occasionally let the prisoners carry a blanket with them for their exercise period. "We were all walking around in a circle with blankets over our heads, looking like a bunch of old Mother Hubbards," stated Jesse DaSilva.

The *Tang* prisoners quickly learned how to disseminate information to other prisoners in their Ofuna barracks. "We weren't allowed to talk to each other, but we could talk to the guards," recalled Floyd Caverly. "When the guard was leading us to some duty, we could talk to him while we were walking. We had picked up a bit of Japanese, but he couldn't quite understand what we were saying." As the prisoners rattled some broken English and Japanese "story" to the guards, they would slip in phrases to the other prisoners about the information that the QKs were seeking that day. "We kept talking to the guards all the time they were walking us, but we were telling the rest of the fellows in the cells what the goons were after," said Caverly. "Everybody else in solitary would have their ears to the door listening to what we had to say."

At night, some of the Ofuna prisoners would strike up conversations with their guards to help pass on information. Others just had fun slipping offensive phrases past certain guards whose command of the English language was poor. Caverly recalled one Ofuna inmate, Francis Joseph O'Gara, who had some fun with the guards.

O'Gara had been a sportswriter for the *Philadelphia Inquirer* but then joined the Merchant Marine as a seaman after the outbreak of war in 1941. He was a survivor of the Liberty Ship SS *Jean Nicolet*, which was torpedoed and sunk by the Japanese submarine *I-8* on 2 July 1944 in the Indian Ocean. Three months earlier, *I-8* had sunk a Dutch merchant ship and her crew had brutally murdered all but six of the 97 survivors.[9]

Jean Nicolet's crew abandoned ship and the majority of the crew was taken on deck of the Japanese submarine to be tortured and murdered. The Americans were forced to run a gauntlet on deck with their hands tied behind their backs while Japanese crewmen beat them with rifles and steel stanchions and stabbed them with bayonets. Before the bloodbath was complete, an Australian PBY approached and forced the sub to dive. Many of those not fatally wounded then drowned or were eaten by sharks, although one resourceful *Jean Nicolet* crewman with a hidden knife managed to cut the ropes from some of his shipmates' bound hands. Twenty-three of the Merchant Marine sailors survived in the water long enough to eventually be rescued.

Before the massacre ensued on *I-8*, the Japanese had taken three American prisoners from *Jean Nicolet* below decks: Captain David Martin Nilsson, radio operator Augustus Tilden, and ship's purser Frank O'Gara. Neither Tilden nor Nilsson would survive the war but former correspondent O'Gara, after much abuse on *I-8*, was taken to Penang and eventually transferred on to Yokohama and to Ofuna.

Bill Leibold recalled that "Frank O'Gara was kept in solitary confinement the entire time we were there. Although we communicated through the wall, we never actually saw him." Caverly enjoyed some of the tricks the former reporter would pull on the guards. "He would get several guards in his cell at a time and make like he was trying to learn Japanese. They would teach him family names like 'Mama-san' and 'Papa-san.'"

The other prisoners knew that O'Gara would eventually pull a fast one on the guards. "We would listen to him giving these guys a long bunch of B.S.," said Caverly. "Pretty soon, he would say right in the middle of his schooling, 'Now, which one of you guards will take a dollar bill to blow a party of six?' We would all start to laugh up and down the brig. It was funny as hell." When the guards looked angry at the sudden outburst, O'Gara would quickly switch gears and return to his broken Japanese/English story. "He had to make up a story quickly to cover the insult he had thrown in," Caverly recalled.

Tang's surviving officers and men became close with one another and learned more about each other than they ever would have aboard their ship during wartime. "I was informed that I had conducted too many inspections," wrote Dick O'Kane, "but that was probably a complaint in any ship." He also learned from Caverly that the radio gang had constructed a homemade still aboard ship to brew alcohol. Many times they had burned their fingers while disassembling hot coils before their skipper could catch them.[10]

Ofuna was rattled by the shocks of several good earthquakes on 8 December. "The first one splashed a quantity of water out of the pool for use in case of fire," recorded Lieutenant Commander Fitzgerald. In a conference that day, the senior leaders decided to ration their Red Cross supplies, with the next package to be saved until nearly Christmas. The cold weather increased and the first half inch of snow fell on 13 December.

The next small Red Cross packages were distributed on 23 December. The camp also received three more submarine survivors that day from a British boat, HMS *Stratagem*. On 19 November, her skipper—Lt. Cdr. Clifford Raymond Pelly—sank a 1,945-ton Japanese cargo vessel south of the port of Malacca. In the same vicinity, *Strategem* was attacked by a Japanese patrol boat on 22 November and lost. Severely battered by depth charges, *Stratagem* hit bottom and began flooding. Pelly ordered his men to blow the main ballast.[11]

As the sub headed toward the surface, diving officer Lt. Donald Cameron Douglas and nine British sailors escaped their doomed submarine by opening a hatch. They were literally blown out of their compartment by the pressurized air and swam for the surface. When they reached the surface, "all of us were suffering from bends," stated Douglas. Eight of these ten sailors were picked up by the Japanese and taken into Singapore for interrogation. Lieutenant Douglas and two seamen were then flown to Japan and transferred to Ofuna.

On Christmas day 1944, the Ofuna prisoners were permitted to conduct a 20-minute service during the morning. In the afternoon, the guards allowed them to play games, with sweet potatoes being the prizes. In addition, everyone received a couple of potatoes. "All hope to be among our home friends next time at Christmas," Fitzgerald wrote in his diary.[12]

Tang's Jesse DaSilva guarded his Red Cross stash carefully, not even venturing to participate in the common practice of trading unwanted food for cigarettes. Bill Leibold left his cell for some free time on Christmas day, only to return and find that his Red Cross food package had been snatched. After some bitter complaining, Leibold was compensated by the Japanese guards with two baked sweet potatoes.[13]

The Japanese celebrated New Year's for several days as 1945 began. They had "lots of food plus saki," wrote Fitzgerald. Lt. George Whiting, the *Grenadier* exec, recalled, "When the guards had a party and a few of them left a half-inch or so of beer in their bottles, Greg Boyington and myself finished them off. Nothing ever tasted so good!"[14]

Pappy Boyington, assigned to the camp galley, managed to sneak extra food to his fellow prisoners. *Tang*'s Larry Savadkin stole ketchup from a bottle in the galley and brought it to his shipmates. One of the POWs urinated in the bottle to make it look full, and Savadkin snuck it back to the galley. He alerted Boyington, who kept the bottle of ill content on the shelf until he could safely throw it away.[15]

With the camp count up to 67 Allied POWs by 11 January, Ofuna's commandant transferred 27 men several days later. John Fitzgerald and George Whiting finally made the cut. "We are to leave Monday morning for Omori, the headquarters camp of the Tokyo area," Fitzgerald wrote. "Having spent twenty and one half months in this camp of seclusion, humiliation and intimidation, it's about time we left, and we hold the record for duration of stay here, exceeding the previous record for time by five weeks." Also leaving was *Sculpin*'s only officer, Lieutenant Brown, who had spent 13 months at Ofuna. The newest draft of transferees departed on 15 January for Omori. "It was a great relief to get away from Ofuna," thought Fitzgerald.[16]

During the winter, Ofuna received ample snow quantities until it remained on the ground. "There was no heat in the cells and you could see right through the cracks in the walls," DaSilva recalled. "We would sit around in a circle and talk about food, food, food, as our rations were getting smaller and smaller. We would stamp our feet and walk as much as possible to keep the circulation going."

A young B-29 flier brought in during the winter had been too badly wounded during his shoot down for the Ofuna pharmacist to keep him alive. "I volunteered as one of the group that was asked to bury him, knowing that by doing this I would get a boiled potato as payment," DaSilva stated. "We had to carry him some distance from the camp in deep snow to a hilly wooded area and then dig a deep hole."

The snow and malnutrition took its toll on Commander O'Kane. He contracted beriberi and developed skin ulcers from scurvy that would not heal. In spite of his illness, O'Kane continued to be a role model for his men. Larry Savadkin felt that his skipper was concerned with keeping discipline to protect his men from the Ofuna guards.[17]

During February 1945, the prisoners witnessed a carrier air strike against Japanese mainland targets—a sign that the Philippines had been taken over by the Americans. "A glance to the skies meant a beating from the guards," recalled O'Kane, "but the sight of torpedo bombers just yards away was worth it." Serving as a mess cook, O'Kane could only place a tray of food in the cell of one captured aviator who could not feed himself due to two broken arms. "My request that one of us be allowed to feed him brought knuckle sandwiches. I was removed from mess cooking and do not know his fate."[18]

During the spring, beriberi became a serious threat and two prisoners on each side of the compound died from their illness. Floyd Caverly celebrated his 28th birthday on 1 March 1945. Bill Leibold turned 22 as a prisoner on 4 April 1945. "I knew what day it was, but it was just another day," he recalled.

On 5 April, the Ofuna prisoners were accused of stealing some Red Cross food boxes stored at one end of the barracks. No one confessed and the guards forced them to stand at attention throughout the day in a rainstorm without lunch. "We knew that if anyone did confess, he would probably be taken away and beaten or shot," recalled Clay Decker. When no one had stepped forward by evening meal time, the guards made them get into push-up positions. "If anyone moved, a guard would hit you with a club across the buttocks," Jesse DaSilva stated. "This didn't work, so they took us back inside the barracks and lined us up." After again refusing to acknowledge who had pilfered the Red Cross food, each man was beaten with a club several times.[19]

The next morning, another 19 men were selected to leave Ofuna—including Pappy Boyington and the *Tang* enlisted men. Many, like Jesse DaSilva, were suffering from diarrhea and beriberi. The 19 transferees were moved by train to Yokohama, and then hiked to the Omori district. This transfer left only six American submariners at Ofuna: Ted Reh, Ray Normand, and Robert Berridge from *Perch*, and *Tang*'s three officers.

Fukuoka: November 1944

The 42 *Grenadier* POWs interned at Fukuoka had lost four of their own as their second winter in this work camp approached. Those not placed in the crude sick bay continued to report to the Yawata Steel Mill for their long shifts and poor treatment.

At the mill one day, Al Rupp traded a Marine leather belt he had acquired for extra food. The Japanese guards hung him from the rafters by his wrists with his feet just off the floor through the night. RM1c Bill Keefe recalled that Rupp received special attention as the Japanese "put him on display" to point out their prowess in the art of "how to make an American behave." When he was brought down the next morning he returned to his bunk with his arms numb.[20]

Chuck Ver Valin, a work detail section leader at Fukuoka, had a better mastery of the basic Japanese language than some. He was instrumental in helping to save Chief Charles Whitlock's life. Whitlock, forced to throw all of his Australian money over the side before abandoning ship, continued to gamble in camp.

"Whitlock and others would use their food rations as gambling antes," Ver Valin said. A winning round could cost another prisoner cigarettes or his daily food rations. After some time, Whitlock owed another non-*Grenadier* prisoner a healthy sum of food rations. The chief was on the verge of starving and pleaded with his buddy to help pay off his debt. "I had managed to collect five hundred yen from my work," Ver Valin said. He agreed to try and help pay off the other prisoner. It took some persuading on his part, however. "I finally convinced this other guy that Whitlock was going to die if he didn't get to eat and that he had better take my money. Otherwise, he wouldn't get anything at all."

A much grateful Whitlock promised Ver Valin that he would one day repay him for saving his life. "Although it would be years before I saw that money, it at least taught him to give up the gambling in camp."

Working in a brick kiln during the winter, Rupp was carried back to camp one day with serious cuts and bruises after he fell from a scaffold. The camp doctor examined him and he was put in his bunk space in the *Grenadier* kuti. Tom Courtney and Bill Cunningham helped feed and take care of him that night and the next day. He claimed to have no feeling in his legs and managed to stay in the sick bay for many weeks.[21]

During the time that Rupp was in the hospital, Gordon Cox was brought in due to injury to his eyes. Part of his work in the Yawata pipe shop was to hold parts steady for the Japanese arc welder. "He didn't like POWs, for he took every chance he could to give me a flash with the arc," Cox related. "He got me good a couple of times one day. I woke up in the middle of the night with my eye burning and watering and was completely blind by morning."[22]

In the barracks, Cox remained for several days with a damp cloth over his eyes to relieve the burns. Cox found that Rupp was stretching his semi-paralyzed legs disability as long as he could. As he lay in bed in the barracks, Cox noted Rupp make a trip to the benjo "and came back without a limp. I never could figure out why he went to such lengths to keep from going to work."[23]

During the first week of December, a new colonel replaced Fukuoka's previous commandant. He appeared to be more humane than his predecessor and spoke some English. "He knew of our celebration of Christmas and would allow each kuti to acquire a tree branch," Rupp wrote. With noon rice on 22 December, work details were canceled and there was an orange per man. "This was the first fruit I had eaten since we were captured," Rupp wrote.[24]

Winter brought on increased sickness and death in camp. "Some guys that got beriberi very bad, their stomachs were swollen up until it looked like they would burst," recalled Cox. The medics tried primitive methods of draining some of the swelling but the number of men who fell ill during the early days of 1945 only increased.[25]

"Everyone had beriberi to varying degrees," Cox wrote. This affliction generally caused a water buildup in the body. "The feet and legs would get large during the day when you were on your feet. At night while laying down, it would run back to the rest of the body. Sometime a person would get up in the morning and one side of their face would be puffed up with beriberi, looking very strange all lop-sided."[26]

A severe case of beriberi caused Bernie Witzke's legs to ache as he walked. "From the mill, we rode coal cars part way back, but then had to walk a mile to our camp," he recalled. "My legs were bothering me terribly and the guards finally got tired of waiting on me to limp along." Witzke was taken off the mill detail and given other work at the Fukuoka camp during the next six months.

Skeeter McCoy continued to find himself in trouble with the Fukuoka guards for his efforts in stealing food. "I was young and daring," he related. On one occasion, he and a Wake Island civilian POW were caught stealing beans from the Japanese storeroom. McCoy was taken outside in the bitter winter weather and thrown into one of the water holding tanks outside the barracks. Shipmate John Gunderson recalled, "They dunked him in the tank and then hung him by his thumbs on tiptoes at the front gate naked for all to see as a lesson." McCoy later reflected, "They intended to teach me a lesson, but I didn't learn a thing. I seemed to be in trouble all the time."[27]

Although the winter weather was brutal, the prisoners could see more frequent signs of Allied progress. As the bombing grew nearer in 1945, the camp leader allowed the men to start eating small portions of Red Cross packages. Through civilian workers at the mill, they learned during February that Manila had been retaken. Tom Courtney scrawled in his diary for 22 March 1945, "Alarms regular now. Nips getting hell now." On 1 April, Courtney noted, "Alarms daily and nightly now. Hitting close. Saw my first B-29."[28]

During April, some of the most physically fit men were marched to work on a little farm site five miles from camp. Three manual plow teams worked the ten-acre plot while others hauled fertilizer and water in buckets from wagons. They planted potatoes, squash, turnips, radish, oriental vegetables, and beets. Walking back through town, the men were heckled by the townspeople, calling them names. One day while returning from the garden, however, Al Rupp heard the people calling, "Roosevelt is dead. We killed Roosevelt."[29]

Tom Courtney wrote for 13 April, "Roosevelt died yesterday. God rest him." Gordon Cox was returning from the mill that evening when he noticed a blackboard in camp that announced President Roosevelt's death. "The Japs cheered," he wrote. "They had the idea that his death might end the war. We heard that from many Japs the next day when we went to work."[30]

The guards made them dig an air raid shelter into the side of a hill at the farm site. "There were so many air raid alarms that we didn't get in a full day's work in the steel mill," Cox recorded. The reconnaissance plane known as Photo Joe was seen on a regular basis as he overflew the Japanese cities taking photos. During one air raid, Cox moved too slowly toward the shelter for one Japanese guard, who smashed him between the shoulders with his rifle butt in frustration. He fell to the dirt, face first. "He then made another run and kicked me as I was trying to get up," Cox recalled. "They liked it when they could knock you down, then kick the hell out of you. I got a cracked rib out of that encounter, but there was no one to complain to."[31]

On 30 May, Tom Courtney logged, "Memorial Day. Nothing happened for several days. Maybe lull before storm. All kinds of scuttlebutt coming in about the war and how soon it will end. But it's all bullshit to me." The air strikes ceased until 10 June, when the air raid sirens began going off again. "God, how I pray this would end," Courtney wrote.[32]

More air strikes moved over the Japanese cities during late June. "Everyone had great hope that something would happen, bringing our situation to an end one way or another," Cox wrote. "When that didn't happen, depression started taking over." Some men lost the will to live and their dysentery led to pneumonia.[33]

By July, the POWs found new hope when they could see carrier-based aircraft on occasion in addition to the long-range B-29s. Some planes conducted incendiary runs to start fires. The POWs were in as much danger as the Japanese as they were often caught heading to work during the raids. "The chow is low and getting cut all the time," Tom Courtney wrote in his diary for 22 July. "Scuttle coming in all the time about invasion. If this thing doesn't end soon, these sons-of-bitches will starve us to death. They are all hungry now, too. Too bad." Courtney tried to keep his mind off his hunger by paying visits to his buddy Angus McGowan, who spent three weeks of July hospitalized with severe pneumonia.[34]

By July 1945, the little crematory had more bodies to burn as POWs wasted away and died. Most *Grenadier* men, on average, weighed between 90 to 95 pounds. Al Rupp celebrated his 19th birthday—his third birthday as a POW—on 7 August 1945.[35]

The most fearful air attack on Fukuoka occurred on 8 August during the day. "We were caught totally by surprise," Courtney wrote. "Blew hell out of factory. Incendiary bombs all over, thousands of them." Gordon Cox, at the Yawata mill this day, later recalled, "The first planes over dropped tons of incendiaries in 500-pound canisters." These bombs were spring-loaded. The canisters sprung open while still in the air, throwing numerous small incendiary bombs all over, which started to burn. "There was no way to put them out," Cox wrote. "The mill and the shacks around it were all on fire."[36]

A number of Japanese were killed by the incendiary raid, as well as Cpl. Francis W. Hickey, who was hit directly in the head by a fire bomb. Another POW had his arm so badly burned that the Japanese had to amputate it. "I heard it was cut off with an old wood saw with no anesthetic," Cox related.[37]

The following day, the Japanese kept the prisoners in their barracks while the damage was assessed. The air raid alarms went off five times during the morning hours but the bombers did not return to the area. Bombs fell again during the next couple of days, increasing the rumors that the war must be ending soon. "We kept waiting for reprisals from the guards, but they never came," noted Cox.[38]

Tom Courtney, down to 127 pounds, began scribbling daily in his diary that the factory detail was knocked off for several days during the worst bombing attacks. "This war about over," he wrote on 12 August. "It is so hard to imagine what it will be like to be free again [in] America that is hot dogs, hamburgers and ball games. Freedom and home, the sweetest words in the world."[39]

While the prospects of being liberated soon seem more promising, the real threat remained of being killed by their guards or by the Allied bombing attacks. Courtney maintained his optimism, but penciled a silent prayer for 14 August, "God help us."

21
Omori's "Special Prisoners"

The Omori district, a man-made island which housed hundreds of Allied POWs during World War II, was located on the western shore of Tokyo Bay. During the winter, Omori offered little protection against the cold sea winds. The first U.S. submarine survivors to be transferred from Ofuna on 3 December 1943 into the Omori camp were 13 *Grenadier* enlisted men: Al Albertson, Davis Andrews, Lester Barker, Clyde Barrington, Jewell Embry, Carlisle Herbert, Judd Hinkson, Joe Knutson, Denny Landrum, John Pianka, Paul Russell, Pappy Shaw, and Max Wilson. Arriving with them were *Pope*'s former skipper Lt. Cdr. Welford Blinn, senior *Houston* survivor Al Maher, and *Perch*'s skipper, Lt. Cdr. Dave Hurt.

Cockroaches, fleas, and lice infested the Omori barracks, where the men had no plumbing and slept on platforms raised knee-high above the dirt floor. Two of the aviators kept at Omori were *Enterprise* VT-10 Avenger aircrewmen Mick Glasser and Tom Nelson. "Mick and I were assigned to a railhead-canal facility," related Nelson. "We moved everything from charcoal to pig iron from rail cars to barges and vice versa. The work was about ten hours long and we only got every tenth day off." Glasser found that sneaking food from the Japanese and sabotaging war efforts while on work detail were two of the ways he and his fellow POWs endured their ordeal.[1]

The men who became the most seriously ill were transferred from Omori to the hospital at Shinagawa until they either died or recovered. In April 1944, EM1c Denny "Slim" Landrum nearly died at the Shinagawa hospital in Tokyo where he was transferred for a suspected acute inflammation of the appendix. Dr. Hiroshi

Fuji selected Maj. Alfred A. Weinstein, an American POW who had some surgical training, to assist him with patients. One night during the first week of April, Dr. Weinstein and several Allied doctors were examining Slim Landrum when Dr. Fuji announced that he wanted to operate. Weinstein and his associates protested that Landrum did not have the symptoms of appendicitis. "Dr. Fuji was half drunk," Weinstein wrote.[2]

Dr. Fuji became outraged at their protests and ordered Landrum to be prepped for surgery. Capt. Alex M. Mohnac, Weinstein's assistant, gave Landrum the spinal anesthesia and then the procedure became a nightmare. "Dr. Fuji clumsily slashed through the abdominal wall over the region of the appendix. He searched for it fruitlessly for thirty minutes. He finally let us find it for him. He cut the appendical artery and was unable to control the bleeding. We did. He ripped the normal appendix out by its roots, tearing a hole in the large bowel to which it was attached. Feces oozed through the hole," Weinstein wrote. "He spread the feces liberally throughout the operative field with his clumsy hands." Dr. Weinstein and his comrades took the surgical instruments from Dr. Fuji and finished the operation. The botched process took two and a half hours to remove a normal appendix before the submariner was closed up. "Landrum developed peritonitis, intestinal obstruction, jaundice, and bilateral broncho pneumonia," Dr. Weinstein later wrote. "The wings of the Angel of Death fluttered about him for two weeks. He finally made the grade."[3]

Although Slim Landrum would return to Omori, his health had been damaged permanently. For refusing to do unneeded surgeries on POWs, Dr. Weinstein was sent from the Shinagawa hospital to Omori during the summer of 1944. There, he met Lieutenant Commander Blinn from *Pope* and Lieutenant Commander Hurt from *Perch*. "Dave Hurt was a tall, gray-haired officer," Dr. Weinstein wrote. "The GIs loved him for his kindness. His brother officers respected him for his failure to crack up under beatings and torture at the Ofuna Naval Questioning Camp. Rank to him meant responsibility, not privilege."[4]

One of the most sadistic guards at Omori during 1944 was Sgt. Matsuhiro Watanabe, alias "The Animal" and "The Bird." Watanabe was known to indoctrinate new arrivals, particularly officers, by lining them up at attention and knocking them down several times. TM1c Al Albertson from *Grenadier* learned to avoid Watanabe. "If you saw the bad sergeant coming, you'd just duck around a building and keep out of the way." In spite of his efforts, he was singled out twice for punishment—once for stealing food and once for talking to his fellow crewmen. "I spotted them and went over to talk to them, and he caught me," Albertson said. "That time they just beat me up."[5]

MM1c Max Wilson, another *Grenadier* survivor, became good friends with VT-10 aviator Mick Glasser. "The beloved Father Al Braun was also at Omori and Wilson approached him for information relative to conversion," recalled Glasser. "Father

Braun had managed to hold on to material from the church in the Philippines and Wilson studied with Father Al." Maj. Albert W. Braun, a 56-year-old army chaplain in both World War I and World War II, was decorated with the Purple Heart and two Silver Stars for his courageous service. Captured during the fall of Corregidor, Father Braun insisted on saying mass for the Omori prisoners despite the prohibitions against such service and the abuse he received during 40 months as a POW.

The next group of U.S. submariners to enter Omori was moved out of Ofuna on 30 September 1944. It included three *Grenadier* lieutenants—Sherry, Toulon, and McIntyre—and one enlisted man, Fred Zufelt. With them were Cliff Kuykendall of *Tullibee*, Tony Duva and Bill Whitemore of *S-44*, and Army 1st Lt. Lou Zamperini. As this new group was brought into the compound, they were lined up for inspection by "the Bird," Sergeant Watanabe.

Watanabe stuck a finger in the face of newly arrived gunner's mate Fred Zufelt and said, "You do not stand at attention! You move!" With that, the Bird threatened to strike Zufelt with his sword, but instead punched him squarely in the mouth. Watanabe then stared straight into the eyes of Lou Zamperini. The young aviator looked over the Bird's shoulder to avoid direct eye contact.[6]

The Bird then knocked Zamperini down. "Why you no look in my eyes?" he shouted. When Zamperini took his feet and began staring directly at the Bird, he punched him in the face again. "You no look at me!" Watanabe shouted.

Although Zamperini and Arthur McIntyre spent months interned at Omori, the other six submariners were quickly moved on out on 3 October to Ashio and other camps. *Grenadier's* Lt. Cdr. John Fitzgerald and Lt. George Whiting, and *Sculpin's* Lt. George Brown arrived at Omori about 1000 on 15 January 1945, from Ofuna. Fitzgerald was placed in a bunk room with Ens. Al Mead from *Enterprise* and Lt. Carlton Clark. He found that across the passageway from him was Dave Hurt, *Pope's* Welford Blinn, and Lt. Cdr. Fort Hammond Callahan, a U.S. Navy Corregidor survivor. Fitzgerald was comforted in the fact that cigarettes and tobacco were more abundant. Talking and smoking were allowed. "The food was an improvement over Ofuna, being about 75% barley and 25% rice. The stews were an improvement, also as more vegetables were obtained, approaching the actual quantity as prescribed for us."[7]

Bones and intestines from a slaughterhouse were delivered once a week to add some flavor to the soup-stews. "Work consisted of administration for about sixteen officers and some of the enlisted men," wrote Fitzgerald. "The balance of the officers had gardening work or leather shop duties; the men worked in various warehouses, ship yards or railroad yards in the Tokyo area."[8]

Grenadier's Pappy Shaw recalled that the POWs occasionally received news on the war's progress from a kindly Japanese family who buried food and notes for them near Omori's main fence. On one occasion, Shaw took a soft rock and wrote his name on a railroad car in the shipyards while on a work detail. A Japanese guard caught him in the act and beat him unconscious. Shaw thereafter did his part to hamper war efforts while unloading iron from cargo ships by dropping iron into the ocean when the guards were not looking his way.[9]

Upon arrival at Omori, George Brown was forced to sign papers he believed would register him as a prisoner of war. "Later events showed that I was never registered officially or unofficially as a prisoner of war, nor was my family ever notified," he recalled. After 14 months of captivity, Lieutenant Brown was thus officially still presumed lost. He was assigned to a small, dirt-floor room with Lt. Red Bullard in the back of an Omori barracks. "We were able to steal four or five discarded rice bags which we used as mattresses or floor covering," he said. They were later issued four small torn and filthy blankets. Bullard and Brown slept in all of their clothes during the bitter winter. Their requests for more clothes, medicine, or fire were met with severe beatings. Their hands and feed were crippled with frostbite and Brown struggled with colds and pneumonia.

"To obtain rations necessary to live, we were forced to work at Omori in a leather shop, which was not heated," he stated. When he overslept for a shift of sewing canteen covers, Brown was "forced to stand at attention for eight hours in front of the administration building. The temperature was about 18 degrees [with] a biting wind." He was soon freezing to death. Another prisoner smuggled a bowl of life-saving hot soup to the officer in the camp head. Years later, Brown related that the cold weather abuse caused him to "get a severe case of pneumonia and I still have scars on my lungs as a result."[10]

Being located right in Tokyo Harbor, Omori's camp was in the line of any incoming Allied bombers. One of the biggest air shows came on 16 February 1945. The prisoners had just sat down to their barley and soup at 0645, when the sirens began sounding. "I rushed out to the fence and found a knothole through which I could see the municipal airport a little over a mile away," wrote Fitzgerald. "What a show that was to see those planes diving on the airport, release their bombs and send the hangars and planes up in pieces and flame." The POWs at Omori were entertained by the carrier strikes for two days.[11]

On 1 March, about 45 officers were transferred from Omori to various other camps. George Brown was transferred to Mitsushima POW Camp 2-D, while John Fitzgerald and 14 others were sent to Camp 4-B at Naoetsu, located about 250 miles northwest of Tokyo. The next American submarine survivors moved into Ofuna were the six *Tang* enlisted men, who arrived in April 1945, along with Pappy Boyington and a dozen airmen. "Upon arrival at Omori, we all were assembled in front of the Omori commandant's building and were directed to remove all clothing that had been provided to us by the IJN at Ofuna," recalled Boats Leibold.

After stripping, the 19 newest Omori prisoners were given used trousers and shirts. "The commandant and his top non-com, Sergeant Ogura, looked us over and advised that we were not POWs but were special prisoners," said Leibold. The American submariners and aviators rated special attention from the Japanese. "Our group was taken to a long building that resembled a warehouse," Leibold continued. The "special prisoners" were watched by two guards, one in the room with them and one posted outside the entrance door.

Meals were served to the submariners in their special barracks three times a day. The most customary dish was a bowl of milo maize grain, mixed with barley or rice, and a bowl of soup—still referred to as "all-dump" by the POWs. "Sometimes we'd get a few pieces of fish, but we never received any meat," recalled Jesse DaSilva. Bill Leibold later described confinement at Ofuna.

> From time to time, we would be lined up in front of the platforms and "visitors" would be brought in to look us over. Their escort would point out individuals such as submarine men, naval flier, etc. The only morale booster was the increasing bombing raids. If a man had need of the toilet, he was to approach the guard, bow, and request, "dozo, benjo kudasai." The guard would then give the individual a small wooden "ticket," call to the outside guard, and open the door. The prisoner would then bow and then hand the outer guard his "ticket" and proceed to the outer door and down the side of the building to the benjo located at the rear, escorted by a guard. Quite an experience for those with dysentery!

The *Tang* men were kept in their barracks during their first month at Omori, although Pappy Boyington lobbied to get them out on work detail. American B-29s lit up the skies over Tokyo during the month with bombing raids. The explosions and anti-aircraft fire could be heard and felt some 800 feet across the channel from the mainland in Omori.[12]

Finally, in early May, the *Tang* prisoners were allowed to go out on work detail to clear debris and work on growing gardens. Sergeant Ogura lectured the special prisoners before they were allowed to go out to work. "If we worked hard, we would get two-thirds of the rations of what they gave the prisoners," Leibold stated. "That was the first time we knew that we were only getting half of what they gave the prisoners."

The POWs expressed their concern to Ogura about working barefooted. When they were lined up outside of their barracks, they found many extra pairs of shoes—taken from men who would not be working that day. "We would go through the shoes and try to get a pair that fit us pretty well," said Leibold. "When we came back in from work, we turned the shoes back in to them. From the time I was captured, I never wore shoes regularly."

From Omori, the prisoners were marched across the island's causeway to the mainland where they worked on clearing up sheet metal, wood, and other debris from the extensive bomb damage the city had suffered. One of the main guards during these work details into the city was nicknamed "Gimpy," an English-speaking Japanese man who had been badly wounded during his Army service.

"Soon after Gimpy took over, he asked why we were so dirty," Leibold related. "Of course, we told him we had no means of bathing. On return to Omori that evening, Gimpy stopped us in front of the Commandant's building." After a discussion with the colonel and Sergeant Ogura, Gimpy was allowed to march the *Tang* enlisted men and their companions to the bathhouse to clean up. It was their first bath in nearly two months.

While out on such work details, Floyd Caverly was stunned to witness the treatment that the Japanese Army officers handed out to their own enlisted men. Standing around a little fire of burning lumber one day to keep warm, he watched a young Japanese on a bicycle stop to light a cigarette on the POWs' fire. A nearby Army private chastised the young Japanese man for approaching the prisoners. Caverly watched as the guard first beat "the hell out of him" and then casually asked how the man's family was doing. Caverly found the whole incident to be very strange but felt such abuse was just "typical Japanese."

Some of the *Grenadier* men were moved from Omori in the late spring. TM3c John Leskovsky related, "On 30 May 1945, I was moved to Camp Ten-D; stayed there until the end of the war. Here I took a severe beating about 10 days before the war was over. He used a club on me and really gave me a bad beating. Yet he had no cause to do so."

In the barracks, *Tang*'s Clay Decker ended up being bunkmates with Pappy Boyington. He later recalled that the former Black Sheep squadron leader used some of his Japanese yen to purchase a fish from a scared Japanese civilian he confronted. Boyington and Decker ate the fish raw—a meal which proved to be the submariner's only meat dish during his entire captivity.[13]

Boyington, Decker, and others worked on a little vegetable garden in a bombed-out area of Yokohama. Fertilized with human excrement which the prisoners dipped from the tanks and hauled to the gardens, the little field provided some nourishment for the prisoners. Those assigned to collect the human waste dubbed themselves "honey dippers" as they cleaned out the cement collection bowls within the ruins of destroyed buildings. Although Jesse DaSilva was not well enough to work, he came along with a five-gallon jug of water to make tea for the others.[14]

Some of the garden workers slipped away one day and acquired fish from a nearby fish market with money. "I boiled them in the can of water," DaSilva said. "We tried to sneak them back into camp for our evening meal, but the smell of the cooked fish alerted the guards." Other times, DaSilva picked through garbage behind buildings. "When you're starving, anything tastes good," he said. One day while on tea break, an old dog wandered by the group, who debated on whether to kill it for food. "None of us had the heart to kill it," he admitted.[15]

In June 1945, the three *Tang* officers—Dick O'Kane, Larry Savadkin, and Hank Flanagan—were finally transferred out of Ofuna to Omori. O'Kane's health was declining rapidly. His work detail at Omori consisted of stacking roof tiles and sheet metal left over from bombing raids.

On Sunday mornings, Dave Hurt used shears and clippers to help barber his fellow inmates. "He quietly told us the news," Dr. Weinstein recalled as he sat before the sub skipper barber. Hurt and Lieutenant Commander Blinn picked up various bits of war intelligence, which they disseminated to their "customers" each Sunday.[16]

The lenient guard nicknamed Gimpy was replaced during the summer by a tough Army guard with thick lips and buck teeth—nicknamed "Horseface" by the POWs. Boats Leibold considered Horseface "a miserable, mean SOB who never missed an opportunity to work a prisoner over" while on work detail. When he caught Larry Savadkin with a pair of pliers that belonged to a civilian, Horseface accused the *Tang* officer of stealing them. He beat Savadkin nearly unconscious with the pliers.[17]

As war drew closer to Omori, some prisoners grew tired of the abuse from the Japanese guards. *Tang*'s Floyd Caverly was struggling one day to haul a cartload of cucumbers for a guard who was not impressed with his speed.

"Kurah!" he hollered for the POW to speed up.

"It was raining, it was damned cold, and it was miserable outside," Caverly recalled. "I said back to him, 'Kurah, my ass. I'm not pushing any harder.'"

The Japanese guard instinctively made a jab at Caverly with his bayonet, thinking the American would jump away. "It was more or less a bluff, but I didn't jump out of the way," he recalled. "I didn't give a damn if he jabbed me with that bayonet or not." The guard's bayonet stuck Caverly in the leg, an injury which would fester and later become infected.

On 5 July, Caverly, Leibold, Royal Navy CPO Charles C. Rogers, and Cpl. Author Hendrix Gill were detailed to go out in a small boat from Omori into the bay. Accompanied by a guard, they were ordered to retrieve large logs and move them ashore onto the beach at their camp. "The guard sat in the bow while one of us would row and the other would capture a log," Leibold described. "Caverly and I were in the same boat and our guard was pretty nervous. I don't think he could swim."

Leibold was allowed to get into the bay and push the heavy logs while Caverly, nursing his bayonet wound, rowed. "Rogers and Gill followed suit, with Gill swimming," said Leibold. "Gill told us later that he had gotten some mussels off the causeway pilings." Corporal Gill, who had been suffering from dysentery and malnutrition, became violently ill that night and died in camp in spite of the fact that

Greg Boyington tried to get him some proper medical aid. Although Captain Lloyd H. Goad, an American doctor being held with the POWs, attempted to revive Gill by administering glucose, it was too late.[18]

"I think it was the mussels that did him in," Leibold offered. "We only did that work one day." Leibold suffered from hepatitis, but he and his skipper continued to be sent out on work details during July. Commander O'Kane was in worse health, suffering from hepatitis, jaundice, and beriberi late in the war.

During mid-July, a work party that included Boyington, O'Kane, and Leibold was detailed to enlarge a cave that would serve as a bomb shelter. The party descended 50 feet into the mountainside and toiled all day digging cross tunnels. "I think this is where some of the timber rescued from the bay was used for shoring," Leibold later stated. O'Kane wrote, "Thirty of us had been detailed for this daylight-to-dark work, but by the end of the second week only ten of us could even walk the six miles to the site."[19]

As war grew closer to Omori, the prisoners witnessed incendiary raids on Yokohama. "It was frightening as bombs were dropping all around and some fragments ended up in camp," DaSilva stated. "There was one consolation in knowing the end must be near." Clay Decker related, "It looked to us like the world was coming to an end. Ashes from the burning buildings fell on our camp like black snow. The guards were not too pleased with what our fliers had done, so they were especially cruel to us over the next couple of weeks."[20]

Pete Narowanski was a member of the daily working parties. During one bombing attack, he and a buddy sneaked into an air raid shelter, where they stole packages of noodles. Narowanski and his friend carried some of these noodles with them on their last work detail before the cease-fire.

As Pappy Boyington worked on digging cave tunnels in early August, one of the Japanese noncoms tried to tell his group about a single bomb dropped on Nagasaki. Although the Japanese guard knew nothing about the previous Hiroshima bomb, he informed them that his family and other people were dying from the effects of one amazing bomb that had wiped out the city.[21]

"I couldn't fathom at first that it was only one bomb he was talking about," recalled Boyington. "I thought it was just some more Japanese propaganda. But he said no, that his family had lived in the city of Nagasaki, and that only one bomb had been dropped on the city." In a matter of days, Omori's resident prisoners of war would find that the mysterious bomb would forever change the course of the war in Japan.

22
The Ashio Mining Camp

Located in the mountains north from Tokyo, Ashio Camp 9-B was a mining camp for Allied POWs that came to house more than three dozen U.S. submarine survivors during 1944 and 1945. The camp was at an elevation of 2,000 feet, located at the headwaters of the Watarase River in Ashio. Total camp strength as of 24 January 1944 was 252 Dutch men, plus one British and one American medical orderly.[1]

Two days later, another 21 POWs were moved to Ashio. The group included 17 U.S. submariners released from Ofuna two days prior. Five were *Grenadier* survivors: Lou Poss, John McBeath, George Stauber, Bill Wise, and Pete Zucco. Another dozen were from *Sculpin*: Cecil Baker, Bill Cooper, Leo Eskildsen, Mike Gorman, Ed Keller, Harry Milbourne, Paul Murphy, Ed Ricketts, Moon Rocek, Harry Toney, Eldon Wright, and Bob Wyatt. A dire need for raw copper had compelled the Japanese to reopen the Ashio mine in 1943 after an eight-year hiatus.[2]

The POW camp at Ashio 9-B was run by 47-year-old Lt. Shigeru Numajiri, a former school principal. "He was about 5 feet 6 inches tall, of heavy build, [and] wore glasses," Pete Zucco recalled of Numajiri.[3]

"We were given three wood pulp Japanese blankets, which were never enough to keep us warm," Zucco stated. The *Grenadier* and *Sculpin* POWs found the barracks to be overrun with rats. "Sanitary conditions, especially outside the latrine, were very dirty and poor, as was medical treatment," stated 18-year-old *Grenadier* fireman Cecil Baker from Indianapolis. "They would not issue any medicine. The barracks floors were of dirt and covered with lice. We slept on straw mats about a foot off the ground. Although they permitted us to write letters, they immediately burned them behind the barracks."

The submariners began mine duty the day after their arrival. Issued carbide head lanterns, 80 POWs were led across a narrow river bridge through the streets of the mining community. The mine entrance, a square hole with railroad tracks leading into it, was at the rear of the little town. At the mine entrance was a Japanese shrine that the prisoners were ordered to bow before, upon entering or leaving the mine. "You asked the shrine to protect you from disasters in the mine each day," recalled Ed Keller. After becoming initiated by the small earthquake tremors that would occasionally be felt within the mine, Moon Rocek related, "we said our own prayers at the shrine."[4]

The POWs were put to work "mucking" ore, breaking it and shoveling it into small mine cars that pulled the rock from the bowels of the mine. "We had to descend about 300 feet, with barely enough air to breathe," said Paul Murphy. "We got one day off every two weeks and on our day off we had to chop wood and haul it in for the Jap guards."

Torpedoman Harry Toney worked as a driller. "There was one boss who always carried a hammer who was very cruel," he recalled. "If you didn't work, you missed out on meals." Bill Cooper, suffering from the back injury incurred in his submarine's sinking, said, "Each man was required to muck eight tons of ore per day. My back was killing me as we loaded those cars."

Rocek found one of the few privileges of being at Ashio was in sending out mail. "Don't worry about me. I am all right," he wrote to his parents. "Think and dream a lot of you and of times past and future." Optimism faded when this proved to be the only letter he was ever allowed to send out.[5]

"You were always leery of the overhead, which occasionally would shed rocks," Rocek related. "One day about five of us were sitting down taking a break and felt sand drifting down from above. We scattered quickly but one man had his leg broken by a huge rock that fell from the overhead."

In order to fill eight mine cars per day, Rocek and his pals "learned to be able sometimes to arrange flat rocks in the copper car to make it appear full. After months of getting away with this, they caught on and they would tap the side of the car. If it sounded hollow, they dumped the car over and made us refill it."

The POWs stole grain as they could and cooked it with their carbide mining lamps. Four of the worst Ashio guards were: Takashi Neishi, a former infantryman; Imajiria Kira, nicknamed "Three Fingers" due to having lost a thumb and small finger in a premature grenade explosion; former army lieutenant Shigeo Eizumi, nicknamed "Four Eyes" due to his thick glasses; and former miner Takayoshi Shinkae, who was known as "Blue Coat."[6]

Four Eyes and another guard nicknamed "The Slugger" frequently beat the POWs who were caught stealing food. Three Fingers, in charge of the Red Cross boxes and clothing, "was responsible for beating several men who exchanged their shirts after they had received an incorrect size," recalled Cecil Baker.

Paul Murphy saw a brutal Japanese sergeant "rope several of the men up by their thumbs, pull their legs, and beat them severely. I saw him beat a fellow for not having his shoes shined. He hit me across the face once with a kit similar to a small traveling bag for having my hands in my pockets."

Grenadier's George Stauber, a non-smoker before the loss of his ship, took up smoking just to deal with the stress. The unsanitary living conditions, strenuous mine labor, poor food rations, cold weather, and rampant illnesses claimed lives during February and March. "When you came to camp at night, if there was a dead man, everybody stood death parade," said Ed Keller. "The POWs would be put in two rows and the cart was pulled between them and you would know who died."[7]

Bill Cooper daydreamed about a plan to escape from Ashio. He considered scaling the camp fence at night, hiking over the mountains, and making his way to the coast with some of his *Sculpin* shipmates. Thoughts of this escape plan vanished when the Japanese guards warned that if any man escaped from camp, all of his friends would be killed.[8]

The next group of 17 prisoners transferred from Ofuna to Ashio arrived in March 1944. Two of these men were U.S. submariners, Lt. Kevin Harty and warrant officer John Walden from *Grenadier*. This brought the number of submariners at Ashio in late March to 12 *Sculpin* men, two *Grenadier* officers, and five *Grenadier* enlisted men.[9]

The March arrivals to Ashio included two American medics and a U.S. Army doctor, 1st Lt. Basil B. Durbin, who had been captured at Bataan in 1942. Dr. Durbin and his fellow corpsmen treated the Ashio prisoners as best they could. Detailed to blast apart a large boulder atop a muck pile, Ed Keller was hurt when the rock split and sent him tumbling down a 30-foot-tall muck pile. He lost some teeth in the fall and smashed one of his hands.[10]

Sculpin's George Rocek appreciated Dr. Durbin. "My wound in the left shinbone area began to get worse and smell," he said. "The Army medic had secreted a few sulfa tablets and used them only in emergencies. He ground one up and sprinkled it on my wound every day, and eventually it healed. A year later, I had a small piece of metal work out of my left knee."[11]

On 15 July 1944, four American officers, four Australian officers, and 22 American enlisted men arrived at Ashio from Ofuna. This group included RAAF pilot Geoffrey Lempriere, *Yorktown* aviators Kal Kalberg and Gordon Marshall, Lt. John Critchlow from *Grenadier*, and enlisted men from two U.S. submarines. From *Grenadier*'s crew, the new arrivals included Lynn Clark, Bob Palmer, Charlie Erishman, Carl Quarterman, Buck Withrow, and Charlie Westerfield. In addition, the balance of *Sculpin*'s enlisted men also arrived: Ed Anderson, Joe Baker,

Bill Haverland, Leo Murray, Julius Peterson, John Rourke, Joe Thomas, and Paul Todd.[12]

This made a total of 34 U.S. submariners at Ashio: all 20 *Sculpin* enlisted men, 11 *Grenadier* enlisted men, and three *Grenadier* officers. "Seven of us went to work at the copper smelter, which was pretty bad work on a man's lungs," stated Joe Baker. "There were lots of gas and sulphur fumes."

Chief Bill Haverland, a 28-year-old *Grenadier* POW from Iowa, found that Ashio contained about 280 prisoners upon his arrival. He found that the POWs' daily food was about "700 grams of dry rice and barley that was split up in three meals, and the soup was practically water. Now and then, you'd get a little piece of fish, once every six weeks or so." The men were occasionally given a half-inch square piece of horse meat. "We were weighed about every month during the time I was there," said Haverland. "I seemed to lose about six pounds per month."

During mid-August, 150 American Army survivors of the Bataan Death March were moved into Ashio. *Sculpin*'s Ed Keller recalled them bringing in "books, instruments, accordions, violins, clarinets, mouth organs, guitars, bongos" and other items which made their evenings more tolerable.[13]

Lieutenant Numajiri found little use for the senior officers at Ashio. On 25 August, all American and Australian officers were transferred with the exception of pilot Geoffrey Lempriere and *Grenadier*'s John Walden. Two lieutenants, Harty and Critchlow, were moved to another camp at Zentsuji.[14]

Two of the newly arrived *Sculpin* POWs, Ed Ricketts and Julian Peterson, protested against working in the Ashio mine. Ricketts stated, "They beat us, then sent us to a factory in the town." Strong winter winds often blew over the sulphur vats, causing some of the Korean workers to pass out. "I got tired of this, so one day Peterson and I decided not to work anymore. We crapped out between the boilers. They wouldn't give us any chow and knocked us around," Ricketts testified. The factory guards could not understand this American arrogance and finally became tired of beating Peterson and Ricketts.

Gunner John Rourke's job was to load and unload copper ore used to feed the blast furnaces. "On numerous occasions while at this work, I was beaten by Japanese civilian work bosses, Honchos," he said. On one occasion—suffering from dysentery—his feet were badly swollen and Rourke complained to a Honcho that he was too sick to work. "To this statement concerning my feet and general condition, the Jap civilian replied that I was not weak and beat me with his fists about the face and body, knocking me to the ground." En route to the mines, Rourke was beaten several other times and he witnessed The Slugger beat Charlie Erishman from *Grenadier* severely on another occasion.

Private Basillio Rodriguez was the first American to die at Ashio on 18 September 1944. He was standing beneath an ore chute when a guard ordered a railcar to be dumped into the chute above him. His cause of death was listed as "fracture of base of cranium and the right head bone." Although a formal investigation cleared the guards, some of the POWs believed that Rodriquez's death was nothing short of murder.[15]

Yeoman Bob Palmer later stated, "General treatment in working camps [was] abhorable. All men who died were cremated. Food conditions during last six months of war were acute. The Jap civilians were starving, too. Morale was rock-bottom and thoughts and dreams were of food."

"I was stealing them blind," Ed Ricketts said. "I worked in the commandant's onion patch and stole all of his onions. We had a gang working that was always outfoxing the Japs. When there would be an air raid, we'd break into the Korean storehouse and steal as much as we could. We'd go to the Japs' mess hall while everyone was in the air raid shelter and steal all their rice. We had a fine crew and the guys really showed the guts they had."

The next group of submarine survivors to reach Ashio 9-B included *Tullibee*'s Cliff Kuykendall, *Grenadier*'s Fred Zufelt and Tony Duva, and Bill Whitemore from *S-44*.

Released from Ofuna on 30 September 1944, they were taken to Omori and remained there until 3 October. Among the officers transferred at the same time as these men were three *Grenadier* officers and Lt. Jim Condit from the *Yorktown* air group. Aboard the train to Ashio, Kuykendall was treated to a rice ball from a courteous Japanese guard. He noticed that it was wrapped in a copy of the English-language *Nippon Times* newspaper. "The rice left a stain, but I read about the Japanese shooting down a bunch of American planes at Saipan and in the Marianas," Kuykendall recalled. The propaganda-slanted news offered the POW his first real outside reporting of the war.

"As long as anyone was at Ofuna, they were never listed as POWs," said Kuykendall. "It was only after we were sent to a labor camp that we were listed as POWs." On 22 October, Whitemore, Duva, and other American and Canadian POWs were able to send short messages over the Tokyo radio via the International Red Cross. "Hello, Mom and Dad," Whitemore said. "I am in good health and look forward to your letters. Say hello to all the family and friends. Notify Allen and his wife that I am all right and hope to be home again. Lots of love. William F. Whitemore, USN."

Twelve different listeners picked up the broadcast and relayed the word back to the United States. Mr. and Mrs. Truman Whitemore in Morrison, Illinois, were informed of the happy news that their son was no longer missing in action but officially a POW. Vice Adm. Randall Jacobs telegrammed the Whitemores on 24 October, "I share in your pleasure because your son's whereabouts has been determined."

Tony Duva sent a personal message back to his brother Joe in Altoona, Pennsylvania. "Dear Joe, I am glad to have the opportunity to send this message letting you know that I am fine. Please don't worry about me." The brief message ended by Duva sending his love to his other family members, Reggie, Ruby, Betty, Vera, and Minnie. Like Whitemore, he was careful to slip in specific family names that would certainly authenticate his message. The *S-44* messages were picked up and printed in both servicemen's hometown papers, the *Whiteside County News* and *Altoona Mirror*.

Shortwave radio operators also heard the name of Cliff Kuykendall from the long-lost *Tullibee* read out during October. Hearing Kuykendall's name and his home address in Wichita Falls, Texas, TSgt. John H. Sanders on Guam sent a letter to Kuykendall's family.

With these latest arrivals, Ashio now housed three dozen former American submariners: 20 *Sculpin* men, two from *S-44*, one from *Tullibee*, 12 *Grenadier* enlisted men, and one warrant officer.

Kuykendall found that Ashio's "barracks were constructed flimsy, full of lice, fleas, rats, and unheated in the winter. Prisoners working in the mine were beaten by the Jap work foremen if they didn't like the way the prisoners were working," he stated.

When the prisoners were allowed a day off work twice a month, they were subjected to barracks inspections. The POWs were made to kneel on their pallets as the guards walked through, smashing a man with their gun butts if his fingers were touching the railings. *Sculpin*'s GM2c Bob Wyatt became angered at this and leapt from his second tier bunk onto the guards. "He convinced them he was crazy," recalled shipmate Ed Keller. "So, from then on, they went down the barracks on the opposite side from Wyatt."[16]

John Walden from *Grenadier* later testified:

> In the fall of 1944, the food was so scarce that about 90 percent of the camp was so sick they could no longer work and about 20 percent of the men lost the use of their legs completely. Then a Japanese doctor from Tokyo examined everyone in the camp and sent about 80 percent of the prisoners back to work. The Japanese would not allow us enough hot water, even an ounce a day, with which to wash the food containers.

George Rocek found that ground-up horse bones were considered a treat. "These were boiled for a week to make them soft and then rationed out to the men," he said. "One of our camp cooks was Tony Duva from the *S-44*. Most had a difficult time adjusting to the food, having the runs quite often."

On Christmas eve 1944, the Ashio inmates received Red Cross parcels. "We prisoners received about 60% of the food and the Japanese commanding officers and

Japanese guards took the rest," said Charlie Erishman, a 37-year-old Pennsylvania native from *Grenadier*. "We prisoners received none of the blankets. We prisoners got vitamin pills but none of the other Red Cross medical supplies."

By early 1945, most all of the *Sculpin* men were suffering from beriberi, dysentery, and diarrhea. U.S. Army doctor Durbin administered B1 shots to help keep the beriberi under control. "For beriberi, they'd starve you out for a couple of days and not give you anything to eat," said Bill Haverland. "My legs would swell up to about twice their normal size. My face would swell up, and my joints would get rather stiff." When the beriberi caused legs to swell too much, the men would be taken off the mine detail for several days.

"We got 450 grams wet rice per meal per person with side dish of fish intestines," said *Grenadier* commissary steward Charlie Westerfield, who worked in the Ashio galley. "Working parties gathered weeds for side dishes and soup." Every two months, Westerfield was issued horse bones for his soup. "The guards got 250 grams of dry rice per meal and all the sugar they wanted." By comparison, between December 1944 and August 1945, Westerfield and his cooks were only allowed 60 pounds of sugar for all inmates.

Shipmate Bob Palmer considered Westerfield "a straight-forward, honest man. His days in the Ashio camp were without heavy incident because Charlie knew how to outsmart the Japanese guards. He kept his mouth shut and did his work."[17]

During the winter, Chief Motor Machinist's Mate Erishman found the prisoners' "clothing was particularly inadequate. Twenty-three Javanese or Dutch prisoners died the first winter because of inadequate clothing, no medical care or heat. In the winter, the temperature at Ashio went as low as 16 degrees Fahrenheit below zero." The prisoners trusted Erishman to dish out the maize fairly and procure a shaving blade. "I never knew how many men shaved with Charlie's blade, but he had a way of sharpening it after each of us used it," said Bob Palmer. "Things never seemed to get too tough for him."[18]

The men worked the Ashio mine each day until their prescribed quota was met. "Near the end of the month, the shifts would be lengthened as much as four hours per shift until the quota was filled," recalled John Walden. Some tried to keep their sense of humor. As *Grenadier*'s Pete Zufelt drilled blower holes in the copper mine, he would draw upon his German ancestry by announcing, "I am Baron von Zufelt of the undersea-bottom, Svinzen." A shipmate recalled him proclaiming such statements "not without a small amount of pride I think, being German and all."[19]

Cliff Kuykendall turned to singing to pass his time in the mine. He worked closely with a British soldier, loading ore cars by hand and pushing them toward the mine entrance. "The only song I could remember the words to was 'Deep Purple,' which is kinda a sad song," he reflected. "The British soldier learned the words to it and sang it with me."

In the smelter, gunner Walden found that "chemicals gave off a dense sulphurous smoke and gas which was very painful to the eyes and lungs. Prisoners were forced to work in this with a mask, with either cotton or gauze as a filter, which was of little or no help. After working a shift, some of the prisoners would be so sick they could not eat."

By early 1945, fewer POWs were able to work due to beriberi. Lieutenant Numajiri lined up the prisoners outside their barracks in the cold for inspection from a senior Japanese doctor. "About twelve men at a time had to line up before him," recalled Moon Rocek. "We were naked and told to do six knee bends. From this, he designated about 30 men that were to work."[20]

The poor treatment led to deaths at Ashio. Bataan survivor Pvt. George Frederic Gallion, suffering from beriberi and malnutrition, was often targeted for abuse. Charlie Erishman watched the demise of Gallion. "A number of times when I saw Gallion he had been beaten at work," he recalled. "He was bruised and had cuts on his face, back and legs." Cecil Baker, a bunkmate of Gallion, recalled the soldier was severely punished for stealing food. "He was beaten and deprived of his rations and because of his weakened condition, he caught pneumonia."

Erishman saw Gallion beaten in the face by a civilian guard with a three-inch leather belt while standing at attention in front of Lieutenant Numajiri's office. Numajiri—known as "The Goat"—also struck Gallion in the face with his hands. John Walden recalled that Gallion "kept losing weight but couldn't get permission to get off work and finally, one night in January 1945, he collapsed."

Sick with a high fever, Gallion was sent into the cold mines on 29 January against the protests of Dr. Durbin. Blue Coat forced him to load coal until he could no longer move. *Sculpin*'s Ed Keller and other POWs helped carry Gallion on his back at 2200. "All the way back, I belittled him because he had traded meals for cigarettes. He was dying of malnutrition. I had the compassion to carry him but I was very angry that he was dying."[21]

Gallion was unsuccessfully worked on by Durbin, two corpsmen, and *Sculpin* pharmacist Paul Todd through the night. "The patient never recovered consciousness and died at 0807 January 30, 1945," logged Dr. Durbin.[22]

"The Japanese said at the time that Gallion had died of a heart attack," said John Rourke. Private Gallion was the second American to die at Ashio. Charlie Erishman took on the grim task of fashioning small, cigar-sized boxes to use for the burial of POW ashes.[23]

"We knew the Japanese interpreter [Kiichi Katoku] by the nickname of 'Quack' or 'The Interpreter,'" recalled Erishman. Guard Shigeo Eizumi ("Four Eyes") "would go out of his way to beat a prisoner," said Walden. "Imajiro Kira ('Three Fingers') was a camp nuisance. He had charge of part of the clothing and would go through all the barracks while the prisoners were at work, removing what he thought they didn't need. When the prisoners' belongings did not check with his books, the prisoners would be beaten." Three Fingers and supply clerk Shozo Takahashi ("The Old Man") were notorious for withholding Red Cross supplies. "The Japanese threw away food many times in their garbage," testified Erishman. "The food was very inadequate, consisting of rice, barley and Korean corn, all of which was mixed up and looked like our chicken feed."

Winter was brutal at Ashio's Camp 9-B. "Due to the fact that there were holes in the roofs, the snow used to pile up on the blankets of the prisoners during the night while they were sleeping," stated John Rourke. "I only had two blankets, so I slept in all my clothes trying to keep warm," recalled Cliff Kuykendall. During the quiet hours in the barracks lying on his top tier bunk, he tried to console some of the more disillusioned Bataan Death March survivors by telling them that America would certainly win the war. During the worst stretch of winter, an army soldier slept beside Kuykendall so they could stay warmer from the shared body heat. "I had never had lice before but after I started bunking beside him, I came down with the lice and never could get rid of them," he related.

Kuykendall was caught stealing wood on one occasion for the camp cooks to use to warm the POWs' food. He broke off boards from a rickety fence near the mess hall, carried them to the Javanese prisoner cook and announced, "We have wood now. Warm that food up." A half hour later, Three Fingers and another guard questioned the cooks on their firewood source.

"They hauled me to the little guard shack by the main gate," Kuykendall recalled. He was locked in a shack to endure the cold winter night's elements. About 15 minutes later, a fellow POW offered him a blanket to ward off pneumonia. Three Fingers and camp interpreter Katoku pulled Kuykendall from his shack and stood him at attention. "Three Fingers lectured me for ten minutes while the interpreter told me what he was saying. He warned me that if I ever stole wood and destroyed a fence again, I would be beaten severely."

Some prisoners received mail at Ashio, but few of the letters they were allowed to write were mailed. Australian Geoffrey Lempriere told John Rourke "he found the remains of torn and burnt postcards that prisoners had written the previous evening for mailing to the United States." Rourke found that the POWs' food "was often filled with maggots, which caused diarrhea and dysentery."

On 1 March 1945, *Grenadier* officer Lt. Arthur McIntyre was moved to Ashio to oversee the camp conditions. He had spent six months at Omori before arriving with PhM John McBeath, who had been sent to the Shinagawa Hospital Camp for treatment of beriberi during the spring. McIntyre was shocked at the conditions upon arrival at Ashio.

Snow was about one or two feet deep on the group, the barracks were cold and dirty; and I was barely able to recognize men whom I had known well only a few months previously. The prisoners looked like wild men. They were not shaven, their hair was extremely long, and both their bodies and their clothes were filthy. They had not been able to take a bath for several weeks because the camp's water supply was disrupted.

McIntyre also found that "the fleas increased to an unbelievable and unbearable number. If I walked at a normal rate from one end of the barracks to the other end inside the building my legs to a point above the knees would be covered with fleas in a concentration of about one per square inch of my skin." At one point, the Japanese provided the prisoners with a weak flea powder. McIntyre tried placing some fleas in the bottle as a test. The next day, however, "the fleas were still spryly hopping around."

Pete Zucco, suffering from dysentery during March, had to make several trips to the latrine one day while working in the Ashio mines. "Blue Coat and the other two guards started slapping me in the face and yelling at me because I was always leaving my work," he stated. "I told them the food the Japanese fed me was no good."

Zucco was beaten with a club by Blue Coat while another guard beat him with a cutress, a tool used for raking the ore. "I was knocked to the ground at least three times and then dragged to my feet and beaten some more," he said. "Several of the blows on my back were so hard that I suffered a severe pain for several months. Several blows were struck while I was lying on the ground." After more than 20 minutes of this abuse, Zucco was dismissed back to work.

In late March, the Ashio guards allowed distribution of some Red Cross clothing that had been received some time before. Japanese guard Takahashi ("The Old Man") dispensed clothing on a merit system, rewarding prisoners whom he felt had worked the hardest. "No consideration was given to the needs of the individual prisoners," related McIntyre. "Attempts to reason with the Japanese on this matter were futile."

Around 1 April, the Japanese distributed Red Cross toothbrushes, shoe polish, tooth powder, toilet paper, razor blades, hair clippers, combs, and shoelaces. Lieutenant McIntyre later convinced his Japanese superiors to allow the men to use two softballs, a softball bat, a basketball, and a violin he had discovered in a storeroom. Around 17 May, he was also able to take delivery of 71 books contributed by the YMCA and Red Cross for the men to read in their off hours.

McIntyre complained to a visiting Japanese colonel during May about the camp food and succeeded in getting extra soybeans distributed to his men. During the spring months, prisoners were allowed to scavenge for tender green leaves to serve as vegetables—which were found to cause much diarrhea. On other occasions, Camp 9-B was given fish heads and entrails of small sand sharks. "This fish was either in a state of decomposition or had been treated with ammonia for it gave off such a strong odor of ammonia that it would almost bring tears to our eyes," said

McIntyre. Most men were unable to stomach the shark heads and entrails because of the diarrhea that they caused. On a few occasions, dried or salted fish "full of maggots and worms" was brought into Ashio.

Pete Zucco developed pneumonia and a high fever from his dysentery in April. When his work in the mines slowed, Blue Coat "started beating me with his fists and club" in the head, arms, and body until he collapsed. Covered with bruises and welts, Zucco was returned to work 15 minutes after his beating. The next day, he was placed on the sick list due to his high fever. "The only treatment which I received was the hot towels administered by the prisoner of war first aid men," Zucco related.

Arthur McIntyre went to Lieutenant Numajiri on 1 June 1945 to request the remainder of the 39 Red Cross food parcels from the storeroom. The previous week, however, Three Fingers told *Grenadier* officer John Walden that only 32 of these packages remained after someone had stolen some of them. Numajiri promised Lieutenant McIntyre that his men would be allowed to have these boxes on the next day as that was McIntyre's birthday. During the late afternoon of 1 June, he noted storekeeper Takahashi and Sgt. Maekawa Kazumasa spending considerable time in the storeroom with the door closed.

On 2 June, Takahashi asked McIntyre to sign for the food boxes stolen by the guards, but the lieutenant refused. The Japanese told McIntyre that his fellow POWs had stolen the Red Cross supplies—in spite of the fact that other prisoners had seen Japanese guards, including Commandant Numajiri, consuming the food. Japanese guards then searched the American Barracks No. 2 and "found" stolen food and cigarettes beneath the bunk of Army Sgt. Wallace Ashley Hall, a 200th Coast Artillery soldier taken prisoner at Bataan in 1942. *Grenadier* radioman Lou Poss and Army private Clay claimed some of the items to try and help out Hall's case.

As Lieutenant McIntyre watched, guards Four Eyes and Three Fingers beat Hall, Clay, and Poss in the face with fists and a leather slipper. "As a result of the beating, Poss was confined to the camp hospital several days because of a mental derangement," stated McIntyre. POW Lt. Jack Jones stated that the beatings left these three men unable to work and that "Lou Poss was irrational for three days." John Walden said the Japanese also tortured Sergeant Hall by starving him and that Hall "was hung by the thumbs and beaten."[24]

Almost as bad as this abuse was the "treatment" the Allied POWs received in the Ashio hospital from Dr. Katoku. Harry Toney recalled, "I turned in with weak legs and he gave me the burn treatment. They used to put a small piece of punk on your leg about the size of a matchstick and burn that completely to cure everything from piles to diarrhea."

Eldon Wright received a hernia while mucking ore in the mine but was forced to keep working. When Wright's condition worsened in January 1945, he was sent to the hospital for treatment from Dr. Katoku. He was smeared in various places with a substance resembling spun glass, which was lit and burned away slowly. "The treatment consisted of three applications of this substance in the same spot each day for a period of about twenty days. It ultimately resulted in a festering sore," Wright related. After leaving the hospital, Wright still had the hernia and new burn scars on his shoulders. *Sculpin* shipmate Paul Murphy said the doctor's crude remedy was like "putting a lighted cigar to the flesh. Often times this resulted in a very raw burn." Ed Keller stated, "The theory was that the burns would produce white corpuscles to fight the illness. If you had beriberi, they would burn you in the affected area. For diarrhea, they would burn you on the stomach."[25]

George Rocek, treated for beriberi, was left with burn scars on his legs. Cliff Kuykendall remembered that Katoku "put the powder over the area where you had beriberi the worst and then burned it. It was supposed to help you, but it couldn't!" John Rourke was hospitalized in mid-1945 because he was worn out from work. "Dr. Katako put men on a water diet, and made the statement that it was healthy," he said. There were also plenty of work-related injuries in the mine for Dr. Katoku to treat. "One man lost an eye, one man lost his right index, and a third man had to be amputated one finger joint as a result of infection," recalled 2nd Lt. Nicholas Maas.[26]

Camp commander Numajiri conducted an inspection of his prisoners one day to determine who could still work. Lieutenant McIntyre said some men were "struck by Numajiri because they did not have their shoes tied or some reason." Against the protests of Allied doctors in camp, some men were deemed fit for work who were clearly unable to fully function. One of these was *Grenadier*'s PhM1c John McBeath, had been previously hospitalized at Shinagawa with severe beriberi. Upon returning to Ashio on 1 March, he was put on medical orderly detail for some time in the dispensary. After the summer inspection, Numajiri deemed McBeath ready to work again despite the protests of others. "After another day or two of work, McBeath was unable to walk and was carried back into camp by two of his fellow prisoners," recalled McIntyre.

After a year of mucking ore, Moon Rocek had worked his way into one of the driller positions. "Occasionally, when we spotted an air drill used by the Japs and no one was in sight, we would pour the carbide dust into the air supply," Rocek said. "The drill would work for a short time and then was put out of commission."[27]

––––––––––

On 6 June 1945, Joe Baker, Cecil Baker, Bill Haverland, and a few others of the *Sculpin* crew were pulled from the Ashio camp with 80 Dutch POWs and marched five miles up the valley to a brand-new prisoner camp, known as Camp 9DB. They joined the other Ashio camp, where they found Lt. Cdr. Dave Hurt in charge as senior POW.

Hurt, who spoke Japanese fairly well, became acquainted with an English-speaking guard at Ashio named George Enomoto in early June. Enomoto wrote a letter to Hurt's family one year later, relating the common bonds the two "enemies" formed. "He told me quite often of you and children, especially of his eldest son and of happy gossips in his younger days, while being confined in the prison camp in the semi-savage country," Enomoto wrote to Hurt's wife.[28]

During the last three months of war, the Ashio mine workers were pushed even harder. TM1c Herb Thomas said, "The work was changed to 12 hours, presumably to keep pace with the stepped up attempt of increased war production." By this time, Thomas had dropped from his normal 150 pounds down to 110 pounds. Paul Murphy dropped from about 180 pounds to 110 pounds.

The guards conducted another barracks inspection due to the handiwork of George Rocek and a fellow inmate. "Two of us had the personal satisfaction of ripping off a Red Cross food package from the Jap CO's room," he related. They hid the package under a floorboard in an outhouse stall. "About four days later, all barracks had to be vacated and the guards ransacked the whole camp," Rocek recalled.[29]

The Japanese guards attacked prisoners with little provocation. When Three Fingers found four prisoners playing cards on a weekday, he called for Lieutenant McIntyre and punched him in the face. Three Fingers then went into "a rage" and punched the other four men in the face repeatedly.

In July 1945, *Sculpin* cook Ed Anderson received a serious beating from Three Fingers. *Yorktown* radioman Kal Kalberg witnessed Kira use a stick of firewood to strike Anderson in the head because the submariner had prepared special food for sick prisoners who could not eat the regular food. "As a result of this beating, Anderson suffered severe headaches from then until the last time I saw him," stated Kalberg. "Andy" Anderson went to Lieutenant McIntyre and asked him to request the Japanese to send him on regular work details. Anderson "had reached the limit of his endurance" with the frequent beatings in the kitchen.[30]

Jose Quintana and another prisoner named Hogue were beaten in the barracks on 14 August for illegal trading. "Quintana was tied to a chair and was beaten severely by the Japanese sergeant," Pete Zucco said. "He was beaten for about half an hour about the head and body with a saber-shaped wooden club." CMoMM Charlie Erishman also witnessed "Quintana being beaten about the face and body with clubs and fists." After the beating of Hogue and Quintana, Lieutenant McIntyre was ordered by Numajiri to compile a list of all his POWs who had traded with the Koreans. The senior American POW stalled for a number of days, believing that the war's end was likely imminent.

During the ensuing barracks searches following the beatings, the guards found a squash that Pete Zucco had stolen from a Japanese woman's garden while he was returning from a work detail. "I was forced to stand at attention in front of the Japanese headquarters, holding the squash at arm's length over my head for at least two hours," he testified. "If I lowered the squash, one or more of the guards would start beating me." Zucco was kept on parade throughout the entire day. "Numajiri, the camp commander, slugged me in the face several times and stood by watching while different guards beat me with their fists and clubs," he said. Three Fingers questioned the *Grenadier* sailor intensely, beating him severely for any answer that did not "suit him."

Although bruised, bloodied and weary at the end of the day on 14 August, Zucco would find good reason to celebrate in less than 24 hours.

23
"They're Gonna Be Here Tomorrow"

Makassar: 1944–1945

"Every day I got up in the morning, I didn't know if I was gonna be alive that night," Bob Lents. The former *Perch* torpedoman and 41 shipmates were quartered in the new jungle camp outside of Makassar during the second half of 1944.

The Americans helped build railroad tracks through swamplands, using only hand tools. They disassembled radio towers from a nearby island and rebuilt them at Makassar. The Japanese decided to move an old Dutch concrete pillbox from the coast back to the front gate of the new camp. "I believe it was about eight feet in diameter and the walls were about one foot thick," said Sam Simpson. "Tom Byrnes was our petty officer in charge." *Perch*'s crew helped dig the pillbox out of the sand and moved it with a system of log rollers and rope. "This thing must have weighed about 25,000 pounds," recalled Turk Turner. "We cut down palm trees to roll it on." Ernie Plantz said "they would beat you with a stick so you would pull harder."[1]

The work parties hauled logs, constructed roads, and hauled dirt and rock with their yo-yo poles. "After a long day's work, some times we were given ten swats on the ass for nothing or perhaps we would be made to do the lizard for fifteen or twenty minutes," Sam Simpson recalled. The "lizard" was a term coined by the prisoners for a day's end stamina test where Japanese guards had the men get down on all fours, keeping their backs straight and their bellies off the ground. "Should your belly touch the ground or your back became too arched, you would get several swats on the butt with a length of rattan," Simpson wrote.[2]

Each Makassar prisoner had a single white cloth uniform for display whenever a touring Japanese official visited their camp. Every other day of the year, the men simply wore the rags that they had owned since being captured. "I had a pair of short pants that were starting to wear out," recalled Alabama Arnette. "I'd find some little scrap of fabric somewhere and I'd patch them by hand. I got to where I was pretty good at it."

Sam Simpson, having been raised on a farm, was put in charge of the camp commandant's private garden. "We cleared the land of grass and brush, dug up the ground and planted seeds," he related. When insects ate all the seeds, Simpson's party built protective tin boxes out of burned-out tin roofing. Suspending the boxes on bamboo in a wet area adjacent to the little pond, the *Perch* men were able to raise plants that could be transplanted to the acre and a half commandant's garden. Tom Byrnes was later given charge of a larger garden that provided for the entire camp.[3]

The bombing grew closer during 1944. As the prisoners took cover during a B-17 air raid one day, several heard the whooshing sound of a dropped object sailing down. "It hit a pile of bamboo stakes we were using to build a bomb-blast shelter," Tom Moore said. The expected blast never occurred, fortunately. "We walked over there and it was an empty beer bottle. Those dirty bastards. If I had a gun, I would have shot them out of the air!"

Alabama Arnette felt bombing getting closer to Celebes was "the most wonderful inspiration." When American PBY floatplanes made appearances late in the war, "we knew that we had conquered some nearby island. Those planes would float around in the air and the Japs were scared to death of them."

One of Moore's cubicle mates was Filipino officer's cook Macario Sarmiento. "He was an old man, and I used to smuggle him extra food," he recalled. Sarmiento and the other *Perch* officer's cook, Alejo Fajotina, were put to work cooking rice with the ship's cooks on most days. "Sometimes they cooked for us what we called morning glories, some kind of greens that just grew up alongside the road," Moore said. "They were horrible. They would throw a piece of pork fat in it. There was no heavy eating. You dropped all your weight quickly."

Turk Turner and some shipmates even resorted to eating monkey on one occasion. They were working at the Makassar hospital when a monkey was seen running about the building. The Japanese guards decided to have fun with their POWs this day, inquiring, "You eat monkey if we kill it?" In their half-starved condition, the Americans were not about to turn down any meal. "We agreed to eat the monkey if the Nips killed it and cooked it for us," Turner said. "After they killed it, I had to skin it to get all the hair off. Once all the hair was off, that's when it hit me—because the monkey looked like a little baby. Anyway, we seasoned it, the Nips cooked it for us and it tasted pretty good."

Tom Moore and his comrades "learned to steal anything you could get your hands on. You just stuffed it in your mouth if it was edible." They ate any animal they could catch and kill, as Moore explained.

> I ate a cat and I didn't sterilize him before I ate him. When I dressed him out, I didn't cut his nuts out and he spoiled the meat. But we ate him anyway. It was horrible. I could burp that for three months. But, I knew how to clean that cat the next time.
>
> We ate dogs. One wandered through there. I love animals, but boy, they saved my life. We ate rats and found that lizards are good. Anything that was edible—if we could get our hands on it, pretty soon it was cleaned out in the camp area, so it was pretty tough to get any meat after that.

Pope destroyerman Bill Penninger agreed that monkey, cat, or "anything with meat on it" was considered edible. He and fellow POWs fashioned and baited a crude trap one night to catch the dog of a Japanese guard. The dog caught his head in the trap while taking the bait and he was secretly cooked late at night in the prisoners' bath area. Penninger and ten of his fellow starved Americans found dog meat to be "pretty good" after adding salt, pepper, onion, and other stolen garnishes they had acquired.

Turk Turner was punished by vicious guard Yoshida on one occasion for stealing sugar while on work detail. "I always counted the licks," he recalled. "I'd count 'em out loud so that I would irritate them a little bit. I can remember counting to twelve, but I don't remember anything after that. I just made sure to stay on my feet even though I was not conscious of what was happening. You got beat even more if you fell down." Shipmates later told him that he had received more than two dozen blows across the buttocks from the Japanese guard. When Turner regained consciousness, Yoshida was exhausted.

As the guard walked by, Turner politely asked him for a drink of water. "You want water?" Yoshida asked.

"Yes," Turner panted as his backside throbbed.

The guard turned and picked up a bucket of water. "I thought he was going to give me a drink of water but instead he threw the whole bucketful in my face."

Quick to take the high road, Turner simply said, "Arrigato," and smiled at his tormentor. "Yoshida looked at me, shook his head and just walked off," he recalled. "He never, ever touched me again after that."

"If one fell down during such a punishment, he was kicked in the guts, face, and back several times," Sam Simpson related. "Their tail would swell up tight and turn black. If the skin got broken, it became a bloody, running sore—awful." Simpson estimated that he received 134 swats during his entire time at Makassar. "The most that I got at one time was twenty." [4]

Alabama Arnette felt that the American prisoners were pushed harder than their Dutch and English counterparts. "The Japanese felt we Americans were hard workers," he said. "When we were assigned to clean the barracks, we would eat food right out of the garbage cans," Arnette admitted. "The Japs would sometimes throw bananas in the garbage and we'd eat them. We looked at it as a means of existence. If you could get a banana, it had vitamins."

The prisoners who worked in the Makassar hospital continued stealing vitamins and during 1944 began slipping out small quantities of medicinal alcohol. "We buried a five-gallon container and slowly filled it with the alcohol as we returned from work parties," related Turk Turner. The *Perch* and *Pope* survivors learned that the guards would rush them right into camp without being searched during the bombing scares. The Americans had learned from Christmas 1942 and Christmas 1943 that the Japanese left them completely alone at Christmastime.

"We filled the alcohol container until Christmastime in 1944," said Turner. "We had enough alkie in there that everyone in our barracks could have something to drink." Other prisoners had stolen a Japanese wok and eggplants from the guard's camp garden. The prisoners built a small fire and heated up the wok in their barracks. "I cooked the eggplant with some rice for our Christmas dinner and it was pretty palatable," Turner stated. "We had a pretty good Christmas."

One of the bombing raids in early 1945 killed a horse on a nearby farm. "They butchered it and brought it into camp," said Turner. The meat was cut into small chunks and distributed to the prisoners at mealtime. "That was the only food I just could not stomach. I don't know if it was the flavor or the tough texture, but I just finally gave mine away."

Following another air raid, some of the prisoners scavenged tobacco and cigarette papers from a badly damaged warehouse. After one man was caught with items stolen from the warehouse, the camp commander created a list of the camp POW thieves. "There were at least 50 guys whose names ended up on the list," Tom Moore recalled.[5]

"Every one of the guys who stole cigarettes had a Japanese partner who beat him unmercifully," related Moore. "They beat them until there was urine, feces and blood all over." The bamboo club beatings did not end until the men were literally broken men, some of whom did not recover from the effects of the abuse.[6]

For Bob Lents, this was just one of the times that he literally had to have his pants cut off of him due to the beatings. "You tried hard not to stay down when you were beaten because they had these hobbled nails in their boots," he related. When the prisoners were allowed to next use their makeshift outdoor showers at the Makassar camp, the evidence of their abuse was all too clear. Lents jokingly chided another shipmate, "I see you're a member of the black-ass club, too."

By 31 December 1944, Ernie Plantz fell ill with malaria as sickness raged through the camp and killed off prisoners daily. "I was going to the bathroom and I just passed out," he said. "They carried me to the hospital and I never knew it."

He lay unconscious for six days in Makassar's bamboo-frame hospital in a malaria-induced coma. During this period, he had a vision of meeting Jesus Christ. He later found that his very religious mother was maintaining an intense prayer vigil for his well-being. "She kept praying for me every day," he recalled. "I'm convinced my mom prayed me right out of that prison camp."[7]

During his period of unconsciousness, Plantz's "bowels were moving so fast they couldn't keep quinine in me long enough to break the fever." His body was down more than 100 pounds during January, when Plantz weighed a mere 75 pounds at the hospital. Seeing that the *Perch* sailor was near death, the Dutch doctor decided it was time to try something to save Plantz. "I was told that he crushed quinine, mixed it with tap water, and gave me an injection directly in the vein with a home-made needle. That's what finally broke my fever."

Bob Lents recalled that the physical abuse only worsened the men's poor health. "All were subjected to heavy beatings with clubs, rope hawsers, shovels, iron bars. This was accompanied by punches in the face, kicks, Judo holds, and other foul methods." Lents was diagnosed with appendicitis and was taken to the Dutch hospital ship *Op ten Noort*. He learned that the Japanese had looted the ship's medical supply of all anesthesia and even sutures. The Dutch surgeon, who spoke no English, grabbed a handful of flesh on Lents' side and squeezed hard.

"Hey, Doc, that hurts like hell!" he complained.

The surgeon merely continued speaking to his nurse in Dutch. The only word he finally made out was "scalpel." With his instrument in hand, the doctor released his painful grip on Lents' flesh and then quickly slashed open the area with his scalpel. As the blood began to flow, "I passed out," Lents said. Throughout the surgery, he lapsed in and out of consciousness. His incision was sutured together with large twine that only remained in the deep incision area for two days. "I was back working again in ten days."

Behind his back, the prisoners called head guard Yoshida "Mad Mark." Lents stated, "At no time were we assured that the U.S. government had been notified of our capture or even knew of our existence." Unlike shipmates taken into Japan, the Makassar inmates received no mail.

Alabama Arnette was one of a group who was moved from the jungle camp to an advanced working camp in early 1945. He had heard through the grapevine that life would be a little easier in the new camp because it was smaller. "I wanted to get up there with my buddy Dan Crist, so I volunteered," recalled Arnette. "I took my little grass mat with me and laid it out beside Crist." Back aboard *Perch*, Crist and Arnette had gotten to know each other when they both volunteered to handle the nightly duty of dumping the garbage off the fantail for "the chance to get fresh air." Reunited with his old garbage-detail buddy more than two years later, Arnette discovered that their new labor camp was no better than the malaria-infested jungle camp. "It was hard labor. They had me working on machines making bombs."

The prisoners also helped to build bomb shelters with vented roofs from coco-nut tree logs. The captives later learned that similar shelters had been used on Palawan to kill large numbers of POWs—including at least two from the subma-rine *Robalo*—toward the war's end, who were doused with gasoline and lit on fire. "They always told us if the Americans landed it would make no difference," Plantz said. "We would never live to see it. I guess they meant to do the same to us."[8]

Those men in the advanced jungle camps took any chance they could to snatch wild fruits. "I was out on a working party once, and someone threw down a stalk of bananas into our party," said Arnette. When the stalk finally reached Arnette, he grabbed two bananas and crammed them in his mouth. "Before I could swallow them, this Jap guard came by and clubbed me a few times and knocked them right out of my mouth," he said. "There went my bananas!"

Ernie Plantz later recalled one humorous event involving a Japanese guard who wanted to take a hot bath. The guard climbed into a steel barrel that had been cut in half and placed above a fire pit. Gunner's mate Earl Harper, who was working as an assistant to the guards, was charged with building the fire and keeping it hot. "It wasn't getting hot enough for this guard, so they kept hollering at Harper, 'Hotter! Hotter!'" said Plantz. Harper kept piling on the wood until the fire was roaring. In short order, the water had almost reached a boil and became far too hot for the Japanese guard. "He hopped out and started to chase Harper," Plantz recalled.

Perch's survivors were in poor health by the spring of 1945. Only one of their fellow crewmen had died during 1944, but *Perch* lost two more sailors in April 1945. CMM Albert Newsome died from the effects of pellagra and malnutrition on 6 April. Newsome's passing was followed by the death of MM2c Charles Brown—known to his buddies as "Brownie"—two weeks later on 18 April. "I never felt I wasn't going to make it," recalled Plantz. "If you felt that way, you usually didn't make it. The guys who had what we called 'give-up-itis,' you knew they'd be gone before long."[9]

Tom Moore agreed that "some of them just gave up." Moore was hospitalized from his own malnutrition and beriberi. "I was a husky guy, short and stocky," he related. "I went from 190 pounds down to 105" as a prisoner. He credited Chief of the Boat Charlie Cross, who worked in the hospital, with helping to keep him alive while he fought his illness. Just being taken to the hospital became a death sentence for some. "Your ration was cut," Moore said. "It was a stinking place. It was primitive and you were taken there to die."

Stephen Orlyk had a severe bout of beriberi that caused his kidneys to shut down. "Orlyk's body began retaining water and he just swelled up to the point that he couldn't even raise his hands to feed himself," Turk Turner recalled. Orlyk's shipmates helped care for him until his kidneys began functioning properly and he was able to lose the water weight he had gained. SM3c Grady "Pete" Burnette of *Pope* found that "it was a daily battle to stay alive and retain your senses."[10]

On 15 June, *Perch*'s FC1c Robert Wilson died from pellagra and bacterial dysentery. Turk Turner was with him at the time. "We had malaria and my legs were paralyzed from what they called malarial paralysis," Turner recalled. "When I tried to walk, I'd fall flat."

As he lay in the hospital bunk beside his buddy, Wilson said one night, "Turk, I just can't take it any more. I quit."

"Wilson, we're getting out of here tomorrow," Turner opined. "They're gonna be here tomorrow."

He tried consoling Wilson, offering him hope that the Allies were on the verge of conquering Japan and they would soon be freed. "I just kept talking to him and I thought I had talked him out of it, but when I woke up the next morning he was dead."

During the late summer of 1945, the Japanese on Celebes were struggling from a lack of military supplies. "The Japs didn't have any aircraft any longer here and at the Japanese military airport they had a number of bombs stored there," Ernie Plantz related. "They couldn't drop them, so they got the bright idea that they would make land mines and hand grenades by having us pulverize the explosives in the bombs."

Due to termites on the island, the Dutch had used four-inch stainless steel pipes for their electricity and light poles. "The Japs had us take those darn things down and replace them with wood," said Plantz. "They cut the steel poles into sections and welded one end shut. They made homemade exploders on the other end and had the prisoners pack them full of explosives from these unused bombs. The men got terrible stuff on them that they couldn't wash off. A number of them got sick."

This improvised mortar-making process caused *Perch*'s MM1c Tom Byrnes, TM1c Sam Simpson, and QM1c Jim Webb to be hospitalized on 22 July with what the Japanese termed "lydite poisoning." Y1c Roland Earlywine and F3c Orville Peterson were also stricken with lydite poisoning during the same week. On 25 July, CPhM Philip Dewes died of pellagra, bringing the number to five who had died at Makassar.

SK3c Bill Penninger from *Pope* was distraught when one of his shipmates died in July. "I was about to give up," he recalled, when SM2c Coffredo Tarquino and MM1c James Fortner intervened. "They took me to the bomb shelter and gave me a talking to," Penninger related. "They made me promise to quit the worrying."[11]

The following day, 200 Makassar prisoners were transferred from Makassar to Batavia Camp No. 1 on the island of Java via Surabaya. Bob Lents was the only *Perch* crewmen pulled, along with 15 Americans from *Pope*, including the only American officer, Lt. (jg) Allen Fisher.

"The trip from Macassar to Surabaya was made under the worst possible conditions on the top side of a small oil tanker along with 200 Japanese Army personnel," Fisher recalled. The POWs were forced to remain in a sitting position under a broiling sun for three days.[12]

"While we were being moved on the oil tanker, we came under a torpedo attack from a Dutch or English submarine, which missed us by only 15 feet or so," Lents recalled. "I was sitting on the bow and I saw it." Each prisoner received less than a half pint of water, two or three ship's biscuits, and two spoonfuls of sugar during this hell ship voyage. In Surabaya, the POWs were placed in a native labor camp while awaiting their transfer orders. "Then followed a two-day train trip under very crowded conditions to Batavia on 9 August," said Lents. "On 20 August, they released us from isolation barracks into the main camp."

The POW camp at Batavia was "a different world," according to *Pope* electrician Bill Seward, who arrived in camp with Lents. "I found that there was fresh water and soap. I took a long bath—the first in three years."[13]

With the movement of these men to Batavia, 122 American POWs remained at Makassar's bamboo camp. CMM Archie Carroll Sawyer from *Pope* was the senior enlisted man in charge. With five deaths at Makassar, *Perch*'s crew on Celebes was down to 37 men plus Bob Lents on Java. At least 26 *Pope* survivors had died in the Makassar camp by this point of the war.

––––––––––

The four largest groups of U.S. submariners being held as prisoners of war by the Japanese during the summer of 1945 were located in camps at Makassar, Ashio, Fukuoka, and Omori. The 17 submarine officers were widely scattered through a number of camps in mainland Japan.

Lt. Cdr. John Fitzgerald, former skipper of *Grenadier*, was transferred by train from Omori through the mountains to Naoetsu, Japan's Camp 4-B on 1 March 1945. Upon arrival on 2 March, Fitzgerald found himself the senior POW. From the train station, the new prisoners hiked more than a mile to their camp through deeply piled snow. "Being on a pair of improvised crutches which were necessary because of a badly infected foot, it was slow going, one crutch or the other sinking into the snow every few steps," he wrote.[14]

The Naoetsu barracks consisted of a large warehouse divided into numerous bunk rooms on two floors. Fitzgerald found that the camp included 231 Australians from Singapore, about 30 Dutchmen, and about another 30 Englishmen, "practically all of who were taken prisoner early in 1942."[15]

About 15 March, the officers were ordered to work in a local factory. Senior POW Fitzgerald refused, saying that the officers would not do manual labor in a Japanese factory. Sergeant Watanabe—known as "The Bird" at Omori in 1944—was furious that the officers refused to work at the factory. "Watanabe went on a rampage which was to continue from time to time until his transfer about the middle of July."[16]

When word reached Japan in April about the death of U.S. President Roosevelt, the Bird was delighted. He demanded that all the POW officers line up in the courtyard so that he could spread the word. Lou Zamperini recalled that Watanabe moved close to Lieutenant Commander Fitzgerald, and said, "Roosevelt-san, he is dead. Dead!"[17]

Around the middle of May, another 400 POWs arrived from Osaka, bringing the camp complement at Naoetsu to about 699 Allied prisoners. During June, Sergeant Watanabe forced the Allied officers to work on barge detail unloading coal ships.[18]

Despite all of the abuse endured in his three years as a POW, "Fitz" Fitzgerald never backed down from complaining to camp officials about working conditions. After insulting the camp commandant in August, he was assigned to "the barge party shoveling coal and iron ore and carrying it in a basket strapped to the back. Frankly, it was a relief to get away from the tension and strain of the camp."

Former *Perch* exec Lt. Bev Van Buskirk had been interned at Yokohama Dispatch No. 1 camp from 4 December 1942. During his first year and a half in this camp, he noted that 44 men died from malnutrition, exposure, mistreatment, unsanitary conditions, and lack of medical treatment.[19]

Evening roll call included beatings for various offenses such as stealing food. "Practically every officer and man from colonel to private received physical violence at the hands of [commandant] Nishizuma or his staff at least once and some many times," Van Buskirk related. He recalled that those men too sick to work were sent up a hill in the mountains to scavenge for weeds to add to the camp's soup mixtures. About once every six months, nearby villagers would slaughter a cow and allow the POWs to have the blood. "When blood is poured into boiling water, it coagulates into large chunks," wrote Van Buskirk. "The cooks would break them into small bits. It would taste just like giblets."

Van Buskirk received a severe beating on 5 June 1945 while cleaning up scrap iron and pipe about the shipyard. A guard attacked him for not working fast enough, beating his face and head with his fists and a club until Van Buskirk passed out. During August, the lieutenant was at a hospital camp at Tokyo in the Shimogawa area, which was "notorious for the ability to reduce men to walking skeletons in record time."

In response to an air assault on the Tokyo area on 12 August, Van Buskirk and the other Shimogawa prisoners were beaten in the face with a leather shoe and forced to perform push-ups until men began collapsing. As the war's end approached, Van Buskirk was one of only three American officers at the Sendai # 8-B Kosaka POW Camp. He was held with 8 British POWs, 99 Dutchmen, and a large group of U.S. Army and Marine Corps enlisted men.

Of the other 15 captured U.S. submarine officers, the three from *Tang* remained at Omori; *Grenadier*'s John Walden was at Ashio; six were placed into camps near Tokyo; and the other five spent time at Zentsuji Camp No. 3.

Lt. George Brown from *Sculpin* was moved from Omori on 1 March 1945 to the Mitsushima Camp 2-D—renamed Tokyo 12-B Tenryu Camp in August 1944—where he became the senior American officer. This camp was run by Japanese Lieutenant Kubo, Sergeant Watanabe (The Bird), a half dozen former Army enlisted men, "and a few civilian guards, the youngest being 14," Brown detailed. "The prisoners, including myself, suffered many severe beatings by clubs, rubber shoes, wooden shoes, wooden swords, belts and clubs."

One day, the guards ordered 20 men with beriberi to go up the mountainside, climbing about 2,000 feet and walking ten miles through snow to bring back logs for camp fuel. As result of this duty "two of these men died of a heart attack upon return to the camp."

Brown was put to work on a farm, carrying wood, and moving refuse from latrines to fertilize the gardens. He endured two chipped teeth from various beatings and suffered from diarrhea, dysentery, and beriberi due to unsanitary drinking water and from eating leaves, weeds, seaweed, and rotten fish. According to Brown, 60 men died from various poor conditions in the Mitsushima camp during 1945.

Lt. (jg) Jake Vandergrift from *Perch* was the first U.S. submariner transferred from Ofuna to Zentsuji, located on the island of Shikoku. Sent with a small group of *Pope* officers, he found that this was a type of propaganda camp that the Japanese allowed the Red Cross to inspect. Soon after their arrival in August 1942, Vandergrift and the *Pope* officers were photographed to show the world the "pleasant" conditions in which they were contained.

During late August, the Zentsuji prisoners were allowed to write a 25-word card to their families. Lt. Jack Ryder was reunited with Vandergrift when he was transferred from Ofuna to Zentsuji during September. During November, Radio Tokyo recorded three-minute broadcasts from some of the camp's prisoners as part of Japan's continuing propaganda effort to show how well they were treating their Allied prisoners. For Christmas 1943, the Zentsuji prisoners had cocoa, rice, beans, corned beef, hard tack, butter, and decent food as the Japanese allowed their "guests" to usher in the Christian holidays.[20]

Perch officer Lt. Ken Schacht and two *Grenadier* officers—lieutenants Kevin Harty and John Critchlow—were transferred into Zentsuji during 1944. Harty arrived in September from Ashio. While food and working conditions were better than what he had experienced at Ofuna and Ashio, he testified that Zentsuji interpreter Kobiyahsi "was known for brutality and mistreatment of prisoners of war. There was also a doctor name Saito, who deserves punishment for neglect and ill treatment."

One of Harty's companions from Ofuna, 1st Lt. Fred Garrett, arrived at Zentsuji on 1 December 1944. Sporting handmade crutches, Garrett was admired by his fellow POWs for the upbeat attitude he maintained in spite of the fact that his injured leg had been amputated by the Japanese.

As the war moved closer to Japan, the camp commandants found less reason to maintain the decent treatment they had offered the Zentsuji inmates. On 23 June 1945, 335 Army, Navy, and Marine prisoners were moved from Zentsuji Camp No. 3, to a new camp to hold the Americans. Harty, Critchlow, Schacht, Vandergrift, and Ryder were among the American officers transferred to Rokuroshi Camp (Osaki Camp No. 11), located in the mountains above Fukui.

"The railroad trip to this camp was made under the worst conditions I had yet observed," said Vandergrift. "One hundred and fifteen officers and their effects [were] in a third class coach." The men took a boat trip across the Inland Sea during this two-day transfer but most of the journey was by train. "Guards further increased the crowding since they had enough room for each guard," Jack Ryder added. Arriving at the Fukui station on 24 June, the POWs were forced to begin a long hike up a mountain trail at 2300 toward Rokuroshi Camp through a driving rainstorm.

"One officer in our group had lost a leg in a plane crash and another had beri-beri so bad that he was crippled and could barely walk with a cane," Ryder said. "Both these officers were forced to climb the 12 kilometers of mountain trail." Army POW Capt. George Edward Steiger noted in his diary that "Fred Garrett (one leg) was not allowed to have our help."[21]

Vandergrift, Harty, Critchlow, Schacht, Ryder, and the 330 other American POWs reached Rokuroshi Camp at 0200 on 25 June, thoroughly exhausted. Upon settling into their barracks, the Americans were farmed out to various work details. Jake Vandergrift said the prisoners "cut brush, de-seeded fields and planted crops, working about four hours a day. In our weakened condition, we could not do more." To their daily rice, Jack Ryder stated that the Japanese added "a spoonful or two of vegetables per meal."

Vandergrift felt the "food allowance was slightly better than Zentsuji, but still inadequate." By 11 July, a ten-man detail was sent to forage the mountainside for soup greens as vegetables were not obtainable. Kevin Harty found that the "food was scarce and rations continuously cut. Men were forced to 'volunteer' to work in order to get enough rice to sustain life."

Captain Steiger's diary entries give some insight into camp life at Rokuroshi.[22]

July 30. Two miles up mountain for fence poles in a.m. "Turk" Critchlow helped me with room duty.

August 1. Hauled firewood from hill clearing in a.m. Issue of quadruple-cooked ox bones.

August 3. Rice cut to 295 grams (10½ oz). Part of national cut? Work stopped. Just when I thought we were about to receive a living ration!

Rokuroshi's only American casualty came six weeks after the officers' arrival, when 2nd Lt. James I. Mallette died from his poor condition. In the war's closing days, the guards showed little sympathy for their prisoners. On 6 August, four Bataan survivors—lieutenants William Elmo Lewis Jr., William Wiley Bird, Paul Alfred Stansbury, and Horace Butare Patterson Jr.—were questioned and stood in the sun all day without food. By 14 August, there was renewed hope throughout the camp as the vapor streams of numerous aircraft could be seen in the distance. Four days later, some of the restrictions were lifted, and the men were allowed to smoke outside in the evening.[23]

"Many think the war is over," Captain Steiger wrote in his diary on 18 August. "I am afraid to think so."

24
Liberation of the Lost

Liberation of Omori

Among the Japanese islands, some 174 prisoner of war camps were run during the war. About 17,000 captives were held in Japan with another 220,000 Allied prisoners held elsewhere in the Japanese Empire. Of the 95,000 American, British, Canadian, Australian, and New Zealand prisoners held, 28 percent died in captivity.[1]

Roughly two dozen U.S. submariners were being held on Omori at war's end. Some of these Omori prisoners were out digging a cave on 15 August some distance from camp. "We were ordered to remove our tools and unstring the light bulbs in the cave," recalled Boats Leibold. "We were told we would return to Omori in the early afternoon; most unusual." He and Dick O'Kane soon heard the Emperor's voice over the radio. O'Kane comprehended the phrase, "The war is over."[2]

As he was carrying tools out of the cave, one of the guards noticed that Leibold was struggling. "I was limping from a damaged foot and leg, thanks to Horseface," he said. "The guard asked about my injury and told me that I would soon receive treatment in a hospital!" When the prisoners reached camp, they were informed that the war was over. "On the news, the Japanese slaughtered an old horse at Omori and carted it with them as they went over the hill," recalled O'Kane. The camp's resourceful cooks scrubbed out the horse's intestines, chopped them up, and mixed them with corn for an "all-dumpo" celebration meal.[3]

The POWs tore down the fence that surrounded the special prisoner building within camp. "That night, a number of the drunken Jap guards made an attempt to enter our building," said Leibold. "The camp master sergeant Ogura, backed by POWs, brought this to a halt. His skill with his sword effectively put one of his men down and we all breathed easier."

The next day, 16 August, the guards had all disappeared from Omori except for one. The prisoners took over camp and waited on liberation. "When the war was over, O'Kane was the senior officer at Omori but was suffering physically," recalled Leibold. "Pappy Boyington continued to carry out O'Kane's direction. In my building, there were 104 men and I can recall cutting a loaf of spam, dropped by a B-29, into 104 pieces. You can bet there were 104 pairs of eyes overseeing my accuracy!"

The colonel commanding Omori had a pig he kept in a fenced enclosure near the galley. During the previous month, Floyd Caverly, Leibold and Charles Rogers had noticed someone dumping food into the pig pen each day. Guards checked on the trio periodically as they cut wood in camp but they were not always supervised. "Caverly made an 'inspection run' and found the pig food to be burned rice that had been scraped from the pot," said Leibold. "After that, Caverly made a daily run to get some of what we termed 'burners,' whacking the pig as necessary. When the war ended, it was decided to butcher the pig. Michael Killain, a CBM in the Royal Navy, whacked the pig with a sledgehammer. Mike, with help, picked the pig up and lowered it into a 55-gallon drum rigged to heat water by the ex-POWs. A pig 'all-dump' was planned."

During the next two weeks, U.S. B-29s rained down canned goods. Some of the heavy drop loads crashed through buildings until O'Kane felt that "Omori looked like a giant salad." The prisoners painted "P.W." in large letters on the Omori buildings' rooftops, including one to let the flyboys know that Medal of Honor winner Boyington was in the camp. Clay Decker added, "Some of our lads got sick gorging themselves on all the food."[4]

Leibold recalled, "Navy planes and B-29s dropped all kinds of goodies—food, clothing, medical supplies, magazines, everything except dancing girls."

On 28 August, Captain Harold Stassen—who had resigned from his third term as governor of Minnesota to serve in the Navy reserves—led a destroyer division that anchored off Omori. Upon Stassen's first visit to the prison camp, he was shocked by the condition of the American POWs. "Commander Stassen told everybody that they were going to look things over and make up a plan to evacuate us in the next few days," recalled Boats Leibold. "About an hour or so later, he called us back and told everybody, 'If you have anything, get it together, because we're leaving right now.'"

A flotilla of landing craft was sent toward Omori to rescue the men. More than 600 men had packed into the island camp by this time, many arriving from other auxiliary camps. Navy photographers stood on the LCMs as they approached Omori's seawalls, where the prisoners were packed in deep rows to watch the arriving liberators. "I was standing on the pier wearing nothing but a loincloth and someone started filming a newsreel," said Jesse DaSilva.[5]

Captured in the photographs and on film were moving images of the smiling, cheering American, Dutch, and British prisoners of war. They triumphantly waved homemade flags of their countries as the landing craft approached. *Grenadier* torpedoman Al Albertson recalled that he, a chief from another small ship, and Slim Landrum helped create an American flag. Their picture was taken by the *Life* photographer. "Slim Landrum was the instigator of it," recalled Albertson. "We made it out of bed sheets with some crayons." Albertson was proud that the photos showed Landrum wildly waving his American flag higher than the Dutch and British flag.

The Japanese colonel in charge protested to the liberators through his interpreter that he had been given no authority from Tokyo to release the prisoners. Boats Leibold recalled, "He was promptly advised, 'You have no authority, PERIOD.'" DaSilva watched as a young American officer stuck a revolver in the guard's face and stated, "This is your Tokyo!"[6]

Caverly and Leibold were aboard one of the first LCMs that churned out into Tokyo Bay. "When we left, the Jap guards were still just patrolling around and around this place, even though the landing craft had smashed down the fencing," recalled Caverly. DaSilva was 100 pounds, some 70 pounds below his normal weight. The *Tang* men were taken on board the hospital ship *Benevolence* (AH-13). Caverly said they were "given a big feed. I had a sore leg from my old bayonet wound but they put our Old Man in a bunk right away and started the intravenous fluids." The *Life* magazine reporter who accompanied Commander Stassen into Omori had an editor who knew of Dick O'Kane. The editor's brother still lived in O'Kane's old hometown and he had his reporter wire Ernestine O'Kane directly from Tokyo to let her know that her husband was alive.[7]

Caverly slept on a Navy mattress in a passageway on *Benevolence* overnight. "The next morning, I went over to another ship where they were trying to round up some whites for us to wear to go over and watch the signing on the battleship *Missouri* in Tokyo Bay." Caverly found it impossible to locate uniforms on the ship that fit him. "We were all so damn skinny," he said. "Nobody in the Navy was as small as we were. I lost 100 pounds. The seat of any trousers I put on came to my knees. I decided the hell with it. I wasn't going over to the *Missouri* looking like that."

Bill Leibold recalled, "A number of men were invited to attend the surrender ceremony, as was I. Most declined as the general feeling was they had had enough of the Japs!" Four Americans POWs from Omori were selected on the evening of 1 September and told that they would be brought aboard *Missouri* to witness the surrender ceremony. All had done time together at Ofuna prior to Omori: 1st Lt. Bill Harris, the son of Brig. Gen. Field Harris who had been captured at Corregidor; Cdr. Al Maher from the cruiser *Houston*; Lt. Jim Condit, *Yorktown* TBF pilot; and

MM2c Pappy Shaw from the submarine *Grenadier*. Of the American submariners who survived their various prisoner of war camps, Shaw was their sole representative on board *Missouri*. While on board *Missouri*, Shaw had a chance to tell Gen. Douglas MacArthur how much the prisoners had enjoyed the burning of Tokyo by Superfortress fire raids. MacArthur said he was "pleased" and sent greetings back with Shaw to San Antonio, the general's former home.[8]

Shaw had been moved from Omori shortly before war's end to a nearby Tokyo Bay–area POW camp at Sumidagawa #20-D where Pop Condit was being held. When the camp was liberated, it was 30 August—Shaw's 32nd birthday. His husky, 200-pound frame had shriveled to less than 90 pounds. Upon being selected to go aboard *Missouri*, Shaw could only borrow another sailor's whites instead of the preferred khaki uniform.

Al Albertson was on one of the first planes that returned to the States, traveling via Kwajalein, Guam, Pearl Harbor, and then Oakland, California. "They really treated us well at each stop," he recalled. "They gave me a physical and what they were really concerned about was dysentery." Albertson passed his test and was allowed to fly commercial class to Shalamar, Great Lakes.

Floyd Caverly heard that two Navy planes were taking off for a flight back to Alameda, California. "They said that anybody who was interested in going to the San Francisco area could get on," he said. "Well, I goddamned near swam over there." Caverly flew in an R4D to Guam. His next flight took him to Pearl Harbor, where the POWs were inspected at the Aiea Naval Hospital. While in Hawaii waiting on his next flight, Caverly had the idea to see what happened to a roll of film he had shot just before *Tang* departed on her fifth patrol in September 1944. "Caverly went to the shop just to check and sure enough, the proprietor had the order ready and waiting, albeit for a year!" recalled Bill Leibold. Caverly's candid snapshots of his crewmen proved to be the last photos taken of many a *Tang* sailor.

From Pearl Harbor, Caverly was flown straight back to San Francisco, where he was eager to find his wife. "My family knew that there were survivors off the *Tang*," he said, "but they didn't know who they were or how many until about the time that I landed at Alameda."

The *Tang* survivors were in poor shape. Pete Narowanski had several teeth caps missing as the result of beatings. Larry Savadkin dropped from 155 pounds to 90 pounds. Dick O'Kane went down to 85 pounds.[9]

Eight of the nine *Tang* survivors were airlifted back to the United States aboard different aircraft. The ninth man, Jesse DaSilva, chose to take a three-week route back to the States on board the hospital ship *Rescue* so that he could fatten up before seeing his family again. Weighing 170 pounds when he was captured in October 1944, he had dropped to around 100 pounds. DaSilva arrived in San Francisco one year to the day after *Tang* had been sunk.

Lieutenant Savadkin took a boat to Yokohama, hitched a ride to the airport and hopped a C-54 to Guam—where he was the first American submariner to arrive from Japan. When word reached Admiral Lockwood that U.S. submariners had indeed been found alive, a car was sent to fetch him. Lockwood chatted with him personally and Savadkin informed ComSubPac that Skipper Dick O'Kane had done the Navy proud by never cracking under the torture he had endured. Savadkin was soon flown to Pearl Harbor, where doctors checked him over at the Aiea Naval Hospital and sent him on to San Francisco. "It was all ad hoc," he recalled of his various flights toward home. After a brief stay in the Oak Knoll Hospital in Oakland, California, the former *Tang* officer arrived by plane in New York City on 10 September.[10]

Clay Decker stuck close to his friend Pappy Boyington after Omori's liberation, riding with him on a landing craft to the hospital ship *Benevolence*. From the Atsugi Air Station, he also boarded a C-54 with Boyington, where Decker found that he was the only enlisted man aboard this flight. His journey finally brought him to the Alameda, California, Naval Air Station. As he looked out the airplane window at the hills and homes around San Francisco Bay, he thought, "I couldn't believe it was actually real—that I was actually home." While overjoyed to finally see his young son again, Decker was dismayed to find that his wife Lucille had divorced and remarried, thinking that he had been lost. "I was shocked to find that I was no longer Papa-san."[11]

Boats Leibold was flown back to California on the same flight with Pete Narowanski and Hayes Trukke. They stopped at Guam, Johnson Island, Kwajalein, and Honolulu. Just as on Guam, a Submarine Force officer met the surviving submariners upon their arrival at Pearl Harbor. Leibold was driven to meet Admiral Lockwood, who offered to put him up at the Royal Hawaiian. Anxious to get home, Leibold instead caught a flight to California, where he was assisted at the Oak Knoll Naval Hospital. "An officer took me to San Francisco to have a blue uniform made. A few days later I was taken to Mare Island, where a suit of greys was tailored at the Exchange Uniform Shop. I am sure that all sub survivors were offered the same." He was then moved closer to home to the Long Beach Naval Hospital, where he was a patient for a time with shipmate Hayes Trukke and two newly promoted survivors from *Grenadier*, CSM Lynn Clark and CGM Bill Wise.[12]

When Dick O'Kane was flown into Guam, Admiral Lockwood found him to be yellow from jaundice and literally just skin and bones. ComSubPac was convinced that *Tang*'s famous skipper would not have survived a few more weeks as a POW. Choosing to make a slow return home via Pearl Harbor so that his body could recover from its frightful condition, O'Kane was nonetheless upbeat about his survival. "Our prayers had been answered and we found our families and loved ones fine," he recalled.[13]

Months before, Ernestine O'Kane had at last received some slim hope that her husband might be alive. Submarine officer Dusty Dornin, an old friend of her husband, knew that O'Kane has survived *Tang*'s sinking and was being held as a prisoner. Against all regulations, Dornin wrote a letter to Ernie O'Kane, telling her that a garbled message had been received saying that an American named Jed O'King was alive in the prison camps and that the only person that the military could closely match to this name was Dick O'Kane. It was far from confessing that he knew O'Kane was alive, but at least he had given his fellow skipper's wife a remote hope to cling to. The wire dispatch from the Omori camp finally confirmed that he was indeed alive.[14]

Ernie O'Kane was reunited with her husband Dick at a train station in 1945 in New Hampshire. "I raced up to him and kissed him," she later recalled. "He looked about 55 years old. He was not yet 35 years old."[15]

O'Kane and his fellow POWs had a new outlook. "At sea or ashore, none of us would ever take our wonderful land with all its freedoms for granted."[16]

Ofuna and Tokyo Camps Liberated

The three *Perch* radiomen were the only U.S. submariners still kept at Ofuna at the time the war ended. According to Ted Reh, U.S. and British radiomen at Ofuna were tasked with training Japanese recruits in operating radios. When Japan surrendered, the prisoners were lined up and told that the war was over. Just as in other camps, Reh noted how quickly the Japanese guards disappeared the next day, leaving the prisoners alone in camp with the gates open.[17]

Grenadier's Lt. Al Toulon remained in a camp opposite from Tokyo until 6 September 1945. Prior to his release from prison camp, he received a laceration to the forehead and cheek when struck by soap dropped from a B-29. Toulon was impressed that his teeth held up as well as they did in spite of the fact that he was without a toothbrush for a full year.

On the morning of 22 August, *Perch*'s Lt. Bev Van Buskirk and his fellow prisoners were ordered out of their Yokohama barracks and told that the war had ended. "The first thing we did was to make a large PW sign on the hill behind our camp out of rocks and then painted it white with a paste of flour and water," he recalled. Carrier-based aircraft dropped supplies and notes to the POWs in the camp on 25 August. The supply drops became more numerous over the following week as B-29s rained down barrels of goods.

On the morning of 11 September, some of the prisoners killed a shaggy old horse that was standing just outside the prison gates. The camp cooks were grilling steaks when they received word to break camp immediately and head for a train that was ready to pick them up at the base of the hill. "As we headed out of the gate, the aroma from the galley brought tears to our eyes," Lieutenant Van Buskirk later wrote. "We knew we were passing up our first opportunity in three and a half years to have a nice juicy steak."[18]

Grenadier skipper Lt. Cdr. John Fitzgerald spent his last weeks of captivity working in Japanese shipyards from camp 4-B at Naoetsu, near Tokyo. On the afternoon of 15 August, the work parties were dismissed, told that there was no power at the factory. Fitzgerald knew right away that the war must be over because the camp still had lights and a radio blasting away.[19]

After the commandant announced on 20 August the war was over, Fitzgerald protested heavily to the camp officials to increase food rations and cigarettes for the POWs. On 25 August, six planes from *Lexington* flew over. "One cannot imagine the joy felt by all hands," he wrote. "The facial expressions were something I'll always remember. Some of the men were crying like infants."[20]

Camp officials gave in to Fitzgerald's requests this day and trucks began rolling into camp carrying Japanese emergency rations, biscuits, canned tangerines, rice, and vegetables. Additional supplies were dropped from aircraft over the next few days. "We began eating like kings," wrote Fitzgerald. Liberation proved to be a dreadfully slow process, so Fitzgerald arranged for railroad transportation of all Naoetsu POWs. He sent the majority of the camp out on 5 September and followed on 6 September with the balance of the POWs.[21]

While waiting to be liberated, Fitzgerald went to great lengths writing reports to document his ordeals as a POW in Japan. His secret diary, taken in Omori, ended up in American hands once again. The interpreter, Private Mono, obtained it from Japanese files and gave it to Lt. Cdr. Dave Hurt before his return. Fitzgerald's diary was passed to Adm. Bill Halsey. Fitzgerald briefed senior officers at Yokohama on 6 September on his ordeal and that of his fellow prisoners. The next evening, he left Japan aboard a C-54 transport plane and arrived in the United States on 12 September.

Liberation day at Mitsushima (Tokyo 12-B Tenryu camp) came on 4 September. Among the 93 American survivors were U.S. Navy survivors captured in the Philippines from the submarine tender *Canopus*, and *Sculpin*'s only officer survivor, Lt. George Brown. During his four-and-a-half months at this camp, Brown had presided over the funerals of 43 Americans who died of pneumonia. "I, as the senior American officer, would say prayers which I had to make up since there was no Bible or prayer book available."[22]

Upon liberation from Mitsushima, George Brown rode a train to the coast along with 43 boxes of ashes of the cremated American POWs. He boarded a U.S. destroyer and soon was reunited with other *Sculpin* shipmates. He was overjoyed to find that all 20 enlisted men who had made it to Japan with him in 1943 had also survived their prison camp ordeals.

Rokuroshi Liberation

At the mountain camp of Rokuroshi, five American submarine officers remained by the time the war ended—Kevin Harty, John Critchlow, Jake Vandergrift, K. G. Schacht, and Jack Ryder. Vandergrift had dropped 60 pounds and was down to about 130 pounds by early September. On 17 August, the Rokuroshi prisoners were allowed to stop working.

Lieutenant Habe gathered the men of Rokuroshi camp on 22 August at 1600 and announced to them that the war was over. On 30 August, Jack Ryder and three other officers were trucked out for Kyoto and they returned the next night with a truckload of supplies from other prisoner camps.[23]

On 2 September, the United States flag was raised over the camp and the men renamed it "Camp Mallette" in honor of the only man to die there. The first rescue teams arrived on 7 September 1945, and the prisoners celebrated with a big bonfire in the evening. Japanese trucks pulled into camp two days later and began evacuating the men from the mountain camp to the town of Fukui. They were moved to Yokohama the following day and arrangements for their transportation home followed.

"The U.S. Army got to us on 8 September and rescued us," recalled Lieutenant Harty from *Grenadier*. "I was in good health, very thin, but good health. I had been about 160 pounds but had gotten down to about 89 pounds." During his entire internment in Japan, his parents had only received one postcard from him in 1944 to know that he was alive. Harty was flown to Guam for interrogation and from there began his long return trip home.

Ashio Liberation

At the time the atomic bombs were dropped on Hiroshima and Nagasaki, the Ashio mining camps were home to more than three dozen submarine survivors from four of the "lost boats." This group included Chief of the Boat Tony Duva and Bill Whitemore from *S-44*, Lt. Cdr. Dave Hurt of *Perch*, Cliff Kuykendall from *Tullibee*, all 20 *Sculpin* enlisted men, and 14 *Grenadier* survivors: Bob Palmer, Lou Poss, George Stauber, Charlie Erishman, Buck Withrow, Charlie Westerfield, Fred Zufelt, Pete Zucco, John Walden, Carl Quarterman, John McBeath, Lynn Clark, and Bill Wise.

Ed Keller was stunned to hear from a kindly Japanese civilian guard in the mine that one bomb had destroyed a whole city. Bill Cooper and Keller had narrowly escaped death in the Ashio mine at war's end when a big rock came loose and tons of rocks crashed down, burying Cooper's drill in the rubble. Paul Murphy recalled, "On the 15th of August, we quit working at noon and they sent a truck to pick us up and ride us back to camp."

Guard George Enomoto, who had become friends with *Perch*'s Dave Hurt, "induced him to join the wild green-picking detail on the afternoon of the 15th August and to go out of the camp." Enomoto had heard Hirohito announce that the war was over but the 213 prisoners of Ashio's Tokyo 9-B Detached Camp could not yet be told. The work party hiked two kilometers from camp, passing across a bridge over a ravine before taking a brief break outside of a rustic tobacco shop. Enomoto carefully leaned in toward Lieutenant Commander Hurt and whispered, "Just for the time being, only between you and me, the war is over." Enomoto recalled that Dave Hurt "just smiled with tears in both his eyes."[24]

The Japanese guards refused to admit the war was over. George Rocek felt that perhaps the Allies had made a landing on Japan and the guards were trying to prevent them from escaping. Determined to find out the truth, some of the POWs decided to break one of the camp's golden rules. "The worst thing you could do was to smoke on your rice mat," recalled Ed Keller. "Fire could destroy the barracks." Two of the prisoners sat in the barracks, smoking cigarettes on their rice mat bedding. Instead of beating them, the guards fetched the interpreter, who pleaded with them, "Please don't smoke on the beds!" Keller stated, "We then knew the war was over."[25]

During the next week, the guards directed the 256 POWs at Ashio's main camp to paint 20-foot-tall "PW" letters on a barracks roof. Commandant Numajiri began distributing food, clothing, and Red Cross rations that had been long withheld from the POWs. "The old guards quickly disappeared from camp and they were replaced by new ones, who were just as nice as they could be," Bill Cooper related. "Japan was scraping the bottom of the barrel at that time," Cliff Kuykendall recalled of the new guards. "They weren't much, but they were friendly. One of them kept smiling and telling me in Japanese, 'friend,' and 'no more war.'"

It was not until 25 August that U.S. pilots located the Ashio mountain camps. Lt. Samuel B. Hibbard of *Bataan*'s VF-47 took his wingmen north from Tokyo to look for additional POW camps. The clouds in the mountains became heavy and Hibbard was preparing to turn back when he spotted a large PW painted on a rooftop through a hole in the clouds. He advised his wingmen to mark his position in case he did not make it back. Hibbard dived his F6F Hellcat through the tight opening and roared over the Ashio camp, dumping candy, cigarettes, and provisions he had in his cockpit for just such an opportunity.[26]

Lieutenant Hibbard narrowly avoided the Ashio mountains but tossed down a hand-scribbled note with his provisions before he departed. Dave Hurt took possession of the note, which read in part, "Greetings!! It won't be long—they are making initial landings today. PEACE should come to you fellows soon." As Sam Hibbard's Grumman roared away, guard George Enomoto watched Lieutenant Commander Hurt shade his eyes from the sun and stare with a face pale with excitement. "I saw tears filling his eyes and a sublime smile on his face."[27]

During the next few days, carrier planes and B-29s unleashed crates over Ashio, some of which crashed through buildings. "We really feasted then, day and night," said Moon Rocek. "We made up a list of the Korean and Japanese mine workers who had treated us decently. They were brought to camp and we gave them all the supplies of clothing, food, etc., that would be left behind. They all left with tears in their eyes."[28]

On 30 August, Bataan survivor William J. La Fitte and four other POWs created an American flag, the first to ever fly over Ashio. "For three weeks, all we did was smoke, eat, and talk about what we would do once we got back home," Bill Cooper recalled.[29]

"The nuclear bombs saved us, I guess," Kuykendall recalled. "We had been told that if America ever invaded Japan, they would kill all of us POWs. The atomic bombs saved my life and everyone else's." As conditions improved, he was able to write a letter to his family back home in Texas on 31 August.

> My dearest family,
> Today I am 21. Am spending my 21st birthday in Ashio, Japan, a Jap prisoner work camp in mountains north of Tokyo 90 miles. Have been here since Oct. 3, 44. Have never heard from you. Have written you about six times. Hope you know I'm alive. Yank planes have been dropping food & clothing. We are certainly a happy bunch of fellows. Am well.
> Cliff

During the American submariners' time at Ashio, two American POWs and 22 Dutch prisoners died. *S-44* survivor Bill Whitemore heard a rumor that the surrender terms of the Japanese were slated to be signed on his birthday, 31 August, although the date was pushed back two days.

Grenadier chief of the boat Buck Withrow was moved by the torture and abuse his skipper had endured during the war to protect his crew and America's military secrets. "I think as much of Fitzgerald, our skipper, as I almost do of my father. He went through hell for us," Withrow stated. "They beat him, jumped on his stomach and tortured him by burning splints under his nails. He never talked. They even had him working in the mines for telling the Jap Commander just what he thought of him."

Loaded with American, Dutch, and British survivors on 5 September, a train moved south toward Yokohama, leaving the mountains behind. Hidden from view far to the south of this area was the worst of the damage caused by the atomic bombs. Ed Keller related, "Maybe if we had seen Hiroshima, we might have felt sorry for them." When the train pulled into its terminal at Yokohama, "the first person to greet us was a U.S. Army nurse with cigarettes and candy bars. What a beautiful sight!" Moon Rocek said. The survivors boarded buses that took them to the city's wharf.[30]

The naval base at Yokohama became a decontamination center and a reunion point for POWs preparing to board ships for passage out of Japan. The 20 *Sculpin* enlisted men happily encountered Lt. George Brown, fresh from his journey out of the Matsushima prison camp. Bob Palmer, *Grenadier*'s yeoman, ran into electrician's mate Ralph Adkins, who was fresh out of Fukuoka Camp No. 3 and busily wolfing down a sandwich in the base cafeteria.[31]

"Hello, there, Ralph L. Adkins," the yeoman called, using the sailor's full name by memory from typing it into muster rolls.

"Well, hello, there, Robert W. Palmer," Adkins shot back, surprising his shipmate with his own memory.

Palmer and shipmates George Stauber and Bill Wise were suffering from dysentery upon their arrival at this base. They found that eating foods like sugar and potatoes tended to make them run for the nearest benjo due to the spastic nature of their illness. Stauber and Wise solved this problem by taking trays of food to the benjo to sit down and eat, where nature could simply take its course. "When we were confronted with all that food, all at once, we went a little crazy," recalled Palmer.[32]

The survivors were decontaminated at the wharf, where hospital ships were moored alongside. Rocek went on board USS *Ozark* (LSV-2), while some—like *Sculpin*'s George Brown, Bill Cooper, and Ed Keller and *S-44*'s Tony Duva—flew directly home. His first plane lost power to an engine and was forced to return. While waiting overnight for another plane, Cooper sifted through a hangar and collected a Japanese rifle and bayonet. His next plane reached Pearl Harbor, where he enjoyed the steak dinners in officers' country. Admiral Nimitz gave each surviving submariner $500 and the Purple Heart. Cornering Cooper, Lockwood asked about the seven survivors. "No, there's 21 of us," he informed ComSubPac. "I've got a list of everybody and their addresses."

Cooper spent two weeks in the Oak Knoll Hospital before he was well enough to transfer to a naval air station hospital near his Memphis home. Cooper was finally reunited with his family after years apart. "My folks never even saw me in a uniform from the time I left home until I came home after prison camp."

The wife of ship's cook Andy Anderson found Cooper in the Oak Knoll Hospital. "As our cook, he had put on some weight before we were lost, so his wife probably thought he now looked very thin." Pharmacist John McBeath also caught a direct flight out to Guam. "When I was repatriated, we were flown over the bombed cities," McBeath recalled, "and they were flat."[33]

Tony Duva was the first of the two *S-44* survivors to reach the United States on 13 September. He gave an account of his ordeal to the local Oakland, California, newspaper while at the Alameda VR-2 base. The reporter found the chief torpedoman to be "unusually healthy looking for a former prisoner" and that Bill Whitemore was due to arrive in a day or so. Duva was eager to return to Pennsylvania to visit his brother Joseph.[34]

Word came out that a third *S-44* survivor had been found in the Japanese camps, Rhollo Rhodney Fees, of Clifton Heights, Pennsylvania. Although Fees' name originally showed up on a Red Cross list as a survivor, Duva and Whitemore discovered that it was a mistake.

Aboard *Ozark*, *Sculpin* survivor Mike Gorman found that his faith had carried him through. A 156-pound teenager when he entered the service in 1943, he weighed 94 pounds on 29 August. Gorman attended a church service on the fantail of *Ozark* and suddenly felt "a tremendous sense of peace and wholeness come over him. God had carried him through."[35]

Rocek, Gorman, and other submarine survivors, including Lou Poss and Fred Zufelt from *Grenadier*, rode *Ozark* from Japan to Guam, arriving there on 12 September. The submariners were treated with great respect and were given a steak dinner in their honor. Some of the men were allowed to send telegrams home to their families. *S-44*'s Bill Whitemore wired his parents back in Illinois from Guam on 12 September, "Rescued by Americans. Am well. Will be home soon. Love, William." The following day, Whitemore dashed off another quick telegram, "Feeling fine. Awaiting transportation."[36]

Ozark departed Guam and traveled to Pearl Harbor for another brief layover. Upon arrival in San Francisco, the submarine men were the first to leave the ship. The Submarine Force had individual cars, with an officer assigned for each submarine POW who was returning. "They took us to a hotel for a large welcome dinner," Rocek recalled. "We were all impressed and proud to be submariners, and knew that we were not forgotten."[37]

After his discharge from Oak Knoll Hospital, Rocek caught a train to Chicago. He called his sister, arranging for her to meet him. "It was heart-wrenching, with all the crying and sobbing," he recalled. In Chicago, he took the elevated train to his dad's tailor shop, where Rocek noted the look of shock as his father viewed his son's skinny body. "My mother heard the commotion in the shop and came running out, crying," he said.[38]

Joe Baker was another *Sculpin* survivor who rode *Ozark* back to California for recovery at the Treasure Island Hospital. Raised in a small town in western Massachusetts, he was eager to call his family in Boston upon his arrival in San Francisco. "They never knew that I was a POW, even after we were liberated in Tokyo Harbor," Baker recalled.

When the phone was answered in Boston, he knew his mother's voice.

"Hi, Mom! This is Joe," Baker said.

"Who?" asked Mrs. Baker.

"This is your son, Joe."

Mrs. Baker fainted. His fourteen-year-old sister snatched up the receiver and demanded, "Just a moment whoever this is. I want to talk to you!"

After a quick explanation that he had indeed survived the sinking of his ship and years as a prisoner of war, Joe Baker convinced his younger sister that he was truly alive. His mother came around and got back on the phone for a joyous reunion. "My name had already been put on the town memorial as lost in war," he recalled. "It was quite a shock for her."

Liberation at Fukuoka

On 15 August—Tom Courtney's 23rd birthday—a reduced number of Fukuoka No. 3 POWs went to work at the Yawata Steel Mill but they returned at noon. The usual rumors flew that perhaps the war was over, but this time there was a new, strange rumor. "Mixed in with the other rumors were ones that the U.S. had dropped bombs that had destroyed whole cities," recalled *Grenadier* sailor Gordon Cox. "We didn't believe anything until it happened; then, you had your doubts."[39]

The first indication Cox and *Grenadier*'s other 37 survivors had that there might be some truth in these rumors was the mannerisms of the usually brutal Japanese guards. When Cox encountered one guard, the Japanese man turned and ran from him. All told, 64 Americans—including four from *Grenadier*—had died at the brutal Fukuoka No. 3 camp, plus 13 British POWs, 50 Dutchmen, 25 Indians, and 6 other nationalities.

"The few men who had gone to work came back and said the war was over," recalled Bill Cunningham. "The Jap guards had gone, but the Americans were told not to leave camp but to wait to be liberated." Some of the POWs went into town to find out if the rumors were true. Cunningham and his companions immediately moved out of their filthy barracks to escape the bedbugs.[40]

The camp interpreter spread the word on 16 August that the war was truly over. "Praise the Lord," Tom Courtney penned in his forbidden diary. "Soon we will get all we want to eat but what I want now is a good night's sleep." Al Rupp recalled, "My mind whirled with the words I had just heard."[41]

Beginning 30 August, B-29s began dropping "cases of chow, candy, cigarettes and gum," wrote Courtney. "It was like Christmas—chow from heaven. A horio's [prisoner's] dream." Angus McGowan—who weighed 140 pounds when *Grenadier* was lost—was down to 89 pounds. "Dropping all that food was the worst thing they could have done," McGowan stated. "We weren't able to digest all those heavy foods and we became sick." Some men explored outside their camp. On the night of 2 September—when the men were officially informed of their freedom—Tom Courtney slipped away to the beach with buddies Joe Price, John Schwartzly, Charles Roskell, and an Army prisoner. "It was dark as hell and I fell in a creek," Courtney wrote. "It was funny."[42]

Some grew tired of waiting on liberation and left camp on their own. Elwood O'Brion and Angus McGowan left camp with Skeeter McCoy and Chuck Ver

Valin. "I didn't stay in my camp to wait for the Yanks and tanks to come and release us," McCoy said. "We just walked out of prison camp and went across the bay to the main island of Japan. We got on a train and got to Hiroshima, where we met a war correspondent named Bob Taylor from the *New York Times*." In need of an interpreter, Taylor asked the *Grenadier* men to accompany him for the next few weeks on his journey through the Tokyo area.

McCoy, Ver Valin, McGowan, and O'Brion eventually flew on a transport plane out of Tokyo to Guam, where they found a transport waiting on them. Upon arrival back at Oak Knoll Hospital in California, they transferred on to hospitals closer to their homes as soon as they were fit. McCoy was less than 100 pounds upon his liberation, down some 70 pounds from his normal size. He was finally able to reunite with his parents while in California.

McCoy left Oak Knoll for home with Ver Valin and McGowan. "We stopped in Texas, where McCoy got off," recalled McGowan. "Chuck got off in Washington and I was flown to the naval hospital in Portsmouth." After a short time recovering in Virginia, McGowan was finally able to make his way back home to Charlotte for a reunion with his mother and family members.

The majority of the Fukuoka prisoners remained in camp during the next week, where supplies began running low. Those in charge managed to come up with enough beer one day for everyone to have a bottle, while others managed to buy extra bottles off the non-drinkers. "There was half a dozen of the submarine crew that had done the same thing," recalled Gordon Cox. "We sat in a circle talking and drank our beer. In our emaciated condition, the beer had a pretty strong effect."[43]

Cox, Joe "Gringo" Ingram, Irving Loftus, and a few others departed camp on foot in ragged clothing the next morning. Loftus struggled with walking due to a badly swollen foot from beriberi. The *Grenadier* men traveled via trains and a ferry to Yokohama, where they were deloused, given showers, clothing, and Red Cross supplies.[44]

Cox, wearing a T-shirt, cut-off dungarees, and an old sailor's cap, went on board USS *Hyde* on 15 September in Tokyo Harbor. He reached Guam on 17 September, and was flown to Pearl Harbor a week later. He arrived in San Francisco two days later, where he spent a week recovering. Reaching home in Yakima via Seattle, he was met at the bus depot on 2 October by his two younger brothers. "The folks had aged a great deal, and Mother's hair was completely gray. The war had been hard on them, also."[45]

Bill Cunningham, Joe Price, and others also left Fukuoka and took a train into Tokyo. "Some went south and some went north, but only a few obeyed orders and remained in camp," Cunningham recalled.[46]

Bernie Witzke, long troubled with beriberi, was among the majority of the *Grenadier* crew who stayed in camp as directed. Down to 98 pounds from his normal

190 pounds, he was much relieved by the continued air drops of supplies. "The Japanese civilians around Fukuoka were also really happy that the war was over," Witzke recalled. "The Japanese military had virtually made prisoners of many of them during the war."

While waiting to leave Japan, Tom Courtney went into the town of Kokura with Rex Evans and John Schwartzly. He obtained a small booklet to copy his diary notes into. "I transposed and enlarged on many items taken from the original, which was largely written in my own code just in case the Japs found it," Courtney related. "The original I gave to Angus McGowan." Some of the original document was literally scraps of paper from cigarette packs that he had kept hidden under a loose board under his sleeping mat in the camp.[47]

Virgil Ouillette, who had lost 80 pounds, recalled: "They picked us up at the shore at Nagasaki and we went on an English carrier. That's where they took care of us and debugged us. Then we went to Okinawa." TM3c Riley Keysor also rode an old steamship back to Treasure Island, where his family finally reunited with him in his California hospital room.

Bill Cunningham, waiting on a transport ship, was called for a flight and was the only submariner on the plane. He was pleased to find a submarine representative on hand at every stop. The first-class treatment for the returning U.S. submariners did not end in the United States. At Alameda, an officer with "a big blue Chrysler with gold dolphins painted on the side" picked up Cunningham and gave the *Grenadier* survivor a tour of Los Angeles.[48]

Liberation of Makassar and Batavia Camps

The last U.S. submarine POWs to be liberated were those from *Perch*, the men who had spent the longest time in captivity since their boat's loss on 3 March 1942.

Turk Turner always held a ray of optimism for his fellow *Perch* shipmates throughout their ordeal. By August 1945, he had gotten out of the hospital from his bout with malaria. He continued to tell his glum shipmates, "Hey, they're gonna be here tomorrow."

Turner was still unable to walk well enough to go on work detail. When he woke up one morning, his electrician buddy Jesse Robison was preparing to go to work. Turner rolled over and said, "Hey, Robbie, something's happened."

Robison pessimistically replied, "Yeah, I know. They're gonna be here tomorrow. You've been saying that for years!"

"I know that," Turner protested. "But Robbie, something has happened. I can feel it!"

Robison shook his head and headed out with the other prisoners to work while Turner remained in his barracks. Around 1000, he saw Robison's working party marching back in through the main gate into camp. Instead of searching the party for illegal contraband this day, the guards instead told the men to run back to their barracks.

"What happened?" someone asked in the barracks.

"The war is over with!" Turner cried triumphantly.

"Aaahh!" shouted several others who had heard their optimistic shipmate one too many times.

Turner confidently repeated, "The war is over with."

The Japanese refused to say anything at first when the work parties were returned. "We knew something was going on," said Seaman Ben Clevinger. The prisoners remained in their barracks for three days after the first atomic bomb was dropped. After the second bomb was dropped, the Japanese commander called all of the men up to the camp's front gate. He climbed up on a chair and announced that the war was over. "There was no cheering, no celebration," Tom Moore recalled. "We were too exhausted."[49]

Pope survivor EM3c Bill Seward got the word on the surrender via a note written in English that someone threw over the wall into the Makassar camp. "There were no horns, bells or any noise at all," Seward recalled, "just a soft hush overall. We all, in our own way, said a prayer that we had survived the last three and a half years."[50]

Alabama Arnette, at work in the bomb-making shop, was worried how much longer his body could hold out when word of the surrender reached him. "This Japanese guy came to the door of our barracks and said, 'The war is over,'" Arnette related. "And then he just turned and left." The Makassar prisoners raided a nearby bombed pig farm and celebrated their newfound freedom with a pork stew and rice dinner. Arnette said, "I had the best pork dinner I've ever had in my life."

Ernie Plantz recalled that their guards suddenly wanted to be friendly. "They stuck out their hands and wanted to shake our hands," he said. "Needless to say, we didn't do any hand shaking. These were the same bastards that held us prisoner for three and a half years." The prisoners were finally paid for their slave labor. "The Japanese thought it was the funniest damn thing in the world, not paying us," Plantz said. "We never saw a penny of it until the war was over and they surrendered. They paid us our ten cents a day for 1,297 days."

During the days which followed, the *Perch* and *Pope* prisoners moved back into town and took over the hospital that the Japanese had operated. Turk Turner managed to steal a large belt of fine cloth as the Japanese guards were packing out of camp. His cloth became an effective bartering item with islanders who passed by with chickens and eggs.

When hostilities ceased in the Pacific, U.S. military forces were initially unaware of the illegal prison camp at Makassar-Celebes. The Asiatic Fleet sailors—among the first to be captured by the Japanese in World War II—were among the last to be discovered.

"On September 13, a B-25 flew over and men ran to get the American flag and show it," recalled Ben Clevinger. "The pilot signaled he saw us and the next day dropped off a radio." The plane carried General Earl Walter Barnes, commander of the 13th Air Force. The POWs related that only 988 Dutch, British and American prisoners remained from more than 2,800 in 1942.[51]

The radio dropped by the B-25 crew became a hot item. Although it had been dropped by Americans, the senior British officer refused to let the *Perch* and *Pope* survivors use it. "So, that night at midnight we put our radioman in there and had him send out a message," said Turk Turner. A short while later, a listener in Australia picked up their dispatch and promised to notify the American military.

Tom Moore and two buddies celebrated the impending arrival of the Air Force by getting drunk. The senior British officer among the former POWs had the trio confined to the brig for their celebration. When General Barnes arrived the next day, a chief petty officer in charge of the American contingent informed him that three American sailors, who had survived more than three years as POWs, were in the brig for celebrating their release.[52]

Barnes demanded that Moore and his buddies be released immediately. "We flew out aboard the general's bomber and were the first three POWs from our camp to make it back to Palawan in the Southern Philippines," Moore related. "We became celebrities. They put us up on a stage before a crowd who cheered when told we had just been released from a Jap prison camp."

When the planes began dropping supplies over the camps, Alabama Arnette once again felt it was "heaven on earth because we had been beaten around so badly. The Japanese had told us we were no better than dogs. When the planes came flying in low, I'll never forget how wonderful it felt to be an American. They dropped us cigarettes, candy, and all sorts of good things to eat."

As the American planes began arriving at Makassar and Batavia, news was flashed back to the United States of the survival of the *Perch* and *Pope* crews. Within days, the liberation process and the circuitous route home commenced on 17 September for the long-lost prisoners. Most went via Borneo, Palawan, Manila, Johnston Island, Guam, and Hawaii to Oakland, California. Upon landing in Manila, the survivors were given physicals, shots, and debriefings concerning their return for home.

"All of us weighed 100 pounds or less when we were rescued," said six-foot-tall Ben Clevinger. Ernie Plantz, having dropped from 175 pounds to 75 during his ailment in January 1945, had managed to "beef up" to 85 pounds by war's end. Bud Harper weighed 76 pounds when he was liberated. Stephen Orlyk was down to 90 pounds, a drop in weight of 100 pounds. In contrast, Turk Turner only dropped to about 140 pounds, which he attributed to his art of stealing any kind of food whenever possible throughout his internment.[53]

The Americans began liberating Batavia's camp on 18 September, where 40 men remained. The prisoners awoke one morning to find a single guard present- ing arms under a Japanese flag at half-mast. "We decided something was going on so we walked up to the front gate," recalled Bob Lents. "The Japanese presented arms to us and we walked through the gate and outside." The American prisoners encountered excited Javanese natives outside the compound. In their crude com- munication to Lents and his comrades, the Javanese "told us there was the 'big boom' and the war was over."

Lents' family found out that he was alive due to a war correspondent named Jack Shelley aboard one of the planes. "This guy used to give the news over the radio station up there in Des Moines, Iowa, before the war," Lents stated.

Shelley moved about, interviewing the American survivors, asking them their names and where they were from. Recognizing the former radioman's voice, Lents walked over and said, "Well, hi there, Jack Shelley."

"How the hell do you know me?" Shelley asked.

"Well, I've heard your news many a times," Lents stated.

The correspondent helped Lents by sending a telegram back to WHO radio station in Des Moines that night. "They announced on the radio that I was alive," Lents said. "My family heard the news while they were eating breakfast. They couldn't hardly believe what they were hearing."

From Batavia, Lents was flown to Calcutta, India, and placed in an Army hospi- tal to recover. From 160 pounds, his weight upon entering the hospital was a mere 80 pounds. "That was even after they had been dropping food in the prison camp and we'd been eating pretty good," Lents recalled. When he was able to travel again, he spent some time recovering and being dewormed in St. Albans Naval Hospital on Long Island before catching a flight and a bus back into his Iowa hometown in November.

Turk Turner was the last of the *Perch* survivors to be flown from Makassar to Balikpapan, where he found "all the beer you could drink. We couldn't drink much, though. Our stomachs were so small that we just couldn't handle it." Turner was next flown to Palawan, where he and Robbie Robison were issued chits for cases of beer. They found themselves very popular with the local troops who were on strict beer rationing. After flights to Saipan and Johnston Island, Turner finally arrived at Pearl Harbor. At the Pearl Harbor Submarine Base, Turner was given his submarine combat pin for the successful war patrols he had made back in early 1942.

Ben Clevinger reached Manila on 18 September, where he was first allowed to call his family back home. Like the other liberated submariners before them, the *Perch* crewmen endured long rehabilitation. Torpedoman Sam Simpson spent some time in Oakland and then was transferred to a hospital closer to home at Quantico,

Virginia. It was early 1946 before Simpson, advanced to chief torpedoman, was sufficiently recovered to continue his naval career.

Torpedoman Bill Atkeison cabled his parents from Manila, saying he was "doing fine. Will be home soon as possible." His parents in Mobile, Alabama, were filled with nervous excitement. News of his return made the front page of the local paper. "We had a letter from Warren the Christmas four years from this coming Christmas," his mother told the *Mobile Press*. "Since that time we were notified by the Navy that he could be presumed lost."[54]

Arnette and his best friend Dan Crist made it aboard the same transport plane from Makassar. After stops at Borneo, Palawan, and Manila, they finally landed at Pearl Harbor—where both were interviewed by intelligence officers on 30 September. "They called Crist and I out of the ranks when we got to Hawaii," Arnette recalled. "We were given the Purple Heart and they took us around the island like special guests. Then, when we got to San Diego, they pulled me and Crist out again and an officer took us out for steak dinners."

The *Perch* officers, radiomen, and machinist's mates who had been moved to mainland Japan in 1942 were liberated prior to their other shipmates on Celebes. In the mining camp of Orio and in the shipyards, the machinists were liberated on 15 September 1945, Bernie Deleman's 25th birthday. Deleman, Rudy Klecky, Joe Foley, Lawrence Dague, Calvin Goodwine, Jim McCray, and Felix Walton from *Perch*'s engine rooms had survived more than two years at Fukuoka 6-B while slaving in the Orio coal mines and nearby shipyards.

Perch skipper Dave Hurt was flown back to Annapolis for a reunion with his family on 12 September, including his wife and three sons. His oldest boy David Hurt Jr. was by then a midshipman at the Naval Academy. When he stepped from his plane, he was wearing the insignia of a lieutenant commander, his rank at the time of his capture. Capt. E. R. Durgin, Director of Training, Bureau of Naval Personnel, presented Hurt with his captain's commission upon his arrival. He received his new four-stripe gray shoulder boards, which were placed on him by his wife, along with a new "scrambled egg" captain's cap. Other officers in his welcoming party, including Capt. Morton Mumma from his Academy class, replenished his uniform with the proper shoulder boards and eagles on his shirt collar and cap.[55]

Hurt's oldest son, 19-year-old Dave Hurt Jr. was deeply moved by the reunion with his "lost" father. The Academy celebrated its 100th anniversary on October 10, 1945. Captain Hurt was present for the homecoming football game, where his son participated as a flag bearer during the halftime ceremonies. The announcer paid tribute to Captain Hurt, saying that he was an Academy man who has just been liberated from Japaneses POW camps. "The tremendous round of applause from the stands in honor of my dad is something I'll never forget," Dave Hurt Jr. recalled.[56]

Perch, Grenadier, Tullibee, Sculpin, S-44, Tang, and *Robalo* were among the 52 U.S. submarines lost during World War II from all causes. These seven submarines are the only ones from which survivors are known to have been directly taken into Japanese prisoner camps. From these seven lost boats, 525 men were listed on their final muster rolls. Of these 525, only 196 men were fortunate enough to be picked up or captured by Japanese forces. Two of them were immediately thrown back into the ocean to die. At least two others were later executed.

Twenty more of these U.S. submariners perished when the aircraft carrier they were aboard en route to Japan was sunk by a U.S. submarine. Fourteen others died in Japanese captivity from various causes. None of the captured *Robalo* men survived their internment. Only Cliff Kuykendall from *Tullibee* survived to tell of his ship's last days. Bill Whitemore and Tony Duva were the only two from *S-44* to be taken as POWs.

From the other boats, 9 men from *Tang* returned to American in 1945 and 21 from *Sculpin* saw their homes again. *Grenadier* and *Perch*'s crews had the greatest number of survivors, although they lost ten men due to the subhuman conditions in the POW camps. Once officially listed as "overdue and presumed lost," these men had gone through unspeakable suffering.

All told, the U.S. Navy lost 374 officers and 3,131 enlisted men of the submarine service during World War II. These men, including those who died after being captured, are now on the honor roll of submariners who are "on eternal patrol." A handful of men who had served on *Sealion* and the sub tender *Canopus* in the Philippines when these islands were overrun were returned from Japan at war's end. From the seven lost boats that had men captured by the Japanese, only 158 men (including 17 officers) out of 525 made it home alive from the prison camps.

Epilogue

The hell ships *Hie Maru* and *Asama Maru,* which transported *Grenadier* and *Perch* survivors, were both torpedoed and sunk by U.S. submarines before the war's end. *Drum* destroyed *Hie Maru* with a spread of four torpedoes fired on 17 November 1943. *Asama Maru* survived until torpedoes from *Atule* finished her off in November 1944. "Enjoyed hearing that they met their end by a sub," *Grenadier* survivor Bill Wise, badly injured during beatings he endured on these ships, later stated. "Poetic justice, I'd say."[1]

Among the men who participated in the war crimes trials in early 1946 and 1947 were Dick O'Kane, Floyd Caverly, and Leibold from *Tang*; John Fitzgerald from *Grenadier*; John Rourke and Cecil Baker from *Sculpin*; and Frank O'Gara, the former newspaper reporter who had been captured by a Japanese submarine. Many other members of the submarine crews were tracked down to give detailed testimony under oath about various war crimes they had endured. Tom Courtney's Fukuoka diary and the extensive notes of Fitzgerald were key pieces of evidence used in some of the war crimes trials. "It wasn't a real pleasant experience," Leibold recalled. "They were dragging their feet as far as I was concerned."

At least 137 Japanese were tried for war crimes, of which 129 were convicted, including one admiral, four vice admirals and two rear admirals. Vice Admiral Wakabayashi, in command of forces at Truk, was convicted for neglect of duty for violations committed by members of his command. His command had beaten and tortured 41 members of *Sculpin*'s crew in 1943 and performed unnecessary amputations on three of these sailors. Two of his Truk commanders were convicted of killing seven prisoners of war on Dublon by stabbing, beating or beheading them. Twelve Japanese were sentenced to death on Guam in May 1947 for their crimes. One of them was a surgeon commander on Truk who had chloroformed one POW and dissected him alive on the operating table.[2]

Two men sentenced to death were from Ofuna: Warrant officer Iida, and "Congo-cho," Pharmacist's Mate Kitamura. Hata, the cook known as "Curly" was given 20 years, while the guards that served Ofuna from 1942 to 1945 were given various sentences ranging from 4 to 40 years. From the Zentsuji camp, Commandant Hosatani was sentenced to 20 years and brutal camp doctor Saito was hanged for the abuse he had handed out to POWs.

Ashio camp commandant Shigeru Numajiri and seven of his guards were tried for war crimes in Yokohama in July 1947. Numajiri was sentenced on 7 August to 18 years of hard labor. Of the guards, Imajira Kira ("Three Fingers") received 15 years; Shigeo Eizumi ("Four Eyes") received 5 years; Takashi Neishi received 5 years; Takayoshi Shinkae ("Blue Coat") received 3 years; and the other three were acquitted.[3]

The *Perch* Survivors

The freedom from prison camp brought an end to 1,298 days of captivity for the *Perch* crew. Ernie Plantz spent ten months recovering in a hospital at Great Lakes, Illinois. He had emerged from Makassar weighing only about 80 pounds with various injuries, including a misshapen wrist from a beating that had shattered many bones. He eventually retired as a lieutenant with more than 30 years of service. He served one stint as chief of the boat of the submarine *Spikefish* in Groton. He married in 1965 and earned his business degree in the 1970s. Plantz settled in Ledyard, Connecticut, where he became active in town politics for years.[4]

In 2005, Ernie Plantz was one of the first ten men selected to receive the Connecticut Veterans Hall of Fame award. "I felt pretty proud to get that honor," he admitted. "The first man inducted was George H. W. Bush, the president." Like others, Plantz simply wanted to get on with his life at first. "I think I felt guilty and a little ashamed," he later stated. "Guilty because I didn't understand why my friends died and I didn't. Ashamed because I worked for the enemy. I didn't feel like I got a chance to do my part." In spite of his feelings, Plantz was later awarded the Bronze Star, 52 years after the loss of his ship. It would be 2006, another seven years, before the Navy pinned the commendation on his chest at age 86.[5]

Bernie Deleman spent more than a year recovering in naval hospitals before his hometown of Wilkes-Barre, Pennsylvania, could throw him a proper hero's welcome celebration in 1946. After retiring from the Navy in 1959, Deleman earned his degree in mechanical engineering and worked as a civilian employee of the

Navy Lab until 1977. He and his wife Aldina "Dee" Deleman traveled extensively and became avid golfers, in spite of an injured leg that Bernie had suffered at the hands of the Japanese during his internment.

Jack Ryder retired as a captain after 30 years in the Navy and was buried in the Arlington National Cemetery with full honors. Kenneth Schacht also retired as a full captain in 1965, when he was serving as Commanding Officer U.S. Naval Station, Annapolis.[6]

Perch's skipper, Dave Hurt, did not live long after the war. He returned to find that his wife Connie had fallen in love with another submariner and wanted a divorce. Hurt went out hunting near Tazewell, Virginia, on 22 November 1945, with two doctors, both first cousins to him. While separated from each other, there was a gunshot and Hurt was found dead. Both of the doctors ruled suicide and no serious investigation was ever made. Hurt's older brother had previously committed suicide, as had two uncles. Around the town of Tazewell, it was generally accepted that the former *Perch* captain had been depressed and shot himself. Publicly, it was labeled as "a hunting accident."[7]

Some later refused to believe that Hurt had taken his own life. K. G. Schacht, who knew his skipper well, considered the stories "lots of gossip." Schacht actually "talked with Dave for 30 minutes the night before his death. He was in excellent spirits. Dave Hurt's death was accidental. That I fully believe." Schacht firmly believed that after surviving three and a half years as a POW, "nothing could be so devastating as to cause him to take his own life."[8]

Jake Vandergrift served as executive officer of *Remora* (SS-487) after the war and then as skipper of *Tilefish* (SS-307). He later commanded Submarine Division 81, Submarine Squadron 6, and the tender *Orion* (AS-18). His last tour was as Commander Naval Station, Annapolis, Maryland, where he was also Commodore of the Naval Academy Sailing Squadron. He retired on 3 February 1969 and passed away that same month. The Naval Academy Sailing Squadron memorialized Vandergrift by naming its maintenance shop in his honor. *Perch*'s executive officer, Bev Van Buskirk, was awarded the Legion of Merit for his combat service and later commanded *Diodon* (SS-349) from 1946–48. He was physically retired in 1951 with the rank of commander and settled in San Diego. Van Buskirk joined a realty firm and later served as a technical advisor on several submarine films.

Ben Clevinger retired from the Navy in 1963 and settled in Ocala, Florida, where he worked for the post office for another 26 years. He remained in contact with many of his *Perch* and *Pope* POW buddies, and helped Ed Van Horn to orchestrate the first reunion in Ocala. Clevinger passed away in 1998 from congestive heart failure due to beriberi cardiomypathy from nutritional defects suffered while in Japan. His son, Dr. Sidney Clevinger, observed the ill effects that his father and several of his former POW buddies suffered in their later years of life.

Alabama Arnette parted ways with the military and studied upholstery and interior design at LaSalle University in Chicago. He became quite proficient in his trade, practicing for many years in San Francisco and Mill Valley, California. Arnette moved his upholstery business back to his home state of Alabama, where he worked until retiring on full disability.

Paul Richter left the Navy and returned to his hometown of San Antonio to work as a master electrician. Ted Reh retired from the Navy in the 1960s as a chief warrant officer. He worked another 20 years for the postal service before retiring to California. Sam Simpson retired as a chief underwater ordinance technician after almost 30 years' service, much of which was in submarines. Ray Normand put in 22 years of military service before moving back to Massachusetts and working as a heating technician. Stephen Orlyk completed 20 years of naval service in 1946 and was buried in the United States Veterans Cemetery in Augusta, Maine, following his death in 1985.[9]

Bob Lents, still suffering from the broken bone in his neck, was discharged from the Navy on 30 December 1946, with the rate of chief torpedoman. Now retired in Arkansas, Lents and his fellow *Perch* crewmates maintained close contact over the years. Chief electrician Pete Pederson put out a newsletter for many years and the survivors orchestrated many reunions. The first reunion in 1982 was attended by 14 *Perch* veterans, most of whom had survived a POW experience: Pederson, Richard Evans, Ken Schacht, Ed Van Horn, Sam Simpson, Paul Richter, Ben Clevinger, Bernie Deleman, Ernie Plantz, and Orvel Peters. "What a great event it was," Pederson wrote. "I met shipmates I hadn't seen since we left Makassar in 1945."[10]

The *Perch* and *Pope* crews continued their combined reunions for many years. Bill Seward of *Pope* took over the newsletter for a number of years, followed by Turk Turner of *Perch*. As of 2007, only six members of the captured *Perch* crew remained alive: Turner, Bob Lents, Alabama Arnette, Ted Reh, Ernie Plantz, and Tom Moore, and Moore passed away in 2009. Their submarine was discovered on Thanksgiving Day, 2006, by a team of Australians who were searching for the remains of the British cruiser HMS *Exeter*. They found the World War II submarine in about 190 feet of water north of Surabaya City. Confirmation of her identity was established when diver Kevin Denlay was able to photograph a plaque on the sub's conning tower. Covered with six decades of marine growth, the large lettering could still be read: U.S.S. PERCH SUBMARINE.

Seeing photos of his submarine in early 2007, Plantz was surprised. "I never thought I'd see it again," he said. These photos reminded him of his horrible experiences as a POW. "I think they bring back more bad memories than good," he told a reporter.[11]

In 1997, Ernine Plantz actually returned to Makassar, Celebes, "to see if that place was as awful as I remembered. I had a Eurasian friend who had grown up there and then become a naturalized American." With his friend, who was fluent in Malaysian, Plantz toured Makassar for ten days. "The original camp that we were in was still there but the Indonesians had converted it into low-rent, subsidized housing. We also went to the waterfront where I had offloaded ships and to places where they had made us do menial chores. It was really something."

Memories of the whole POW experience would long trouble some of the *Perch* survivors. Warren Atkeison's wife later reflected, "Nights were the worst time for him. When he did sleep, many times he had nightmares and spoke Japanese."[12]

Reflecting on his three and a half years as a POW, Alabama Arnette felt that his Japanese captors were "100 percent inhumane. They had no respect for us at all." In spite of this, he maintains no bitter feelings toward Japanese. "It's a funny thing," Arnette related. "I have a neutral feeling toward them. They were fighting a war and so were we. We had to obey their rules, but their rules and their way of fighting were different from our way."

The *Grenadier* Survivors

The effects of malnutrition and abuse sustained as POWs took their toll on some of the *Grenadier* men throughout their postwar lives. Bill Wise, who retired from the Navy as a commander, suffered from breathing problems in the 1980s, attributed to his working in the Ashio mines. Railroad Leslie spent much time in hospitals and had his back fused above his buttocks in the early 1980s to help him recover from his beatings. Denny Landrum, who had survived a botched appendix operation at Omori, returned to Richmond, Virginia, to work as an electrical contractor. He developed a heart condition attributed to the beriberi he had suffered and died at age 56 in 1980.[13]

Chuck Ver Valin remained in the Navy for 30 years, serving in Vietnam before retiring in 1970 as a lieutenant commander. Years after the war, he was shocked to open a letter one day and find more than $300 from shipmate Charles Whitlock. At Fukuoka, Ver Valin had paid off another prisoner to erase his chief's gambling debt—one that would have cost him so many days worth of food rations that he would not have survived the malnutrition. "I mailed it back to him and told him not to worry about it," Ver Valin said. "Whitlock mailed it back to me and told me to keep it. He said he had twenty years' service and had taken on a good-paying job back home, so I should take the money. He thanked me for saving his life back in the camp."

In the 1970s, the strong bond of the *Grenadier* crew's experiences brought the submarine crew back together. Bob Palmer, the former yeoman, began a monthly newsletter in mid-1981 with co-editor Ben Fulton and the crew began to have reunions. *Sculpin* survivor George Brown paid the *Grenadier* crew a visit during their 1982 Hartford reunion.

While some never fully recovered mentally from some of the abuse they endured, they moved on with life. Tom Courtney reflected in 1986, "We can all truly say that when we die, we will all go to heaven as we have already served our time in hell."[14]

To commemorate their years as POWs, many—including Al Albertson, Joe Minton, Lou Poss, Bob Palmer, Lyle Swatzke, Dempsey McGowan, and Bill Keefe—bought automobile license plates with "POW" as part of the number. Some chose "POW 210" in honor of *Grenadier*'s hull number. "I have never been stopped," Keefe wrote in 1982. "One trooper on a routine check just looked and said nothing."[15]

The convent community at Penang remained in the dark about the fate of the submarine crew until Al Toulon and Carlisle Herbert visited the school in the early 1980s. In 1982, the *Grenadier* men began sending money to the convent to support its work, and Palmer started writing to former principal and subsequent school board chairman Sister Francis de Sales. Sister Francis wrote one reply to Palmer, "For many years, the 'writing on the wall' which we regard with such reverence was, to a certain extent, shrouded in mystery. All we knew was that these brave men were the crew of an American submarine, who suffered cruel torture on our premises at the hands of the Japanese."[16]

Palmer and his wife made a trip to Penang in early 1988 after corresponding with Sister de Sales for some time. At the convent, Sister de Sales and another nun were waiting with orchids for the submarine veteran and his wife. When they were led into the the Catholic convent's gymnasium, they were met by thundering applause from 200 girls, "standing on their chairs applauding."[17]

Sister de Sales toured the Palmers about the school, taking them through the classrooms where Bob had spent so many days. The small cells behind the classrooms remained, as did the little building where John Fitzgerald had been tortured. When the sisters were allowed to begin using the convent again after the war, they had the unpleasant task of scrubbing blood and desperate messages from the walls. Where names were found carved into walls and doors, the sisters opted to leave them as permanent reminders of what had gone on in their school in World War II. The school in Convent Light collected memorabilia from *Grenadier* and built a permanent display case there.

Palmer summed up what Sister de Sales' school meant to *Grenadier* men: "To evolve from the hazards of a submariner in wartime to the agonies of being a prisoner of war, then to be able to touch hands with someone and something related to that experience, well, it is both exciting and soul-satisfying."[18]

Ben Fulton, wrote that the contact with the sisters led to closer family ties. "The children look on their parents with new pride and respect." Children from the school have felt the mark of the *Grenadier* men's generosity. Student Christine Kohr, daughter of a Malay newspaper editor, wrote to Bob Palmer: "I remember how reverently the nuns would tell us to pray alike for all those concerned—from the U.S. soldiers to their captors." *Grenadier* co-editor Fulton passed away in November

1989 and Palmer passed away in 2006.[19]

The *Grenadier* case remains on display, along with the names carved in the walls and door. "Visitors to the school are very interested in the etchings and displays," school principal Chan Gaik Ngoh said in 2000. "All of them, including a good number of Japanese tourists, want to see the room."[20]

Charles "Skeeter" McCoy stayed in the Navy and played football on the Submarine Force Pacific Fleet team. "I picked up the monicker 'Tim' while playing football, and it has stuck with me," McCoy said. He retired from the Navy in 1965 as a lieutenant and settled in Austin, Texas, where he became marketing director for National Western Life Insurance Company. In 1972, McCoy started his own insurance company, which his son now runs. Not content to take things easy, Tim McCoy still puts in a half day of work.

McCoy is philosophical on the POWs' experiences. "I believe God has a plan for you," he said. "You have to get on with your life and put this behind you. Life is very funny. The bad times seem to fade away and our minds only dwell on the good times." McCoy, often asked to speak of his experiences as a POW, quickly realized that he had to let the past go. "If you walk around with hate in your heart, the only person that really ever hurts is you," he said. "Yesterday is history and tomorrow is a mystery unless you get on with your life today."

Kevin Harty, reflecting on recent events involving American soldiers humiliating their prisoners of war in Abu Ghraib, said, "Some of what happens to prisoners is just a question of human actions." In the case of the Japanese treatment of the American submarine POWs in World War II, however, their actions went much further than mere humiliation. The fatal beatings, starvations, severe torture, forced labor, unnecessary amputations, and even medical experiments on Allied POWs betrayed civilized behavior by any country's standards.

Joe Price, who lost 50 pounds as a POW, said of his survival, "I guess I just numbed myself to what was going on. I just refused to believe it was happening. That was my only protection." Price stayed in the Navy until his retirement and then worked the remainder of his career in civil service. Price and shipmates John McBeath and Bill Cunningham all became brothers-in-law after the war when Price and McBeath married two of Cunningham's sisters.

John Fitzgerald, the much-abused skipper of *Grenadier*, continued a successful naval career. After participating in the war crimes trials during 1946, he returned to submarines and commanded task groups and squadrons. Fitzgerald commanded the oiler *Pawcatuck* before taking on assignments that stationed him in Turkey and Madrid, Spain, during the 1950s. He retired 1 November 1959 and was advanced to the rank of rear admiral. For his efforts to save *Grenadier* and for "unflinchingly withstanding the cruelties of his captors in various Japanese prison camps for two years and five months," Fitzgerald received the Navy Cross. His crew felt he was worthy of the Congressional Medal of Honor.

Admiral Fitzgerald passed away on Friday, 7 July 1990, and was buried in the Annapolis cemetery. Bob Palmer later wrote of his skipper, "His strength, moral character and dogged determination saved many of us from, in many cases, extreme pain and suffering. His gallant face-to-face arguments with our captors for better conditions [resulted in] punishment he bore with such dignity and strength. He was a fine Naval Officer who never ceased to command our respect and admiration."[21]

George Whiting was awarded the Silver Star for *Grenadier*'s last patrol and for his steadfast resolve to resist divulging information during the various means of torture he endured as a POW. After rehabilitation, he returned to submarines, commanding USS *Medregal* for two years, and later Submarine Squadron Six during 1960–61. Revisiting Ofuna in 1956, he found Japanese guard "Metal Mouth," who was living close to the former camp. "Had some of that excellent Japanese beer in his house as we talked about old times," Whiting recalled. After retiring from the Navy in 1966 as a captain, he started his own optometry practice in North Carolina. "I bear no hard feelings toward our captors," Whiting stated, "but I can never find any room in my heart to forgive those particular bastards who hurt my shipmates and other fellow POWs."[22]

Al Toulon went on to command destroyers, an oiler, and the submarine *Sablefish* (SS-303) after the war, in addition to a three-year stint teaching navigation at Annapolis. After retiring from the Navy in 1962, Toulon opened a successful real estate office on Kauai—his wife Betsey's home island in Hawaii—where they have since retired. John Critchlow also took up real estate after retiring from the Navy. Harmon Sherry retired as a rear admiral and passed away in 1983 at West Point, New York. Lt. Cdr. Arthur McIntyre returned to Ashio in October 1946, visiting the guard shack, galley, and the brig, where he found inscriptions written by some who did not return.[23]

Many of *Grenadier*'s enlisted men, such as Charlie Roskell and Joe Knutson, careered in the Navy. Bernie Witzke put in 30 years and 28 days, retiring as a lieutenant. When he attended officers' school, he graduated fourth from a class of 226. Joe "Baby Duck" Minton retired from the Navy as a lieutenant in 1964, after spending all but five years in submarines. Dempsey "Angus" McGowan remained in the Navy, retiring as a chief engineman in 1961. He went on to work in federal service, finishing his last seven years as building engineer at the new FBI Academy at Quantico, Virginia.[24]

John McBeath retired from the Navy in 1958 and worked for the Campbell's Soup Company until his retirement in 1981. McBeath then finished his postwar career by serving as a security guard for a computer corporation in Moorestown, Virginia. Thomas Trigg, *Grenadier*'s only African American survivor, worked at Thomas Jefferson High School in his hometown of Dallas, Texas, and later was called into ministry. Trigg admired his former skipper and wrote that "if I had to do it all over again, I would serve under him."[25]

Gordon Cox was recovering in a Seattle hospital when the Navy pushed through his long-overdue rating advancement. When asked what he wanted, he elected photographer's mate. "I was fooling with cameras then, so that's what they gave me. I didn't know what the hell I was doing." Cox left the Navy in March 1946, and took a graveyard shift job with United Airlines. He later took a job in custom plastic fabrication in Portland, where he made a career out of fabricating plastic faces for signs.

Judd Hinkson worked in civil service and at age 60 passed the health exam for the Merchant Marines. Buck Withrow worked for Honeywell Corporation after the Navy and retired in Illinois. Joe Ingram, nicknamed "Gringo" and "Chili Bean" by his shipmates, later put his Yawata Steel Mill factory experience to use. After retiring from the Navy as a chief petty officer, he became a pipefitter and instrument installer for the state of Alabama.[26]

Johnny Johnson, who put in 21 years in the Navy, requested assignment aboard the new submarine *Grenadier* (SS-525) and was her chief electrician when she was commissioned in 1951. The second *Grenadier* was christened by Mrs. John Fitzgerald. Torpedoman Al Albertson, who reached warrant officer during his 30 years in the Navy, went into civil service working on missiles before retiring to his current home state of Nevada. Al Rupp, the youngest of the *Grenadier* survivors, penned two books about his POW experiences before passing away in January 1989.

Lyle Sawatzke, an accomplished high school boxer, returned home to Crofton, Nebraska, where he spent many years building homes and coaching wrestling, winning many honors for himself and his wrestlers. Two of his children received scholarships to college from U.S. SubVets of World War II.[27]

Lee "Pappy" Shaw, having attended the surrender ceremonies on board the battleship *Missouri* on 2 September 1945, was flown from Kisaru on the eastern shores of Tokyo Bay to the Marianas. After stops at Guam and Honolulu, he arrived at the Oakland Airport on 7 September with 44 other Navy and Marine ex-POWs on board two large C-54 transport planes. They were the first U.S. POWs to be flown directly home. When long-lost Uncle Lee Shaw returned home to Texas, he became known as "Uncle Sailor" to his nieces and nephews. "When he returned from the Japanese POW camps, he would load the nieces and nephews up to go to the farmer's market in San Antonio to buy stalks of bananas, crate of oranges and grapefruit," recalled niece Sandy Stacy. "He said that he missed the fresh fruit so much during his stay in the POW camps." After putting in a career with the Navy, Shaw helped break horses for area farmers in Texas, charging only a couple dollars each. "Uncle Sailor died too young, age 53 years," said Stacy. "His POW experience and some bad genes—his mother died at 46—probably had a lot to do with that."[28]

Riley Keysor stayed in the Navy and retired as a chief torpedoman after 37 years' service. During his service he was stationed in the Philippines for a year and also served under Captain Fitzgerald again in Key West, Florida, when the skipper was running the base there. He found a commemorative plaque of the loss of *Grenadier* in a Navy salvage yard in Pearl Harbor in 1986. He brought the plaque home and mounted it on his barbecue pit until he could dedicate it to the Naval Submarine Base, Bangor, in a ceremony on 19 September 1986. In 1993, on the 50-year anniversary of *Grenadier's* loss, Keysor delivered a speech at the Trident Training Facility about the day his submarine was lost.

As for Orientals, Keysor says "I won't talk to them." He has no like for anyone Japanese or Korean to this day and generally avoids talking about his POW experiences. As of this writing, Keysor still raises and lowers a flag every day at his home in honor of World War II submariners on eternal patrol.[29]

The *Sculpin* Survivors

Sculpin earned eight battle starts under two skippers during World War II. John Cromwell, the division commander who chose to ride *Sculpin* down versus being captured, was posthumously awarded the Congressional Medal of Honor. His citation read in part: "Determined to sacrifice himself rather than risk capture and subsequent danger of revealing plans under Japanese torture or use of drugs, he stoically remained aboard the mortally wounded vessel as she plunged to her death. Preserving the security of his mission at the cost of his own life, he had served his country as he had served the Navy, with deep integrity and an uncompromising devotion to duty."

The only surviving *Sculpin* officer, George Brown, became a successful businessman after retiring from the Navy. George "Moon" Rocek, who passed away in August 2007, returned to submarines in 1946 and was assigned to *Sea Leopard* (SS-483). In later years, he became involved in joint reunions held among the *Sculpin*, *Squalus,* and *Sailfish* crews.[30]

Bill Cooper said, "They say cats have nine lives. I've got a lot more than that." He was proud of the accomplishments of the U.S. submarine service. "On a percentage basis, we only represented 1.667 percent of the Navy and on a percentage basis we had the highest mortality rate of any combat organization in World War II. But we sank more ships than our regular Navy, the Naval Air, Army Air Corps, and Marines combined."

Cooper left the Navy and started back to school briefly before he decided to go to work selling college courses by correspondence. His boss tried to convince him that signing up GIs would be easy money. "You can fool a lot of GIs, this guy told me," said Cooper. "I told him, 'I'm one of them, and you don't want to fool with them.' So, I never went back with him." He instead opted for a career selling insurance for Allstate throughout some of the southern states. The government did give him partial disability for his back and intestinal ailments, but Cooper remained troubled with various pains from his POW days. Nonetheless, he became active in *Sculpin/Sailfish* reunions long after the war.

Joe Baker was pinned with the Bronze Star by Admiral Chester Nimitz in 1947. "Nimitz and several other admirals tried to talk me into staying in the Navy and going to Annapolis," Baker said. "But I had already been accepted to Dartmouth and that's where I went." He chose to leave the Navy behind and became a bank executive after graduation.

Herb Thomas left the Navy after extensive recovery time in a Great Lakes hospital and put in his career with John Deere in Iowa. Mike Gorman retired from the Navy in 1963. The secret interrogation camp of Ofuna certainly had an impact on radioman Julius Peterson. Discharged from the Navy in January 1946, he attended the University of Idaho, became an attorney, and subsequently served as a special FBI agent from 1954 to 1976.[31]

The *S-44* and *Tullibee* Survivors

Both Tony Duva and William Whitemore, now deceased, returned to their naval careers after rehabilitation. Whitemore completed 30 years, retiring as a lieutenant in 1972. He served on other submarines, including the *Nautilus* and *Razorback*. His last assignment was director of the radioman school at San Diego. He passed away in 1995, never relating much of his POW experiences to his family.

Following liberation, *Tullibee*'s sole survivor Cliff Kuykendall was put into the Oak Knoll Naval Hospital. He was having his five busted teeth repaired during an all-day surgery when he was told that an admiral wanted him to fly to Washington for a meeting. The night before leaving, Kuykendall took an offer from fellow sub POW chief Tony Duva of *S-44* to go out for drinks. He found his body was still weak from being a POW and he could not handle the liquor like Duva. He hitched a ride back to the hospital in a taxi with two Marines. In his room, Kuykendall got sick. Later, one of his nurses chastised him, and then showed him the bed pan that he had vomited in. "I had worms from the prison camps that I was still passing."

Kuykendall flew to Washington where he found that Rear Admiral Crane wanted-ed to see him, since he was a *Tullibee* survivor. Crane's daughter had been married to Lt. David Wilson, the *Tullibee* engineering officer. Unfortunately, he could not offer Crane much information on Wilson, but told him what he could. Kuykendall, wanting to be near his home in Wichita Falls, finished his recovery in a temporary Navy hospital in Norman, Oklahoma.

When Kuykendall eventually retired from the Navy, he served 15 years in an Army branch of the Department of Defense's intelligence agency, mostly in the Washington, DC, area. He was wounded on duty and retired for disability. He

retired to North Texas, splitting his time between homes in Wichita Falls and the
small town of Nocona before settling permanently in Wichita Falls. He remains
very approachable on his experiences and maintains a very positive outlook on life.
"After the war, I tried to put it out of my mind," Kuykendall reflected more than 60
years later. "However, some of it still returns as though it happened yesterday."

Certainly the life belt he almost refused to wear on 26 March 1944 played a role
in saving his life. "Many people have asked me over the years how I ended up being
the only survivor of *Tullibee*," Cliff states. "I realized long ago it is impossible for
me to explain."

The *Tang* Survivors

Each *Tang* survivor received an award after returning from Omori. Two con-
ning tower officers, Frank Springer and Larry Savadkin, were awarded the Navy
Cross. Officers Ed Beaumont, Mel Enos, Hank Flanagan, John Heubeck, Dick
Kroth, Paul Wines, and Basil Pearce each were awarded a Silver Star. Silver Stars
also went to four of the men lost or washed from *Tang*'s bridge when she was
hit: Floyd Caverly, Lawrence Erickson, Bill Leibold, and James White. Lookout
Charles Andriolo received the Navy's Letter of Commendation. Jesse DaSilva,
Clay Decker, Pete Narowanski, and Hayes Trukee also earned Silver Stars, as did
five men who did not survive *Tang*'s sinking: James Culp, Paul Larson, John Parker,
Leland Weekley, and George Zofcin.

Pete Narowanski was pinned by Vice Admiral Lockwood in Pearl Harbor with
the Silver Star. Dick O'Kane received the Congressional Medal of Honor from
President Harry Truman at a White House ceremony on 27 March 1946. He
commanded submarine squadrons and was officer in charge of the submarine
school at Groton, before being assigned to the Navy Department in Washington
in 1956. Unhappy with his assignment, O'Kane retired in 1957 and was given the
"tombstone" rank of rear admiral. After working for several years in New York,
he settled on a horse ranch in Sebastopol, California, where he wrote best-selling
books on *Wahoo* and *Tang* in his later years. Stricken with Alzheimer's disease, Dick
O'Kane passed away on 16 February 1994, at the age of 83. The Navy honored
the Medal of Honor recipient by naming the Arleigh Burke–class destroyer USS
O'Kane (DDG-77) in his honor in 1994.[32]

Bill Leibold recalled, "We tried to call and get ahold of Pete on the East Coast.
They got his daughter, who said that he had just passed away the night before,
which was the same day the skipper had passed away." Jesse DaSilva and Pete
Narowanski left the Navy and returned to civilian careers. Narowanski worked as
a technical representative for AIA Corporation, an electronics firm in Baltimore.
DaSilva became a press supervisor for the *Los Angeles Times* and was the treasurer

of the Los Angeles chapter of the United State Submarine Veterans of World War II.[33]

Seven *Tang* survivors were married during the war but at the time of their repatriation, only three—Caverly, O'Kane, and Leibold—remained married. Leibold's wife Grace and Caverly's wife Leone have passed away while O'Kane's wife Ernestine remains alive as of this writing. "My wife Grace was one of the three who felt their husbands would return, despite the 'overdue and presumed lost' message," said Leibold. "These were strong marriages with strong women."

Hank Flanagan, divorced after the war, was stationed for some time at the sub base at New London and eventually remarried. He died in 1957, believed by some of his shipmates as a result of the health issues he incurred as a POW. Hayes Trukee was promoted to chief petty officer and assigned to duty at NAS, North Island, San Diego, after the war. After leaving the Navy, he joined the Los Angeles Police Department and remarried.

Clay Decker returned home to find that his wife had remarried and that another man was the replacement father for his young son. He left the Navy, working for Skelly Oil for 15 years before starting his own successful trash business in his home state of Colorado. Although placed on full disability and on 100 percent oxygen, Decker still managed to attend numerous submarine conventions before his death in 2003.[34]

Larry Savadkin careered in the Navy, where he spent more years in submarines before taking on various shore duties, including assignments in Belgium and Istanbul. He retired in 1972 to California, and passed away on 1 April 2007. Clay Decker, Jesse DaSilva, and their wives were very active in the SubVets of World War II organization. The *Tang* survivors held periodic reunions at the homes of O'Kane, Caverly, Decker, and Leibold. During one of their last reunions, seven of the survivors and their wives visited the Palomar Observatory in California.

With the passing of Larry Savadkin, only two *Tang* survivors are living as of this writing. Former radio technician Floyd Caverly remained in the Navy and retired to Oregon, where he turned 91 on 1 March 2008. Former chief bosun's mate Bill Leibold is now 87 and in good health. He became a warrant officer and retired with the rank of lieutenant commander, having commanded two ships during his service. During his service, he was able to maintain relationships with other *Grenadier* and *Perch* ex-POWs, including Lynn Clark, who was Leibold's relief at the Bureau of Naval Personnel and also of command of the submarine rescue ship *Greenlet* (ASR-10).

After retiring from the Navy in 1969, Leibold managed a Mercedes-Benz service dealership for ten years while raising three children with his wife Grace. Leibold has opted to stay away from the World War II veteran organizations. For some veterans, he feels "this may be a means of overcoming those dark days. The stigma of being a 'special prisoner' has never disappeared. To this day, I awaken in the middle of the night and I'm back at Ofuna—not a pleasant experience and I know I am not alone."

Appendix A: U.S. Submarine POWs of World War II

SURVIVORS, ALL BOATS

Name	Rank/ Rate	Submarine	POW Camps
Adkins, Ralph L.	EM1	*Grenadier*	Penang, Singapore, Fukuoka
Albertson, Norman A.	TM1	*Grenadier*	Penang, Singapore, Ofuna, Omori
Alboney, Francis	TM3	*Perch*	Makassar
Anderson, Edward N.	SC2	*Sculpin*	Truk, Ofuna, Ashio
Andrews, Davis "J"	TM1c	*Grenadier*	Penang, Singapore, Ofuna, Omori
Arnette, Elbert H.	F1	*Perch*	Makassar
Atkeison, Warren I.	TM2	*Perch*	Makassar
Baker, Cecil E.	F1	*Sculpin*	Truk, Ofuna, Ashio
Baker, Joseph N.	F1c	*Sculpin*	Truk, Ofuna, Ashio
Barker, Lester L.	EM2	*Grenadier*	Penang, Singapore, Ofuna, Omori
Barrington, Clyde W.	TM3c	*Grenadier*	Penang, Singapore, Ofuna, Omori
Berridge, Robert C.	RM3c	*Perch*	Makassar, Ofuna
Boersma, Sidney H.	CQM(A)	*Perch*	Makassar
Bolden, Sidney	SC3	*Perch*	Makassar
Bolton, Vernon	SC2	*Perch*	Makassar
Brown, George E., Jr.	LT	*Sculpin*	Truk, Ofuna, Omori, Mitsumishi
Byrnes, Thomas F., Jr.	MM1	*Perch*	Makassar
Caverly, Floyd M.	RT1	*Tang*	Formosa, Ofuna, Omori
Clark, Lynn R.	SM1	*Grenadier*	Penang, Singapore, Ofuna, Omori, Ashio
Clevinger, Gordon B.	S1	*Perch*	Makassar
Cooper, Billie M.	QM2	*Sculpin*	Truk, Ofuna, Ashio
Courtney, Thomas R.	S2	*Grenadier*	Penang, Singapore, Fukuoka
Cox, Gordon C.	S1	*Grenadier*	Penang, Singapore, Fukuoka

Name	Rank/ Rate	Submarine	POW Camps
Crist, Daniel	EM2	*Perch*	Makassar
Critchlow, John N., Jr.	LT	*Grenadier*	Penang, Singapore, Ofuna, Omori, Ashio, Zintsuji, Rokuroshi
Cross, Charles L., Jr.	CTM(A)	*Perch*	Makassar
Cunningham, William M.	S2	*Grenadier*	Penang, Singapore, Fukuoka
Dague, Lawrence W.	MM2	*Perch*	Makassar, Fukuoka, Orio
DaSilva, Jesse B.	MoMM2	*Tang*	Formosa, Ofuna, Omori
Decker, Clayton O.	MoMM3	*Tang*	Formosa, Ofuna, Omori
Deleman, Bernard	MM2	*Perch*	Makassar, Fukuoka, Orio
Duva, Ernest A.	CTM	*S-44*	Paramushiro, Ofuna, Ashio
Earlywine, Roland I.	Y1c	*Perch*	Makassar
Earlywine, Virgil E.	GM1	*Perch*	Makassar
Embry, Jewell C.	MoMM1	*Grenadier*	Penang, Singapore, Ofuna, Omori
Erishman, Charles A.	CMoMM	*Grenadier*	Penang, Singapore, Ofuna, Omori, Ashio
Eskildsen, Leo A.	F1	*Sculpin*	Truk, Ofuna, Ashio
Evans, Rex R.	RM3	*Grenadier*	Penang, Singapore, Fukuoka
Evans, Richard M.	TM3	*Perch*	Makassar
Evans, Robert E.	SC3	*Grenadier*	Penang, Singapore, Fukuoka
Fajotina, Alejo	CK3	*Perch*	Makassar
Fitzgerald, John A.	Lt. Cdr.	*Grenadier*	Penang, Ofuna, Omori, Naoetsu
Flanagan, Henry J.	Lt. (jg)	*Tang*	Formosa, Ofuna, Omori
Foley, Joseph A., Jr.	MM1	*Perch*	Makassar, Fukuoka, Orio
Fourre, Glen R.	EM2	*Grenadier*	Penang, Singapore, Fukuoka
Fulton, Ben H.	EM2	*Grenadier*	Penang, Singapore, Fukuoka
Garrison, Randolph J.	SC1	*Grenadier*	Penang, Singapore, Fukuoka
Gill, Benjamin S.	F1	*Perch*	Makassar
Goodwine, Calvin E.	MM1	*Perch*	Makassar, Fukuoka, Orio
Gorman, Michael T.	S2	*Sculpin*	Truk, Ofuna, Ashio
Greco, John	TM3	*Perch*	Makassar
Gunderson, Julian H.	S1	*Grenadier*	Penang, Singapore, Fukuoka
Harper, Earl R.	GM3	*Perch*	Makassar
Harty, Kevin D.	Lt.	*Grenadier*	Penang, Ofuna, Ashio, Zentsuji, Rokuroshi
Haverland, William H.	CMoMM	*Sculpin*	Truk, Ofuna, Ashio
Herbert, Carlisle W.	F1	*Grenadier*	Penang, Singapore, Ofuna, Omori
Hinkson, Richard J.	EM2	*Grenadier*	Penang, Singapore, Ofuna, Omori
Hurt, Albert D., Sr.	Lt. Cdr.	*Perch*	Makassar, Ofuna, Omori, Ashio
Ingram, Joe G.	MM2	*Grenadier*	Penang, Singapore, Fukuoka
Johnson, Charles E.	EM3	*Grenadier*	Penang, Singapore, Fukuoka
Keefe, William H.	RM1	*Grenadier*	Penang, Singapore, Fukuoka
Keller, Edwin K. F.	S2	*Sculpin*	Truk, Ofuna, Ashio
Kerich, Thomas L.	F2	*Perch*	Makassar
Keysor, Riley H.	TM3	*Grenadier*	Penang, Singapore, Fukuoka
Klecky, Rudolph	MM2	*Perch*	Makassar, Fukuoka, Orio
Knutson, Joseph S.	RM1	*Grenadier*	Penang, Singapore, Ofuna, Omori
Kuykendall, Clifford W.	GM2	*Tullibee*	Palau, Saipan, Ofuna, Ashio
Landrum, James D.	EM1	*Grenadier*	Penang, Singapore, Ofuna, Omori
Leibold, William R.	CBM	*Tang*	Formosa, Ofuna, Omori
Lents, Robert W.	TM3	*Perch*	Makassar

Name	Rank/Rate	Submarine	POW Camps
Leskovsky, John	TM3	*Grenadier*	Penang, Singapore, Ofuna, Omori
Leslie, Ramon G.	MoMM1	*Grenadier*	Penang, Singapore, Fukuoka
Loftus, Irving C.	F2	*Grenadier*	Penang, Singapore, Fukuoka
Liebold, William R.	CBM	*Tang*	Formosa, Ofuna, Omori
McBeath, John J.	PhM1	*Grenadier*	Penang, Singapore, Ofuna, Omori, Ashio
McCoy, Charles "H"	S1	*Grenadier*	Penang, Singapore, Fukuoka
McCray, James G.	CMM	*Perch*	Makassar, Fukuoka, Orio
McGowan, Dempsey E.	F1	*Grenadier*	Penang, Singapore, Fukuoka
McIntyre, Arthur G.	Lt.	*Grenadier*	Penang, Singapore, Ofuna, Omori, Ashio
Milbourn, Harry S., Jr.	MM3	*Sculpin*	Truk, Ofuna, Ashio
Minton, Joseph A.	QM3	*Grenadier*	Penang, Singapore, Fukuoka
Monroe, Elmo P.	EM2	*Perch*	Makassar
Moore, Thomas (n)	S1	*Perch*	Makassar
Murphy, Paul L.	F1	*Sculpin*	Truk, Ofuna, Ashio
Murray, Leo J.	MoMM1	*Sculpin*	Truk, Ofuna, Ashio
Narowanski, Peter	TM3	*Tang*	Formosa, Ofuna, Omori
Normand, Joseph R.	RM2	*Perch*	Makassar, Ofuna
O'Brion, Elwood A.	EM1	*Grenadier*	Penang, Singapore, Fukuoka
O'Kane, Richard H.	Cdr.	*Tang*	Formosa, Ofuna, Omori
Orlyk, Stephen M.	MM1	*Perch*	Makassar
Osborne, Robert W.	S1c	*Perch*	Makassar
Palmer, Robert W.	Y1	*Grenadier*	Penang, Singapore, Ofuna, Ashio
Pederson, Victor S.	CEM	*Perch*	Makassar
Peters, Orville V.	F3	*Perch*	Makassar
Peterson, Julius G.	RM2	*Sculpin*	Truk, Ofuna, Ashio
Pianka, John K.	MoMM1	*Grenadier*	Penang, Singapore, Ofuna, Omori
Pierce, Miner B.	S1	*Grenadier*	Penang, Singapore, Fukuoka
Plantz, Ernest V.	EM3	*Perch*	Makassar, Batavia
Poss, Edgar L.	RM1	*Grenadier*	Penang, Singapore, Ofuna, Ashio
Price, Joseph T.	F1	*Grenadier*	Penang, Singapore, Fukuoka
Quarterman, Carl O.	CQM	*Grenadier*	Penang, Singapore, Ofuna, Omori, Ashio
Quillette, Virgil A.	F1	*Grenadier*	Penang, Singapore, Fukuoka
Rae, Thomas J.	S1	*Grenadier*	Penang, Singapore, Fukuoka
Reh, Theodore J.	RM1	*Perch*	Makassar, Ofuna
Richter, Paul R., Jr.	EM2	*Perch*	Makassar
Ricketts, Edward F.	MoMM2	*Sculpin*	Truk, Ofuna, Ashio
Roberts, Warren E.	TM2	*Grenadier*	Penang, Singapore, Fukuoka
Robison, Jesse H.	EM2	*Perch*	Makassar
Rocek, George (n)	MoMM1	*Sculpin*	Truk, Ofuna, Ashio
Roskell, Charles (n)	F2	*Grenadier*	Penang, Singapore, Fukuoka
Rourke, John P.	GM2	*Sculpin*	Truk, Ofuna, Ashio
Rupp, Albert J.	S1	*Grenadier*	Penang, Singapore, Fukuoka
Russell, Paul D.	F3	*Grenadier*	Penang, Singapore, Ofuna, Omori
Rutkowski, Henry W.	S1	*Grenadier*	Penang, Singapore, Fukuoka
Ryder, John F.	Lt.	*Perch*	Makassar, Ofuna, Zentsuji, Rokuroshi
Sarmiento, Macario	CK1	*Perch*	Makassar
Savadkin, Lawrence	Lt.	*Tang*	Formosa, Ofuna, Omori
Sawatzke, Lyle L.	F2	*Grenadier*	Penang, Singapore, Fukuoka

Name	Rank/ Rate	Submarine	POW Camps
Schacht, Kenneth G.	Lt.	*Perch*	Makassar, Ofuna, Yokohama, Zentsuji, Rokuroshi
Schwartzly, John F.	F1	*Grenadier*	Penang, Singapore, Fukuoka
Shaefer, Gilbert E.	TM3	*Perch*	Makassar
Shaw, Lee C.	MoMM2	*Grenadier*	Penang, Singapore, Ofuna, Omori
Sherry, Harmon B.	Lt.	*Grenadier*	Penang, Singapore, Ofuna, Omori, Tokyo-area camps
Shoemaker, Dean B.	TM2	*Grenadier*	Penang, Singapore, Fukuoka
Simpson, John E.	S1	*Grenadier*	Penang, Singapore, Fukuoka
Simpson, Samuel F.	TM1	*Perch*	Makassar
Stafford, Frankland F., Jr.	SM2	*Perch*	Makassar
Stauber, George F.	MM2	*Grenadier*	Penang, Singapore, Ofuna, Omori, Ashio
Taylor, Glenn E.	TM1	*Perch*	Makassar
Taylor, Orville A.	FC2	*Grenadier*	Penang, Singapore, Fukuoka
Thomas, Herbert J.	TM1	*Sculpin*	Truk, Ofuna, Ashio
Todd, Paul A.	PhM1	*Sculpin*	Truk, Ofuna, Ashio
Toney, Harry F.	TM3	*Sculpin*	Truk, Ofuna, Ashio
Toulon, Alfred J., Jr.	Lt.	*Grenadier*	Penang, Singapore, Ofuna, Omori
Trigg, Thomas J.	Matt1	*Grenadier*	Penang, Singapore, Fukuoka
Trukke, Hayes O.	TM2	*Tang*	Formosa, Ofuna, Omori
Turner, Marion M.	EM2	*Perch*	Makassar
Van Buskirk, Beverly R.	Lt.	*Perch*	Makassar, Ofuna, Yokohama
Vandergrift, Jacob J., Jr.	Lt. (jg)	*Perch*	Makassar, Ofuna, Zentsuji, Rokuroshi
Van Horn, Edward (n)	EM1	*Perch*	Makassar
Ver Valin, Charles H.	MoMM1	*Grenadier*	Penang, Singapore, Fukuoka
Walden, John S.	GUN	*Grenadier*	Penang, Singapore, Ofuna, Omori, Ashio
Walton, Felix B.	MM2	*Perch*	Makassar, Fukuoka, Orio
Webb, James F.	QM1c	*Perch*	Makassar
Westerfield, Charles W.	CCS	*Grenadier*	Penang, Singapore, Ofuna, Omori, Ashio
Whiting, George H.	Lt. Cdr.	*Grenadier*	Penang, Ofuna, Omori
Whitlock, Charles H.	CEM	*Grenadier*	Penang, Singapore, Fukuoka
Whitemore, William F.	RM3c	*S-44*	Paramushiro, Ofuna, Ashio
Wilson, Charles M.	MM1c	*Grenadier*	Penang, Singapore, Ofuna, Omori
Winger, Ancil W.	EM2c	*Perch*	Makassar
Wise, William E.	GM2c	*Grenadier*	Penang, Singapore, Ofuna, Ashio
Withrow, William C.	CTM	*Grenadier*	Penang, Singapore, Ofuna, Omori, Ashio
Witzke, Bernard W.	MM3c	*Grenadier*	Penang, Singapore, Fukuoka
Wright, Eldon	EM3c	*Sculpin*	Truk, Ofuna, Ashio
Wyatt, Robert O.	GM2c	*Sculpin*	Truk, Ofuna, Ashio
Yates, Henry S.	CMM	*Perch*	Makassar
York, Robert F.	EM2c	*Grenadier*	Penang, Singapore, Fukuoka
Zucco, Peter	S1c	*Grenadier*	Penang, Singapore, Ofuna, Omori, Ashio
Zufelt, Fred	GM1c	*Grenadier*	Penang, Singapore, Ofuna, Omori, Ashio

CAPTURED U.S. SUBMARINERS WHO DIED WHILE POWS

Name	Rank/Rate	Submarine
Baglien, Jerome W.	RM3	*Sculpin*
Barrera, Maximo	Ck1	*Sculpin*

Name	Rank/Rate	Submarine
Berry, Warren R.	TM1	*Sculpin*
Brannum, Bill C.	F1	*Sculpin*
Brown, Charles N	MM2	*Perch*
Brown, Thomas V.	S2	*Sculpin*
Carter, Robert W.	S2	*Sculpin*
DeLisle, Maurice S.	F1	*Sculpin*
Doyle, Charlie	MoMM1	*Grenadier*
Dewes, Philip J.	PHAR	*Perch*
Edwards, Houston E.	CEM	*Perch*
Elliott, Henry L.	F1	*Sculpin*
Gamel, John W.	Ens.	*Sculpin*
Guico, Justiniano G.	StM1	*Grenadier*
Kennon, John B., Jr.	SC3	*Sculpin*
Kimmel, Manning M.	Lt. Cdr.	*Robalo*
Laman, Harold D.	MoMM2	*Sculpin*
Larson, Paul L.	CPhM	*Tang*
Laughlin, Floyd G.	QM1	*Robalo*
Linder, Charles Freeman	MM2	*Grenadier*
Martin, Wallace K.	SM3	*Robalo*
McCartney, James W.	EM3	*Sculpin*
McCreary, Frank E.	MM1	*Perch*
Moore, Weldon E.	CSM	*Sculpin*
Morrilly, Robert M.	EM3	*Sculpin*
Newsome, Albert K.	CMM	*Perch*
Parr, John	RM3	*Sculpin*
Pitser, Charles E.	TM2	*Sculpin*
Poston, Mason C.	TM1	*Robalo*
Smith, Charles G., Jr.	Ens.	*Sculpin*
Snyder, George W., Jr.	MM3	*Grenadier*
Taylor, Clifford T.	RM3	*Sculpin*
Tucker, Samuel L.	Ens.	*Robalo*
Van Beest, Henry	S1	*Sculpin*
Welsh, William H.	S1	*Sculpin*
White, Duane J.	MoMM2	*Sculpin*
Wilson, Robert A.	FC1	*Perch*

Note: At least one other unknown man from *Robalo* is believed to have died as a POW.

Key: n = no middle name

In addition to the men from the seven lost submarines covered in this book, other men of the U.S. Submarine Force were captured by the Japanese in World War II. The submarine tender *Canopus* (AS-9) was heavily damaged by Japanese bombers in December 1941 and was scuttled in Manila Bay. Six of the *Canopus* crew were killed in the attack, while another 70 died in the Philippine Islands, during transport aboard hell ships or as POWs. Also captured were two submariners who had served on *Sealion* before she was destroyed at Manila: Herbert Raymond Conser and Howard Firth. Conser survived the war but Firth died as a POW.

Appendix B: The Lost Boat Rosters

USS *Perch* (SS-176) Roster for Second War Patrol
Lost at Sea 3 March 1942

Name	Rank/Rate
Alboney, Francis	TM3
Arnette, Elbert Hugh	F1
Atkeison, Warren Ingram	TM2
Berridge, Robert Channing	RM3
Boersma, Sidney Henry	CQM(A)
Bolden, Sidney	SC3
Bolton, Vernon	SC2
Brown, Charles Newton *	MM2
Byrnes, Thomas Francis, Jr.	MM1
Clevinger, Gordon Bennett	S1
Crist, Daniel (n)	EM2
Cross, Charles Leonard, Jr.	CTM(A)
Dague, Lawrence William	MM2
Deleman, Bernard	MM2
Dewes, Philip James *	Phar
Earlywine, Roland Ilo	Y1c
Earlywine, Virgil Elmo	GM1
Edwards, Houston Ernest *	CEM
Evans, Richard Mains	TM3
Fajotina, Alejo	CK3
Foley, Joseph Albert, Jr.	MM1
Gill, Benjamin Swartz	F1
Goodwine, Calvin Eugene	MM1
Greco, John	TM3
Harper, Earl Rector	GM3
Hurt, Albert David, Sr.	Lt. Cdr.
Kerich, Thomas Leslie	F2
Klecky, Rudolph	MM2
Lents, Robert Wayne	TM3
McCray, James George	CMM
McCreary, Frank Elmer *	MM1
Monroe, Elmo Paul	EM2
Moore, Thomas (n)	S1
Newsome, Albert Kenneth *	CMM(A)
Normand, Joseph Raymond	RM2
Orlyk, Stephen Michael	MM1
Osborne, Robert Willie	S1c
Pederson, Victor Sigward	CEM
Peters, Orville Vincent	F3
Plantz, Ernest Virgil	EM3
Reh, Theodore John	RM1
Richter, Paul Richard, Jr.	EM2
Robison, Jesse Holland	EM2
Ryder, John French	Lt.
Sarmiento, Macario	CK1
Schacht, Kenneth George	Lt.
Shaefer, Gilbert Eugene	TM3
Simpson, Samuel Ford	TM1
Stafford, Frankland Fish, Jr.	SM2
Taylor, Glenn Elmo	TM1
Turner, Marion McDaniel	EM2
Van Buskirk, Beverly Robinson	Lt.
Vandergrift, Jacob Jay, Jr.	Lt. (jg)
Van Horn, Edward (n)	EM1
Walton, Felix Burrell	MM2
Webb, James Francis	QM1
Wilson, Robert Archibald *	FC1
Winger, Ancil Wayne	EM2
Yates, Henry Strickland	CMM

* Died while in POW camps.

59 men total: 53 survivors

USS *Grenadier* (SS-210) Roster for Sixth War Patrol
Lost at Sea 22 April 1943

Name	Rank/Rate
Adkins, Ralph Langley	EM1
Albertson, Norman Arthur	TM1
Andrews, Davis "J"	TM1
Barker, Lester Leroy	EM2
Barrington, Clyde W.	TM3
Clark, Lynn Reginald	SM1
Courtney, Thomas Robert	S2
Cox, Gordon Charles	S1
Critchlow, John Nisbit, Jr.	Lt.
Cunningham, William Michael	S2
Doyle, Charles *	MoMM1
Embry, Jewell Creston	MoMM1
Erishman, Charles Alexander	CMoMM
Evans, Rex Richard	RM3
Evans, Robert Eugene	SC3
Fitzgerald, John Allison	Lt. Cdr.
Fourre, Glen Raymond	EM2
Fulton, Ben Harold	EM2
Garrison, Randolph Jefferson	SC1
Guico, Justiniano Garcia *	StM1
Gunderson, John Henry	S1
Harty, Kevin Dennis	Lt.
Herbert, Carlisle Willie	F1
Hinkson, Richard Judd	EM2
Ingram, Joe Garza	MM2
Johnson, Charles Eugene	EM3
Keefe, William Harrold	RM1
Keysor, Riley Huntsman	TM3
Knutson, Joseph Sheldon	RM1
Landrum, James Dennis	EM1
Leskovsky, John	TM3
Leslie, Raymond Grant	MoMM1
Linder, Charles Freeman *	MM2
Loftus, Irving Charles	F2
McBeath, John Joseph	PhM1
McCoy, Charles "H"	S1
McGowan, Dempsey Ernest	F1
McIntyre, Arthur Greenville	Lt.
Minton, Joseph Ardell	QM3
O'Brion, Elwood Allen	EM1
Ouillette, Virgil Angers	F1
Palmer, Robert Wiley	Y1
Pianka, John Kazimier	MoMM1
Pierce, Miner Bryan	S1
Poss, Edgar Louis	RM1
Price, Joseph Thomas	F1
Quarterman, Carl Owen	CQM
Rae, Thomas Johnnie	S1
Roberts, Warren Edgar	TM2
Roskell, Charles	F2
Rupp, Albert John	S1
Russell, Paul Delbert	F3
Rutkowski, Henry William	S1
Sawatzke, Lyle Lane	F2
Schwartzly, John Francis	F1
Shaw, Lee Clifford	MoMM2
Sherry, Harmon Bradford	Lt.
Shoemaker, Dean Boyd	TM2
Simpson, John Edward	S1
Snyder, George William, Jr.*	MM3
Stauber, George Frederick	MM2
Taylor, Orville Anderson	FC2
Toulon, Alfred Joseph, Jr.	Lt.
Trigg, Thomas James	Matt1
Ver Valin, Charles Henry	MoMM1
Walden, John Shawhan	Gunner
Westerfield, Charles William	CCS
Whiting, George Harris	Lt. Cdr.
Whitlock, Charles Howard	CEM
Wilson, Charles Maxwell	MM1
Wise, William Edgar	GM2
Withrow, William Clyde	CTM
Witzke, Bernard William	MM3
York, Robert Francis	EM2
Zucco, Peter (n)	S1
Zufelt, Fred (n)	GM1

* Died in POW camps.

76 men total: 72 survivors

USS *S-44* (SS-155) Roster for Fifth War Patrol
Lost at Sea 7 October 1943

Name	Rank/Rate
Beck, Billy Mac	S1
Biller, Tobias Raphael	S1
Brown, Francis Elwood	Lt. Cdr.
Butters, Leo Elmer	CSC
Calvert, Charles Franklin	MoMM2
Carrier, Patrick Anthony	EM3
Cleverdon, Tom (n)	CPhM
Cooper, Thomas O'Don	S2
Cutright, Paul Parker	MoMM1
Dillow, William (n)	CMoMM
Duva, Ernest Anthony *	CTM
Ellis, William Henry	EM3
Erhart, William Edward	S1
Erico, Daniel Benjamin	CBM
Fees, Rhollo Rhodney	MoMM1
Ferrell, Earl Dean	Y2
Gander, David Earl	F1
George, Frank (n)	F1
Giles, Fred Jr.	F1
Gillen, Frederick Earl, Jr.	S2
Glenn, Curtis (n)	SC2
Godfrey, Edward William	MoMM2
Goodin, Tommie Lewis	F2
Green, Lonzo Junior	F2
Harasimowicz, Anthony (n)	CEM
Howard, Holly Jackson	MoMM2
Hugyo, Nicholas Andrew	MoMM1
Jaworski, Philip James	GM2
Johnston, Clidie Numan	MoMM2
Klink, Lyle Nelson	MoMM2
Miller, Arthur Leverne	CMoMM
Mitchell, Herman Mondell	StM2
Morris, William Ira, Sr.	TM3
Moss, Clarence Elmore	GM1
Nash, Benjamin Marion	Ens.
Parr, Thomas Sheridan, Jr.	SM2
Queen, Billy Muriel	SC2
Queen, Frederick Kyle	Lt. (jg)
Quinn, Robert Groves	Lt.
Rauch, Eugene Marion	EM3
Rodgers, Russell George	MoMM2
Rodin, Lloyd Jean	S2
Rosenberg, Harry (n)	RM3
Rubits, John Victor	MoMM2
Sloan, James Hill, Jr.	F1
Smith, Arthur Eugene	TM3
Smith, Charles Wayne	EM1
Smith, George Francis	CSM
Stephens, John Raymond	RM1
Stephenson, James Thomas, Jr.	Lt. (jg)
Stromsoe, Harold Arvid	CTM
Thompson, Dale Robert	MoMM2
Turner, Frank Alvin, Jr.	QM3
Velebny, Joe Albert	TM1
Warburton, Robert Lee	S1
Wester, George Seaman	S1
Whitemore, William Francis *	RM3
Wood, John Charles	F1

* Recovered from POW camps.

58 men total: 2 survivors

USS *Sculpin* (SS-191) Roster for Ninth War Patrol
Lost at Sea 18 November 1943

Allen, John Nelson [1]	Lt.	Martin, Merlin Guy	FC3
Anderson, Edward Niles [3]	SC2	McCartney, James William [2]	EM3
Apostol, Eugenio [1]	Ck1	McTavish, John Francis	S1
Arnath, Eugene	S2	Milbourn, Harry Smith, Jr. [3]	MM3
Baglien, Jerome Warren [2]	RM3	Miller, Charles Edward	TM3
Baker, Cecil Eugene [3]	F2	Moore, Weldon Edward [2]	CSM
Baker, Joseph Nicholas, Jr. [3]	F2	Moreton, Arnold Frank	EM1
Barrera, Maximo [2]	Ck1	Morrilly, Robert Michael [2]	EM3
Beidleman, Edgar Melrose, Jr.	RT2	Murphy, Paul Louis [3]	F1
Bentson, Fred George	S2	Murray, Elmon Truett	SM3
Berry, Warren Rawling [2]	TM1	Murray, Leo Joseph [3]	MoMM1
Blum, Arthur George	EM3	Parr, John [2]	RM3
Brannum, Bill Clifton [2]	F1	Partin, William Henry	S1
Brown, George Estabrook, Jr. [3]	Lt.	Peterson, Julius Grant [3]	RM2
Brown, Thomas Vincent [2]	S2	Pitser, Charles Earl [2]	TM2
Carter, Robert William [2]	S2	Ricketts, Edward Forest [3]	MoMM2
Clements, Kenneth Burl	MoMM2	Rocek, George [3]	MoMM1
Coleman, Charles Steele	MoMM1	Rourke, John Paul [3]	GM2
Connaway, Fred [5]	Cdr.	Salava, Frank	FC3
Cooper, Billie Minor [3]	QM2	Schnell, Elmer Virgil	TM3
Cromwell, John Phillip [1]	Capt.	Schroeder, Delbert Eugene [5]	Y2
Daylong, James Edwin	MoMM2	Shirley, Dowdey Buel [5]	SM3
DeFrees, Joseph Rollie, Jr. [5]	Lt.	Smith, Charles Gold, Jr. [2]	Ens.
De Lisle, Maurice Simon [2]	F1	Smith, Larcy Harold	EM2
Diederich, Donald Lawrence	EM3	Suel, James Thomas	S1
Elliott, Henry Leonidas [2]	F1	Swift, John Barlow	EM1
Embury, George Roderic [5]	Lt. (jg)	Taylor, Clifford Gene [2]	RM3
Eskildsen, Leo Aage [3]	F1	Taylor, Russel Hershel	S1
Fiedler, Wendell Max [1]	Ens.	Thomas, Herbert Joseph [3]	TM1
Gabrunas, Philip Joseph [1]	CMoMM	Todd, Paul Allen [3]	PhM1
Gamel, John Worth [2]	Ens.	Toney, Harry Ford [3]	TM3
Goorabian, George [1]	S1	Van Beest, Henry [2]	S1
Gorman, Michael Thomas [3]	S2	Warren, Ellis Edward	EM2
Guillot, Alexander Benjamin [1]	F1	Weade, Claiborne Hoyt [1]	CTM
Harper, James Quinton [1]	TM3	Welsh, William Henry [4]	S1
Haverland, William Herbert [3]	CMoMM	White, Duane Joseph [2]	MoMM2
Hemphill, Richard Earl [1]	CMM	Wright, Eldon [3]	EM3
Holland, Ervin Raymond	MoMM1	Wyatt, Robert Orlin [3]	GM2
Johnson, Gordon Everett	MoMM2		
Kanocz, Steve	EM3		
Keller, Edwin Karl Frederick [3]	S2		
Kennon, John Bowers, Jr. [2]	SC3		
Laman, Harold Dewitt [2]	MoMM2		
Lawton, Clifford Joseph	F1		
Maguire, Stanley Wayne	EM2		
Marcus, Grover Wade	RM3		

[1] Killed or went down with *Sculpin*.
[2] Died in *Chuyo* sinking.
[3] Recovered from POW camps.
[4] Wounded; thrown overboard by Japanese destroyermen.
[5] Killed/mortally wounded by gunfire.

84 men total: 21 survivors

USS *Tullibee* (SS-284) Roster for Fourth War Patrol
Lost at Sea 26 March 1944

Name	Rank/Rate	Name	Rank/Rate
Abnet, Paul Ray	S1	Kisman, Frederick Herman	RM2
Anderson, William Robert	TM3	Kuykendall, Clifford Weldon *	GM2
Arnold, Don Trenton	QM1	Landon, Clayton Lloyd	MoMM1
Barcoozy, John, Jr.	QM2	Lindsay, Frank (n)	F1
Beehler, Russell Edward	MoMM2	Lovett, Carl Marvin	EM3
Betsill, John Earl	MoMM2	Mann, Donald Raymond	MoMM2
Blanchard, Lionel Phillip	SC2	McConnell, Ramsey Farley	EM3
Brindupke, Charles Frederic	Cdr.	McDonald, Warren Glenn	EM3
Britt, Melvin Louis	TM3	McFadden, Melvin LeRoy	MoMM1
Brocklesby, Albert Fremont	SM1	Moffit, John Joseph	RM2
Brown, John Chris	MoMM2	Muoio, Charles Joseph	F1
Burasco, Nugent Anthony	S2	Nicholas, Eugene Ross	F1
Butler, David (n)	Ens.	Nopper, Allen Walter	RT1
Ciraldo, Frank (n)	MoMM3	Pattee, Clifton Eugene	EM1
Clay, Joseph Peter	TM2	Pawlik, Matthew Stanley	EM2
Clifford, George Clifford	F1	Peterson, Richard Hermal	Lt. (jg)
Crane, Lomon Bruce	TM3	Reger, Fred "B"	EM3
Crossman, Russell Harrison, Jr.	EM2	Rehn, Carl (n)	EM2
Deetz, Hugh Waldo	MoMM2	Roby, Robert Hamlin	MoMM1
Degenhardt, Charles Herman	RM1	Saterfield, Powell Tilman	Ens.
Delaney, Thomas Morris	CGM(A)	Schoenrock, Walter Leonard	CCS
Douglas, Clifford (n)	S2	Seibert, Howard Donald	F1
Duncan, Greer Assheton, Jr.	Lt. Cdr.	Smith, Albert Frances	F1
Dzik, Edward Howard	SC1	Stearns, Kirk Comstock	EM1
Ellis, LeRoy (n)	ST1	Strachan, Howard Lee	S2
Evans, William Arthur	Lt.(jg)	Sullivan, Hugh E.	CMoMM
Farley, Edward Michel, Jr.	S1	Symkiewicz, Arthur Alexander	TM1
Frank, William John	TM2	Thacker, Henry Lafayette	PhM1
Gage, Clarence Silas	MoMM1	Ticknor, George Oran	CEM
Graham, Donald Adair	S1	Trytko, Stanley (n)	RM3
Grenier, Raymond Alfred	RT1	Vigeant, Paul Roland	TM3
Grosz, John Neil	FCS2	Wagner, John Jay	Y1
Hall, Marvin John	MoMM3	Wallis, George Clement	SM3
Heath, Charles Newton, Jr.	F1	Washington, Ripley, Jr. (n)	StM1
Henkel, Francis Milton	F1	Wendt, Robert Joseph	TM3
Hicks, Carl James	TM2	Wilson, David Spencer	Lt.
Hieronimus, Louis Joseph	EM1	Wiser, Harold Judson	FC3
Hoefler, William Edward	S1c	Wood, John Kenneth	Lt. (jg)
Irwin, Henry Taylor, Jr.	Lt.		
Joder, Wilmot Burgess	CMoMM(A)	* Recovered from POW camps.	
Keating, Henry Francis	MoMM1		
Keener, Theodore McCoy, Jr.	TM3	80 men total: 1 survivor	

USS *Robalo* (SS-273) Roster for Third War Patrol
Lost at Sea 26 July 1944

Name	Rank/Rate
Ackley, James William	S1
Bailey, John Billy	TM2
Bell, Robert William	SM1
Boehles, Jerome Peter	TM1
Breeden, Charles Edward	EM3
Brereton, Walter Allen	MoMM1
Brokman, Gilbert	S1
Cagle, Columbus L., Jr.	MoMM1
Carter, Hubert Earl	Lt. Cdr.
Changary, Stephen John	MoMM3
Clark, Edward Omer	S1
Clifford, Marvin "D" "R"	S1
Cooperman, Herman Marx	RT2
Cotterman, Stanley N.	PhM1
Cress, Donald Clifford	RM3
Dickerson, Darrell Ellroy	CMoMM
Dittman, Calvin Lee	TM2
Downey, Wallace Lamont	MoMM2
Dvoracek, James Louis, Jr.	F1
Ervin, Lyle Franklin	MoMM1
Fell, Charles Woodford	Lt. Cdr.
Fink, Dean Elwood	RM3
Flanaghan, Arthur James	GM2
Fondon, George Melvin	F1
Fricker, John Joseph	SC2
Gerdes, Herman John, Jr.	Ens.
Gleaton, Elliott, Jr.	SC2
Graham, Kimball Elwood	EM1
Hamilton, Howard Leon, Jr.	TM3
Hart, James Francis, Jr.	TM3
Hood, Harley Truman	TM3
Hurst, Jack Akers	MoMM2
Ivey, Holly Berry	RT1
Jackson, Nyle Milton	TM2
Jambor, William Edward	GM1
Johnson, Emil Herman	MoMM1
Johnson, Nathan Young	SC1
Kesterson, William George	MoMM2
Kimmel, Manning Marius *	Lt. Cdr.
Konen, Arthur Carl	S2
Laughlin, Floyd George *	QM1
Leahey, Richard Jeremiah	SC3
LeFebvre, John Warren	CEM
Levy, Donald Judell	MoMM3
Lovell, Denzel Walter	EM1
Lutman, Joseph Arnold	Ens.
Martin, Ray Eugene	EM2
Martin, Wallace Keet *	SM3
Marx, Marvin Jerome	EM2
Matthews, William George	Y1
McKnight, Hugh Ferguson, Jr.	Lt. (jg)
Nichols, Harvey Edward	F1
Niclas, John Richard	MoMM2
O'Brien, John Joseph	MoMM2
O'Rourke, Edward Peter	F1
Paw, Edward Joseph	FC2
Phelps, Billy Brite	TM1
Poston, Mason Collie *	EM2
Priddis, John Frederick	CEM
Proseus, Reginald John	Lt.
Ramsier, Harold Leon	MoMM1
Root, Charles Alfred	MoMM1
Russell, Stanley Joel	F2
Smith, Stephen William	GM3
Sonemann, Walter Frank	RM3
Speener, Russell William	S1
Spencer, Samuel Elliot	CTM
Taylor, Herschel Paul	MoMM1
Tucker, Samuel Lombard *	Ens.
Usealman, Harold Elmer	S2
VanDeurzen, Joseph Reinard	MoMM3
Varney, Elmer Grayson	S1
Virga, Ciro Robert	F1
Vogel, Frederick Paul	TM3
Wilkerson, Dale Francis	MoMM2
Williams, Davie Lee	StM1
Wilson, Frederick Joseph	CMoMM
Winnan, Roland Oliver	EM3
Wlodarczyk, Sigmund Julius	F1
Wood, Claude Eugene, Jr.	QM3
Zea, Calvin Kenneth	TM3

* Died while a captive of the Japanese.

81 men total: no survivors

USS *Tang* (SS-306) Roster for Fifth War Patrol
Lost at Sea 24 October 1944

Name	Rank/Rate
Accardy, John George	SM3
Adams, Ralph Francis	StM1
Allen, Dwayne Dale	MoMM2
Anderson, Phillip Edward	TM3
Andriolo, Charles	RM2
Anthony, Homer	F1
Ballinger, William Franklin	CTM
Bauer, Edwin Clarence	Y3
Beaumont, Edward Huntley	Lt.
Bergman, Edwin Frederick	RM1
Bisogno, Frederick Nicholas	TM3
Boucher, Wilfred Joseph	TM3
Bresette, Bernard Vincent	QM3
Bush, John	EM2
Caverly, Floyd Merle *	RT1
Chiavetta, Benjamin	Y3
Clark, Walter Junior	QM3
Coffin, Robert James	EM3
Culp, James Henry	CEM
Darienzo, Arthur John	EM2
Dasilva, Jesse Borges *	MoMM2
Decker, Clayton Oliver *	MoMM3
De Lapp, Marvin Verle	CMoMM
Dorsey, William Edwin	MoMM1
Enos, Fred Melvin, Jr.	Lt.(jg)
Ericksen, Lawrence Hall	F1
Fellicetty, Daniel Clyde	Y3
Finckbone, Bruce Hampton	EM2
Flanagan, Henry James *	Lt. (jg)
Fluker, John William	TM1
Foster, John Morris	TM1
Galloway, William Carter	TM2
Gentle, Thomas Edison	F1
Gorab, George Jacob, Jr.	EM3
Gregg, Osmer Dinnis	Cox
Hainline, Howard Wayne	QM3
Harms, Frank George	MoMM2
Haws, Glen Olen	MoMM2
Henry, John Francis	F1
Heubeck, John Henry	Lt. (jg)
Hudson, Albert Leroy	CMoMM
Ijames, Homer Wesley, Jr.	RM3
Imwold, Stewart Samuel	MoMM3
Jenkins, Donald Morgan	Y3
Jones, Sidney William	CQM
Kaiser, Louis Charles	MoMM3
Kanagy, John Theodore	EM1
Kassube, John Thomas	Cox
Key, John Andrew	SC3
Knapp, Ralph B.	FC3
Kroth, Richard Jerome	Lt. (jg)
Lane, Leroy Richard	EM1
Larson, Paul Lewis	CPhM
Lee, Robert Peter	RM3
Leibold, William Rudolf *	CBM
Llewellyn, Lindley Herbert	RM2
London, Charles William	F1
Loveless, Chester	EM1
Lytton, Ellroy	MoMM1
McMorrow, Robert Vance	MoMM1
McNabb, John Joseph	F1
Narowanski, Pete *	TM3
O'Kane, Richard H. *	Cdr.
Parker, John Jefferson	CCS
Pearce, Basil Charles, Jr.	Ens.
Raiford, Rubin MacNiel	Ck2
Reabuck, Francis John	F1
Rector, Darrell Dean	GM3
Reinhardt, Ernest	F1
Roberts, James Lester	SC3
Robertson, George Louis	MoMM2
Savadkin, Lawrence *	Lt.
Smith, Seymour Golding, Jr.	QM3
Springer, Frank Howard	Lt.
Stepien, Edward Frank	F1
Sunday, Fred Lois	EM3
Trukke, Hayes Oliver *	TM2
Vaughn, Paul Benton, Jr.	Cox
Wadsworth, Charles Waite	TM3
Walker, Howard Madison	StM1
Weekley, Leland Stanford	CTM
Welch, Robert Edward	QM2
White, James Milton	GM1
Williams, Walter Herman	Y2
Wines, Paul Thornton	Lt. (jg)
Wukovich, George	MoMM1
Zofcin, George	MoMM1

* Returned from POW camps.

87 men total: 9 survivors

Chapter Notes

CHAPTER 1

***PERCH* IN PERIL**

Primary sources were interviews with Elbert H. Arnette, Robert W. Lents, Marion Turner, Ernest V. Plantz, and Thomas Moore. *Perch* survivor statements referenced: EM3c Daniel Crist, Lt. Kenneth G. Schacht, and Lt. B. H. Van Buskirk.

1. *United States Submarine Veterans of World War II. A History of the Veterans of the United States Naval Submarine Fleet.* Dallas: Taylor Publishing Company, 1984–90. Vol I: 400.

2. Van Buskirk, Cdr. B. R., USN (Ret.) "Laughing With a Prisoner of War." *Polaris*, October 1983.

3. Schacht, Capt. K. G., USN (Ret.) "Loss of the *Perch* (SS-176)." *Shipmate*, February 1972, 21.

4. Ibid.

5. Alden, Cdr. John D., USN (Ret.) *U.S. Submarine Attacks During World War II.* Annapolis: Naval Institute Press, 1989, 2.

6. Schacht, "Loss of the *Perch*," 22.

7. Ibid.

8. Parkin, Robert Sinclair. *Blood on the Sea. American Destroyers Lost in World War II.* New York: Sarpedon, 1995, 38–42.

9. Hara, Capt. Tameichi. *Japanese Destroyer Captain.* New York: Ballentine Books, 1961. Reprint: 1978, 88.

10. Schacht, "Loss of the *Perch*," 22.

11. Ibid.

12. "The Loss of the *Perch*." Report of Lt. B. R. Van Buskirk, courtesy of Submarine Force Museum. This handwritten report, later transcribed, was originally compiled by the officers and CPOs of *Perch* during their early days as POWs.

13. Schacht, "Loss of the *Perch*," 22.

14. "Going to Make It: Former Submariner Never Gave Up Hope After Being Taken Prisoner by Japanese." *New London Day*, 14 September 2004, A5.

15. "Seventy Five Blows." *Looking Aft.* West Virginia Chapter Newsletter, U.S. Submarine Veterans WWII. Volume 10: Issue 1 (March 2003), 1–3.

16. Schacht, "Loss of the *Perch*," 22.

17. Schacht letter of 7 June 1982, to newsletter editor Pete Pederson, USS *Perch* Newsletter, Vol. 11.

18. Hara, *Japanese Destroyer Captain*, 89. In attempting to piece together the Japanese destroyers that attacked *Perch* at different times over several days, Captain Hara's narrative was particularly helpful in setting the record straight. He wrote that his *Amatsukaze* and *Hatsukaze* encountered the American submarine and made an unsuccessful attempt to sink her late on 1 March. Hara further wrote that it was his same two destroyers that encountered *Perch* again after 0300 on 2 March.

19. Hara, *Japanese Destroyer Captain*, 89–90. Hackett, Bob, and Sander Kingsepp, "Last Days of USS *Perch* (SS-176)." Accessed http://www.combinedfleet.com/Perch.htm on 30 May 2007.

20. Schacht, "Loss of the *Perch*," 22.

21. Ibid., 23.

22. Ibid., 22.

23. *U.S. Submarine Veterans of World War II*, I: 354. Haldin, Ken. "POWs Gather for Reunion." *Ocala Star-Banner*, 15 April 1984, 1A.

24. Hackett and Kingsepp, "Last Days of USS *Perch* (SS-176)"; Hara, *Japanese Destroyer Captain*, 90.

CHAPTER 2
"A MIRACLE WAS NEEDED"

Primary sources were interviews with *Perch* veterans Arnette, Lents, Turner, Plantz, and Moore. *Perch* survivor statements referenced: Crist, Schacht, Van Buskirk, and Lt. (jg) J. J. Vandergrift Jr.

1.   Schacht, "Loss of the *Perch*," 22.

2.   *U.S. Submarine Veterans of World War II*, II: 172.

3.   "USS *Perch* Sunk by Japanese." Thomas Moore interview by Don Moore. Accessed http://www.perch-base.org/ on 23 July 2007.

4.   "The Loss of the *Perch*," Report of Lieutenant Van Buskirk, 5.

5.   Blair, Clay, Jr. *Silent Victory. The U.S. Submarine War Against Japan*. Philadelphia: J. B. Lippincott Company, 1975. Two-volume reprint, I: 165.

6.   Schacht, "Loss of the *Perch*," 24.

7.   Ibid.

8.   Hackett and Kingsepp, "Last Days of USS *Perch* (SS-176)."

9.   Schacht, "Loss of the *Perch*," 25.

10. *United States Submarine Veterans of World War II*, IV: 60–61; Samuel F. Simpson POW experiences, correspondence with author Gregory Michno of 20 January 1999, p. 6.

11. Blair, *Silent Victory*, I: 166.

12. Schacht, "Loss of the *Perch*," 25.

13. *United States Submarine Veterans of World War II*, IV: 61.

14. DeVore, Frances. "A Forgotten Prisoner." *Ocala Star Banner*, 20 June 1990, 1E.

15. "Memories Surface With Sub's Discovery." *New London Day*, 5 February 2007, A1, A8.

16. Van Buskirk, Cdr. B. R., USN (Ret.) "Laughing With a Prisoner of War." *Polaris*, October 1983.

17. Simpson to Michno, 20 January 1999, 7.

18. Hara, *Japanese Destroyer Captain*, 90. Michno, Gregory F. *Death on the Hellships: Prisoners at Sea in the Pacific War*. Annapolis: Naval Institute Press, 2001, 13.

19. "Japanese Destroyer *Ushio*." Accessed http://en.wikipedia.org/wiki/Japanese_destroyer_Ushio on 30 May 2007.

20. "USS *Perch* Sunk by Japanese."

21. Van Buskirk, "Laughing With a Prisoner of War."

22. Schacht, "Loss of the *Perch*," 25.

23. Michno, *Death on the Hellships*, 9, 14.

24. "Going to Make It," A5.

25. Van Buskirk, "Laughing With a Prisoner of War."

26. Michel, John J. A. *Mr. Michel's War. From Manila to Mukden: An American Navy Officer's War With the Japanese, 1941–1945.* Novato, CA: Presidio Press, 1998, 100.

27. "Going to Make It," A5.

28. Michel, *Mr. Michel's War,* 101–2.

29. Ibid., 103.

30. Ibid., 103–4.

31. Michno, *Death on the Hellships,* 14–15.

CHAPTER 3
THE FIRST MONTHS OF HELL

Primary sources were interviews with *Perch* veterans Arnette, Lents, Plantz, Turner, and Moore. *Perch* survivor statements referenced: Crist, Lt. Cdr. David A. Hurt, MM2c R. Klecky, Lt. John French Ryder, Schacht, Van Buskirk, and Vandergrift.

1.   Van Buskirk, "Laughing With a Prisoner of War." Zamperini, Louis, and David Rensin. *Devil at My Heels. A Heroic Olympian's Astonishing Story of Survival as a Japanese POW in World War II.* New York: Perennial, 2004, 134.

2.   Ibid.

3.   Ibid. This remains the key source until otherwise noted.

4.   Michel, *Mr. Michel's War,* 183.

5.   Van Buskirk, "Laughing With a Prisoner of War."

6.   Ibid.

7.   Armstrong, Jim. *From POW to Blue Angel: The Story of Commander Dusty Rhodes.* Norman: University of Oklahoma Press, 2006, 45.

8.   Ibid., 54–57.

9.   Ibid., 57, 71–75.

10. Ibid., 75–76.

11. Phaneuf, Keith M. "Some Memories are Horrifying But Camaraderie is Still Strong." *New London Day,* 22 June 1989, B1, B8.

12. Michel, *Mr. Michel's War,* 109–10.

13. Ibid., 111.

14. Ibid.; Simpson to Michno, 20 January 1999, p. 8; Samuel F. Simpson recollections of 13 January 1986, courtesy of Gregory Michno, 8.

15. Phaneuf, "Some Memories Are Horrifying But Camaraderie Is Still Strong," B8.

16. "USS *Perch* Sunk By Japanese. Tom Moore Spent 3 $\frac{1}{2}$ Years as a POW."

17. Phaneuf, "Some Memories Are Horrifying But Camaraderie Is Still Strong," B1, B8; Simpson to Michno, 20 January 1999, p. 5.

18. Michel, *Mr. Michel's War,* 112.

19. Ibid., 111; also, http://www.homeofheroes.com/brotherhood/antrim.html, accessed on 17 May 2007.

20. Michel, *Mr. Michel's War,* 113.

21. Michel, *Mr. Michel's War,* 114–29.

22. Ibid.

23. Ibid., 131.

24. Michel, *Mr. Michel's War,* 132.

25. Ibid., 133–34.

26. Michno, *Death on the Hellships,* 55.

CHAPTER 4
"HARD LABOR, POOR CONDITIONS"

Primary sources were interviews with *Perch* veterans Arnette, Lents, Plantz, Turner, and Moore. *Perch* survivor statements referenced: F1c E. H. Arnette, Crist, Schacht, Van Buskirk, and Vandergrift.

1. Michel, *Mr. Michel's War*, 139–42.
2. Ibid., 142–43.
3. Ibid., 143.
4. Ibid., 145.
5. Ibid., 148.
6. Ibid., 162.
7. Ibid., 163–67.
8. Van Buskirk, "Laughing With a Prisoner of War."
9. *Sub-Base Gazette* newspaper clippings of 27 March, 10 July, and 21 August 1943, Submarine Force Museum, New London, Conn.
10. Simpson to Michno, 20 January 1999, p. 10.
11. Ibid., 3.
12. Ibid., 4; Simpson to Michno, 3 February 1999.
13. Simpson to Michno, 3 February 1999.
14. Kennedy, Don. "Turk: Navy Vet Recalls Years as POW." *The Flagship* (Norfolk, Va), 30 March 2000, A8; Simpson to Michno, 3 February 1999.
15. Simpson to Michno, 20 January 1999, 2.
16. Ibid., 3.
17. Simpson to Michno, 3 February 1999.

CHAPTER 5

THE FIGHT TO SAVE *GRENADIER*

Primary sources were interviews with *Grenadier* veterans Norman A. Albertson, Gordon C. Cox, Kevin D. Harty, Riley H. Keysor, Charles H. McCoy, Dempsey E. McGowan, Virgil A. Ouillette, Alfred J. Toulon Jr., Charles H. Ver Valin, and Bernard W. Witzke. *Grenadier* survivor statements referenced: Lt. K. D. Harty, CY Robert W. Palmer, and GM1c Fred Zufelt.
1. 1945 diary of Lt. Cdr. J. A. Fitzgerald, 2, courtesy of Charles H. "Tim" McCoy. Hereafter referenced as Fitzgerald diary.
2. Capt. John A. Fitzgerald biography, U.S. Navy Office of Information, 2 June 1958.
3. John A. Fitzgerald correspondence with Clay Blair, author of *Silent Victory*. Clay Blair Collection #8295. Box 67, Folder 11. American Heritage Center, University of Wyoming. See also Blair, *Silent Victory*, I: 207.
4. "History of USS *Grenadier* (SS 210)." Office of Naval Records and History, Ships' Histories Section. Courtesy of Charles H. "Tim" McCoy.
5. Gordon C. Cox memoirs, 1940–46, 17. Hereafter referenced as Cox memoirs.
6. Ibid., 1.
7. Ibid., 2.
8. Ibid., 5.
9. Ibid., 6–15.
10. Ibid., 15.
11. Fitzgerald report of 1945.
12. Fitzgerald diary, 2.
13. Cox memoirs, 16.
14. Fitzgerald diary, 2–3.
15. Ibid., 3.
16. *Grenadier* Newsletter, 4: December 1981.
17. Ibid., 9: May 1982. *U.S. Submarine Veterans of World War II*, IV: 335–36.
18. *Grenadier* Newsletter, 9: May 1982.
19. Rupp, Albert. *Threshold of Hell.*. Long Beach, Ca.: Almar Press, 1985, 22–23, 1–3.
20. Ibid., 7–8, 22–23.
21. Cox memoirs, 17; *Grenadier* Newsletter, 31: February 1985.

22. Fitzgerald diary, 3.

23. *Grenadier* Newsletter, 12: August 1982.

24. Cox memoirs, 17.

25. Ibid.

26. Fitzgerald diary, 4.

27. *Grenadier* Newsletter, 14: November 1982.

28. *Grenadier* Newsletter, 16: January 1983; 5: December 1982.

29. Cox memoirs, 20–21.

30. Ibid., 20: July 1983.

31. Fitzgerald diary, 5.

32. Ibid.

33. Ibid.; Rupp, *Threshold of Hell*, 28. Knarr, Jack. "Recalling Horror as War Began." *Burlington County Times*, 7 December 1998, A1, A5.

34. Knarr, "Recalling Horror as War Began," A5.

35. Lee C. Shaw biographical information courtesy of Peggy Pepper and Pat Havel.

36. Fitzgerald diary, 5.

37. Cox memoirs, 21.

38. William Michael Cunningham oral history. Interviewed 10 February 1955, by L. P. Lyman. Courtesy of Charles H. McCoy.

39. Ibid.

40. Fitzgerald diary, 5.

41. Ibid., 6.

42. Cox memoirs, 21.

43. Rupp, *Threshold of Hell*, 28.

44. *Grenadier* Newsletter, 11: July 1982; Cox memoirs, 21.

45. *Grenadier* Newsletter, 9: May 1982.

46. Ibid., 11: July 1982.

47. Rupp, *Threshold of Hell*, 29.

48. Cox memoirs, 21.

CHAPTER 6
"WHERE HELL STARTED"

Primary sources were interviews with *Grenadier* veterans Albertson, Cox, Harty, Keysor, McCoy, McGowan, Joseph T. Price, Ouillette, Toulon, Ver Valin, and Witzke. *Grenadier* survivor statements referenced: Harty, Palmer, RM1c E. L. Poss, TM2c Warren Roberts, Lt. A. J. Toulon, CTM William Clyde Withrow, and Zufelt.

1. *Grenadier* Newsletter, 3: November 1981.

2. Cunningham interview with L. P. Lyman.

3. Cox memoirs, 1.

4. Ibid., 22.

5. Ibid.

6. *Grenadier* Newsletter, 39: April 1986.

7. Rupp, *Threshold of Hell*, 31.

8. Fitzgerald diary, 6–7.

9. Rupp, *Threshold of Hell*, 32.

10. Fitzgerald diary, 7; Rupp, *Threshold of Hell*, 33; Cunningham interview, 10 February 1955.

11. Rupp, *Threshold of Hell*, 34.

12. Thomas Courtney diary, courtesy of Charles H. "Tim" McCoy.

13. Fitzgerald diary, 7.

14. Cox memoirs, 23; *Grenadier* Newsletter, 29: November 1984.

15. Rupp, *Threshold of Hell*, 34–36.

16. Ibid., 36.

17. Ibid., 36–37.

18. Fitzgerald diary, 7–8.

19. Cox memoirs, 24.

20. Ibid.

21. Cunningham interview, 10 February 1955.

22. Rupp, *Threshold of Hell*, 38–39.

23. Ibid., 40.

24. Cunningham interview, 10 February 1955.

25. Rupp, *Threshold of Hell*, 41; *Grenadier* Newsletter, 19: June 1983.

26. Rupp, *Threshold of Hell*, 41–42.

27. "Former POW Dies Here at 56," *Richmond Times Dispatch*, 12 April 1980, B8; Lee Shaw recollections to niece Sandra Fahnert Wofford Stacy; Cox memoirs, 23.

28. Rupp, *Threshold of Hell*, 42; Cox memoirs, 23.

29. Fitzgerald diary, 8–9.

30. Ibid. This diary is the source for the paragraph that follows.

31. Rupp, *Threshold of Hell*, 43.

32. Ibid., 45–46.

33. Ibid., 46–47.

34. Cunningham interview, 10 February 1955.

35. "MacArthur Sends Greetings to San Antonio by Sailor Rescued from Japanese." AP story of 7 September 1945, from Oakland, Ca. Courtesy of Sandy Stacy via Pat Havel.

36. Cox memoirs, 25.

37. Rupp, *Threshold of Hell*, 47.

38. Cox memoirs, 25–26.

39. *Grenadier* Newsletter, 9: May 1982.

40. Ibid., 44: January 1987.

CHAPTER 7
"WE BECAME TERRIFIC LIARS"

Primary sources were interviews with *Grenadier* veterans Albertson, Cox, Harty, Keysor, McCoy, McGowan, Price, Ouillette, Ver Valin, and Witzke. *Grenadier* survivor statements referenced: S2c Thomas Robert Courtney, Harty, TM2c John Leskovsky, Palmer, Poss, Roberts, Toulon, Withrow, Zufelt, and a 17-man group interview of the following *Grenadier* enlisted men: CEM C. H. Whitlock, S1c J. H. Gunderson, S1c M. B. Pierce, S1c J. E. Simpson, SC1c R. J. Garrison, QM3c J. A. Minton, TM2c D. B. Shoemaker, S1c R. W. Rutkowski, EM3c C. E. Johnson, F1c L. L. Sawatzke, RM3c R. R. Evans, F1c B. W. Witzke, EM2c B. H. Fulton, F1c C. Roskell, F1c V. A. Ouillette, RM2c W. H. Keefe, TM2c J. Leskovsky, F1c J. G. Ingram, StM1c T. J. Trigg, EM3c L. L. Barker, and TM3c R. H. Keysor. Also referenced: 11 July 1946 war crimes statements of Cdr. John A. Fitzgerald.

1. Fitzgerald diary, 9.

2. Cox memoirs, 26.

3. Fitzgerald diary, 9–10.

4. Ibid., 12.

5. Ibid.

6. Ibid., 11.

7. Ibid., 10.

8. Ibid., 12–13.

9. Ibid., 16.

10. Statement of Cdr. Arthur Lawrence Maher, Box 514, Ofuna Depositions, National Records Center, courtesy of Carl LaVO.

11. Fitzgerald diary, 13–14.

12. Reynolds, Clark G. *The Fighting Lady. The New Yorktown in the Pacific War.* Missoula, Mont: Pictorial Histories Publishing Co., 1986. Reprint: 1993, 39–45. Statement of Lt. James E. Condit, Box 514, Ofuna Depositions, National Records Center, courtesy of Carl LaVO. See also Fitzgerald diary, 14.

13. Fitzgerald diary, 15.

14. Ibid., 14; Statement of Louis Silva Zamperini, Box 514, Ofuna Depositions, National Records Center, courtesy of Carl LaVO. Zamperini, Louis, and David Rensin. *Devil at My Heels. A Heroic Olympian's Astonishing Story of Survival as a Japanese POW in World War II.* New York: Perennial, 2004, 131–37.

15. Fitzgerald diary, 15–16.

16. *Grenadier* Newsletter, 39: April 1986.

17. Ibid., 40: June 1986.

18. Rupp, *Threshold of Hell*, 49.

19. Cox memoirs, 26–27.

20. Rupp, *Threshold of Hell*, 50–51.

21. Cox memoirs, 27; Rupp, *Threshold of Hell*, 52.

22. Rupp, *Threshold of Hell*, 53.

23. Cunningham interview with L. P. Lyman, 10 February 1955.

24. Ibid.

25. *Grenadier* Newsletter, 39: April 1986.

26. Cox memoirs, 25–27; Rupp, *Threshold of Hell*, 62.

27. Cox memoirs, 27.

28. Ibid., 28.

29. Ibid.

30. Cunningham interview, 10 February 1955.

31. *Grenadier* Newsletter, 14: November 1982; 15: December 1982.

32. *Grenadier* Newsletter, 14: November 1982.

33. Cunningham interview, 10 February 1955.

34. Cox memoirs, 28.

35. Rupp, *Threshold of Hell*, 55.

CHAPTER 8
HELL SHIPS AND HARD TIMES

Primary sources were interviews with *Grenadier* veterans Albertson, Cox, Harty, Keysor, McCoy, McGowan, Price, Ouillette, Ver Valin, and Witzke. *Grenadier* survivor statements referenced: Courtney, Palmer, Poss, Roberts, Toulon, Withrow, and Zufelt.

1. Cox memoirs, 30.

2. *Grenadier* Newsletter, 6: January 1982; Rupp, *Threshold of Hell*, 56.

3. Cox memoirs, 30.

4. Ibid.

5. *Grenadier* Newsletter, 6: January 1982; Rupp, *Threshold of Hell*, 57.

6. Rupp, *Threshold of Hell*, 58.

7. Rupp, *Threshold of Hell*, 58; Cox memoirs, 30–31.

8. Rupp, *Threshold of Hell*, 59; Cox memoirs, 31.

9. Rupp, *Threshold of Hell*, 60.

10. Cunningham interview, 10 February 1955.

11. Rupp, *Threshold of Hell*, 61–62.

12. Ibid., 61.

13. Cox memoirs, 31; Rupp, *Threshold of Hell*, 63–64.

14. Cox memoirs, 33.

15. Ibid., 32.

16. Rupp, *Threshold of Hell*, 68.

17. Cox memoirs, 33; Rupp, *Threshold of Hell*, 69.

18. Rupp, *Threshold of Hell*, 70; Fitzgerald diary; *Grenadier* Newsletter, 18: May 1983.

19. Michno, *Death on the Hellships*, 55; Cox memoirs, 33; Fitzgerald diary, 17.

20 Michno, *Death on the Hellships*, 55–56; Rupp, *Threshold of Hell*, 72.

21. Rupp, *Threshold of Hell*, 73; Cox memoirs, 33–34.

22. Rupp, *Threshold of Hell*, 73.

23. Ibid., 74; Cox memoirs, 34.

24. Cox memoirs, 34–35.

25. Rupp, *Threshold of Hell*, 74.

26. *Grenadier* Newsletter, 7: March 1982; 6: January 1982.

27. Cox memoirs, 35.

28. Fitzgerald diary, 17.

29. Cox memoirs, 51.

30. *Grenadier* Newsletter, 44: January 1987.

31. Rupp, *Threshold of Hell*, 74.

32. Cunningham interview, 10 February 1955.

33. Rupp, *Threshold of Hell*, 74; Cox memoirs, 35.

34. *Grenadier* Newsletter, 16: January 1983; 14: November 1982.

35. Rupp, *Threshold of Hell*, 75; Cox memoirs, 35.

36. Rupp, *Threshold of Hell*, 74.

37. Ibid., 76.

38. Cox memoirs, 35.

CHAPTER 9
"THE CASTLE" AT FUKUOKA

Primary sources were interviews with *Grenadier* veterans Albertson, Cox, Harty, Keysor, McCoy, McGowan, Price, Ouillette, Ver Valin, and Witzke. *Grenadier* survivor statements referenced: Courtney, Lt. Arthur Greenville McIntyre, Palmer, Poss, Roberts, Toulon, Withrow, and Zufelt.

1. Rupp, *Threshold of Hell*, 76.

2. Cox memoirs, 36.

3. Ibid., 36; Rupp, *Threshold of Hell*, 78.

4. Rupp, *Threshold of Hell*, 76–78.

5. Ibid., 79.

6. Cox memoirs, 37; *Grenadier* Newsletter, 9: May 1982.

7. Michael M. Glasser Confederate Air Force Oral History Program, 28, courtesy of Mick Glasser and interviewer William J. Shinneman. Additional information supplied by Glasser during interviews and correspondence in 1996 and 2007.

8. Cox memoirs, 37.

9. Cunningham interview, 10 February 1955.

10. Courtney diary, 4.

11. Cox memoirs, 38.

12. Ibid.

13. Rupp, *Threshold of Hell*, 82–83.

14. Cunningham interview, 10 February 1955.

15. Rupp, *Threshold of Hell*, 87.

16. Ibid., 84–87.

17. Cox memoirs, 39.

18. Rupp, *Threshold of Hell*, 87; *U.S. Submarine Veterans of World War II*, IV: 388.
19. Cox memoirs, 39.
20. Ibid.
21. Rupp, *Threshold of Hell*, 92.
22. Courtney diary, 4.
23. Rupp, *Threshold of Hell*, 94.
24. Ibid.
25. Cox memoirs, 39.
26. Ibid., 45.
27. Ibid.
28. Ibid.
29. Ibid., 46–47.
30. Ibid., 47; Courtney diary, 4.
31. Rupp, *Threshold of Hell*, 101–3.
32. Cunningham interview, 10 February 1955.
33. Rupp, *Threshold of Hell*, 103.
34. Ibid., 102–6.
35. Ibid., 108–9.
36. Cox memoirs, 48.
37. Rupp, *Threshold of Hell*, 117.
38. Courtney diary, 4.
39. Cox memoirs, 48.

CHAPTER 10
S-44's FINAL FIGHT

Primary sources for this chapter were the *S-44* survivor's statements of CTM Ernest Arthur Duva and RM3c William F. Whitemore (courtesy of John Crouse of the St. Mary's Submarine Museum in Georgia) and correspondence with Robert Whitemore, son of survivor Bill Whitemore.

1. Gugliotta, Bobette. *Pigboat 39. An American Sub Goes to War*. Lexington: The University of Kentucky Press, 1984, 173.
2. Holmes, Harry. *The Last Patrol*. Shrewsbury, England: Airlife Publishing Ltd., 1994, 26–27; Blair, *Silent Victory*: I: 275.
3. Roscoe, *Submarine Operations*, 245.
4. Cleverdon information from correspondence with Cleverdon relative Jamie Hulsey and Jack Cleverdon, Tom Cleverdon's younger brother.
5. "Doomed Sub's Survivor Tells of Jap Attack." *Oakland* (Ca.) *Tribune*, 14 September 1945. Courtesy of Robert Whitemore.
6. Robert Whitemore interview, 12 May 2007.
7. "Doomed Sub's Survivor Tells of Jap Attack." Information on Phil Jaworski was provided by his niece, Janet M. David, who stated that Phil's mother Viola Jaworski was visited after the war by one of the two *S-44* survivors, likely Bill Whitemore. He told her that Jaworksi exited the hatch right behind him but that he was either subsequently shot or drowned in the freezing water.
8. Cleverdon being one of those killed is related by one of his relatives on a website in which he described *S-44* survivors later coming to visit Cleverdon's parents. They explained that their son had been among those killed while trying to escape the sinking ship. I accessed http://restraininorder. blogspot.com/2005/08/dumpster-dans-story-unravels.html in May 2007. For Fees being among the escapees, Robert Whitemore provided various letters and clippings that his grandparents had saved in which Fees was originally thought to have survived Japanese POW camps.
9. Blair, *Silent Victory*, I: 393.
10. *Grenadier* Newsletter, 60: August 1990.
11. Fitzgerald diary, 18.

12. Glasser CAF Oral History, 28–29.

13. Moore, *The Buzzard Brigade*, 94.

CHAPTER 11
SCULPIN'S LAST BATTLE SURFACE

Primary sources were interviews and correspondence with *Sculpin* veterans Joseph Baker, Bill Cooper, Herbert Thomas, and George Rocek. *Sculpin* survivor statements and war crimes testimony referenced: F2c Cecil Eugene Baker, F1c J. N. Baker, Lt. George E. Brown, CMoMM William Herbert Haverland, F1c Paul Louis Murphy, RM2c J. G. Peterson, MoMM2c Edward F. Ricketts, MoMM1c George Rocek, GM2c John Paul Rourke, TM1c Herbert Joseph Thomas, PhM1c Paul A. Todd, TM3c Harry Ford Toney, EM3c Eldon Wright, and GM2c R. O. Wyatt.

1. Blair, *Silent Victory*, I: 495; LaVO, Carl. *Back From the Deep. The Strange Story of the Sister Subs Squalus and Sculpin*. Annapolis: Naval Institute Press, 1994, 124.

2. LaVO, *Back From the Deep*, 125.

3. Ibid. Accessed http://www.combinedfleet.com/Chogei_t.htm, 2 June 2007.

4. Accessed http://en.wikipedia.org/wiki/Japanese_destroyer_Yamagumo_(1938) on 2 June 2007.

5. LaVO, *Back From the Deep*, 122, 126.

6. Ibid., 127.

7. Ibid.

8. Ibid., 128.

9. Ibid., 130.

10. Mendenhall, Rear Adm. Corwin, USN (Ret.). *Submarine Diary. The Silent Stalking of Japan*. Chapel Hill, N.C.: Algonquin Books, 1991, 138.

11. LaVO, *Back From the Deep*, 131.

12. Ibid., 133.

13. Ibid.

14. Ibid., 134.

15. Ibid.; *U.S. Submarine Veterans of World War II*, IV: 362.

CHAPTER 12
TEN DAYS ON TRUK

Primary sources were interviews and correspondence with *Sculpin* veterans Baker, Cooper, Thomas, and Rocek. *Sculpin* survivor statements and war crimes testimony referenced: F2c Cecil Baker, F1c J. N. Baker, Brown, Haverland, Murphy, Peterson, Ricketts, Rocek, Rourke, Thomas, Todd, Toney, Wright, and Wyatt. Of particular detail were four sets of 1948 war crimes testimony given by Julius Peterson, Cecil Baker, Joe Baker, and John Rourke, plus 10 July 1946 testimony of Lt. Cdr. George Brown.

1. LaVO, Carl. "Footprints in the Sand." *Proceedings*, January 1986, 85–87; *U.S. Submarine Veterans of World War II*, I: 244.

2. LaVO, *Back From the Deep*, 135.

3. In an interview with Billie Cooper by the author on 9 May 2007, he identified the man thrown over as a young sailor who was striking for quartermaster. He concluded that his previous statements calling this man "Weade" were a mistake, since Weade had many years of service and was a chief torpedoman. Herb Thomas also stated in May 2007 that his after torpedo room boss, Chief Torpedoman Weade, did not escape the sinking of *Sculpin*.

4. LaVO, *Back From the Deep*, 135.

5. Ibid.

6. Michno, *Death on the Hellships*, 143.

7. LaVO, *Back From the Deep*, 137.

8. Ibid., 138.

9. Ibid., 139.

10. Ibid., 138.

11. Ibid., 139.

12. Ibid., 138.

13. Ibid., 139.

14. Ibid., 140.

15. Stewart, William H. *Ghost Fleet of the Truk Lagoon.* Missoula, Mont: Pictorial Histories Publishing Co., 1985, Fourth printing 1991, 65.

16. Michno, *Death on the Hellships*, 143.

17. LaVO, *Back From the Deep*, 141.

CHAPTER 13
CHUYO'S SOLE SURVIVOR

Primary sources were interviews and correspondence with *Sculpin* veterans Baker, Cooper, Thomas, and Rocek. *Sculpin* survivor statements and war crimes testimony referenced: F2c Cecil Baker, F1c Joe Baker, Brown, Haverland, Murphy, Peterson, Ricketts, Rocek, Rourke, Thomas, Todd, Toney, Wright, and Wyatt.

1. LaVO, *Back From the Deep*, 141.

2. Wittmer, Paul. "The Story of the Men of USS *Sculpin* (SS-191)." Accessed www.subvetpaul.com/Sculpin.html on August 28, 2008.

3. LaVO, *Back From the Deep*, 141.

4. Blair, *Silent Victory*, I: 497.

5. Ibid.; I: 434–36, 497–98; LaVO, *Back From the Deep*, 169.

6. Rocek, "Saga of a *Sculpin* Survivor"; LaVO, *Back From the Deep*, 146.

7. Rocek, "Saga of a *Sculpin* Survivor"; Wittmer, "The Story of the Men of USS *Sculpin.*"

8. Rocek, "Saga of a *Sculpin* Survivor"; Wittmer, "The Story of the Men of USS *Sculpin.*"

9. Blair, *Silent Victory*, I: 499.

10. Rocek, "Saga of a *Sculpin* Survivor."

11. Ibid.

12. Michno, *Death on the Hellships*, 147.

13. Rocek, "Saga of a *Sculpin* Survivor."

14. LaVO, *Back From the Deep*, 153.

15. Rocek, "Saga of a *Sculpin* Survivor."

16. Ibid.

CHAPTER 14
"NO ONE KNOWS YOU'RE ALIVE"

Primary sources were interviews and correspondence with *Sculpin* veterans Baker, Cooper, Rocek and Thomas. Survivor and war crimes statements used are listed by ship. *Grenadier*: Harty, McIntyre, and Palmer. *Sculpin*: F2c Baker, F1c Baker, Brown, Haverland, Murphy, Peterson, Ricketts, Rocek, Rourke, Thomas, Todd, Toney, Wright, and Wyatt. *Perch:* Arnette, Lents, Plantz, and Turner. USS *Pope*: William R. Penninger.

1. Fitzgerald diary, 19.

2. LaVO, *Back From the Deep*, 155.

3. Ibid., 154.

4. Ibid.

5. Ibid., 155.

6. Ibid., 156.

7. Ibid., 157.

8. Fitzgerald diary, 19.

9. Ibid., 20.

10. Ibid., 20–21.

11. *Grenadier* Newsletter, 7: March 1982.

12. Fitzgerald diary, 21.

13. *Grenadier* Newsletter, 7: March 1982.

14. LaVO, *Back From the Deep*, 156–57.

15. Fitzgerald diary, 21–22; *Grenadier* Newsletter, 29: November 1984; LaVO, *Back From the Deep*, 156.

16. Fitzgerald diary, 21; Zamperini, *Devil at My Heels*, 146.

17. Fitzgerald diary, 21–22.

18. Fitzgerald diary, 21. *Grenadier* Newsletter, 9: May 1982.

19. LaVO, *Back From the Deep*, 158.

20. *Grenadier* Newsletter, 7: March 1982.

21. Fitzgerald diary, 22–23.

22. Ibid., 24.

23. Ibid., 25.

24. Ibid.

25. Gamble, Bruce. *Black Sheep One. The Life of Gregory "Pappy" Boyington.* New York: Ballentine Books, 2000, 357; *Grenadier* Newsletter, 4: December 1981.

26. Gamble, *Black Sheep One*, 357; *Grenadier* Newsletter, 4: December 1981.

27. Fitzgerald diary, 25.

28. 15 April 1946 prisoner of war testimony of Lt. (jg) A. J. Fisher, an officer from the destroyer *Pope* who became Makassar's senior American POW.

29. 15 April 1946 report of Lieutenant Commander Fisher.

30. "Seventy Five Blows." *Looking Aft*, West Virginia Chapter Newsletter, U.S. Submarine Veterans WWII, Volume 10: Issue 1 (March 2003), 3.

CHAPTER 15

TULLIBEE'S SOLE SURVIVOR

Primary sources were interviews and correspondence with Clifford W. Kuykendall. *Tullibee* survivor statement referenced: GM2c Clifford Weldon Kuykendall, taken 9 September 1945 on Guam.

1. Kuykendall's 1945 statement puts the time of radar contact as 0800, but he says this is a mistake or a typographical error. "The time radar contact was made was around 2000 hours, not 0800," he wrote on 27 March 2007.

2. Once again, Kuykendall does not agree with the 1945 statement that was taken from him. In statements to the author and in a letter of 26 March 2007, he wrote: "One thing was interpreted incorrectly on the statement. It was around 25 seconds after firing that the tremendous explosion occurred. They may have made an error typing it or possibly by the shorthand. They made a few mistakes in September 1945."

3. Lindemann, Klaus. *Desecrate 1. Operations Against Palau by Carrier Task Force 58, 30 and 31 March 1944, and the Shipwrecks of World War II.* Belleville, Mich.: Pacific Press Publications, 1988, 73, 259.

4. Ibid., 73, 147, 259, 318.

CHAPTER 16

LOSS OF *ROBALO*

Primary sources were interviews and correspondence with *Tullibee* veteran Kuykendall and *Grenadier* veterans Cox, McCoy, Ouillette, and Ver Valin. Survivors statement referenced: *Tullibee*'s Kuykendall and *Grenadier*'s Roberts. War crimes testimony of Lieutenant Commander Brown of *Sculpin*, 10 July 1946.

1. Gamble, *Black Sheep One*, 352–53.

2. Fitzgerald diary, 26.

3. Belote, James H. and William M. Belote. *Titans of the Seas. The Development and Operations of Japanese and American Carrier Task Forces During World War II.* New York: Harper & Row, 1975, 261.

4. Fitzgerald diary, 27–28.
5. Ibid., 28.
6. *Grenadier* Newsletter, 7: March 1982.
7. Fitzgerald diary, 29–32. This diary remains the key source until otherwise noted.
8. Zamperini, *Devil at My Heels*, 140.
9. Ibid., 136, 143.
10. Fitzgerald diary, 35.
11. Ibid.
12. Bradley, James. *Flyboys*, 183–97.
13. Fitzgerald diary, 36; Gamble, *Black Sheep One*, 358.
14. Fitzgerald diary, 36–37.
15. Ibid., 37–39.
16. Ibid., 39–41.
17. Cox memoirs, 48.
18. Ibid., 49.
19. Ibid.
20. Rupp, *Threshold of Hell*, 124, 133, 120.
21. Cox memoirs, 50.
22. Ibid., 52–53.
23. Ibid.
24. Ibid., 54.
25. Rupp, *Threshold of Hell*, 137.
26. Michno, *Death on the Hellships*, 170.
27. Holmes, *The Last Patrol*, 114.
28. Blair, *Silent Victory*, II: 660.
29. Ibid.
30. Roscoe, *United States Submarine Operations in World War II*, 348.
31. Blair, *Silent Victory*, II: 661.
32. Sturma, Michael. *The USS Flier. Death and Survival on a World War II Submarine*. Lexington: The University Press of Kentucky, 2008, 65–123.
33. "Record of Proceedings of an Investigation conducted at the headquarters of the Commander Submarines Seventh Fleet by order of The Commander in Chief, United States Fleet and The Chief of Naval Operations to investigate the circumstances connected with the loss of the U.S.S. *Robalo* and the loss of the U.S.S. *Flier*," 14 September 1994 (previously classified).
34. Ibid.
35. Roscoe, *United States Submarine Operations in World War II*, 348.
36. Blair, *Silent Victory*, II: 661; Michno, *Death on the Hellships*, 241.
37. Michno, *Death on the Hellships*, 273.
38. Ibid., 225, 333.

CHAPTER 17
"ALL HANDS WERE ON EDGE"
Primary sources were interviews and correspondence with *Tullibee* veteran Kuykendall and *Perch* veterans Arnette, Plantz, Lents, Moore, and Turner. *Perch* survivor statement referenced: Crist.
1. Simpson to Michno, 20 January 1999, 9.
2. 15 April 1946 report of Lieutenant Commander Fisher.
3. Simpson to Michno, 3 February 1999.
4. DeVore, "A Forgotten Prisoner," 2E.
5. "USS *Perch* Sunk by Japanese."
6. Ibid.
7. Haldin, "POWs Gather for Reunion," 12A.

8.   Simpson to Michno, 20 January 1999, 1–2.

9.   *Ex-POWs: USS Pope (DD-225)/USS Perch (SS-176) Newsletter.* December 1994. Additional details on Paul Richter's ordeal furnished by his sisters, Frances Richter Swinny and Marguerite Richter Nemky.

10. Fitzgerald diary, 42.

11. Ibid.

12. Fitzgerald diary, 43; Zamperini, *Devil at My Heels*, 144–45.

13. Zamperini, *Devil at My Heels*, 145.

14. Ibid.

15. Fitzgerald diary, 43–44.

16. Ibid., 44–45.

17. Gamble, *Black Sheep One*, 359–60.

18. Zamperini, *Devil at My Heels*, 146–47.

19. Fitzgerald diary, 45–47.

20. Gamble, *Black Sheep One*, 358–59.

21. William A. Dixon, 2nd Lt., AAF, deposition, courtesy of Carl LaVO from National Records Center.

22. Fitzgerald diary, 49–50.

CHAPTER 18
TANG'S TRAGIC TWENTY-FOURTH

Primary sources were interviews and correspondence with *Tang* veterans William R. Leibold and Floyd M. Caverly. *Tang* survivor statements referenced: Cdr. Richard Hetherington O'Kane, Lt. Lawrence Savadkin, Lt. (jg) Henry J. Flanagan, MoMM2c Jesse Borges DaSilva, TM2c Hayes Oliver Trukke, and TM3c Pete Narowanski.

1.   Moore, *The Buzzard Brigade*, 180–85.

2.   DeRose, *Unrestricted Warfare*, 282–83.

3.   Ibid., 209.

4.   O'Kane, *Clear the Bridge!*, 25.

5.   Ibid., 33, 457.

6.   Erickson, cited for a commendation for the ship's final patrol, is likely the other bridge lookout. Due to the six decades that have passed, however, neither Floyd Caverly nor Bill Leibold can say this certainty. Although one recent book on *Tang* lists James White as being below decks at this time, Leibold and Caverly are certain that he was on the bridge (Leibold to author, 30 April 2008 and 1 May 2008).

7.   O'Kane, *Clear the Bridge!*, 384–86.

8.   Ibid., 455.

9.   Ibid.

10. Ibid.

11. Ibid.

12. DeRose, *Unrestricted Warfare*, 214.

CHAPTER 19
ESCAPE FROM 30 FATHOMS

Primary sources were interviews and correspondence with *Tang* veterans Leibold and Caverly. *Tang* survivor statements referenced: O'Kane, Savadkin, Flanagan, DaSilva, Trukke, and Narowanski.

1.   Adams, Cindy. "USS *Tang* Survivors." *Polaris*, February 1981; O'Kane, *Clear the Bridge!*, 460.

2.   Ibid.

3.   *U.S. Submarine Veterans of World War II*, I: 204; Adams, "USS *Tang* Survivors."

4.   DeRose, *Unrestricted Warfare*, 219.

5.   *U.S. Submarine Veterans of World War II*, I: 208. Whitlock, Flint, and Ron Smith. *The Depths of Courage.*

American Submariners at War with Japan, 1941–1945. New York: Berkley Caliber, 2007, 246–47.

6. Whitlock and Smith, *The Depths of Courage*, 320–21.

7. Tuohy, *The Bravest Man*, 326.

8. DeRose, *Unrestricted Warfare*, 218; Tuohy, *The Bravest Man*, 327.

9. Knoblock, Glenn A. *Black Submariners in the United States Navy, 1940–1975.* Jefferson, N.C.: McFarland & Company, 2005, 70–72.

10. Other accounts list this man as Howard Walker. Knoblock, *Black Submariners in the United States Navy*, 71, calls on a 1998 account by Jesse DaSilva in which he specifically remembered this man as Rubin Raiford. "Hank Flanagan clearly stated it was Raiford," Bill Leibold related to author on 30 April 2008. Floyd Caverly agreed on this being Raiford (Leibold to author, 1 May 2008). Leibold and Caverly agree that Raiford was the mess attendant with the smashed face who later reached the surface.

11. Whitlock and Smith, *The Depths of Courage*, 325.

12. DeRose, *Unrestricted Warfare*, 291; Whitlock and Smith, *The Depths of Courage*, 325.

13. DeRose, *Unrestricted Warfare*, 221, 291.

14. Hayes Trukke specifically names Chief Weekley as being in the second properly organized escape party, or the third overall group to leave. As with many disaster recollections, few survivors generally recall events to have occurred in precisely the same fashion or sequence.

15. DeRose, *Unrestricted Warfare*, 221.

16. Ibid.

17. Burgess, Tom. "First Man Up, Last Man Out: Clayton O. Decker." *Historical Diver*, Vol. 10, Issue 2 (Spring 2002, No. 31), 34.

18. Ibid.; 32, 35–36. Monroe-Jones, Edward. *Submarine Escape and Rescue: An Anthology from 1851 through 2005.* Bangor, Wa.: Submarine Research Center, 2007, 19–24.

19. Tuohy, *The Bravest Man*, 330–31.

20. Kershaw, Alex. *Escape From the Deep.* Philadelphia: De Capo Press, 2008, 124.

21. Knoblock, *Black Submariners in the United States Navy*, 72; Leibold to author, 30 April 2008.

22. DeRose, *Unrestricted Warfare*, 224.

23. Tuohy, *The Bravest Man*, 333.

24. O'Kane, *Clear the Bridge!*, 459.

25. Tuohy, *The Bravest Man*, 337.

26. O'Kane, "Report of the Loss of the U.S.S. *Tang* (SS306)," September 1945; contained in O'Kane, *Clear the Bridge!*, 458.

27. Ibid., 459.

28. "The Silent Service." Set #1 DVD, Disc 1: *The Boats of WWII/The Captains of WWII.* Documentary, 2000, A&E Television Network.

29. O'Kane, *Clear the Bridge!*, 460.

30. Ibid.

31. Ibid., 460–61.

32. Ibid., 462.

33. DeRose, *Unrestricted Warfare*, 226.

34. "The Silent Service." Set #1 DVD, Disc 1: *The Boats of WWII/The Captains of WWII.*

CHAPTER 20
"GOD HELP US"

Primary sources were interviews and correspondence with *Tang* veterans Leibold and Caverly and *Grenadier* veterans Cox, McCoy, McGowan, and Ver Valin. Also, *Tang* survivor statement of DaSilva.

1. O'Kane, *Clear the Bridge!*, 462–63.

2. Fitzgerald diary, 52–53.

3. Ibid., 53; O'Kane, *Clear the Bridge!*, 463.

4. Tuohy, *The Bravest Man*, 359.

5. Ibid., 361, 365–66.

6. Ibid., 360.

7. Fitzgerald diary, 54.

8. Ibid.

9. "Japanese Atrocities—The S.S. *Jean Nicolet*." Referenced http://www.armed-guard.com/ag87. html on 18 July 2007. Also referenced http://veterans.house.gov/hearings/schedule110/apr07/04-18-07-am/record/4-18-07flury.shtml on 18 July 2007 for statement of *Jean Nicolet* survivor William B. Flury.

10. O'Kane, *Clear the Bridge!*, 464.

11. "Report on the Loss of HM *Submarine Stratagem*." August 1945 statement of Lt. D. C. Douglas. Accessed http://www.cofepow.org.uk/pages/ships_stratagem.httm on 29 May 2007.

12. Fitzgerald diary, 55.

13. DeRose, *Unrestricted Warfare*, 244.

14. Fitzgerald diary, 56; *Grenadier* Newsletter, 7: March 1982.

15. Tuohy, *The Bravest Man*, 367.

16. Fitzgerald diary, 56–57.

17. Tuohy, *The Bravest Man*, 365.

18. O'Kane, *Clear the Bridge!*, 465.

19. Whitlock and Smith, *The Depths of Courage*, 356–57.

20. Rupp, *Threshold of Hell*, 141; *Grenadier* Newsletter, 9: May 1982.

21. Rupp, *Threshold of Hell*, 144–47.

22. Cox memoirs, 51.

23. Ibid.

24. Rupp, *Threshold of Hell*, 149–51.

25. Cox memoirs, 56.

26. Ibid., 56–57.

27. *Grenadier* Newsletter, 11: July 1982.

28. Courtney diary, 4.

29. Rupp, *Threshold of Hell*, 159–61.

30. Cox memoirs, 58.

31. Ibid., 58–59.

32. Courtney diary, 5.

33. Cox memoirs, 59.

34. Courtney diary, 6.

35. Rupp, *Threshold of Hell*, 173–74.

36. Courtney diary, 6; Cox memoirs, 60.

37. Cox memoirs, 60.

38. Ibid.

39. Courtney diary, 6.

CHAPTER 21
OMORI'S "SPECIAL PRISONERS"

Primary sources were interviews and correspondence with *Tang* veterans Leibold and Caverly, *Grenadier* veteran Albertson and VT-10 veterans Michael Glasser and Thomas C. Nelson Jr. Also, *Tang* survivor statement of DaSilva.

1. Moore, *The Buzzard Brigade*, 186.

2. Weinstein, Alfred A., M.D. *Barbed-Wire Surgeon*. New York: The MacMillan Company: 1947. Reprint, 1961, 206–7.

3. Ibid., 207.

4. Ibid., 231.

5. Fitzgerald diary, 58.

6. Zamperini, *Devil at My Heels*, 151.
7. Fitzgerald diary, 57.
8. Ibid., 58.
9. Lee Shaw recollections as told to his niece, Peggy Pepper.
10. LaVO, *Back From the Deep*, 194.
11. Fitzgerald diary, 58–59.
12. Gamble, *Black Sheep One*, 366.
13. DeRose, *Unrestricted Warfare*, 250.
14. Gamble, *Black Sheep One*, 367.
15. Adams, "USS *Tang* Survivors."
16. Weinstein, *Barbed-Wire Surgeon*, 231.
17. Gamble, *Black Sheep One*, 367.
18. Ibid., 367–68.
19. Ibid., 368; O'Kane, *Clear the Bridge!*, 466.
20. Whitlock and Smith, *The Depths of Courage*, 361.
21. Gamble, *Black Sheep One*, 368.

CHAPTER 22
THE ASHIO MINING CAMP

Primary sources were interviews and correspondence with *Tullibee* veteran Kuykendall and *Sculpin* veterans Baker, Cooper, Rocek, and Thomas. Survivor and war crimes statements used are listed by ship. *Grenadier*: CMoMM Charles A. Erishman, McIntyre, Palmer, Gunner John S. Walden, CCS Charles W. Westerfield, and S1c Peter Zucco. *Sculpin*: F2c Cecil Baker, Haverland, Murphy, Ricketts, Rourke, Toney, and Wright. *Tullibee*: Kuykendall. *S-44*: Duva and Whitemore.

1. Lt. Nicholas Maas POW testimonial courtesy of Carl LaVO.
2. LaVO, *Back From the Deep*, 159–61.
3. Ibid., 162.
4. Ibid., 163–64.
5. Rocek, "Saga of a *Sculpin* Survivor."
6. LaVO, *Back From the Deep*, 163.
7. *Grenadier* Newsletter, 9: May 1982; LaVO, *Back From the Deep*, 165.
8. LaVO, *Back From the Deep*, 167, 179.
9. Maas POW testimonial.
10. LaVO, *Back From the Deep*, 181.
11. Rocek, "Saga of a *Sculpin* Survivor."
12. Maas POW testimonial.
13. LaVO, *Back From the Deep*, 181.
14. Maas POW testimonial.
15. LaVO, *Back From the Deep*, 181.
16. Ibid., 184.
17. *Grenadier* Newsletter, 58: January 1990.
18. *Grenadier* Newsletter, 5: December 1982.
19. Ibid., 16: January 1983.
20. Rocek, "Saga of a *Sculpin* Survivor."
21. War crimes deposition of Estil J. Cohorn; LaVO, *Back From the Deep*, 185.
22. War crimes depositions of Captain Basil B. Durbin and Cpl. Darrell W. Summers, courtesy of Carl LaVO.
23. *Grenadier* Newsletter, 37: December 1985.
24. Lt. Jack Jessie Jones testimony, courtesy of Carl LaVO.
25. LaVO, "Footprints in the Sand," 88.
26. Maas POW testimonial.

27. Rocek, "Saga of a *Sculpin* Survivor."

28. George Enomoto to Mrs. David Hurt, 5 June 1946, courtesy of David A. Hurt Jr.

29. Rocek, "Saga of a *Sculpin* Survivor."

30. Kenneth Oscar Kalberg war crimes deposition, courtesy of Carl LaVO.

CHAPTER 23
"THEY'RE GONNA BE HERE TOMORROW"

Primary sources were interviews and correspondence with *Perch* veterans Arnette, Plantz, Lents, Moore, and Turner, and *Pope* veteran Penninger. *Perch* survivor statements referenced: Ryder and Vandergrift.

1. Hamilton, "Going to Make It," A5; Simpson to Michno, 3 February 1999.

2. Simpson narrative, 13 January 1986, 6.

3. Simpson to Michno, letters of January 20 and 3 February 1999.

4. Simpson narrative, 13 January 1986, 6; Simpson to Michno, 3 February 1999.

5. Moore narrative in "USS *Perch* Sunk by Japanese."

6. Ibid.

7. Hamilton, "Going to Make It," A5.

8. Ibid.

9. Ibid.

10. Miller, Ted. "A Retreat to Golf." *Marietta Daily Journal*, September 1995.

11. Penninger to Seward in *Perch-Pope Ex-POWs* Newsletter, 2001.

12. 15 April 1946 report of Lieutenant Commander Fisher, courtesy of Robert Lents.

13. Seward in *Perch-Pope Ex-POWs* Newsletter, October/November 2001 issue.

14. Fitzgerald diary, 59.

15. Ibid.

16. Ibid., 60.

17. Zamperini, *Devil at My Heels*, 177.

18. Fitzgerald diary, 60–61.

19. Van Buskirk, "Laughing With a Prisoner of War."

20. "POW Diary of Captain George Steiger." Accessed http://www.fsteiger.com/gsteipow.html on 12 July 2007.

21. Ibid.

22. Ibid.

23. Ibid.

CHAPTER 24
LIBERATION OF THE LOST

Primary sources were interviews and correspondence with: *Tullibee* veteran Kuykendall; *Sculpin* veterans Baker, Cooper, Rocek, and Thomas; *Tang* veterans Caverly and Leibold; *Perch* veterans Arnette, Plantz, Lents, Moore, and Turner; and *Grenadier* veterans Albertson, Cox, Harty, Keysor, McCoy, McGowan, Price, Ouillette, Toulon, Ver Valin, and Witzke. Survivor and war crimes statements used are listed by ship. *Grenadier*: Harty, McIntyre, Poss, Toulon, Withrow, and Zucco. *S-44*: Duva. *Sculpin*: Murphy. *Tullibee*: Kuykendall. *Perch*: Ryder and Vandergrift.

1. LaVO, "Footprints in the Sand," 88.

2. DeRose, *Unrestricted Warfare*, 257.

3. O'Kane, *Clear the Bridge!*, 466.

4. Ibid.; Whitlock and Smith, *The Depths of Courage*, 370.

5. Gamble, *Black Sheep One*, 372.

6. Adams, "USS *Tang* Survivors."

7. DeRose, *Unrestricted Warfare*, 258.

8. See http://www.nps.gov/archive/wapa/indepth/extContent/usmc/pcn-190-003143-00/

sec1b.htm, accessed on 9 July 2007. "MacArthur Sends Greetings to San Antonio by Sailor Rescued From Japanese"; courtesy of Sandy Stacy via Pat Havel.

9.   Adams, "USS *Tang* Survivors."

10.   Tuohy, *The Bravest Man*, 392–93.

11.   Ibid., 393; Whitlock and Smith, *The Depths of Courage*, 374.

12.   Tuohy, *The Bravest Man*, 393–94.

13.   O'Kane, *Clear the Bridge!*, 466.

14.   DeRose, *Unrestricted Warfare*, 253.

15.   "The Silent Service." DVD, Disc 1. *The Boats of WWII/The Captains of WWII.*

16.   O'Kane, *Clear the Bridge!*, 466.

17.   Ken Lohmann to author on 9 May 2007, concerning his interview with his uncle Ted.

18.   Van Buskirk, "Laughing With a Prisoner of War."

19.   Fitzgerald diary, 61.

20.   Ibid., 62.

21.   Ibid., 62–63.

22.   LaVO, *Back From the Deep*, 194.

23.   "POW Diary of Captain George Steiger." Accessed http://www.fsteiger.com/gsteipow.html on 12 July 2007.

24.   George Enomoto to Mrs. David Hurt, 5 June 1946, courtesy of David A. Hurt Jr.

25.   LaVO, *Back From the Deep*, 191.

26.   Samuel T. Hibbard recollections to David A. Hurt Jr.

27.   George Enomoto to Mrs. David Hurt, 5 June 1946, courtesy of David A. Hurt Jr.

28.   Rocek, "Saga of a *Sculpin* Survivor"; LaVO, *Back From the Deep*, 191.

29.   Undated La Fitte letter to Carl LaVO.

30.   Rocek, "Saga of a *Sculpin* Survivor."

31.   *Grenadier* Newsletter, 23: October 1983.

32.   Ibid., 12: August 1982.

33.   Knarr, "Recalling Horror as War Began," A5.

34.   "Doomed Sub's Survivor Tells of Jap Attack." *Oakland* (Ca.) *Tribune*, 14 September 1945. Courtesy of Robert Whitemore.

35.   LaVO, "Footsteps in the Sand," 87.

36.   LaVO, *Back From the Deep*, 195.

37.   Rocek, "Saga of a *Sculpin* Survivor."

38.   LaVO, *Back From the Deep*, 195.

39.   Cox memoirs, 60–61.

40.   Cunningham interview, 10 February 1955.

41.   Courtney diary, 6–7; Rupp, *Threshold of Hell*, 175.

42.   Courtney diary, 10.

43.   Cox memoirs, 62.

44.   Ibid., 62–63.

45.   Ibid., 64–66.

46.   Cunningham interview, 10 February 1955.

47.   *Grenadier* Newsletter, 39: August 1986.

48.   Cunningham interview, 10 February 1955.

49.   DeVore, "A Forgotten Prisoner," 2E; Moore testimony from "USS *Perch* Sunk by Japanese."

50.   Seward in *Pope-Perch* Newsletter, September 1995.

51.   DeVore, "A Forgotten Prisoner," 2E.

52.   Moore testimony from "USS *Perch* Sunk by Japanese."

53.   DeVore, "A Forgotten Prisoner," 1E.

54.   "Mobilian Presumed Lost Since Sub Disappeared Nearly 4 Years Ago Cables Parents He Is Safe." *Mobile Press*, 25 September 1945. Courtesy of Bill Atkeison.

55. 13 September 1945 press release, courtesy Submarine Force Museum, New London, Conn.

56. David A. Hurt. Jr. interview with author, 7 June 2008.

CHAPTER 25

EPILOGUE

Primary sources were interviews and correspondence with: *Tullibee* veteran Kuykendall; *Sculpin* veterans Baker, Cooper, Rocek, and Thomas; *Tang* veterans Caverly and Leibold; *Perch* veterans Arnette, Plantz, Lents, Moore, and Turner; and *Grenadier* veterans Albertson, Cox, Harty, Keysor, McCoy, McGowan, Price, Ouillette, Toulon, Ver Valin, and Witzke.

1. *Grenadier* Newsletter, 7: March 1982.

2. Stewart, *Ghost Fleet of the Truk Lagoon*, 101–5.

3. LaVO, *Back From the Deep*, 201–2.

4. Hamilton, "Going to Make It," A5.

5. Ibid.; "After Six Decades, WWII Vet Finally Gets His Bronze Star." *The Day*, 1 July 2006.

6. Schacht, "Loss of the *Perch*," 25.

7. Blair to Schacht letter, 21 March 1972; Clay Blair papers.

8. Schacht to Blair, 9 February 1972, Clay Blair papers.

9. *U.S. Submarine Veterans of World War II*, II: 172, I: 354.

10. *Perch* Newsletter, 11, June 1982.

11. Harrington, Rachel. "Memories Surface With Sub's Discovery." *The Day* (New London, Conn.), 5 February 2007, A1, A8.

12. Charlene Atkeison to W. R. Seward, 16 July 2001, in *Perch* newsletter.

13. *Grenadier* Newsletter, 7: March 1982; "Former POW Dies Here at 56." *Richmond Times Dispatch*, 12 April 1980, B-8.

14. *Grenadier* Newsletter, 12: August 1982.

15. Ibid.; 7: March 1982; 14: November 1982; 22: September 1983.

16. Shen, Hwa Mei. "From Pain to Gain." *The Star Online* (Malaysia), 4 September 2000.

17. *Grenadier* Newsletter, 50: March 1988.

18. Shen, "From Pain to Gain."

19. Ibid.

20. Ibid.

21. *Grenadier* Newsletter, 59: June 1990.

22. Ibid., 14: November 1982.

23. LaVO, *Back From the Deep*, 200–1.

24. *Grenadier* Newsletter, 6: January 1982; 8: April 1982.

25. *Grenadier* Newsletter, 3: November 1981; 22: September 1983.

26. Ibid., 12: August 1982.

27. *U.S. Submarine Veterans of World War II*, IV: 388; *Grenadier* Newsletter, 19: June 1983.

28. Sandra Fahnert Wofford Stacy recollections, 30 May 2008. "MacArthur Sends Greetings to San Antonio by Sailor Rescued From Japanese," courtesy of Sandy Stacy via Pat Havel.

29. Seltzer, JOSA Fred W. "Survivor Commemorates 50th Anniversary of USS *Grenadier*'s Sinking at TRITRAFAC." *Trident Tides*, 30 April 1993, A13.

30. LaVO, *Back From the Deep*, 200–2.

31. *U.S. Submarine Veterans of World War II*, IV: 362.

32. DeRose, *Unrestricted Warfare*, 265–67.

33. Adams, "USS *Tang* Survivors."

34. DeRose, *Unrestricted Warfare*, 253.

Bibliography

OFFICIAL REPORTS

Duff, Ivan F., Cdr., USNR. "Medical Study of the Experiences of Submariners as Recorded in 1,471 Submarine Patrol Reports in World War II." Navy Department, Washington Bureau of Medicine and Surgery, 1947.

USS *Grenadier*. Statements of survivors taken by Navy intelligence upon return from POW camps and war crimes testimony. Those referenced: S2c Thomas Robert Courtney; CMoMM Charles A. Erishman; Lt. K. D. Harty, USNR, taken at Guam; TM2c John Leskovsky, taken October 1945; Lt. Arthur Greenville McIntyre; CY Robert W. Palmer, taken 12 September 1945; RM1c E. L. Poss, taken at Guam; TM2c Warren E. Roberts, taken October 1945; Lt. A. J. Toulon; Gunner John S. Walden; CCS Charles W. Westerfield; CTM William Clyde Withrow, taken at Guam; S1c Peter Zucco; GM1c Fred Zufelt, taken at Guam; and a 17-man group interview of the following *Grenadier* enlisted men: CEM C. H. Whitlock, S1c J. H. Gunderson, S1c M. B. Pierce, S1c J. E. Simpson, SC1c R. J. Garrison, QM3c J. A. Minton, TM2c D. B. Shoemaker, S1c R. W. Rutkowski, EM3c C. E. Johnson, F1c L. L. Sawatzke, RM3c R. R. Evans, F1c B. W. Witzke, EM2c B. H. Fulton, F1c C. Roskell, F1c V. A. Ouillette, RM2c W. H. Keefe, TM2c J. Leskovsky, F1c J. G. Ingram, StM1c T. J. Trigg, EM3c L. L. Barker, and TM3c R. H. Keysor.

USS *Grenadier* (SS-210) War Patrol Reports. Courtesy of Charles H. "Tim" McCoy.

"History of USS *Grenadier* (SS–210)." Office of Naval Records and History, Ships' Histories Section. Courtesy of Charles H. "Tim" McCoy.

"The Loss of the *Perch*." Report of Lt. B. R. Van Buskirk, courtesy of Submarine Force Museum. This handwritten report, later transcribed, was originally compiled by the officers and CPOs of *Perch* during their early days as POWs.

USS *Perch*. Statements of survivors taken by Navy intelligence upon return from POW camps. Those referenced: F1c E. H. Arnette; EM3c Daniel Crist, USN, taken 30 September 1945; Lt. Cdr. David A. Hurt; MM2c R. Klecky; Lt. John French

Ryder; Lt. Kenneth G. Schacht; and Lt. (jg) J. J. Vandergrift, Jr., USN, taken 14
September 1945.

"Record of Proceedings of an Investigation conducted at the headquarters of the
Commander Submarines Seventh Fleet by order of The Commander in Chief,
United States Fleet and The Chief of Naval Operations to investigate the circumstances connected with the loss of the U.S.S. *Robalo* and the loss of the U.S.S. *Flier*,"
14 September 1994 (previously classified).

USS *S-44*. Statements of CTM Ernest Arthur Duva, interviewed 1 October 1945,
and RM3c William F. Whitemore, courtesy John Crouse, St. Mary's Submarine
Museum in Georgia.

USS *Sculpin*. Statements of survivors taken by Navy intelligence upon return from
POW camps and various war crimes testimony take under oath. Those referenced:
F2c Cecil Eugene Baker; F1c J. N. Baker; Lt. George E. Brown; CMoMM William
Herbert Haverland; F1c Paul Louis Murphy; RM2c J. G. Peterson; MoMM2c
Edward F. Ricketts; MoMM1c George Rocek; GM2c John Paul Rourke; TM1c
Herbert Joseph Thomas; PhM1c Paul A. Todd; TM3c Harry Ford Toney; EM3c
Eldon Wright; and GM2c R. O Wyatt. Also, additional war crimes testimony of
Lt. Cdr. George Estabrook Brown Jr. (10 July 1946 in New York) and 1948 deposi-
tions of Cecil Baker, Joseph Baker, Julian Peterson, and John Rourke.

USS *Tang*. Statements of survivors taken by Navy intelligence upon return from Omori
POW camp. Those referenced: MoMM2c Jesse Borges DaSilva; Lt. (jg) Henry
J. Flanagan; DaSilva; TM3c Pete Narowanski; Cdr. Richard H. O'Kane; Lt.
Lawrence Savadkin; and TM2c Hayes Oliver Trukke.

USS *Tullibee*. Statement of GM2c Clifford Weldon Kuykendall, interviewed on 9
September 1945.

INTERVIEWS

Albertson, Norman A. USS *Grenadier*. Interviewed by the author, 4 February and 2
June 2007.

Arnette, Elbert H. USS *Perch*. Interviewed by the author, 1 December 2007.

Baker, Joseph R. USS *Sculpin*. Interviewed by the author, 7 February 2007; various
correspondence and follow-up calls.

Caverly, Floyd M. USS *Tang*. Interviewed by the author, 10 February 2007; various
correspondence.

Cooper, Billie M. USS *Sculpin*. Interviewed by the author, 4 February 2007; various
correspondence and follow-up calls.

Cox, Gordon C. USS *Grenadier*. Interviewed by the author, 4 February 2007; various
correspondence and follow-up calls. Gordon also furnished copies of his detailed,
unpublished memoirs and family history.

Cunningham, William Michael. Interview by L. P. Lyman, 10 February 1955. Courtesy
of Submarine Force Museum Archives. Groton, Ct. Wendy S. Gulley, archivist.

David, Janet M. Niece of *S-44*'s GM2c Philip James Jaworski. Email correspodence,
October 14–15, 2008.

Decker, Clayton O. USS *Tang*. "Sinking of the *Tang*." Video interview by Rocky Mountain
(Co.) Base, Submarine Veterans, 2003. Courtesy of W. G. "Doc" Sweany.

Deleman, Aldina N. Wife of USS *Perch*'s Bernard Deleman. Interviewed by the author
12 November 2007.

Glasser, Murray "Mick." VT-10 aviator interviewed by the author in 1995 and follow-up correspondence through 10 August 2007.

Harty, Kevin D. USS *Grenadier*. Interviewed by the author, 30 January 2007; various correspondence and follow-up calls.

Hurt, Cdr. David A., Jr., USN (Ret.). Son of Lt. Cdr. David A. Hurt, USS *Perch*. Various mail and email correspondence, June 2008. Dave kindly shared photos, recollections and correspondence he has gathered concerning his father.

Johnson, Charles E. USS *Grenadier*. Interviewed by his daughter, Kim Reed, on 22 June 2005. Courtesy of Pat Havel.

Keysor, Riley H. USS *Grenadier*. Interviewed by the author, 7 February 2007.

Kuykendall, Clifford W. Sr. USS *Tullibee*. Interviewed by the author, 20 and 29 January 2007; various correspondence and follow-up calls.

Leibold, William R. USS *Tang*. Interviewed by the author, 29 January 2007; various email correspondence and follow-up calls.

Lents, Robert W. USS *Perch*. Interviewed by the author, 1 October 2005, and 23 January 2007; various correspondence.

McBeath, John J. USS *Grenadier*. Interviewed by daughter Veronica Mayo during September 2007.

McCoy, Charles H. USS *Grenadier*. Interviewed by the author, 27 January, 15 February, and 26 July 2007; various correspondence.

McGowan, Dempsey E. USS *Grenadier*. Interviewed by author, 11 March 2008.

Moore, Thomas. USS *Perch*. Interviewed by the author, 27 January 2007.

Nelson, Thomas C., Jr. VT-10 aviator interviewed by the author in 1995 for *The Buzzard Brigade*.

Penninger, William R. USS *Pope*. Interviewed by author, 6 September 2008.

Plantz, Ernest V. USS *Perch*. Interviewed by the author, 6 November 2007.

Price, Joseph T. USS *Grenadier*. Interviewed by the author, 30 January 2007.

Ouillette, Virgil A. USS *Grenadier*. Interviewed by the author, 4 February 2007.

Reh, Theodore J. USS *Perch*. Interviewed by his nephew, Kendall D. Lohmann, during May 2007.

Rocek, George. USS *Sculpin*. Interviewed by the author, February 7, 2007.

Ryder, Lee K. Daughter of USS *Perch's* John F. Ryder. Telephone conversations and emails from 17 February–May 2008.

Shaw, Lee C. USS *Grenadier*. Interviewed by his niece, Sandra Fahnert Wofford Stacy, during the late 1950s. Other Shaw testimony from nieces Peggy Pepper and Pat Havel, who shared stories, letters, and photos with author in May 2008.

Simpson, Samuel F.. USS *Perch*. Various papers and correspondence with author Gregory F. Michno, circa 1986–99.

Swinny, Frances Richter. Sister of USS *Perch's* Paul R. Richter, Jr. Interviewed by author, 6 August 2008. Other information on Paul Richter furnished by his other sister, Marguerite Richter Nemky.

Thomas, Herbert J. USS *Sculpin*. Interviewed by the author, 20 May 2007; various correspondence and follow-up calls.

Toulon, Alfred J. Jr. and Betsey Toulon. USS *Grenadier*. Joint telephone interview by the author, 21 June 2008, and subsequent correspondence.

Turner, Marion M. USS *Perch*. Interviewed by the author, 25 January and 30 May 2007; various correspondence and follow-up calls.

Ver Valin, Charles H. USS *Grenadier*. Interviewed by the author, January 30, 2007; various correspondence and follow-up calls.

Whitemore, Wendy and Robert Whitemore. Children of *S-44*'s William F. Whitemore. Interviewed by the author, 17 February 2007.

Witzke, Bernard W. USS *Grenadier*. Interviewed by the author, 19 May 2007.

BOOKS

Alden, Cdr. John D., USN (Ret.). *U.S. Submarine Attacks During World War II.* Annapolis: Naval Institute Press, 1989.

————. *United States and Allied Submarine Successes in the Pacific and Far East During World War II.* Chronological Listing. Pleasantville, N.Y.: Self-published, second edition, October 1999.

Armstrong, Jim. *From POW to Blue Angel: The Story of Commander Dusty Rhodes.* Norman: University of Oklahoma Press, 2006.

Belote, James H. and William M. Belote. *Titans of the Seas. The Development and Operations of Japanese and American Carrier Task Forces During World War II.* New York: Harper & Row, 1975.

Blair, Clay, Jr. *Silent Victory. The U.S. Submarine War Against Japan.* Philadelphia: J. B. Lippincott Company, 1975. Two-volume reprint.

Bouslog, Dave. *Maru Killer. War Patrols of the USS Seahorse.* Placentia, Calif.: R.A. Cline Publishing, 1996. Second Printing, 2001.

Calvert, Vice Adm. James F. USN (Ret.). *Silent Running. My Years on a World War II Attack Submarine.* New York: John Wiley & Sons, Inc., 1995.

DeRose, James F. *Unrestricted Warfare. How a New Breed of Officers Led the Submarine Force to Victory in World War II.* New York: John Wiley & Sons, Inc., 2000.

Fluckey, Adm. Eugene B. *Thunder Below! The USS Barb Revolutionizes Submarine Warfare in World War II.* Chicago: University of Illinois Press, 1992.

Galatin, Adm. I. J., USN (Ret.). *Take Her Deep! A Submarine Against Japan in World War II.* New York: Pocket Books, 1988.

Gamble, Bruce. *Black Sheep One. The Life of Gregory "Pappy" Boyington.* New York: Ballentine Books, 2000.

Gugliotta, Bobette. *Pigboat 39. An American Sub Goes to War.* Lexington: The University of Kentucky Press, 1984.

Hara, Capt. Tameichi. *Japanese Destroyer Captain.* New York: Ballentine Books, 1961. Reprint: 1978.

Hinkle, David Randall (editor). *United States Submarines.* New York: Barnes and Noble Books, 2002.

Holmes, Harry. *The Last Patrol.* Shrewsbury, England: Airlife Publishing Ltd., 1994.

Hornfischer, James D. *Ship of Ghosts. The Story of the USS Houston, FDR's Legendary Lost Cruiser, and the Epic Saga of her Survivors.* New York: Bantam Books, 2006.

Kershaw, Alex. *Escape From the Deep.* Philadelphia: De Capo Press, 2008.

Kimmett, Larry, and Margaret Regis. *U.S. Submarines in World War II. An Illustrated History.* Seattle: Navigator Publishing, 1996.

Knoblock, Glenn A. *Black Submariners in the United States Navy, 1940–1975.* Jefferson, N.C.: McFarland & Company, 2005.

LaVO, Carl. *Back From the Deep. The Strange Story of the Sister Subs Squalus and Sculpin.* Annapolis: Naval Institute Press, 1994.

Lindemann, Klaus. *Desecrate 1. Operations Against Palau by Carrier Task Force 58, 30 and 31 March 1944, and the Shipwrecks of World War II.* Belleville, Mich.: Pacific Press Publications, 1988.

Lockwood, Vice Adm. Charles A., USN, (Ret.). *Sink 'Em All. Submarine Warfare in the Pacific.* New York: E. P. Dutton & Co., Inc., 1951.

Maas, Peter. *The Terrible Hours. The Man Behind the Greatest Submarine Rescue in History.* New York: Harper Torch, 2000.

Mendenhall, Rear Adm. Corwin, USN (Ret.). *Submarine Diary. The Silent Stalking of Japan.* Chapel Hill, N.C.: Algonquin Books, 1991.

Michel, John J. A. *Mr. Michel's War. From Manila to Mukden: An American Navy Officer's War With the Japanese, 1941–1945.* Novato, Calif.: Presidio Press, 1998.

Michno, Gregory F. *Death on the Hellships: Prisoners at Sea in the Pacific War.* Annapolis: Naval Institute Press, 2001.

———. *USS Pampanito: Killer-Angel.* Norman: University of Oklahoma Press, 2000.

Monroe-Jones, Edward. *Submarine Escape and Rescue: An Anthology from 1851 through 2005.* Bangor, WA: Submarine Research Center, 2007.

Moore, Stephen L., with William J. Shinneman and Robert W. Gruebel. *The Buzzard Brigade: Torpedo Squadron Ten at War.* Missoula, Mont.: Pictorial Histories Publishing Co., 1996.

O'Kane, Rear Adm. Richard H., USN (Ret.). *Clear the Bridge! The War Patrols of the U.S.S. Tang.* Rand McNally & Company, 1977.

Ostlund, Mike. *Find 'Em, Chase 'Em, Sink 'Em. The Mysterious Loss of the WWII Submarine USS Gudgeon.* Guilford, Conn.: The Lyons Press, 2006.

Parkin, Robert Sinclair. *Blood on the Sea. American Destroyers Lost in World War II.* New York: Sarpedon, 1995.

Reynolds, Clark G. *The Fighting Lady. The New Yorktown in the Pacific War.* Missoula, Mont.: Pictorial Histories Publishing Co., 1986. Reprint: 1993.

Roscoe, Theodore. *United States Submarine Operations in World War II.* Annapolis: Naval Institute Press, 1949.

Ruhe, Capt. William J., USN (Ret.). *War in the Boats. My WWII Submarine Battles.* McLean, Va.: Brassey's Inc., 1994.

Rupp, Albert. *Beyond the Threshold.* Long Beach, Calif.: Almar Press, 1985.

———. *Threshold of Hell.* Long Beach, Calif.: Almar Press, 1985.

Schratz, Capt. Paul R., USN (Ret.) *Submarine Commander. A Story of World War II and Korea.* Lexington: The University Press of Kentucky, 1988.

Stewart, William H. *Ghost Fleet of the Truk Lagoon.* Missoula, Mont.: Pictorial Histories Publishing Co., 1985, Fourth printing 1991.

Sturma, Michael. *The USS Flier. Death and Survival on a World War II Submarine.* Lexington: The University Press of Kentucky, 2008.

Tuohy, William. *The Bravest Man. The Story of Richard O'Kane & U.S. Submarines in the Pacific War.* Phoenix Mill: Sutton Publishing, 2001.

U. S. Submarine Losses. World War II. Prepared by The Commander Submarine Force, U.S. Pacific Fleet. Washington, DC, 1946.

United States Submarine Veterans of World War II. A History of the Veterans of the United States Naval Submarine Fleet. Dallas: Taylor Publishing Company, 1984–90. Four volumes.

Whitlock, Flint, and Ron Smith. *The Depths of Courage. American Submariners at War with Japan, 1941–1945.* New York: Berkley Caliber, 2007.

Zamperini, Louis, and David Rensin. *Devil at My Heels. A Heroic Olympian's Astonishing Story of Survival as a Japanese POW in World War II*. New York: Perennial, 2004.

ARTICLES

Burgess, Tom. "First Man Up, Last Man Out: Clayton O. Decker." *Historical Diver*, Vol. 10, Issue 2 (Spring 2002, No. 31), 34.

"Doomed Sub's Survivor Tells of Jap Attack." *Oakland* (Calif.) *Tribune*, 14 September 1945. Courtesy of Robert Whitemore.

Ex-POWs: USS Pope (DD-225)/USS Perch (SS-176) Newsletters. Various issues, 1983–2004. Courtesy of Marion "Turk" Turner.

Feuer, A. B. "The Strange Saga of the USS *Perch*." December 1992, 24–29.

DeVore, Frances. "A Forgotten Prisoner." *Ocala Star Banner*, 20 June 1990, 1E-2E.

"Former POW Dies Here at 56." *Richmond Times Dispatch*, 12 April 1980, B-8.

"Going to Make It: Former Submariner Never Gave Up Hope After Being Taken Prisoner by Japanese." *New London Day*, 14 September 2004.

Haldin, Ken. "POWs Gather for Reunion." *Ocala Star-Banner*, 15 April 1984, 1A, 12A.

Harrington, Rachel. "Memories Surface With Sub's Discovery." *The Day* (New London, Conn.), 5 February 2007, A1, A8.

Kennedy, Don. "Turk: Navy Vet Recalls Years as POW." *The Flagship* (Norfolk, Va.), 30 March 2000, A4, A8.

Knarr, Jack. "Recalling Horror as War Began." *Burlington County Times*, 7 December 1998, A1, A5.

LaVO, Carl. "Footprints in the Sand." *Proceedings*, Vol. 112: January 1986, 85–88.

"MacArthur Sends Greetings to San Antonio by Sailor Rescued From Japanese." AP story of 7 September 1945, from Oakland, Calif. Courtesy of Lee Shaw's niece, Sandra Fahnert Stacey.

"Memories Surface With Sub's Discovery." *New London Day*, 5 February 2007, A1, A8.

Miller, Ted. "A Retreat to Golf." *Marietta Daily Journal*, September 1995.

"Mobilian Presumed Lost Since Sub Disappeared Nearly 4 Years Ago Cables Parents He Is Safe." *Mobile Press*, 25 September 1945. Courtesy of Bill Atkeison.

Moore, Don. "War Tales" interview with Thomas Moore. Accessed http://www.perch-base.org/ on 23 July 2007. Article: "USS *Perch* Sunk by Japanese."

Palmer, Robert W. "The Sinking of the USS *Grenadier* SS 210." *Polaris*, April 1983, 16–18.

Phaneuf, Keith M. "Some Memories are Horrifying But Camaraderie Is Still Strong." *New London Day*, 22 June 1989, B1, B8.

Schacht, Capt. K. G., USN (Ret.). "Loss of the *Perch* (SS-176)." *Shipmate*, February 1972, 21–25.

Seltzer, JOSA Fred W. "Survivor Commemorates 50th Anniversary of USS *Grenadier's* Sinking at TRITRAFAC." *Trident Tides*, 30 April 1993, A13.

"Seventy Five Blows." *Looking Aft*. West Virginia Chapter Newsletter, U.S. Submarine Veterans WWII. Volume 10: Issue 1 (March 2003), 1–3.

Shen, Hwa Mei. "From Pain to Gain." *The Star Online* (Malaysia), 4 September 2000.

Van Buskirk, Cdr. B. R., USN (Ret.). "Laughing With a Prisoner of War." *Polaris*, October 1983.

Index

ABOUT THE AUTHOR

Stephen L. Moore, a sixth generation Texan, is the author of eight previous books on World War II and Texas history. His recent submarine service titles include *Spadefish* (2006) and *War of the Wolf* (2008), the story of the *USS Seawolf*. His Texas history titles include *Savage Frontier*, a multi-volume chronology of the early Texas Rangers, and *Eighteen Minutes: The Battle of San Jacinto and the Texas Independence Campaign* (2004). Moore is a frequent speaker at Texas book events and conferences and writes for local historical journals, including *The Texas Ranger Dispatch*. He, his wife Cindy and their three children live north of Dallas in Lantana, Texas.

The Naval Institute Press is the book-publishing arm of the U.S. Naval Institute, a private, nonprofit, membership society for sea service professionals and others who share an interest in naval and maritime affairs. Established in 1873 at the U.S. Naval Academy in Annapolis, Maryland, where its offices remain today, the Naval Institute has members worldwide.

Members of the Naval Institute support the education programs of the society and receive the influential monthly magazine *Proceedings* or the colorful bimonthly magazine *Naval History* and discounts on fine nautical prints and on ship and aircraft photos. They also have access to the transcripts of the Institute's Oral History Program and get discounted admission to any of the Institute-sponsored seminars offered around the country.

The Naval Institute's book-publishing program, begun in 1898 with basic guides to naval practices, has broadened its scope to include books of more general interest. Now the Naval Institute Press publishes about seventy titles each year, ranging from how-to books on boating and navigation to battle histories, biographies, ship and aircraft guides, and novels. Institute members receive significant discounts on the Press's more than eight hundred books in print.

Full-time students are eligible for special half-price membership rates. Life memberships are also available.

For a free catalog describing Naval Institute Press books currently available, and for further information about joining the U.S. Naval Institute, please write to:

Member Services
U.S. Naval Institute
291 Wood Road
Annapolis, MD 21402-5034
Telephone: (800) 233-8764
Fax: (410) 571-1703
Web address: www.usni.org